Mestizaje and Globalization

Mestizaje and Globalization

Transformations of Identity and Power

Edited by
STEFANIE WICKSTROM AND
PHILIP D. YOUNG

THE UNIVERSITY OF
ARIZONA PRESS

TUCSON

The University of Arizona Press
www.uapress.arizona.edu

We respectfully acknowledge the University of Arizona is on the land and
territories of Indigenous peoples. Today, Arizona is home to twenty-two federally
recognized tribes, with Tucson being home to the O'odham and the Yaqui.
Committed to diversity and inclusion, the University strives to build sustainable
relationships with sovereign Native Nations and Indigenous communities through
education offerings, partnerships, and community service.

ISBN-13: 978-0-8165-3090-8 (cloth)
ISBN-13: 978-0-8165-5547-5 (paper)
ISBN-13: 978-0-8165-9857-1 (ebook)

Cover designed by Leigh McDonald
Cover art by Kansuet (Panama, 1974), *Cautiva / Captive*, 66×61 cm, oil and acrylic
on canvas, 2011. Khajetoorians Brown Collection. Represented by Allegro Galeria
(Panama).

Publication of this book was made possible in part by funding from the Office of
Research and Sponsored Programs at Central Washington University.

Library of Congress Cataloging-in-Publication Data
Mestizaje and globalization : transformations of identity and power / edited by
Stefanie Wickstrom and Philip D. Young.
    pages cm
  ISBN 978-0-8165-3090-8 (hardback)
 1. Mestizaje—Latin America. 2. Mestizaje—United States. 3. Mestizos—
Latin America—Ethnic identity 4. Mestizos—United States—Ethnic identity.
5. Ethnicity—Latin America. 6. Ethnicity—United States. 7. Globalization—
Social aspects—Latin America. 8. Globalization—Social aspects—United
States. I. Wickstrom, Stefanie, editor of compilation. II. Young, Philip D.,
editor of compilation.
  GN562.M48 2014
  305.8098—dc23

                    2014007754

Printed in the United States of America
♾ This paper meets the requirements of ANSI/NISO Z39.48-1992 (Permanence of
Paper).

Phil Young in the field in the Ngäbe-Buglé Comarca in Western Panama with Ngäbe friends in 2013

Phil Young was a perceptive and compassionate observer of globalization. Born in 1936, he had seven-and-a-half decades to consider and participate in change in the world. Service in the U.S. Army in Panama in the 1950s took him into Ngäbe territory. He went back to conduct his dissertation research with the Ngäbe in 1964–1965. He loved the people and the place, and he returned many times to be with the friends and families who hosted and supported him in his fieldwork. Witnessing transformation there enriched his life.

His career gave him many opportunities to enrich the lives of others through leadership and collaboration as a scholar, teacher, advisor, and development consultant. I and many others were lucky to have his support and guidance in graduate studies and professional work.

Since he died unexpectedly on June 30, 2013, the completion of this book has become a project dedicated to him. I have missed his collaboration in preparing the final copy of the manuscript but, more than that, his good company. I am more fully responsible than I would have been otherwise for any errors, but I think Phil would be happy with what you have here, which is as much his intellectual work as it is mine and that of the authors.

—*Stefanie Wickstrom, August 30, 2013*

CONTENTS

Preface   ix

Acknowledgments   xi

Introduction to Key Concepts   3
STEFANIE WICKSTROM AND PHILIP D. YOUNG

I. CONSTRUCTING *MESTIZAJE*

1. The Revolutionary Encounter   25
   REX WIRTH

2. *Mestizaje* in Colonial Mexican Art   43
   SOFÍA IRENE VELARDE CRUZ

3. The Tradition of La Chaya in Vallenar, Chile: The Search
   for Imaginaries in the Nineteenth and Twentieth Centuries   56
   IVÁN PIZARRO DÍAZ

II. BARRIERS TO EMPOWERMENT
THROUGH IDENTITY

4. Born Indigenous, Growing Up Mestizos: Schooling
   and Youth in Arequipa, Peru   77
   MARIELLA I. ARREDONDO

5. Questioning the Nation: Affirmative Action and Racial
   Quotas in Brazilian Universities   92
   PAULO ALBERTO DOS SANTOS VIEIRA

6. Political Subjectification, *Mestizaje*, and Globalization:
   Constructing Citizenship in Aid and Development
   Programs in the Peruvian Andes   107
   JORGE LEGOAS P. AND FABRIZIO ARENAS BARCHI

7. The Door to the Future: Cultural Change and the
   Cheyenne Sun Dance   124
   JENNIFER WHITEMAN

III. EMPOWERMENT

8. From Mestizos to Mashikuna: Global Influences on
   Discursive, Spatial, and Performed Realizations of
   Indigeneity in Urban Quito   145
   KATHLEEN S. FINE-DARE

9. Indigenous Peoples as a New Category of Transnational
   Social Actors: An Analysis Based on the Case of Argentina   164
   SABINE KRADOLFER

10. Divine Design: Crafting and Consuming the Sacred
    in Afro-Brazilian Candomblé   180
    ANGELA CASTAÑEDA

11. Women's Roles and Responses to Globalization in
    Ngäbe Communities   193
    PHILIP D. YOUNG

12. Politicizing Ethnicity: Strategies in Panama and Ecuador   212
    VÍCTOR BRETÓN SOLO DE ZALDÍVAR AND MÒNICA MARTÍNEZ MAURI

13. Beyond *Mestizaje*: Andean Interculturality in Ecuador   234
    JOHN STOLLE-MCALLISTER

References   249
Contributors   273
Index   277

PREFACE

The Spanish word *mestizaje* does not easily translate into English. Its meaning and significance have been debated for centuries, since colonization of the Americas by European powers began. Its simplest definition is "mixing." Norms and ideas about racial and cultural mixing have been imagined, imposed, questioned, rejected, and given new meanings by different people and peoples, ethnic groups, classes, races, organizations, and institutions at different times in different places. The chapters of this book present an array of perspectives on the realization of these processes, fundamental in establishing and transforming relations of power.

The chapters here answer a number of interrelated questions: How have identities been imposed, constructed, negotiated, and interpreted in the Americas throughout the course of globalization? What kinds of challenges to identity (re)construction do the peoples of the Americas confront as they respond to globalization? How do they use identity to empower themselves in a globalizing world? Can autonomous reconstructions of identity and meaning enable disempowered peoples to solve problems inherent to globalization?

The authors' inquiries are fundamentally interconnected. Whether they consider experiences of conquerors or conquered, in history or present times, their chapters illustrate that the politics of identity is central to understanding globalization—and vice versa. The chapters in this book do not pretend to present a unified theoretical perspective. As with all research and writing, there is theoretical perspective embedded in each work. Some authors make their perspective explicit; others do not.

Several of the chapters here are based on papers originally presented at the Fifty-Third International Congress of Americanists symposium, "Reconstructing Mestizaje: Political Identities and Responses to Crises of Globalization," convened in Mexico City in July 2009. Symposium participants undertook critical analyses of "mestizaje" and "globalization," abstractions often accepted as neutral descriptors of processes seemingly inevitable. They were inspired by the exchange of ideas and wanted to further develop their work. Later, other scholars interested in mestizaje and globalization were invited to contribute chapters.

ACKNOWLEDGMENTS

Thanks go first and foremost to the authors. The rewarding process of working together to better comprehend *mestizaje* and globalization and share our insights has been sustained by commitment over time to the project. Authors John Stolle-McAllister, Mònica Martínez Mauri, and Jorge Legoas P. provided extra assistance that is much appreciated. Essential support has also come from Kathleen Black and Rex Wirth. Advice, encouragement, and ideas have come from many good colleagues and friends, among them Gilberto García, John Peña, Jennifer Hackett, John Bort, Bill Harp, Philip Garrison, and Dan Herman. We also acknowledge the helpful comments of the four anonymous reviewers who generously gave their time to provide feedback and suggestions.

Mestizaje and Globalization

Introduction to Key Concepts

STEFANIE WICKSTROM AND PHILIP D. YOUNG

Among their traditional beliefs, Quechua and Aymara peoples of the Andes hold the concept of *pachakuti*, "literally, the turning about of the times . . . a change of direction" (Delgado-P. 1994, 77), as a turning or reversal of the world (Skar 1994). The Andeans view the pachakuti as a process that does not necessarily take place in a brief span of time but rather builds to a point of climax, of rapid, profound sociocultural change and the emergence of a new world order that has lasting consequences far into the future. Related in Andean Indigenous belief to a world turning or emergence of a new order is the idea of parallel worlds, older worlds that continue to exist alongside the new (see Skar 1994).[1] The changes brought about by a pachakuti are not necessarily good or bad; they are radical changes that result in life in a world vastly different from the world that preceded it.

A great turning took place, they say, with the ascendance of the Inca. The last great turning occurred with the arrival of the Spaniards, the overthrow of the Inca Empire, and the imposition of colonialism.[2] The world is turning again now, they say. The impact of recent changes and reactions to them, beginning after World War II and accelerating from about 1990 on, makes it appear that this is indeed the case. Although variable from region to region and country to country, the Americas (along with the rest of the world) have undergone social, political, and economic changes in the past three decades at a seemingly unprecedented pace.[3] Economists and other scholars refer to this recent period of rapid change as globalization.

Following World War II, infrastructural and agricultural projects were introduced in many countries of the Americas as globalization opened

3

more avenues for economic, social, political, and technological change.
Such development projects have usually been imposed and have had destructive impacts on Indigenous peoples and other disempowered populations that are in the way. Most, maybe all, Indigenous peoples are not
against development projects per se, but they would like them to proceed
(or not) on their terms, not those of the nation-states or multinational corporations driving them. And therein resides the core of the problem. Numerous nation-states have signed agreements (e.g., ILO Convention No.
169, the UN Declaration on the Rights of Indigenous Peoples) to protect
the human rights and property of Indigenous peoples. Many nation-states
also have provisions in their own constitutions or laws that supposedly
protect Indigenous rights and give Indigenous peoples a say in development projects within their territories. But, in the course of planning and
implementing development projects, governments (including that of the
United States) and multinationals regularly ignore Native rights, often using the "greater good for the greater number" argument.

At the same time, processes of globalization have given Indigenous
groups, rural dwellers, and other disempowered populations knowledge of
and access to high-speed communications and media-making technology,
providing them with the means to communicate rapidly with each other
and with national and international news media, as well as organizations
and audiences supportive of their causes. In this way, globalization helps
to make processes of social and cultural *mestizaje* more evident to more
people. It also reveals political and economic consequences that have long
been evolving in response to processes of mestizaje, throughout an historical trajectory instigated by the European invasion of the Americas.

Today, many marginalized groups are consciously responding to mestizaje as something central to politics and the imposition or transformation of cultural, social, and economic change. Since the 1970s, there has
been a shift from the use of (mostly) passive resistance, i.e., "weapons of
the weak" (Scott 1985), to more frequent proactive resistance—public
protests, media campaigns, organizational networking, internationally legal actions, etc.—which expose to the world the often harsh human rights
violations committed by governments and multinationals in the course of
implementing development projects such as ever-expanding agri-industry
plantations, open-pit mines, hydroelectric mega-dams, and oil production
facilities. Disempowered peoples have recognized the power of asserting
an ethnic identity and engaging in a politics of identity in resistance.

Grappling with Globalization

The chapters in this book examine ways in which economic, social, political, and technological aspects of globalization have influenced the identities of the peoples of the Americas, particularly Indigenous groups, and

how they have responded. What, exactly, is globalization and when did it begin? Literally hundreds of books and thousands of articles have been written about globalization.[4] The term itself does not have a definition that scholars, politicians, or anyone else seem able to agree on (Steger 2003) nor is there much agreement about when it began. There is also little agreement on whether it is beneficial or not.

Globalization involves "almost unrestrained flows of capital, consumer goods, information, and people around the globe" (Brumann 1998, 496), the expansion of networks of social and economic relations, and an increase in interdependencies among political entities that fosters "in people a growing awareness of deepening connections between the local and the distant" (Steger 2003, 13).

We might say that, on a global scale, the period beginning in the late 1980s marks the beginning of the current wave of globalization. The dissolution of the USSR and the fall of the Berlin Wall erased Cold War barriers to the internationalization of capital and financial markets. At the same time, technological innovations had been ushering in vast improvements in communication and transportation, with increases in speed and reach and decreases in cost.[5] Academic debates in dependency theory and world-systems analysis take a longer view, but when economists and politicians debate the definition of globalization and its costs and benefits, it is this contemporary period upon which most tend to focus, rather than earlier historical periods that displayed parallel economic and social changes and reactions.

It is this contemporary period that some Indigenous leaders have referred to as "the new colonialism" (see Gandhi 2001). Some scholars, particularly neo-Marxist sociologists like James Petras and Henry Veltmeyer, have called it, with considerable justification, "the new imperialism" (Petras and Veltmeyer 2004).

Whether we take the long view, that globalization begins with the arrival of Europeans, or the short view, that globalization begins about 1989, it has had dramatic and multitudinous effects. It has affected different strata of populations in different ways. Its impacts in urban areas have been different from those in the countryside. It has different effects among different ethnic and racial communities, classes, age groups, and genders.

Critics of globalization range from mild to moderate to radical. The latter see no good whatsoever in the processes and policies of the current phase of neoliberal globalization (often referred to as the "Washington consensus," for obvious reasons). Proponents range from those who see some problems with the current (economic) process (Stiglitz 2001) to those who think that every aspect of globalization is inherently beneficial (e.g., Bhagwati 2004; M. Wolf 2004). The latter often also seem to believe that there actually is, in the real world, something called a free-market economy.[6] For a brief but excellent general introduction that goes beyond economic aspects of globalization to consider political, cultural, and ideological dimensions as well, see Steger 2003.

By the 1990s, it had become obvious that earlier predictions about the disappearance of nation-states, or a considerable weakening of their economic and political power, had not come to pass and in all likelihood would not occur (Held at al. 1999). Fears that economic globalization would lead to cultural homogenization had also dissipated in the face of mounting evidence that, in fact, even the opposite could happen (Brumann 1998). Social movements that strengthened group identity—Indigenous social movements, for example—were taking center stage and were focused more often than not on social and political issues rather than economic ones. A renewed emphasis on ethnic and cultural identity, a sharpening of the boundaries of the local as a reaction to the impositions of the global, has emerged.

Much of the globalization literature views processes and interactions of globalization from the top down, as it is often initiated and managed by nation-states, governments, transnationals, and multilateral financial and development institutions, but it is analytically more enlightening to view globalization as a series of adaptive processes that involve interchanges between the global and the local. People as individuals and small groups in communities and localities adapt to these impositions. Those "at the top," in turn, adjust and adapt their own strategies and policies in response to adaptations from below, especially those that take the form of resistance. Globalization is multidimensional, shaped by planned and spontaneous responses, and it involves an ongoing series of adjustments from the global to the local and back again. Globalization may be viewed as both evolutionary and revolutionary.

Mestizaje

What is mestizaje? The word does not easily translate to English. A language dictionary will define it as "miscegenation," a term associated with illegitimacy and taboo. Miscegenation refers to race. Mestizaje can be biological or cultural. It can be considered an ideology or a movement, and it has been influential in drawing attention to identity and power in evolving intercultural relations in Latin America. Norms and ideas about racial and cultural mixing throughout the Americas have been constructed and imposed by many different kinds of social, political, legal, religious, and economic institutions, among others. As they have defined them, institutions have also responded for centuries to the sometimes constructive and sometimes destructive influences of intercultural relations and identity politics.

The struggle to make sense of mestizaje is ongoing. It is beyond the scope of this chapter to describe its numerous and often conflictual meanings as it is interpreted throughout the Americas and elsewhere (see, for example, Gruzinski 2002; M. Miller 2004; Pérez-Torres 2006). Our objective here is to provide an introduction to help the reader interpret mestizaje in the chapters that follow. Many chapters in this book treat mestizaje as a cultural phenomenon and a political endeavor tied to identity, but it is important to note that mestizaje continues to be examined as a racial phenomenon (although defining race is now generally understood to be a cultural or political endeavor).

Given its own historical, geographical, and demographic profiles at the time it launched its colonial enterprise, Spain was obsessed with biological mestizaje. In Latin America, given what took place there as worlds collided during colonization, the obsession endured and relations of power were constructed on understandings of race and identity espoused by powerful people and colonial institutions. After independence, mestizaje was appropriated by nation-states to legitimize and assimilate chosen expressions of non-European cultures.

The work of Spanish ethnologist Claudio Esteva-Fabregat is a twentieth-century example of a scholar's attempts to interpret culture on the basis of nineteenth-century ideas about biological evolution and the influence of climate on cultural development.[7] He has struggled to set forth an interpretive framework that accounts in some part for the influences of genetics on the development of a pluralistic society in Ibero-America. He contends (as have others interested in biological mestizaje) that the mestizo has an advantageous genetic makeup that promotes survival. In addition, he believes that, given the right climactic and social conditions, mestizaje enables the exertion of an energy that can transform "culture" itself for better adaptive advantage. In the aftermath of the upheavals of colonization, the more fit mestizos grew in numbers while Indigenous peoples were "driven to frustrations of personality that carried with them the mark of confused identity, the loss of control over their reality, and the awareness that their existential style had been stripped of its cultural coherence" (Esteva-Fabregat 1995, 271). He asserts that, given the typical superior genetic makeup of the adventurer-migrant (from Spain or Portugal), the adaptive advantages conveyed by their societies, and a number of other variables resulting from the biological hybridization of the human populations of the region (with the exception of a very few isolated groups), "the native tribes of Ibero-America can be considered today as mestizoized aggregations" (Esteva-Fabregat 1995, 194). He goes on to explain that "under these circumstances, as the Hispanic cultural style tended to reproduce itself and expand on American soil within the framework of political, religious, economic, social, and technological institutions, and as it achieved dominance in the heart of interracial relations, the Natives found refuge in the *reducciones* run by the missionaries, settlements whose isolation shielded them from the total breakdown of their traditional milieu" (271).

Whether they "found refuge" or were enslaved or targeted for assimilation, they and other disempowered peoples of the Americas posed no real problem to development so long as expressions of their cultural heritages did not preclude their directed participation in the new society and economy. Where they survived as slaves, indentured servants, or tenant farmers, their mestizoized identities became acknowledged components of the cultural landscapes of the new nations of Latin America. What many interpreters of mestizaje may leave out of the analysis is agency. Indians, slaves, and campesinos are not simply byproducts of genetic processes and historical transformations. They are people who interpret and influence what is happening to and around them.

One particularly fit specimen of Mexico's mestizo intellectual elite—philosopher, educator, and politician José María Albino Vasconcelos Calderón—popularized a thesis that was to impact thinkers and writers throughout the Americas for decades to come. In *La raza cósmica: Misión de la raza Iberoamericana (The Cosmic Race: Mission of the Ibero-American Race),*[8] published in 1925, drawing upon ideas emerging from his involvement with the pre-revolutionary intellectual group Ateneo de la Juventud,[9] José Vasconcelos claimed that, with the blood of all the peoples of the world, Latin Americans were a "cosmic race," able to redeem themselves from the ravages of colonialism through powers conveyed by a pan-mestizo identity, which would pave the way for humanity to create a more utopian life than could be established by conquest and empire. Building the future of Latin American nations was up to the mestizos. As were many philosophers of his time, Vasconcelos was influenced by the ideas of Alexander von Humboldt, Charles Darwin, and Herbert Spencer and their work on biological evolution.

After writing the treatise for which he would be remembered and that would greatly influence understandings of the importance of mestizaje for years to come, Vasconcelos continued to struggle to make sense of the changing American experience and the respective influences of race, language, civilization, imperialism, nationality, and culture. He eventually concluded that "it is proved that evolution may affect species, but has no influence on the development of man and of cultural processes" and rejected *The Cosmic Race* as an error (Vasconcelos 1963, 81). Perhaps it is fitting that he ultimately discarded the influence of biology, as Vasconcelos's lifetime (1882–1959) is concurrent with the emergence of the widespread understanding throughout Latin America that mestizaje is as much a cultural phenomenon as a biological one.

Interpretations of Identity and Power

Mestizaje has often been an imposed assimilative force that denies people the power inherent in their identities. Today, Indigenous peoples reject the mestizo label and insist on their Indigenous identities. Other disempowered racial and ethnic groups and their movements have also questioned and rejected mestizaje as they claim their own identities and engage in politics. States, multinationals, and other elite institutions and powers have responded to identity-based movements that challenge the status quo by co-opting leaders and creating internal factionalism that undermines identity and group solidarity, and thereby political effectiveness.

Indigenismo

Indigenismo is not translated into English without losing its most important congeries of connotations. It has been used to connote certain views of Indigenous cultures in Latin America largely imposed from the outside by literati and government officials. It is widely understood to be linked with mestizaje. From the early part of the twentieth century until the 1970s, indigenismo was most visible and prominent as a literary genre in Mexico and the central Andean countries (Ecuador, Peru, and Bolivia), and as government policy in Mexico.[10] Variations of indigenismo influencing incorporation of Indigenes into the mainstream culture of the nation-state exist in many Latin American countries. Mainstream culture is idealized as mestizo, although "mestizo" is not always a term in common usage (e.g., in Panama the term *latino* is the common one; in Guatemala, *ladino*).

In literary works, indigenismo conveys "a romantic, folkloric image of the Indian as stoic, abject, and mysterious . . . the Indian as a residual figure—an anomaly—and the mestizo as a modern citizen" (Taylor 2009, 3). Government laws and policies may portray Indigenous cultures as premodern (to put it politely), largely out of touch with the modern world and often manifesting resistance to development and change, i.e., as backward and ignorant (to put it more bluntly). They refused to become mestizo, even though, in the view of the non-Indigenous observer, becoming mestizo would be in the best interests of the nation-state and the Indigenes themselves. This is a view that prevailed until the 1970s and that is still expressed in some nations, in the policies of some governments, and in the writings of some intellectuals.

By the end of the 1960s, Indigenous social movements had emerged and were gaining strength throughout the Americas, including in the United States.[11] In Latin America, tenets of indigenismo were questioned and criticized by some anthropologists, mostly Mexican, who rejected imposed policies of mestizaje as the means for incorporation into the nation. They argued that Indigenous peoples should be unburdened from the yoke of integrationist policies and have rights to self-determination within multicultural states, with equal rights of citizenship and perhaps special considerations by virtue of their indigeneity.

Propositions along these lines were formally set forth in the first (1971) and second (1977) Declarations of Barbados.[12] And, as Varese (1982) points out, these criticisms came from not only social scientists but also various Indigenous organizations emerging in the 1970s, and they have continued to gain strength. New Indigenous organizations—from local to regional and in some cases national (e.g., Ecuador)—came into being, as did Indigenous social movements in their own right (not beholden to labor unions or peasant unions or other class-based organizations as in the past). These were and are based on self-identification as Indigenous and culturally distinct from majority national, typically mestizo, cultures. They are movements based in indigeneity.[13]

Indigeneity

Indigeneity currently refers to self-identification as Indigenous and to a largely, though not entirely, internally imposed means of conceptualizing one's ethnicity as distinct from non-Indigenous. This contrasts with and may be opposed to externally imposed indigenismo. In Spanish it is rendered as *indianidad*[14] (Groupe de Recherches sur l'Amérique Latine Toulouse-Perpignan 1988; Herbert 1977) and sometimes as *indianismo*, the latter seemingly a revival of the use of the term before indigenismo.

Identity and Power North of the Rio Grande

As the field of Latin American Studies expanded in the United States in the mid-twentieth century, North American chroniclers of development in Latin America typically characterized Indigenous and other marginalized peoples as detrimental to progress (even though their coerced economic and social roles were increasingly indispensable). One interesting example is Martin C. Needler.[15] Expressing in 1963 one of the predominant points of view of the time, the young Harvard-trained political scientist wrote: "It can hardly escape observation that the most highly developed countries of Latin America politically are at the same time among the most European in the ancestry of their population. . . . The most Indian and African states, on the other hand, are more frequently found toward the lower end of anyone's scale of development . . . according to any index used—literacy, level of income, newspaper circulation, or any other" (1963, 19). He allowed that race should not be viewed as an innate biological characteristic but claimed it was an indicator of "a certain cultural history and, even today, a distinctive way of life" (1963, 19).

Howard Wiarda, still a prominent scholar of Latin American politics and international relations in the United States, also conveys a story focused on the European contributions to mestizo culture. In his widely read *The Soul of Latin America*, he asserts the existence of a tradition of political thought in Latin America, "a virtually unbroken string for more than two thousand years" (2001, 350) that originated in Greece, shaped political development of the Iberian Peninsula, and then later influenced and came to Latin America by way of Europe. Like many other elite scholars in the United States and Europe, he believes this tradition of thought defines political culture in the Americas, and he offers constructed interpretations of the history of the major pre-Hispanic civilizations of the Americas as background for understanding development in Latin America. Wiarda mentions Indian labor as a commodity, Indigenous populations as inspiration for ideas of some (mestizo) political theorists (for example, José Mariátegui in Peru), and in the contemporary context, Indigenous people as social movement actors who are now contributing to social, political, and economic development in Latin America. Wiarda's Latin America "has shown positive genius in absorbing, accommodating, and coopting new ideologies, pressures, and social movements to its dominant and often still prevailing historic political tradition" (2001, 354).

In the United States, accommodation of Indigenous identity was rare. The cultures of immigrant peoples who settled Indigenous territories characterized national identity, and the ideologies of non-Indigenous peoples were the basis for the construction of nationhood.[16] Native Americans were killed, forcibly assimilated, or confined to reservations as their nations were occupied and their lands and resources expropriated for development throughout the process of nation-building by the new arrivals. Miscegenation was prohibited by norms of the dominant culture and sometimes by law (see Wickstrom 2005 inter alia). Assimilative processes in the United States were likened favorably to a melting pot.[17] But that which emerged from the melting pot would be influenced little by Indigenous identities, histories, or cosmovisions.

In the aftermath of the civil rights movement, proponents of multiculturalism rejected the melting-pot metaphor and called for respect for "diversity" and acceptance of a multicultural national identity, sometimes represented metaphorically by political theorists as a "salad bowl." For a time, in the United States, Canada, and Brazil,[18] affirmative action policies that took into account race, color, religion, sex, and national origin (but not the notion of "occupied nations") were implemented to correct for discriminatory politics and socioeconomic development.

In U.S. popular culture, identities of American Indians, newly arrived immigrants, and minority populations are assimilated together into an imagined culture supposedly native to the place. Nonetheless, many peoples—from Métis people and tribal nations living across borders to Chicanos from Aztlán—are engaged in cultural survival, claiming their identities and pre-conquest imaginations, and impacting identity politics:

> History is myth. Myth is story. Story makes medicine. I am in daily search of these acts of remembering of who we once were because I believe they will save our pueblos from extinction. I believe our pre-

conquest imaginations offer strategies for building self-sustaining societies today, societies that can disrupt the mass suicide of global consumption.[19]

Interculturalidad

Relations of power in the Americas are persistently influenced by culture and identity as globalization proceeds. In Latin America, the "plurinational state" has begun to talk the talk of "multiculturalism." Now enshrined in constitutions and special legislation of a number of Latin American states,[20] neoliberal multiculturalism accords some de jure recognition of Indigenous peoples' autonomy. How such accommodations actually impact Indigenous peoples remains to be seen.[21]

From 1990 onwards, many Indigenous movements have defined and promoted *interculturalidad*.[22] A 1997 publication of the Confederation of Indigenous Nationalities of Ecuador (La Confederación de Nacionalidades Indígenas del Ecuador, CONAIE) explains: "The principle of interculturalidad respects the diversity of indigenous peoples and nationalities and other Ecuadorian social sectors, but at the same time demands unity amongst these in economic, social, cultural and political arenas to transform existing structures and construct a new plurinational state, characterized by equal rights, mutual respect, peace and harmony between nationalities" (CONAIE in Walsh 2007, 179).

Unlike mestizaje, affirmative action, or neoliberal multiculturality, which promote national unity by giving minorities a chance to participate on imposed terms, interculturalidad emerges from critical interpretation of political, social, and economic development. Whitten and Whitten describe the consciousness of interculturality as "diasporic, global, and dynamic" (2008, 238). Interculturalidad is transformative. It calls for the deconstruction of economic, political, social, and cognitive realities. This deconstruction is prerequisite to reconstruction of sustainable and emancipatory lifeways, formulated with direct input from Indigenous people, based on their experiences and cosmovisions.

Indigenous leaders, activists, and organizations throughout the Americas are asserting their world views as essential to making politics, development, and intercultural relations sustainable.[23] Variants of interculturalidad are influencing social movements in Ecuador, Peru, and Bolivia; in other parts of Latin America; in the United States; and beyond. Movements based in critical or decolonial interculturalidad demand recognition of the destructive impacts of the assimilation and subjugation of the peoples of the Americas throughout the course of globalization. The endeavor is not *multi*cultural, but *inter*cultural, demanding movement from one cultural system to another (Whitten and Whitten 2008). It is a transition to something new.

What Lies Ahead?

Part I—Constructing Mestizaje

The chapters in Part I use historical perspective to help interpret the construction of mestizaje in the Americas. They provide insight into the clashes between world views and understandings of them that would be manifest throughout the process of the emergence of nations and mestizo cultures in the "new" world. They offer interpretations of imposed constructions of identity that continue to influence relations of power and expressions of culture.

Mexican identity has been created from a partly mythologized past tied to civilizations that battled for control of the Valley of Mexico even before Rome's empirical project was well underway across the globe. From the "Romanization" of Western Europe and the battles for the Iberian Peninsula between Christians and Moors, through the conquest and Hispanicization of the Americas, to the emergence of pluralism as a normative political ideal in the United States, Rex Wirth contrasts mestizaje with pluralism in chapter 1. He traces the political evolution of what is today Mexico and the construction of mestizaje against the backdrop of evolving European political systems and the emergence of nationhood in the United States rooted in Anglo pluralism. He argues that constructed mestizaje, seen as the basis of cultural identity in Mexico, can also be a basis for interpreting predominant political ideologies. In turn, pluralism, considered to be a political ideology, should be recognized as a basis of constructed cultural identity in the United States.

In chapter 2, Sofía Irene Velarde Cruz also looks as far back as ancient Rome in her exploration of mestizaje and cultural legitimacy as she considers how the mixing of Spanish and Indian styles in the religious art of New Spain has been and should be characterized. Her exploration reflects imposed acculturation—then and now—and raises questions about resistance on the part of Indigenous artists in New Spain. Knowing what to make of the pre-Hispanic iconography employed in devotional works of the Catholic faith in the sixteenth century remains a challenge as the peoples of Mexico continue to wrestle with identity.

In chapter 3, Iván Pizarro Díaz illustrates changing representations in late nineteenth- and early twentieth-century Chilean newspaper editorials about "el juego de la Chaya." Considered by Hispanic observers to be an element of Carnaval, La Chaya is likely an Indigenous festivity with roots in Aymara traditions incorporated into the Christian celebration. Perceptions and judgments of it changed over time through constructions of imaginaries by Chilean social, economic, and political elites engineering the process of nation-building. Pizarro Díaz suggests that its eventual disappearance was brought about not so much by direct repression as by economic changes accompanying globalization, especially immigration to urban areas.

Part II—Barriers to Empowerment Through Identity

The vast assortment of racial, ethnic, and cultural identities of the peoples of the Americas has been reduced to manageability by assimilative mechanisms such as mestizaje and the melting pot. Laws and policies directed at transforming the lives of disempowered peoples are based on imposed identity constructs. In the Americas today, education, development aid, affirmative action, and Indian policy are based on and reinforce ideologies of dominant cultures. Cases examined here suggest these ideologies themselves must be confronted in struggles for well-being, justice, and cultural survival. As we consider how imposed notions of identity distort history, exclude participation, and stand in the way of cultural survival in Peru, in Brazil, and in Cheyenne territory in what today is the United States, we come to better understand common barriers to empowerment through identity.

In chapter 4, Mariella I. Arredondo explores the formation, endurance, and reproduction of class- and race-based hierarchies through her interviews with students in middle-class and elite private schools in the city of Arequipa, Peru. She analyzes high school students' perceptions of intersections among ethnicity, race, class, and culture in Arequipa. She finds that, as rural-urban migration of Indigenous people has intensified, the students' perceptions are helping perpetuate the exclusion of Indigenous peoples from participation as legitimate citizens—unless they abandon their identities. In the context of globalization and rapid change, urban Ariquipeños of all ages embrace their own unique construction of mestizaje. It does not, however, include immigrants arriving from the surrounding rural regions, who supposedly have no culture. This disguises ethnic and racial prejudice as "cultural difference" and facilitates assimilation on terms imposed by the dominant culture, undermining attempts to implement intercultural education aimed at constructing a just and inclusive society.

In chapter 5, Paulo Alberto dos Santos Vieira explores imposed understandings of equal opportunity in his discussion of affirmative action in Brazilian universities. He deconstructs the Brazilian state's paradigm of "racial democracy," which has obscured the racist nature of Brazilian society and undermined awareness and redress of racial inequality. He believes contemporary policies of affirmative action have transformative potential, but that transformation also depends on the black movement's ongoing challenge to a system that has long prevented subaltern social groups from accessing spaces of power.

Jorge Legoas P. and Fabrizio Arenas Barchi consider the experiences of rural campesino-Indigenous communities in Peru in chapter 6. They find that, as Peru's economic and governing systems adapt to international economic and political contexts and accompanying ideologies, in recent years political participation of Indigenous people as citizens in a "culturally diverse" society remains based on a predominant "mestizing" imaginary. They critically examine notions of citizenship and participation imposed by the Peruvian state and non-governmental organizations. They find that discourses of development and democracy continue to characterize rural Andean communities, their members, and their Indigenous, peasant ways of life as "poor" and encourage their transformation and, ultimately, assimilation.

In chapter 7, Jennifer Whiteman outlines the forced adaptation of the Cheyenne to changing material conditions during the conquest of the Americas and in what is today the United States. She finds that Cheyenne kinship, ceremony, and spirituality convey collective memory and promote the survival of collective identity even as the Cheyenne continue to be forced to adapt to superstructural changes imposed throughout the processes of globalization. She considers the interpretive significance of historical materialism and mestizaje as a lived process. Marxist theory can help explain what has happened to the Cheyenne, but it does not adequately consider or explain that which "makes a Cheyenne a Cheyenne." Whiteman's chapter, focused on forced adaptation and enduring cultural survival, is the transition to Part III.

Part III—Empowerment

The chapters in Part III illustrate that autonomous identity (re)creation continues to take place as ideologies related to identity continue to be imposed "from above" and sometimes manipulated for exploitative purposes. Disempowered peoples and their movements can be empowered through their interpretations of change and understanding of their own cultures and identities and of the significance of it all in a globalizing world.

In chapter 8, Kathleen S. Fine-Dare warns against the tendency to equate change with loss. She explores the identity politics of cultural performances in Quito, Ecuador. She describes the ongoing construction of indigeneity taking place as people try to make sense of change. She finds that the indigeneity of residents of Quito is largely self rather than outsider imposed. While this affords them greater agency, it has also created new conflicts based in Indigenous identity. In Quito, identity politics is both "realizing and frustrating" the goals of Indigenous organizations.

Sabine Kradolfer, in chapter 9, describes another way things are changing for Indigenous people in Argentina. She focuses mostly on the experiences of the Mapuche, who are becoming empowered through their mobilizations in the international arena. Situating their own struggles in the larger frame of the transnationalization of Indigenous movements, they are demanding recognition and respect. The "melting pot" in Argentina is made up of European immigrant identities. The state never embraced a notion of mestizaje, but international Indigenous rights movements coupled with human rights movements and Indigenous mobilizations in Argentina have compelled it to take multiculturalism into account.

In chapter 10, Angela Castañeda introduces us to women who consciously appropriate symbols of Candomblé, a "religion of survival," to make a living in a global marketplace. She draws attention to the agency of the artist, the entrepreneur, the consumer, herself as a Latina ethnographer in Brazil, and even *orixá* imagery itself. Mestizaje should be considered a lived process, drawing attention to ways people deal with racial-cultural mixture on a daily basis. Castañeda asks whether Candomblé as a lived practice, and even the orixá themselves as they are marketed, traded, and possessed, might enliven a transformative process of intercultural communication about the sacred and the secular within the global community.

In chapter 11, Philip D. Young describes changes he observed in Ngäbe communities and families over the course of the past fifty years in Panama. As contact with the dominant society has increased, he finds that educational opportunities, Ngäbe dependence on wage labor in a changing market, and access to cell phones and computers have made Ngäbe women today more independent and more assertive than they were when he began working with Ngäbe people in 1964. The women he has consulted are aware of and claim these changes.

In chapter 12, Víctor Bretón Solo de Zaldívar and Mònica Martínez Mauri ask what accounts for the relative success of Indigenous social movements. They compare and contrast Indigenous movements in Ecuador and Panama. They illustrate the transformative power of identity-based collectives, an "Indigenous us," and the rejection of mestizaje in Ecuador. They show how, despite a similar rejection of mestizo identity in Panama, Indigenous groups in Panama have been handicapped in their attempts to transform national identity politics by their lack of success so far in forming a collective identity.

Finally, in chapter 13, John Stolle-McAllister describes the emergence of the Indigenous interculturalidad movement in Ecuador and its impact on national and local politics. As Indigenous movements and thinkers consciously challenge mestizaje, they are boosting a new praxis that may encourage awareness and transformation of the identities of the peoples of the Americas—not just Indigenous peoples—and promote clearer understanding of exploitative forces of globalization. He believes Indigenous interculturalidad may be a transformative force that can empower communities to advance sustainable and equitable development strategies.

Chapters in Parts I, II, and III interpret the construction of mestizaje, disempowered peoples' responses to it and other identity constructs, barriers to empowerment through identity, and transformations in relations of power throughout the course of development as identity facilitates empowerment. Different theoretical perspectives and methodologies influence the inquiries of the authors of the chapters that follow. We invite readers to consider the research and findings of the authors and draw their own conclusions about transformations of identity and power. This is a good thing, and it will contribute to better understandings of mestizaje, globalization, and the experiences of the diverse peoples of the Americas.

Notes

1. We use the non-standard capitalization of "Indigenous" throughout the book when referencing descendants of the original inhabitants of the Americas, although, where possible, we refer to people by their more specific group names. The term is widely employed by Indigenous people to mark themselves as culturally, socially, and politically distinct from dominant mestizo society, and it is not merely a descriptor of an endemic population. This usage complies with the desires expressed by such groups as the South and Meso American Indian Rights Center to be named in such a way and follows similar standard practices in referring to "Native" Americans and national groups.

2. Since colonial times, the belief has existed that at the time of the next pachakuti the Inca will return.

3. It should be noted, however, that the first fifty years after European contact and colonization of what is now Latin America and the Caribbean was a period during which change was at least as rapid as the current wave of rapid change—and in ways more traumatic and devastating for the Indigenous populations.

4. In 1997, Young supervised an MA-level exit paper by a student in the International Studies Program at the University of Oregon entitled "Globalization: Advocates, Opponents and Rebels" (Bryer 1997), a 110-page review of a sizable sample of the definitions and debates about globalization in the literature of the time—not all of the extant literature, for even then the student found the quantity to be overwhelming. Remarkably, the range of definitions continues to be extensive, and the contentious debates continue.

5. Some scholars, particularly economists, argue that the new technology of communication and transportation is not necessarily a part of the phenomenon of globalization. In a very strict sense, this may be true. However, even globalization characterized as only economic phenomena could not have occurred nor continue to occur without the technological innovations of the late twentieth and early twenty-first centuries.

6. In reality, completely free markets, in which prices are governed only by the laws of supply and demand, do not exist. This is different from free trade, which, in theory, means that goods flow freely across national borders without tariffs or subsidies or other government restrictions being imposed. Free trade is sometimes given a wider meaning to include the free movement of labor, services,

and capital as well. International Monetary Fund (IMF) structural adjustment policies generally include, in addition to the free movement of goods, the free movement of services and of capital (called direct foreign investment) but not labor. In reality, whether narrowly or broadly defined, there is no completely "free" trade.

7. The editors wish to make it clear that we do not espouse Esteva-Fabregat's views.

8. See Vasconcelos 1997.

9. Young People's Cultural Association—literally "Youth Athenaeum." Athenae are clubs, mostly elite intellectual associations dedicated to culture, art, and literature. They take their name from the sanctuary of the goddess Athena, the goddess of wisdom, the arts, etc. One prominent example, still in existence, was established in 1824 as a private gentlemen's club in London.

10. The historical trajectory of indigenismo in the Central Andean countries, and especially Peru, differs from that of Mexico. These differences are not explored here. A good source, though not available in English, is Marzal (1993). An English summary of the historical differences between Peruvian and Mexican indigenismo is Jordan-Ramos (2010b), chap. 2.

11. One stimulus to the pan-Indian movement was arguably the publication of Vine Deloria Jr.'s *Custer Died for Your Sins* in the United States in 1969.

12. Global recognition of the rights of Indigenous peoples was finally agreed upon, after years of debate, by the United Nations in the Declaration on the Rights of Indigenous Peoples, adopted by General Assembly Resolution 61/295 on September 13, 2007.

13. Indigenous social movements have been discussed widely within the conceptual frameworks of the politics of identity (see Brysk 2000; Van Cott 2005; Yashar 1998, 2005 inter alia).

14. There is some question as to whether indigeneity was translated into Spanish as indianidad or vice versa. We currently suggest that indigeneity is an English translation of indianidad, based on the fact that Peruvian intellectual José Uriel García used the term in 1937 to convey what appears to be its contemporary meaning.

15. Needler received his PhD from Harvard in 1960 and went on to teach political science as a Latin Americanist (R. Gomez 1967). His academic career included serving as dean of the School of International Studies at the University of the Pacific in Stockton, California, and teaching in the Department of Political Science at the University of New Mexico.

16. Scheckel (1998) provides an engaging analysis of American Indians and national identity in what is today the United States.

17. In use since the end of the eighteenth century, the term became popular after a 1909 play of the same name by Israel Zangwill.

18. For more on affirmative action in Brazil, see chapter 5 by dos Santos Vieira in this volume.

19. Cherríe Moraga, "The (W)rite to Remember: Indígena as Scribe 2004–5 (an excerpt)" in Flores and Rosaldo (2007, 377).

20. Argentina, Bolivia, Brazil, Colombia, Ecuador, Guatemala, Mexico, Nicaragua, Panama, Paraguay, and Venezuela (Stavenhagen 2006, 2008)

21. An excellent compilation of recent scholarship assessing Indigenous autonomy is González Pérez, Burguete Cal y Mayor, and Ortiz-T., 2010.

22. Interculturalidad translates to English as "interculturality." We use the Spanish in this chapter for two reasons: first, because we are citing scholars and organizations in Latin America that use the term interculturalidad and share at least a similar understanding of the tenets of interculturalidad employed in Indigenous resistance movements; and second, because the term "interculturality" in English has been used in different disciplines and by different writers to mean a number of different things. The study of critical interculturalidad is becoming more widespread, is being undertaken by more Latin American Studies scholars, and is interpreted and approached from a variety of perspectives. Besides those cited in this chapter, recommended sources on interculturalidad include Dembicz (2004), Saavedra (2007), and Viaña Uzieda et al. (2009). For more on different understandings of interculturalidad, see the introduction to chapter 13 by Stolle-McAllister in this volume.

23. Good examples have been set forth in the Declaration of Quito (First Continental Encounter of Indigenous Peoples 1990) and, more recently, by the Indigenous Peoples Working Group of the World People's Conference on Climate Change and the Rights of Mother Earth, convened by Bolivian President Evo Morales in Bolivia in 2010. The Working Group declared: "This . . . is a space in which to channel the voices, wisdom, and reclamation of our origins that are present today in Indigenous and First Nations peoples. We aim to encourage and promote Indigenous visions, practices, and relationships of harmony with nature, and to share proposals regarding climate change and the defense of Mother Earth" (Working Group 7 2010). For more on the World People's Conference on Climate Change and the Rights of Mother Earth, see Schipani and Vidal (2010) and Lovato (2010).

PART ONE

Constructing *Mestizaje*

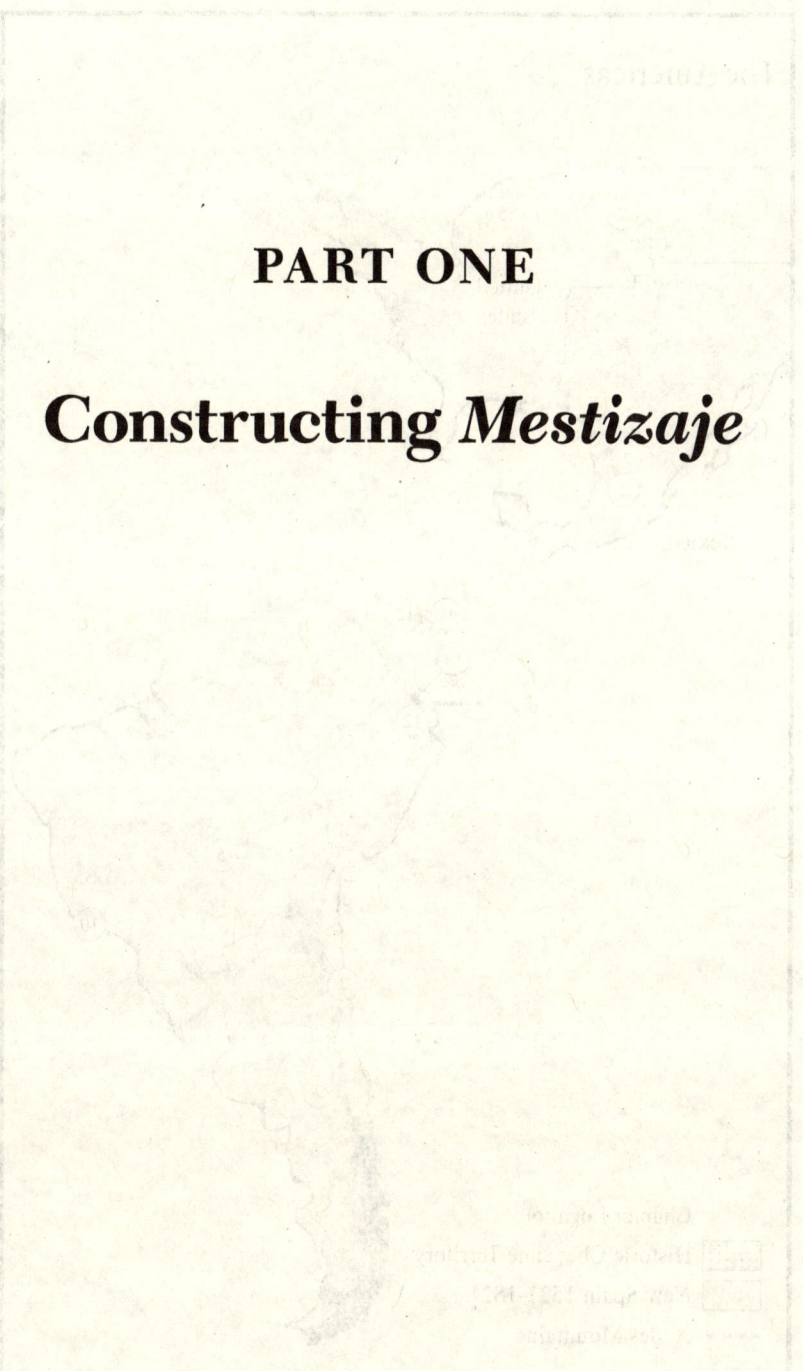

The Americas

United
States

Mexico

7

1
2

11 12

13

8   12

6
4

5

10

3

9

○ Chapter Location
▦ Historic Cheyenne Territory
▨ New Spain 1521-1821
---- Andes Mountains

FIGURE I.IA AND FIGURE I.IB. Map of the Americas. Jennifer Hackett,
Manastash Mapping LLC.

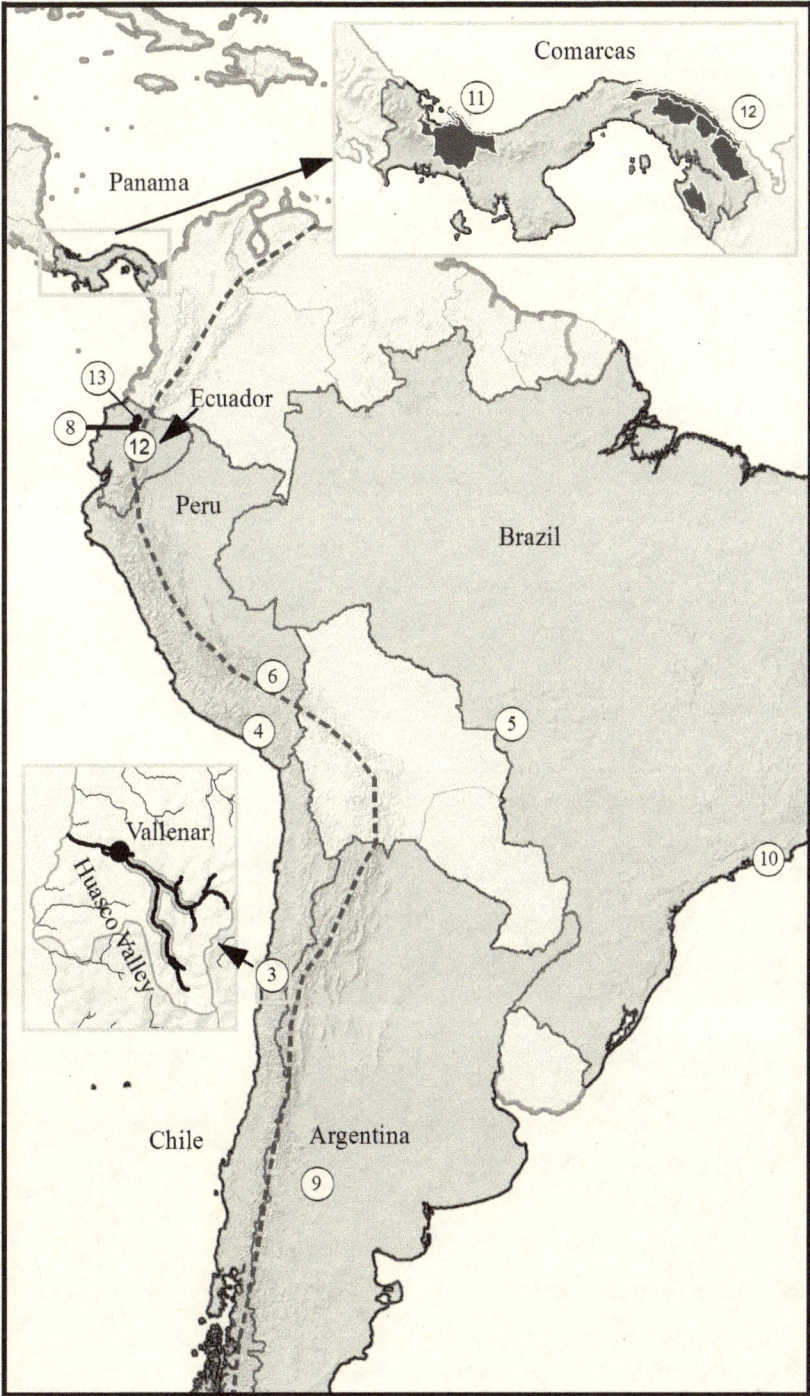

Comarcas

(11)
(12)

Panama

(13)
(8)
(12)
Ecuador

Peru

Brazil

(6)
(4)
(5)

(10)

Vallenar

Huasco Valley

(3)

Chile

Argentina

(9)

CHAPTER ONE

The Revolutionary Encounter

REX WIRTH

People have been living in the Valley of Mexico for a very long time. The cities of the valley have ranked among the top ten in population in the world since the time of the Roman Empire. Today, Mexico City is one the largest cities in the world. This is a phenomenal comeback because only five hundred years ago the valley suffered catastrophic depopulation as a result of the Spanish Conquest.

The decline bottomed out in the mid-1600s, leaving the population base upon which modern Mexico was built: Spaniards who become permanent residents, survivors of African slavery, and the Indigenous population. There is controversy about the numbers, but most agree on the proportions. Eric Wolf (1959), who explored in depth aspects of several of the paths explored in this chapter, synthesized the various estimates and established base populations: the Indigenous population, after a loss of six-sevenths (6/7) of its pre-conquest base, was set at around 2,000,000, Spaniards at 300,000, and blacks at 250,000.

Of all of the states in the Americas with both large land areas and populations, Mexico is unique in that the current mestizo population of over 100,000,000 is largely a result of the mixing of the three groups in this original base. This mixing is *mestizaje*. Mixing and melting are not confined to genetics, but the genetic aspect is of particular importance in instances where it is appropriated and incorporated through political action into the culture. Identities are cultural creations, and it is the mixing of these identities over time that defines a people or a nation.

The nations of the United States and Mexico are neighbors, but the population of the United States results from continuous immigration and annexation, whereas that of Mexico developed in situ. Because they represent polar extremes on this dimension in the Americas, the uniqueness of the Mexican experience will be developed by contrasting it with that of the United States.

The two countries developed in very different conditions because of temporal differences. Mexico was more or less an established cultural entity before the upheavals that ushered in modernity, and those who were Mexicans adapted to change as it took place around them. In the north, culture was built anew.

The perspective of "pluralism," be it melting pot or salad bowl, provides the best window on cultural politics in the United States, but pluralism is a theory, a normative ideal, not a cultural identity. Mestizaje, on the other hand, is a cultural identity that has become a lens for examining existing and emerging patterns of the mixing of peoples and cultures in Mexico. Political scientists frequently use "pluralism" in the construction of general typologies of state governance (usually relating it to some aspect of "democracy") to classify societies. Mestizaje has not been used in the construction of such typologies. The purpose of the explorations in this chapter is to find out why this has been the case. After a quick trip down the essential historical paths in search of clues, patterns, similarities, and differences, the mestizaje concept will be revisited, reconfigured, and fitted into a more inclusive typology.

All Roads Lead to Anáhuac

By 200 BC, Rome had defeated Carthage in the Punic Wars, and the Celtic peoples of Italy to the north and south of the city had been Romanized, while in the Valley of Mexico, Teotihuacán was emerging as a comparable center of civilization whose influence and legend would develop parallel to that of Rome. The conquests, conflicts, and migrations that swirled around these centers in Mexico and the Mediterranean as they expanded, divided, were invaded, and were displaced by successor states would shape the identities, spawn the legends, and engender the gods of their offspring whose paths meet at Lake Texcoco 1,500 years later.

Caesar to Cortés

The last leg of the journey to Tenochtitlán, the Aztec capital on the lake, starts in the recently reconquered Moorish city of Seville in that part of Spain still known as the "Land of the Vandals." To understand the clash of cultures that took place when Hernán Cortés arrived, the origins and paths in Europe that brought the peoples of Spain together on the eve of Columbus's "discovery" of the Americas must be revisited.

Even though people had been there for a long time, our journey will begin as control of the Iberian Peninsula passed from Carthage to Rome at the end of the Punic Wars (264 BC–146 BC). Southern France and Catalonia had important maritime centers, but the rest of the area was marginal to the Romans, who concentrated their efforts on expansion into Gaul. With the completion of Julius Caesar's conquest of Gaul (50 BC) and its "Latinization," or inclusion into the Roman world, the history of the Western Empire began. Some three hundred years later, it came into its own when Constantine made Christianity the state religion of the empire and then moved his seat of government to Turkey, leaving Rome as the center of the Catholic Church and the Western Empire. From this point on, the history of empire in the West, though there were still emperors, is pretty much the story of the popes at Rome—the Holy See.

Throughout the fifth century, Europe was threatened by the Huns. By 450, the Hunnic Empire covered all of Central Europe, stretching from Russia to Turkey. Given the choice between fighting Romans or Huns, the Vandals, who lived in the area of Silesia, chose the Romans and crossed over into Gaul in the fourth century. After some involvement as allies of Rome against the Huns, they moved on into Spain where they established themselves in what is today Andalusia, the Land of the Vandals. Later, when the Romans and their Visigoth allies began to harass them, they attacked the Roman ports, assembled a Teutonic fleet in the Mediterranean, raided coastal areas, and ultimately established an empire in North Africa. They took Carthage in 435 and were living there in oriental splendor when, in 455, they launched their famous sack of Rome.

The Vandals were finally defeated and the royal family exiled in Turkey as a result of the "reconquest" of Africa launched by Emperor Justinian of the Eastern Empire in 533. During the Vandal reign, many Moors served in the multiethnic armies they commanded, and it appears that no small amount of mixing took place. Mestizaje, it seems, has a long history. In addition to being scattered throughout North Africa, no doubt many descendants of the Vandals remained in Southern Spain and others returned as part of the Moorish conquest.

The Visigoths in Spain were quickly dispatched by an Islamic army out of North Africa in 711, and the advance of the Moors was not stopped until they were turned back outside of Paris by Charles Martel, grandfather of Charlemagne. After coming to the Frankish throne, Charlemagne reestablished the borders of France and set up a series of buffer states (counties), known as the Spanish marches, along the Pyrenees to contain Islam in Iberia. He restored Italy, and the pope crowned him Holy Roman Emperor in 800.

Although the Reconquista (reconquest) of Spain is often seen as starting within a couple of decades after the initial invasion with the first Moorish setback, it really started much later after it had fermented in the Spanish marches. During this period, the Goths became more Catholic than the pope, and the local fervor to free Christian Europe from Islam exceeded that of the Crusades.

The bones of Santiago (Saint James) were discovered on the coast of Galicia in 814, and he was soon elevated to the status of the patron saint of Spain and, particularly, of the Reconquista. Revered as Santiago Matamoros ("Moor Slayer"), he lived as an active presence on the battlefield. Pilgrims began to flock to the site, and a succession of ever-larger churches were constructed to house the remains. This became too much for the Moors, and they burned the cathedral at Compostela in 997 and forced resident Catholics to carry the gates and bells south, where they were incorporated into the Alhambra mosque. In 1026, Christian forces under the protection of Santiago Matamoros took Córdoba and forced the Muslims to carry the gates and bells to Toledo. And so it went, back and forth, with escalating mysticism and animosity. The present-day cathedral of Santiago de Compostela in Galicia in northwest Spain was completed during the career of Spain's greatest hero, the legendary El Cid. When, as a boy at the movies, I saw Charlton Heston riding down the beach as El Cid, I assumed that he was working for Ferdinand and Isabella and that his ride drove the last Moor out of Spain. But that would have to wait another four hundred years, during which time the legends of El Cid grew as Christian soldiers under the protection of Santiago Matamoros waged a holy war that seesawed southward as the Spanish kingdoms consolidated in the north, and the Way of Saint James, to Santiago de Compostela, became the most traveled pilgrimage route in the world.

Victory over the Moors was achieved in 1492 by Ferdinand and Isabella. Their marriage had united Leon/Castile and Aragon, bringing the kingdoms that had grown out of Charlemagne's marches into a unified Spain. With the Moors out of the way and Columbus on his way to the Indies, it is time to turn our attention to the consolidation of Catholic Spain and the cultural mythology that grew up around the unemployed conquistadors and their successors, like Cortés, who would carry it to the New World.

Safe from harm and doubt, thanks to Santiago Matamoros, Catholic Spain had no need for scientific justifications. In spite of this, what we call today "blood quantum" became the cultural mechanism for state control and security, and the consolidation and cleansing of the new nation. It was a strange notion. In Baroque Spain, "blood quantum" was a religious concept equated with a natural propensity to accept Christ. Spanish blood, of course, endowed one with the highest propensity, while Moorish blood made it difficult for one to see the light. Bad blood could be overcome with great effort, but beyond a certain point, the absence of good blood would make conversion nearly impossible. Because of this, Moors who had accepted the gospel initially could remain in Spain. By 1515, however, laws were in place that required the removal of all Moors, as had been the case with Jews since 1492. Anyone lacking sufficient good blood had to go. Any bad blood, and it is safe to assume that everyone had some, could still corrupt the rest and ferment heresy inside a person, so the defense of the Church and the people required exceptional spiritual force, skill, and will—the Inquisition.

Hernán Cortés de Monroy y Pizarro was born into this world in 1485. He set out for the Americas in 1504, carrying with him all the heavy baggage of victorious Spanish Christendom. Guided and protected by Santiago Mataíndios ("Indian Slayer"), Cortés sailed from Cuba and landed on the coast of Mexico in 1519, hooked up with La Malinche (his female translator and guide), and made his way to Lake Texcoco, where our Old World road from the Mediterranean ends.

Aztlán to Texcoco

It is certain that there were people living throughout central and southern Mexico before the Nahua and the Maya. What they contribute to the cultural mix might be roughly comparable to the pre-Roman peoples of Italy or pre-Carthaginian peoples of Spain and is equally hard to ascertain. Legends and accounts of the early Spanish chroniclers and modern revisionists all reveal a similar pattern. It is the general pattern framed in its mythical context, not the factual details, that is of interest here.

The Chicano movement's revival of the myth of Aztlán with a second "fertile crescent" formed by the Rio Grande and the Rio Gila seems like a good place to start. It is the legendary source of the migration of the Nahua peoples and of successive migrations southward to Anáhuac, the former lake basin areas of the Valley of Mexico, around what is today Mexico City. The Aztecs (Mexica) encountered by Cortés were the last of several Nahua groups to make the trip. Their conquest of the Valley of Mexico took place about the time of the Crusades in Europe. Their route followed the Pacific coast south to the homeland of the Tarascans, today Michoacán, whence they climbed up to the Central Mexican Plateau. By the fifteenth century, they had consolidated their control of most of the plateau and exercised dominion over an extensive empire. Its capital, Tenochtitlán, was, during the 1400s, one of the largest cities in the world— some say the largest, while others say it was Córdoba. By any count, it was in the top seven and, according to Cortés, the cleanest and perhaps the most beautiful.

Although it is probable that people came to the Americas by routes other than the land bridge, the official story told at the Museo Nacional de Antropología (National Museum of Anthropology) in Mexico City is based on the land bridge. Understandings of paths, numbers, magnitudes, accomplishments, consequences, and legends that grew out of the various southward migrations are varied and changing. Chroniclers, historians, and scientific observers of all kinds are plentiful along the full length of the route. For present purposes, Mexican chronicler Justo Sierra (1969) is the best guide for the New World roads that led to Lake Texcoco because his vantage point during the heady days of Porfirio Díaz's triumphant Mexicanism represents a mythical reality that provides continuity with legends of Santiago Matamoros in Spain up to the Mexican Revolution.

Sierra's mystical Mexican adventure, the details of which differ from accepted contemporary archeological and historical accounts, starts in the north. He tells of the population spreading southward over time. As some of the cliff dwellers of the Rio Grande/Rio Gila move eastward toward the land of the Mound Builders of the Mississippi River valley, others head down the Pacific coast. The Mound Builders move southward by land and sea. The seagoing groups settle the Antilles and move on to the Yucatán Peninsula to catalyze Mayan development, while the others move down the coast and up to the Central Mexican Plateau to the area of Teotihuacán. Those who move eastward out of the vicinity of the Rio Grande and Rio Gila merge with westward flows from the Mississippi Valley to form the Chichimeca and move southward through central Mexico. Had the Spaniards not destroyed their entire written record, it seems probable that the rise-and-fall stories of civilizations in the Central Mexican Plateau and the Yucatán Peninsula would be as intricate and inspiring as our "Romantic" notions of Mediterranean civilizations.

By the middle of the first century BC, the Yucatán had become one of the most densely populated areas ever. Studies using the latest sensing technology support Sierra's contention that "scarcely an inch of earth, it seems, was left uncultivated" (Sierra 1969, 36). After a succession of empires, alternating between those of Nahua peoples and others, the Nahua-based Toltec Empire (800–1200) emerged in the basin areas of the Valley of Mexico and spread to cover all of the ancient sites, including Teotihuacán. It set in motion new mythical and religious dynamics that continue to form the nexus of conflict at all levels down to the individual in Mexico to this day. The influence of Santiago Matamoros pales in the face of the mythical Quetzalcoatl, the god-king, prophet-saint of the Toltecs and of modern Mexico.

Sometime around the tenth century AD, as Toltec civilization reached its pinnacle, the old blood rites, often associated with cannibalism, were replaced by a New World gospel of light. The social fissure opened by the reforms of Quetzalcoatl led to protracted civil war that was ultimately the undoing of the Toltecs. With the eventual triumph of evil over good, Quetzalcoatl departed, but promised to return. It's hard to say whether or not the people of Tenochtitlán held the vision of a white god whose return was anticipated when Cortés arrived, but as it was told by subsequent clergy and chroniclers, there was no doubt.

As the Old World and New World paths drew ever closer to Anáhuac, the last wave of Nahua, the Aztecs, made their way up to the Central Mexican Plateau. By the eleventh century, they had settled around Lake Texcoco, eventually on two islands in the lake, after being involved in numerous intrigues and conflicts with the Tepaneca, who had emerged victorious out of the fray that undid the Toltecs. The Aztecs mixed and allied with the remnants of Tolteca and began to build their cities and wait for a new day. Their new day was ushered in by Montezuma I, who ruled the Aztec from 1440 to 1469, reestablished Nahua control of the whole Valley of Mexico, and scored military victories throughout the lands as far south as Guatemala. Although he established some colonies, he never attempted to consolidate his conquests. His main interest seemed to be the safety of Aztec merchants and the flow of goods to Tenochtitlán.

Fifty years later, Cortés arrived at Anáhuac and entered the domain of Montezuma II. Accompanied by Santiago and wearing the mantle of Quetzalcoatl, he claimed the empire, the prize the conquistadors deserved for returning Spain to Christendom.

Mestizaje: The Birth of a Nation

Cortés entered the game of musical chairs that had been going on for centuries in the Valley of Mexico. The general pattern seemed to revolve around triple alliances. An alliance would form to unseat a dominant power, after which one of the parties to the alliance would consolidate its power and emerge as the imperial center, only to be undone by the next alliance. Aztecs had consolidated their power, except for the Tlaxcalteca, who were waiting their turn to form the next alliance when Cortés arrived, recruited them, and started a new game.

Wrapped in the myth of Quetzalcoatl and through the consummate use of terror and diplomacy, an isolated band of a few hundred Spaniards under the conquistador undid the last empire of Anáhuac. After the fall of Tenochtitlán, the rest of the empire and even the undefeated Tarascans fell like dominos. Within three years, victory was complete and with Cuauhtémoc, the last Aztec emperor, reduced to a figurehead, Cortés began to build his capital on the ruins of Tenochtitlán.

The revolution (the undoing of the understanding of "who we are"), precipitated by the wrath of the god-king Quetzalcoatl and the taking of the prize for Christendom, might have led to consolidation, but Cortés was first and foremost the conquistador. When a challenge arose in the south, he felt compelled to launch what turned out to be an ill-fated campaign. By leaving the consolidation of the center to others, he broke the momentum. Completion of the revolution was left to future generations, and New Spain became the project of churchmen and bureaucrats.

Although he recovered and eventually returned from Spain as the marquis of the Valley of Oaxaca, Cortés's moment had passed. He and La Malinche had a son named Martín (Krauze 1997), not the first mestizo but certainly the archetype. Accepted as a legitimate heir by the conquistador, he was educated in Spain, which included being in service to the future king. He returned to Mexico with his half brother (better born), also Martín, the second marquis. As Martín the Mestizo, he helped spark the revolutionary struggle of blood and culture that continues today.

As the officials of the Real Audiencia took over the government of New Spain, and the clerical orders set out to convert the Indians, the conquest of New Spain in what is today northern Mexico continued. But it was the Indians who lead the conquest. Wearing full armor and carrying the title of captain-general, Indigenous leaders set out to pacify the savage Chichimeca and secure mines and territories for the Crown, worn by the Holy Roman emperor. They rode, as the conquistadors before them, with Santiago and prepared the way for the new gospel of Quetzalcoatl.

Cast into the revolutionary caldron, the friars wove a new and powerful mythology. Quetzalcoatl wasn't Cortés or any other adventurer: he was Saint Thomas (the doubting disciple of Christ), who had moved on from his mission in India centuries before to bring Christianity to the Toltecs. Some versions have him doing Columbus in reverse, but most involve supernatural means. However he got to the Americas, when the Toltecs rejected his message, he departed in the company of the Virgin of Guadalupe to continue his work in the Yucatán. With the Virgin's return in 1531, both of them were now back among the friars, at the head of the missionary forces consolidating the work of Santiago.

With souls to save and evil to eradicate, the old order was re-created in New Spain and the question of "blood" re-emerged. Bartolomé de las Casas made the case for the Indians, essentially arguing "innocent blood," but the other side took up the Reconquista position of "bad blood." Although the Indians emerged innocent from the theological wars, they were defined as minor children until they could be trained up. This licensed the Creoles, those born in the Americas to the Spanish, to launch the exploitative caste system. The advantages conferred on whites (Creoles) by blood left the Indians with a status similar to minor children at the other pole of the main axis of mixing/non-mixing that centered on Martín Cortés (the Mestizo). Mestizaje became the center of the revolutionary struggle.

Black Legends

The intensely religious nature of the struggles for emancipation and domination within Spain and between Spain and the rest of the world was conducive to a black-white dichotomy where the only test of virtue was victory. Defeat arose from corruption and victory vindicated anything. Godlike heroes riding a string of triumphs became devils when they suffered a defeat, and contemporary problems were laid at the feet of the fallen as they were sucked into the caldron of the "Black Legend." Cortés was vilified as he had vilified Montezuma and his priests. When his sons returned to Mexico and took up the cause of the Creoles, the second marquis of Oaxaca was arrested with his brother, Martín the Mestizo, and tortured by the Spanish authorities. The Mestizo was spared by the king and lived to see the defeat of the Spanish Armada, which ended the glory days and plunged Spain itself into the realm of the Black Legend as the British and Dutch painted it as retrograde, savage, and bloodthirsty.

New Spain

Before the end of the eighteenth century, the creative and contending forces that would shape Mexico were in place. The Crown had used the Church as the means of pacification and Christianization of the Indians in New Spain. Sierra lays out the pattern of this enterprise by describing the career of the "Peacemakers" (the two apostles who landed in 1523 and the four great bishops: Bartolomé de las Casas, Juan de Zumárraga, Sebastián Ramírez de Fuenleal, and Vasco de Quiroga). It was officially launched when a contingent of twelve friars, the apostles, was sent to establish colonial outposts. Their numbers multiplied along with the area controlled by the orders, and they amassed wealth over the three centuries until independence. The land-use patterns resulting from their efforts were superimposed upon existing patterns produced by the conquest. Encomiendas had been established when the conquistadors distributed prerogatives and control over Indian labor in specific areas to their men. Their children, the Creoles, came to see themselves as the only legitimate heirs of the conquest and the natural nobility of New Spain. Interest and exclusivity put the Creoles at odds with the ecclesiastical Peacemakers, but their mythological baggage kept them loyal to the Church and the Crown. Finally, universities, established in conjunction with the evangelical and colonizing mission and shunned by the Creoles, became the breeding ground for a new mestizo intellectual class. As the mestizo population grew, these intellectuals were augmented by a petit bourgeois of mestizo shopkeepers and traders. The three elements combined in fruitful ways outside of the center, especially in Michoacán, but external forces in Europe kept the capital in turmoil.

When I began this project, I assumed that wars and the displacements they caused would be the key factors, but it turns out to be not war, but marriage. The Hapsburgs had realized this long before Ferdinand and Isabella united the kingdoms of Aragon and Castile that sprang from Charlemagne's marches. The imperial family of the Holy Roman Empire was

quick to marry into the new line, and by the mid-sixteenth century, Hapsburgs were on the Spanish throne and Mexico was part of the Holy Roman
Empire. Charlemagne's empire, once the Kingdom of the Franks, had
passed to Hapsburg control and, with the incorporation of the Low Countries through marriage, encircled Bourbon France. The result of the
Hapsburgs' successful marriage campaign was an empire that included
the Low Countries, Portugal, Spain, the Hapsburg domains in the east,
and holdings in Italy's and Spain's American colonies.

Tensions caused by the encirclement of France, combined with the English plunder of gold on the high seas and growing Dutch discontent with
their absentee Hapsburg rulers, resulted in continuous warfare that required an ever-larger flow of gold from the Spanish Main to Antwerp. The
Hapsburg king of Spain responded with severe measures, involving special emissaries with absolute power and the Inquisition, to stem the in-
surrection in the north and extract needed resources from the Americas.
Viceroys, visitors, bishops, and strong men from the Audiencias and other
institutions parlayed success in amassing gold reserves into tremendous
personal power, only to be displaced by a new appointee when the gold
flow was insufficient. As the sixteenth century drew to a close, the Dutch
achieved virtual independence during a truce in the Eighty Years' War,
but the Hapsburg Empire renewed its efforts to retain control of the Low
Countries, which continued until 1648 when both the Thirty Years' War
and the Eighty Years' War ended. Spain lost the Northern Netherlands,
and the Spanish (or Southern) Netherlands were cut off from the sea when
the Dutch closed the river to Antwerp.

As the Westphalian world of the nation-state emerged, Hapsburg
Spain was on the ropes. When the Bourbons, through marriage, seized
the Spanish throne in 1714, it was over. As the clock ticked down to the
French Revolution, the Bourbons completed the construction of the
breeding ground for future "strong men" in the New World by intro-
ducing French-style centralized government and a standing army into
Mexico.

As things disintegrated under the pressure of the French Revolution,
the British and Americans planned to take over and divide Spanish holdings in the Americas. These plans were upset not so much by Bonaparte's success on the battlefield as by "family affairs." Napoleon's Caesarism
made him an instant hit with the descendants of the conquistadors, but
his replacement of the Spanish king with his brother Joseph was an as-
sault on Spanish Christendom that could not be tolerated on either side
of the ocean. This upheaval left Portugal open to conquest. The English,
who could not resist the easy pickings, abandoned their projects in the
Americas. Having been hermetically sealed in the bubble of the Reconquista for three hundred years, Mexicans could not accept the idea that
they were subject to the will of the "people of Spain": king, yes; committee, never! This, coupled with the scrapping of U.S./English plans for the

rest of America, triggered the movement for independence in Mexico, which spread throughout Spanish America in 1810.

As the strong-man tradition of military heroes and peacemakers alike turned messianic, the only test of virtue remained success, and the fallen kept the caldron of the Black Legend boiling. When independence was achieved after two decades of struggle, three contenders for the title "Father of the Country" were dead at the hands of their countrymen, and Mexico was under the protection of the Monroe Doctrine.

Mexicans, Mestizos, Mexicanism, and Mestizaje

After independence the new nation began to work out its identity. To the north, the "Americans" were developing a national identity, "Americanism," which incorporated considerable diversity in terms of European origins but would exclude slaves and what was left of the Indigenous peoples. In Mexico, the preponderance of the population was drawn from pre-conquest Indigenous civilizations. The United States of America spun off of the juggernaut of the British Empire while it was soaring to its heights, whereas the United States of Mexico was launched from the final crash that shattered the Spanish enterprise. Born of the Enlightenment, Americanism was built upon the new set of ideas that came to define the Age of Reason, whereas Mexicanism was built upon the cultural remains of two shattered empires and the first truly global system that had grown out of Rome and, in the end, centered on the Spanish Main, through which the wealth of the Far East and the Americas had been funneled to Europe and squandered in the death throes of the Old World order.

Roads to Anáhuac Revisited

Systems of representative government that have emerged out of the European Renaissance and Enlightenments have been classified by political analysts in many different ways. Fig. 1.1 presents three of the dominant types (elitist, corporatist, and pluralist) and a fourth (statist) as they relate to developmental conditions and processes.

The cell labeled statist has been problematic. Statism is usually considered to be beyond the range of "democracy" and is omitted from consideration, but as observed earlier with the ideas of mestizaje and pluralism, unlike the other established types, the statist type has not been backed by corresponding normative and/or explanatory theories of democracy and civil society. As illustrated in fig. 1.1, England, Germany, France, and the United States are empirical examples of the modal types. Theories of corporatism, elitism, and pluralism are in place to explain the respective

	Endogenous	Exogenous
	ELITIST (Accommodation)	PLURALIST (Assimilation)
−	England	United States
Accessibility		
	CORPORATIST (Adaptation)	STATIST (Homogenization)
+	Germany	France

FIGURE 1.1. Western systems typology

patterns of representative republican government and civil society, but comparable statist theories have yet to emerge. As a consequence, pluralist analyses have produced negative images of both France and Mexico.

So far we have examined mestizaje in terms of its origins in Mexico. Now it will be contrasted with pluralism in the United States. Mexico must be located in the above matrix with the big four. Since a substantial portion of the Old World road to Anáhuac involved France, the developmental sketches of France and Mexico will be revisited in search of patterns upon which to base the elaboration of the required theoretical perspectives, place Mexico in the statist tradition, and lay the basis for a more comprehensive comparative framework and a better understanding of the differences between the United States and Mexico.

The first task is to distinguish between different types of acculturation: the pluralist process of assimilation results in an incorporation of diverse individuals under a common creed, while the statist type rests on a more pervasive multidimensional mixing best characterized as homogenization. On the road to Anáhuac, we passed through France with the Vandals as Attila was making his push into Roman territory. At that time, Roman acculturation had been moving forward for over three hundred years. This Latinization was comparable to the Hispanicization of Mexico. Since both of these developments were completed before contemporary theorizing about democracy began during the settlement of North America, they were incorporated, along with feudalism, as part of the constellation of oppression targeted by Enlightenment thought. As the Enlightenment shifted the focus of attention from the corporate group to the individual, rational theories about the establishment and organization of societies began to challenge old notions of social order.

Most of the theorists presented in fig. 1.2 based their rational orders (theories of human nature, society, and government) on speculation about

	Hierarchical	
Pre-state (evolution)		Anti-state (progress)
CONSERVATIVE (Burke)		LIBERAL (Locke)
Cooperative		Competitive
Stateless (cooperation)		Statist (revolution)
SOCIALIST (Rousseau)		ANARCHIST (Hobbes)
	Egalitarian	

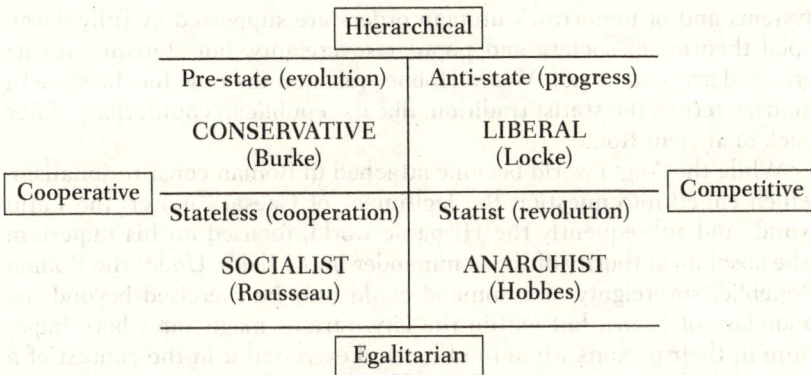

FIGURE 1.2. Democratization of cultures

pre-societal conditions in a "state of nature" and imagined that rational individuals had entered into contracts to improve their lot. The different conceptions of the original condition lead to competing conclusions about what is possible and desirable for organized human society.

The first of these theorists emerged out of the turmoil (anarchy) of the English Civil War (1642–1651). For Thomas Hobbes (1588–1679), the state of nature was war of "all against all" and "life was nasty, brutish and short." The only sure cure was the all-powerful state. Such ideas were unattractive to Enlightenment thinkers, but being both rational and individualist, they set the mold for the more optimistic theorists who followed.

As the Glorious Revolution brought a new king and prosperity to an England where Commons was supreme, John Locke (1632–1704) was able to imagine a more benign state of nature where people were basically nice and got on well most of the time, but scarcity could still cause problems. In these zero-sum and negative-sum instances, the state was needed as an impartial referee, but only in the case of irreconcilable differences between individuals. Because it served merely to ameliorate the already favorable conditions in the state of nature, the state had limited range and could not be allowed to exceed the bounds of necessity.

Edmund Burke (1729–1797) defended tradition against notions of contracts, while Jean-Jacques Rousseau (1712–1778) put forth a contract as the basis of a community. For him, it was not a question of individuals giving up the right of self-defense to create the state in order to secure better protection. Rather, the contract was a social agreement where each would surrender all rights in equal measure to all, making the defense of the rights of others the defense of one's actual rights. Such an arrangement would not require a state. The conservative, liberal, and socialist cultures that are the basis of the partisan competitions in today's representative systems and of tomorrow's utopian orders are supported by fully developed theories of society and popular sovereignty, but statism with its pre-modern roots is not. While Hobbes restated the case for the state in modern terms, the statist tradition, like its republican counterpart, dates back to ancient Rome.

While the Anglo world became attached to Roman constitutionalism, which called into question the legitimacy of Caesar's power, the Latin world, and subsequently the Hispanic world, focused on his imperium (the absolute authority of the commander in the field). Under the Roman Republic, sovereignty of command could only be exercised beyond the boundary of Rome, but within the city, various magistrates bore imperium in their persons while in office and exercised it in the context of a hierarchy and a system of checks and balances. The exception to this was the granting of emergency power to a dictator who held absolute power (imperium) over all officials, even in the city. Such power was constitutionally limited to six months, but Caesar ultimately became dictator for life. Was he ambitious? Did he subvert the constitution? Or was he above it and politics, protecting the city as his most recent successor, Charles de Gaulle, and subsequent presidents of France protect their country?

Dictator (President) for Life carries an ancient, sometimes honorable heritage, but today "dictator" has become the favorite pejorative in the United States. It has replaced the Black Legend as the mechanism for villainizing and controlling foreign states and leaders. This approach seems to have become current in the Porfirio Díaz era and is now the favorite, not only of Americans but also of constitutionalists everywhere. Dictators often hide behind sham constitutions and elections, but true republicans can detect such deceptions and protect the peoples of the world from them. Such threats to the freedom of the Mexican people have been a constant concern of American policy makers, especially after the Mexican Revolution of 1910.

The Latin World

The world of Caesar's imperium included all of the Celtic peoples of continental Europe. As with Italy, their incorporation was complete. They became Roman and spoke Latin. Although there was no great physiological distinction between the people of Italy and Gaul, the Celtic tongues had to give way to Latin to forge a single Roman patrimony that would eventually center on France and persist in various forms to the dawn of the twentieth century. Spain, as part of the Carthaginian and Islamic domains during the Roman era, was never fully incorporated, although Spanish, like French and Italian, is a Romance language.

France and Italy became the Latin world. But the Americas are a different story. It was Spanish that became the imperial language and the

glue of the new nations, not Latin. Spain and the imperium of the conquistadors should get the credit, not the Romans (Esteva-Fabregat 1995).

The New World

Although Spanish and Portuguese are the languages of most of the nations of Latin America, only in Mexico do we find conditions for Hispan-
ization that are comparable to those of Latinization in Roman Gaul.
Cortés's conquest of New Spain is even more spectacular than Caesar's
of Gaul, and the catastrophic depopulation of Mexico combined with the
lack of immigration created a situation that produced patterns of consolidation and governance similar to those of Gaul. Admittedly, the problem of creating a new race from the remnants of several old ones in a
depopulated area is more difficult than melting together remnants of dispersed groups to consolidate their land base, but both Romans and Spaniards faced similar problems and, consequently, followed similar paths. The
argument here is that the Latinization in Europe that produced contemporary French culture and institutions is similar to the Hispanicization
that produced the Mexican institutions and culture. In both cases the result is a political culture based on identity and propelled by a revolutionary ethic that emphasizes equality for all, unlike pluralism with its emphasis on interests and individual freedom.

Contemporary Paths

Mestizaje is primarily an endogenous phenomenon, whereas pluralism
is exogenous. The division here seems to be mostly between settlers
and agents of acculturation. It was never a question of Romans clearing the land and settling Gaul. When Augustus set up the colonial
towns of his Roman Empire, the goal was acculturation and incorporation of the Indigenous population, as was the case with the missions in
Mexico. In both cases, over a period of about three hundred years, the
imperial language gave a new nation its identity. As endogenous myths
grew up around universal Christendom, the Holy See provided the glue
that held both together during their transition into the post-Westphalian
world and precipitated in both protracted struggles against clerical
domination.

Settlers in what is today the United States, on the other hand, were
looking for a new home because of population pressure, displacement, or
cultural conflict. Born in the Age of Reason and the era of the nation-
state, many of the settlements were founded by radical Protestant groups
seeking religious freedom. For them this meant freedom to establish
their own exclusive religious political order and precluded freedom for

anyone who disagreed. Colonial governments were not characterized by tolerance; many sought out heretics with zeal equal to that of the Inquisition. For Indigenous peoples, it was conversion or eradication. Pluralism as elaborated by James Madison (Dahl 1967) became the mechanism for forging stability and unity out of this chaos. As applied to religion, it comes down to this: the more sects there are and the more radical they are, the better. All that is required is that they be divested of police power—separation of church and state—so that individuals can live anywhere, join any sect, and start new ones as they wish. All churches and non-churches remain active in the political arena, but they can't hang Quakers in Massachusetts anymore. Tax law provides for the official pluralistic establishment, and the faithful are out fighting for truth, justice, and their American Way: "Interest cancels interest and the whole remains undisturbed." There are no more popes, kings, or dictators, not even the sovereign people: only the individual and the rational pursuit of self-interest, a new mythical basis for the "First New Nation" (Lipset 1996).

Statist France

France and Mexico were established cultural entities before the upheavals that ushered in modernity. Rather than building anew, they had to adapt to change as it took place around them. On the Old World road to Anáhuac, we passed quickly through France a couple of times on the way to Spain. It's time to go back to what was happening there. During the four hundred years that Rome survived after Caesar, Christianity became the state religion. Over time Catholicism gelled into the glue of Latin Gaul. As the last vestiges of Roman authority crumbled, the Franks began to consolidate in Belgium, and, ultimately, in the late fifth century, Clovis converted to Roman Catholicism and united all of France under his rule. This established the state so firmly upon the three hundred years of acculturation that two hundred years of feuding among his sons and successors could not undo it. During this time, the Western Empire had all but disappeared and Italy had been overrun. In the face of this pressure on their way of life, a new dynasty emerged in France to contain the Moors, preserve Christendom, and, ultimately, under Charlemagne, establish the Holy Roman Empire. Imperium and Universal Christendom returned to the West when he was crowned emperor in 800 at Rome.

After royal succession had been securely established in Catholic France, the battle over emperorship shifted to the east. The pressure of events and ideas (the Enlightenment) finally sparked a revolution in France that sought a return to republicanism and made the people the vessel of sovereignty. This was the beginning of the French cultural adaptation to modernity. Extremism, chaos, and misery that followed revolutionary upheaval were finally contained by a return to imperium. Military prowess translated into governing power as Bonaparte became First Counsel of the French Republic for Life and ultimately Emperor of the French People. As with Cortés, spreading revolution took precedence over consolidation, and the French Empire was quickly undone by the combined force of the other powers of Europe. This triggered a succession of regimes that dramatized the conflict between republicanism, and the monarchy and the Church. By the end of the nineteenth century, with the establishment of the Third Republic, republicanism had triumphed, but Bonapartism (Caesarism) and confidence in the state adapted well to the new understanding (Rémond 1969). After a battering at the hands of the Germans and another experiment with radical democracy, de Gaulle put it all together in the Fifth Republic.

Conclusion

After World War II, with the emergence of democracy and the social economy in Germany, the materials to construct the anticipated typology of democracies based on four distinct origins and dynamics were in place. It turns out that the problem with pluralism and mestizaje is not that they are different, but that they are the same. Neither of them translates directly into a system type that reflects existing civil society, as do elitism and corporatism. Rather, as suggested in fig. 1.3, they result from pro-state and anti-state orientations that produce different societal structures and lead to anti-statist and statist types. Both patterns relate to the mixing of peoples, but the kinds of peoples involved and the conditions in which the mixing takes place are different for each pattern.

Post-Enlightenment settlers pursuing their interests by clearing new lands of forests and people produced pluralist patterns in the United States. Pre-Enlightenment conquerors claiming just rewards and spreading benefits of higher culture and/or religion to other peoples produced

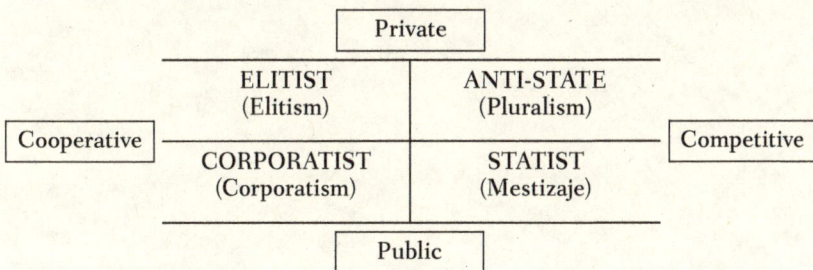

FIGURE I.3. Western democracies

mestizaje. The settlers made it "on their own" and feared state power. They needed the state only to protect their individual gains. The conquerors and priests were state power and sought to use it to spread civilization equally to everyone.

From the exile of the first emperor, through the elected imperium of Antonio López de Santa Anna, the Indigenous presidency of Benito Juárez, and the dictatorship of Porfirio Díaz, the groundwork was laid for the Mexican Revolution. As Mexico developed under pressure from the north, the implementation of American ideals using French methods produced the national consciousness that underpins the "Institutionalized Revolution." Whether the Institutional Revolutionary Party (Partido Revolucionario Institucional, PRI) and its imperial presidency can survive in the new more competitive framework remains to be seen, but there is little doubt that during the last century a Mexican mestizo identity born of Cortés's imperium and the synthesis of Christendom and the ancient empires of Anáhuac and Yucatán has created a new nation that supports a statist democracy.

CHAPTER TWO

Mestizaje in Colonial Mexican Art

SOFÍA IRENE VELARDE CRUZ

TRANSLATED BY STEFANIE WICKSTROM

Addressing ambivalence in established categories of colonial art in Mexico, this chapter proposes a "mestizo" category to characterize works of visual art elaborated during the Viceroyalty of New Spain, mainly in the sixteenth century. Those works of interest here are devotional paintings, sculptures, and the doors and façades of a number of architectural complexes, which integrate aesthetic and iconographic elements common to Western European art and pre-Columbian art of Mesoamerica. I address the connection between *mestizaje* and culture in art, although mestizaje in Mexico often refers to race.

The Indigenous and the Spanish in the Art of New Spain

After the Spanish Conquest of Mexico and imposition of a new religion for the Indigenous population, we begin to see the emergence of a new type of art fusing symbolic and aesthetic elements of Mesoamerican civilizations with Spanish art, making appreciable the participation and influence of Indigenous artists. The inclusion of elements of cultural and religious significance to the Indigenous population in devotional works of the Catholic faith is one of the means by which Indigenous peoples could preserve an important part of their historical and cultural memories. Iconographic elements of Mesoamerican civilization were invariably incorporated in the visual arts and religious architectural complexes, most of which were created by the Indigenous inhabitants of the Viceroyalty of New Spain at the bidding and under the supervision of monks of several religious orders who arrived in Mexico with the purpose of building and adorning places of worship.

In the first half of the twentieth century, Mexican and foreign scholars began studying Mexican art from the period of the Viceroyalty of New Spain that manifested elements neither strictly Indigenous nor Spanish, which could be considered artistic mestizaje of both civilizations. Students of Mexican art who focused on works of the colonial period were faced with the problem of deciding if such artistic manifestations, with unique characteristics illustrating the intervention of Indigenous artists, could be defined as a new modality, outside the bounds of existing categories.

This gave academics a glimpse into the complex process of mestizaje depicted in art that, although heavily influenced by Western European iconographic models, also included important cultural and aesthetic features of Mesoamerican civilization. This meant that specialists began to use terminology to differentiate these works from traditional styles already identified at the time. New terminology sought to describe the mix of elements from Spanish culture and from the Indigenous cultures of Mexico. Terms emerging from analysis of a number of works include "symbiosis," "hybridization," "fusion," "amalgamation," "*mexicanidad*," and the actual category of "mestizo."

It is important to point out that it was not just in Mexico that the study of colonial art involved interpretation of unique traits depicting aesthetic and symbolic characteristics related to both Spanish and Indigenous cultures. It occurred elsewhere in Latin America as well. In Peru, Ecuador, and Bolivia, scholars have given attention to a range of artistic works elaborated during the Spanish rule of America. Important authors whose studies on colonial art are worthy of attention include Ángel Guido, Mario Buschiazzo, Harold E. Wethey, Emilio Harth-Terré, Teresa Gisbert, and José de Mesa. They use the concept of mestizaje to characterize works of art from the colonial period in America that illustrate cultural and aesthetic fusion of the Spanish and the Indigenous. This indicates that processes in colonial art related to mestizaje were not exclusive to Mexico. We find parallel processes in several territories that comprised Spanish America. Here I focus on examples of art in New Spain that suggest that the concept of "mestizo art" best describes some of the art forms elaborated there.

Scholarly Descriptions of Mexican Art

It is important to review the perceptions of several academics who pio-neered the study of Mexican art, in particular those who influenced the study of works of unique character. I briefly review their scholarly descrip-tions of relevant works of art, with attention to terms and categories that have been used, in order to defend the concept of mestizaje I propose in this chapter.

Among the first findings based on analysis of works of art in New Spain combining elements from Spanish and Indigenous art are those of Agustín Velázquez Chávez in *Three Centuries of Mexican Colonial Painting* (1939).[1] He observed that post-conquest art was "entwined with the Hispanic spirit and imparted to colonial art the genius of the indigenous." Velázquez believed that "there were elements of indigenous culture that could iden-tify with the spirit of the Spanish," making studies that clarified the "Mexican" in art especially important. He pointed out, for example, that in the oldest post-Cortesian codices, dating from 1523, it is possible to observe the mixing of two cultures in conflict (Indian and Spanish), as well as transformation and reciprocal influence. Alongside Indigenous glyphs appear European figures painted in a new way, characterized by the simple forms and bright and colorful backgrounds elaborated by art-ists indigenous to the heartland of Aztec Mexico (Anáhuac) (Velázquez Chávez 1939, 5–25).

The historian Manuel Toussaint, in *Mexico and Culture* (1946),[2] de-scribed Churrigueresque art in Mexico as mestizo art and maintained in *The Art in New Spain* (1946)[3] that artistic works from the colonial period were the product of an amalgam of elements (Fernández 1970). Justino Fernández, in his analysis of Toussaint's scholarship, explains that in Toussaint's time Mexico had begun to turn its eyes upon itself in order to recover the essence of its being and its historical past, which was charac-terized by both the Indigenous and the colonial. According to Fernández, this inspired in Toussaint an interest in *mexicanismo* and mestizo art, which he considered to be a paradigm in itself. Toussaint was one of the first scholars who considered using the term mestizo to characterize ar-tistic expression emerging from the colonial period with the aim of in-cluding the participation of Indigenous people in Mexican colonial art (Fernández 1970).

Although these scholars of the 1930s and 1940s had identified the fu-sion in colonial art of elements clearly Spanish and Indigenous in both symbolic and cultural senses, they did not pursue developing a category to designate such manifestations. This is why the work of José Moreno Villa is significant. In 1942, in *Mexican Colonial Sculpture*,[4] he proposed the term Tequitqui be used to categorize works expressing this fusion of elements. Even today the term is used to describe art that was the result of the cultural mixing of the Spaniards and Indigenous peoples.

According to Moreno Villa, it was during the sixteenth century that the most interesting sculpture was produced in Mexico and that "from contact between different races emerged a style that, by analogy with *mudéjar* [Moorish art in Christian Spain], I call 'Tequitqui'" (Moreno Villa 1942, 10). His analogy between mudéjar art of the Middle Ages and Tequitqui art springs from the idea that the works of art born in Mexico during the sixteenth century that merged the Spanish and the Indigenous—each with their own traditions—were akin to those born in Spain. They constituted a "mudejarismo that had to be baptized in some way" (Moreno Villa 1942, 16). As the Muslim who stayed in Spain during the Reconquista (the reconquest of Spain) was a vassal paying tribute to Christian monarchs without surrendering his religion, the Indian in the Viceroyalty of New Spain was a vassal paying tribute who did not surrender his. Moreno Villa sought out the equivalent of the word mudéjar in the Aztec language so as to "baptize the works that exhibit characteristics of this special amalgam of styles with that name" (Moreno Villa 1942, 16). He proposed Tequitqui, which in Nahuatl means "tributary," although he also invited those who knew Indigenous languages to propose a better one.

Tequitqui manifests itself in masonry and stone reliefs, where the Indian artist introduced atavistic idolatrous symbols, "just in case" (*"por si acaso"*). Moreno Villa considered atrial crosses made during the sixteenth century, such as the one in San Felipe de los Alzates in Michoacán, to be examples. According to him, anyone could recognize in them the style he characterized as Tequitqui. The sculptor does not portray the physical traits of Christ, but rather symbols of passion, carved in flattened stone reliefs, which can be regarded as distinctly Indigenous. Moreno Villa points out the inclusion of a disk of obsidian in the piece and explains that obsidian was used with great frequency by Indigenous Mexicans in their monuments and images of their gods. According to their mythology, its purpose was to give life to a representation of divinity. According to Moreno Villa, "these idolatrous reminiscences achieved the presentation of an Indigenous calendar through Christian inscription" (Moreno Villa 1942, 18–19).

The term Tequitqui was accepted by academics of Moreno Villa's time to refer to works of art with elements of significant religious and symbolic content of both Indigenous peoples' religions and Western Christianity. There are reasons, however, to beware of this categorization. First, I believe the inclusion of content with powerful religious symbolism for pre-Hispanic peoples should not be considered simply atavistic ornamentation inherited from the past, as Moreno Villa suggests. This inclusion was accomplished over the course of centuries by some of the pre-Hispanic cultures in Mexico to maintain their complex religious and cultural symbolism. Second, I don't believe the term Tequitqui is analogous to mudéjar (art by Muslims paying tribute to Spanish monarchs) because, in the Viceroyalty of New Spain, Indigenous peoples were forced to convert to Catholicism.

Six years after he published his reflections in *Mexican Colonial Sculpture*, Moreno Villa published a book entitled *The Mexican in the Visual Arts* (1948).[5] Therein he said that in his earlier work he had only wished to present an orderly selection of religious sculpture pieces scattered throughout Mexico and to identify their stylistic lines. He suggested that he had simply dared to qualify with the Aztec name Tequitqui the mestizo art emerging in America as Indigenous peoples interpreted images of an imported religion (Moreno Villa 1948). He mentions having realized later that the mixture manifested in what he called Tequitqui does not contain Indigenous elements. It is, instead, a mixture of styles from three different eras in the history of European art: Romanic, Gothic, and Renaissance. He claims to have reached this conclusion through analysis of a number of sculptural pieces. Having sculpted so many Christian themes using many different techniques and materials, the Indigenous sculptor apprentice in New Spain could achieve in a short period of time what it had taken humanity centuries to perfect, though he had the same lack of technical tradition as the Romanesque apprentice (Moreno Villa 1948).

Ultimately, Moreno Villa throws out the Indigenous contribution to sixteenth-century sculpture in colonial Mexico. He attributes to the Indigenous artist the simple role of reproducing European works arriving in Mexico and explains the phenomenon of the difference in styles as a consequence of skills developed by producing accurate reproductions of European works using tools provided by the European conquerors. But, despite these findings, Moreno Villa's category of Tequitqui prevailed in Mexican art history to refer to art that clearly differed from Western European art.

Eventually some scholars would be inspired to undertake the search for different categories to delimit essential characteristics of works of art in which the mixture of elements of Indigenous and European culture is observed. Unfortunately, in their analyses of works of art from New Spain exhibiting this mix, they did not argue for the use of the term mestizo to define them. Instead, they continued to accept Tequitqui and Moreno Villa's interpretations.

Such was the case with Pedro Rojas in his 1956 work on the Iglesia de Santa María Tonantzintla. Rojas described certain manifestations of Mexican colonial art as the art of the oppressed, referring to Moreno Villa and his Tequitqui analogy to mudéjar art—the art of vassals. However, Rojas also proposed other categories by which to define certain manifestations of mestizo art. Among them stand out those that he used to focus on fusion and mestizaje in the conceptualization of Mexican folk art. Rojas

regarded Mexican folk art as an "index of fusion or prototype of synthesis" and as "a mestizo creation simmering on the coals of a smothered
fire" (Fernández 1970, 288).

Rojas's work touched on mestizaje but, nonetheless, illustrates again
the disqualification of works made by Indigenous hands, these being characterized as folk art in comparison with works of art resembling European
styles. Although this attitude was widespread among academics of the
first half of the twentieth century, some did begin questioning assumptions about Mexican art arrived at by judging according to aesthetic
standards of Western European art and sought to determine the true
essence of works by pre-Hispanic cultures of Mesoamerica and the infil-
tration of its elements into the art of New Spain.

Justino Fernández, in his voluminous analysis of critiques of Mexican
art by both Mexican and foreign scholars, concluded that Pedro Rojas's
commentaries represented the self-conscience of Mexico, which arrived
at a definition of the Indigenous through mestizaje, looking for characteristics of "the mestizo way of being" that could be distinguished from
the European. Fernández claimed that if we begin with the assumption
that one of the universal human needs "is to express oneself in order to
remain and endure," we cannot accept Rojas's proposal, which suggests
that Indigenous people "expressed themselves through art that was daz-
zlingly barbaric, while foreign oppressors in New Spain created magnifi-
cent art." This is equivalent to believing that the oppressed (Indigenous
people) "lived on the margins and timidly created art that was in part an
echo of what had come before and in part an adoption of the foreign,"
the foreign being European. The balance tips in favor of the contributions of the Europeans over those of the Indians (Fernández 1970, 288).

Fernández spoke out against the ongoing use of the term "barbaric" to
characterize Indigenous art, noting that it was unjust and erroneous to
use the term unless, he claimed, one wants "to use it to elevate the concept of barbarism to a supreme position, turning the world upside down."
The philosopher decided that "throughout the historical process of mestizaje, which is ever more pronounced, the boundaries between the familiar and the other tend to disappear, making room for creation that is
original, mestizo, Tequitqui" (Fernández 1970, 288).

Fernández's discussion reflects the revaluation of the art of pre-
Hispanic Mexico taking place in the second half of the twentieth century.
His revaluation promoted recognition of Indigenous features that infil-
trated the art of colonial Mexico and recognition of the cultural mix inherent in the art of New Spain. In this mix, he distinguished a profound
fusion of aesthetic elements, suggesting to him that art could not be studied from a single perspective, neither as a work of the Indigenous artist
somehow "pure" in character nor as a mere reproduction of Western European models. Fernández realized that art should be analyzed in context by a process that clearly takes into consideration mestizaje in both

cultures and that liberates works of art from boundaries that characterize them simplistically as "ours" or "theirs," so they might be understood as expressions of the fusion of different aesthetic values. Such liberation gives birth to a new modality that can be characterized as mestizo art of New Spain elaborated in the sixteenth century in what is now Mexico.

Although Fernández introduced the term mestizo, he did not develop it as a category on a par with Tequitqui. In spite of the preponderance of its use, its ambiguities and inconsistencies led other scholars to continue the search for an appropriate characterization of the style reflecting aesthetic values of both Indigenous and Spanish cultures. In 1978, Constantino Reyes-Valerio proposed designating artwork that blended symbolic elements of Christian and pre-Hispanic character "*indocristiano.*"

Reyes-Valerio refers to sacred art of the sixteenth century made by Indians using Christian themes as monastic art because it emerged in monasteries and convents of various religious orders. He believes that the inclusion of pre-conquest icons reveals the hand of the Indian artist and stresses the appropriateness of the term indocristiano, because it was Indigenous artists who created the sculpture and paintings in Christian monasteries and convents (Reyes-Valerio 2000).

He decided that icons demarcating the indocristiano style are more than ornamental elements, as Moreno Villa had concluded, and sought to clarify several questions about the meanings that Indigenous artists might have given these symbols that were inserted in architectural works constructed in colonial Mexico (fig. 2.1). Reyes-Valerio wondered whether they might have been used intentionally to convey messages to the Indigenous population to keep alive their traditions after the Spanish Conquest or if, on the contrary, a great many symbols lost their meaning after conquest. He pondered why Church authorities would have permitted the inclusion of powerful reminders of Indigenous culture in architectural complexes of worship designed to propagate the Catholic religion (Reyes-Valerio 2000).

Reyes-Valerio conjectured that the friars were not capable of recognizing the immense variety of pre-Hispanic iconography and that evangelizing may not have been as effective as might be expected. He concludes that the symbols conveyed a veiled message to a certain group who understood it. He believed that artwork in monasteries and convents expresses the symbiosis of the histories of two cultures: pre-Columbian and Spanish (Reyes-Valerio 2000).

I argue that the term indocristiano should not be used to refer to works of art that conjoined important symbols of Indian and Spanish culture. From the early years of Spanish colonization of Mexico, there were two processes by which Indigenous artists were involved in sacred art, and we must distinguish one from the other. The first is the one by which the Indians made true copies of Christian images they were shown

FIGURE 2.1. Graphite drawing by John Peña of corncob sculpted in stone on the first Franciscan convent complex built in Tzintzuntzan, Michoacán (in the sixteenth century). Tzintzuntzan was a capital and ceremonial center of the pre-Hispanic Purépecha (Tarascan) empire. The iconography of the corncob had important religious and cultural meanings to pre-Hispanic peoples of Mexico.

by Church authorities. The second involved Indigenous artists changing the Christian iconography by including their own cultural symbols. Therefore, if we use the term indocristiano, we confuse works of mestizo art, which have important symbolic and cultural meaning, with copies of Christian iconography made by Indigenous artists. Moreover, Reyes-Valerio primarily studied stone sculptures on the building façades of monasteries and convents and, to a lesser extent, on the murals painted in the same architectural complexes. There are other works of sacred art in other materials, such as wood and cornstalk-paste sculptures, in which we observe the introduction of pre-Hispanic icons and symbols.

Finally, Reyes-Valerio's analysis serves primarily to disentangle pre-Hispanic symbols from artistic works, isolating them from the context in which they were created. This context also contains a Western Christian thread. We must keep in mind that Christian symbolism also changed as it came into contact with new cultural elements. This is how mestizo art comes into being.

The Concept of Mestizaje Applied to Art

To delve into the etymology of the word mestizo, we begin by referring to its literal meaning, which is "mixed." It seems reasonable to infer that all cultures have used and understood this notion in accordance with their conceptions of the world, applying it in the specific reality of their culture. Throughout history the term has been used in several ways. One is as a biological category denoting a hybrid of two racial types. The term has also been associated with social contexts, and from the first half of the twentieth century in Mexico, the notion of mestizaje began to be applied to certain cultural phenomena.

The meaning related to biological hybrids comes from ancient Rome. Pliny the Elder believed that hybrids emerged in the first place in the animal world.[6] He also believed the notion could be extended to humans, the hybrid being the result of the mixing of two races: one domestic and one savage (Bernard 2001).

Anthropologist and historian Carmen Bernard suggests that hybrid metaphors convey an opposition between the savage and the domesticated or civilized encountered in vocabulary pertaining to family and heritage. The term "*borde*" conveys the idea of the manifestation of a *mezcla baja* (inferior mix) of characteristics, as well as the marginal status of the hybrid. According to a medieval dictionary still in use during the sixteenth century, the word "borde" comes from the Latin word "burdus," which means mule and was used to designate bastards, children born out of wedlock. According to Bernard, the Covarrubias dictionary, published in the early seventeenth century, states:

> Bastard corresponds to inferior or uncouth—that which is done without order, reason, or rules—given that only the identity of the mother is known with certainty and the child is conceived of uncertain seed, the mother having been with many. The child born of an unmarried mother and father, however, may be considered legitimate, given that the subsequent marriage of the parents is deemed legitimate. (Bernard 2001, 108)

Bernard suggests bastard and borde approximate "mestizo," which, according to the Covarrubias dictionary, means "one begotten of diverse animal species."

In addition to definitions, we should consider the ideological connotation of *mixto*, which appears in the sixteenth century, when interpretations of the Reconquista were being formulated. It is then that, for the first time, we find a meaning for the word mestizo that goes beyond its biological connotation.

Bernard identified the categories used to describe the Spanish population during the sixteenth century in a text written by the monk Augustín

Salucio. He divided the Spanish population into four categories: conquerors, conquered, neither conquerors nor conquered, and descendants of the conquerors. Of particular interest here is the third: neither conquerors nor conquered. In it Salucio included the group that allied with the Moors against Ruderic, the last Visgothic king of Hispania. They paid tribute to an infidel lord and were despised by the Christians of the Cantabrian Mountain region in what is today Spain.[7] They were designated as "*mistos*" or "*metis*" for their mixed religion (Bernard 2001). In this context the term mestizo referred to disloyalty to the legitimate lord, not to biology.

The *Dictionary of the Spanish Language* (Real Academia Española 2001) defines mestizo as that which is mixed (mixto) or a mixture (mezcla).[8] There are three different meanings associated with the term mestizo. One is "said of culture, of spirituality, etc.; hailing from the mixture of different cultures." That the Royal Spanish Academy links the term mestizo to culture reflects the fact that the inclusion of culture in the description of mestizo is accepted in the popular imagination and in academic circles.

After the Spanish Conquest of the Americas, mestizo was used to designate individuals who were the product of sexual union between Spanish and Indigenous people. While the laws of New Spain considered mestizos to be products of illegitimate unions, illegitimacy also derived from their doubtful loyalty to the king. Although they served the king, they also served an Indigenous lord (Bernard 2001). The term mestizo ceased to be used in Mexico to refer to legally recognized racial types in the 1820s, the territory's independence from Spain then complete.

The notion of mestizaje was again revived in the early twentieth century, with the study of Mexican culture. We find the terms mestizo and mestizaje used to characterize Mexican ways of being, customs, and traditions. Academic works on mestizaje abound. Among the most famous are the reflections of José Vasconcelos in his book *The Cosmic Race* (1925 [1997]).[9] Many academics working in different disciplines have considered the cultural connotations of mestizaje. Examples of prominent scholars who have contributed to development of the concept of mestizo culture or cultural mestizaje are Elsa Cecilia Frost, Gonzalo Aguirre Beltrán, and Serge Gruzinsky.

Cultural mestizaje is essential, even if some scholars might still argue for a more biologically based interpretation of mestizaje. Mestizaje has been used to define social phenomena since the sixteenth century and, in Latin America, especially in Mexico, to characterize important cultural processes. Néstor García Canclini asserts concepts of hybridity and mestizaje should be used to consider inter*cultural* mixing and that interpreting composition of all of what makes up the Americas requires the use of mestizaje in both the biological and the cultural spheres (García Canclini 2003).[10]

A growing number of studies of colonial art carried out in Mexico and Latin America draw attention to aesthetic mestizaje evident in works that undeniably bear the seal of the Spanish and the Indigenous. Miguel León-Portilla is one who associates mestizo culture with art from the colonial period. Considering mestizaje in diverse artistic processes, León-Portilla notes:

> Another major issue is the development of forms, classifiable as mestizo, in painting, sculpture, ceramics, architecture, a wide range of crafts, as well as in literature, music and dance. In the monasteries, convents and churches of the sixteenth century, where elements of Spanish Renaissance art can be perceived, the presence of the indigenous hand is also revealed. The same is evident later in the lush flowering of the Baroque. (León-Portilla 2003)

Mario Vargas Llosa, in his prologue to the catalog for the exhibition *Revelaciones: Las artes en América Latina, 1492–1820* (*Revelations: The Arts in Latin America 1492–1820*), notes:

> The colonial system imposed new beliefs and modes of behavior, changing appearances but not souls, to which ancient gods, customs, devotions, and mythologies fled, and whence, despite the artists themselves, began to surreptitiously impregnate all manifestations of colonial art, imprinting their own nuances. Not breaking entirely with prototypes brought along with the colonizer, the indigenous artist would renovate them with Native idiosyncrasies. The façades of churches, altars, pulpits, altarpieces, frescoes and sculptures were subtly Americanized with irrepressible eruptions of native flowers and fruits. Virgins and angels became mestizos, were indianized by their skin, facial and bodily features, clothes, through colors and by the landscapes around them; the disarray of perspective and the syncretism of Christianity and abolished religions. It would be a mistake to attribute this mestizaje only to indigenous artists. Europeans transplanted in the colonies were soon mestizo-ized. (Vargas Llosa 2007, xxv)

I believe the concept of mestizaje should be applied in reference to works of visual art with religious meaning in which we find a mixture of cultural and aesthetic elements from Indigenous and Spanish cultures. When I refer to mestizo art, I am referring specifically to works that present patterns distinguishing them from the Spanish style by their polychromic nature or their symbology with an invariably strong religious-cultural connotation in Mesoamerica. Many works, according to their iconography, belong in the mestizo category. To best value the richness of each piece and to give this type of art its rightful place in art history, it is essential to characterize it accurately.

Final Reflections

One of the main objectives in developing concepts that characterize the various artistic styles that have emerged throughout human history is to expand or reflect upon the modern concept of art, so that it might come to include sentient expressions of any culture of the world at different historical moments, considering that people in all times and places have elaborated art in accordance with their particular ways of conceiving of and perceiving the world. Doing so, we can discern works that are similar or different in relation to others without their differences being reduced to subjective notions of superiority or inferiority and encourage reflection on their differences that might convey understanding of the cultures that created them.

Characterizing artistic works in Mexico from the colonial period with strong cultural roots in the Spanish and the Indigenous as "mestizo" addresses the lack of an accurate term. Doing so validates contributions of academics from different disciplines over the years to establishing meanings of culture. Using the term can help us perceive in a holistic context a style of Mexican art comprised of contributions of Spanish and Indigenous artists expressing the distinctive elements of their cultures, without granting supremacy to the contributions of one sector or another.

Today, the influences of globalization have provoked the dilution of important historical memories of virtually all the world's cultures. With respect to Mexico, it is increasingly difficult for its people to recall the meanings of the important iconography persisting in architectural and artistic works that allude to the historical past. Using concepts that integrate reference to the nature of our historical development contributes to our appreciation and preservation of the customs, traditions, and myths of Mexico. Determining appropriate terms must be done in contexts defined by the complexities of other cultures. It must allow us to recognize and respect diverse characteristics of our complex multicultural society so that we may rise to the challenges of the present and engender a stronger commitment to respect for what is distinct about our culture and other cultures of the world.

Notes

1. *Tres siglos de pintura colonial mexicana*
2. *México y la cultura*
3. *El arte en la Nueva España*
4. *La escultura colonial mexicana*
5. *Lo mexicano en las artes plásticas*
6. His groundbreaking encyclopedia entitled *Naturalis Historiæ* (Pliny and Mayhoff 1967) was published circa AD 77–79.

7. *Cristianos montañeses*
8. *Diccionario de la lengua española*
9. *La raza cósmica*
10. García Canclini's work goes beyond mestizaje, encompassing a broader cultural spectrum and focusing on naming and explaining more modern forms of interculturality. He holds that hybridization "is more malleable for denominating these mixes, which combine not only ethnic and religious elements, but become enmeshed in products of advanced technologies and modern or postmodern social processes" (García Canclini 2003).

CHAPTER THREE

The Tradition of La Chaya in Vallenar, Chile

The Search for Imaginaries in the Nineteenth and Twentieth Centuries

IVÁN PIZARRO DÍAZ

TRANSLATED BY STEFANIE WICKSTROM

AND PHILIP D. YOUNG

I esas enloquecedoras miradas i esos rostros risueños . . .
¡Oh! El Carnaval es una gran fiesta.
¡Alegría i felicidad, lectores!
And the enchanted looks in the eyes and the smiling faces . . .
Oh! Carnaval is a grand festival.
Joy and happiness, readers!
—*"Carnaval,"* El Pololo, *1917*

La Chaya persisted in the valleys of the Norte Chico of Chile into the twentieth century. It was a tradition with Indigenous origins that took place in the context of the religious celebration of Carnaval. This chapter explores the dynamics of cultural and racial *mestizaje* in these isolated regions of the nascent Chilean Republic. It is based on analysis of daily and weekly newspapers from the late nineteenth and early twentieth centuries published in the town of Vallenar in the Huasco River valley.[1]

This period was foundational in the history of the Chilean nation, with the War of the Pacific, the occupation of the region of Araucanía, and the colonization of Chile's southernmost reaches, among other important events. It was then that the ideology for this long, narrow strip of the nation was defined.

The nineteenth century witnessed a proliferation of newspapers, as newsprint became the authorized medium, accounting for regional realities. From the mid-nineteenth century into the early decades of the twentieth century, daily and weekly periodicals flourished in the region's cities, villages, and towns. In Vallenar, then just a small city in the relatively remote Norte Chico, nearly fifty newspapers of various types were published during this period.

Today in Chile, the press is a monopolized means of transmitting images from the capital, with the exception of a few major city newspapers in some regions. In contrast, the media of this earlier period appear to have been more democratic, giving voice to more people in more places. Nonetheless, the majority of these voices were those of the elites. They represent the moralist Christian and conservative views of those who exercised power and influence over local decision-making. There are exceptions, however. Along with newspapers that represented the interests of Vallenar's elite, there emerged satirical, sarcastic, and humorous dailies expressing dissident voices. These sources provide information on regional histories, revealing contrary local, regional, and decentralized visions and conveying debates about the virtues and excesses of La Chaya.

Settlement of the Norte Chico

Pre-Hispanic Andean settlement patterns were organized by Tawantinsuyu, provinces or "suyos" that comprised the Inca Empire. They established a dual allocation of space (*hanan* and *hurin*—upper and lower) and located populations in various productive niches in different environmental zones (*mitmaq*) and multiethnic villages in areas removed from the main political and administrative center. The use and ownership of land were arranged according to a hierarchical order of relevant entities (*inti, inka, kuraka, ayllu*), and there were collective, communal labor production systems known as *ayni*. This general system, widely disseminated by the expansion of the Inca Empire, was transformed after the arrival of the Europeans. Along with the institutional breakdown of the Inca Empire came demographic collapse and the imposition of a new social, economic, and religious order.

A new reality for the Indigenous population was ordered into existence by Francisco de Toledo, viceroy of Peru, during his administration (1569–1581). He implemented the system of *reducciones*, the crucible of the colonial vision for the Natives of America. The Indigenes were forcibly relocated throughout the Viceroyalty of Peru, including in the viceroyalty's Chilean Governorate. Reducciones were places of confinement. Abuse provoked by tributes of "personal service," the wide dispersal of Native settlements, the difficulty of evangelizing the Indigenes, and the need for an efficacious method to collect monetary tribute were some of the arguments for their implementation. The system was regulated through *visitas generales* by *visitadores de tierras*, authorities of the viceroyalty.

The Huasco River valley is in the southern part of the Norte Chico, in the Atacama region to the north of Chile's Central Valley. The region was occupied early, pacified violently, and placed under jurisdiction of the Kingdom of Chile. Eventually, the Indigenous peoples of the Huasco River valley were assigned to three main *pueblos de índios*: Huasco Bajo on the coast, Paitanasa in the central part of the valley, and Huasco Alto in the Andes.

The Spanish system of occupation facilitated urban residence in the prominent cities. Rural areas were dominated by haciendas and estates. Santa Rosa del Huasco (now Freirina), established in 1752, was an urban space where the families of estate owners and Spanish administrators maintained residences. Spanish colonial society was centered on Santa Rosa del Huasco until the founding of the city of Vallenar[2] in 1793 at Paitanasa.

Mestizaje was the foundation of the society of the non-Spanish population, that is, those who carried out the main tasks of city life: tailors, blacksmiths, shoemakers, workers, town criers, and domestic servants, among others. The importation of black slaves and the presence of Indigenes, free or indentured, were the main engines driving the social mestizaje that configured the spirit of Chile's common people. Mestizos, cholos, sambos, and mulattos were absorbed by colonial Spanish society, raised according to Spanish norms, and, in some cases, achieved social advancement through their own or inherited wealth (cf. Lipschutz 1963). Mainly, however, they comprised the working class

In the Norte Chico and Central Valley, extensive mining activity required an extensive labor force. The growing cities of Copiapó and La Serena attracted wealthy families who, at the end of the eighteenth and beginning of the nineteenth century, demanded black slaves to attend to their needs. Local Indigenous populations worked in the least profitable economic sectors in the urban areas and were used as indentured laborers in mining. These transformations led to the creation of a melting pot of identities in the mining works and the nascent cities of the north. Records of official surveys of mines and "visits" to Indigenous communities, as well as the population censuses of the eighteenth century, testify to the obvious presence of mestizos, blacks, sambos, and other *castas*.

Carnaval and La Chaya

Born in the cities and towns of Europe in the Middle Ages, Carnaval came to South America with Catholicism. The two-week-long celebration came before Lent in the Christian calendar—summer in Chile. It is a time of liberty and license before the strict rigor imposed during the forty days of Lent preceding Easter. Lent is directed at carnality, prohibiting the consumption of meat and generally calling for suppression of all carnal appetites so as to purify the bodies of the faithful in preparation for the passion of Christ and his resurrection.

Padre Alonso de Ovalle's stories of religious possessions on the Feast of Corpus Christi, or Holy Thursday, of singular beauty, convey a unique appreciation of mestizaje in the making (Ovalle 1888). Brotherhoods of Indians and castas were characteristic of traditions extrapolated from European guilds and Catholic traditions. The celebration included a number of festive pagan activities such as dances, the use of costumes and masks, and horse-riding competitions.

Carnaval was practiced in the capital city of the Kingdom of Chile, Santiago de Nueva Extremadura, throughout the colonial period. It spread to the towns and cities in the Norte Chico and Central Valley (cf. Salinas 2001).

The celebration generated a re-creation of and a connection with pre-existing ceremonies and festivals of the original peoples of America. The worship of their own divinities and the performance of their religious ceremonies were camouflaged in the festivities of Carnaval, something widely addressed by various Andean authors (cf. Marzal 1983) and recognized as religious syncretism.

The La Chaya tradition embedded in Carnaval was a festivity that consisted mainly of casting water with other ingredients (including flour, confetti, colorings, fragrances, and rotten eggs) at the celebrants. It lasted three continuous days. It has been argued (cf. Godoy Orellana 2007; Salinas 2001) that the tradition has ancient roots and its name comes from the Aymara *chayar*, meaning to make offerings to *Pachamama* (goddess of the world or earth) with sprinklings of water and flour.[3]

> Carnaval is a unique festival that takes part in the majority of the Catholic and civilized world. No one can remain serious during those three days. The best-ordered minds falter, gravity is unbalanced, and the prudence and severity of sensible men changes character.
>
> Carnaval provides for the tastes of all: *guazos*[4] mounted on their best horses, their best accoutrements shining and with great mugs of chicha in hand, show off their skills at *la vara*;[5] coaches festooned in green with fragrant basil roam the towns; dances, masks, *la chaya*, pastries, *choclos cocidos*,[6] *humitas*[7] and casseroles are the order of Carnaval.

The old and the young, ignorant and wise, women, all participate in these celebrations of human folly. ("El Carnaval," *El Derecho*, February 9, 1888)

Carnaval may represent "human folly" or perhaps the turning of the world upside down, *pachakuti*. Pachakuti is the end of the world or great destruction (González Holguín 1608). In the Andean tradition, the Incas waited for the next pachakuti or tumultuous turning of the world when a radical new order would arise, emerging from the head of the decapitated Inca, to reign over Tawantinsuyu. During Carnaval it is permissible to cross the boundaries of common sense, offend authorities by taking on their roles in fun and mocking them: in short, to level the playing field—*tinku*. Tinku is the joining of two things (González Holguín 1608). The Andean communities of Peru and Bolivia still practice the ritual rivalry of tinku, between upper- and lower-status groups, a ritual dispute not lacking in drama and violence. The festival can be interpreted, using codes from traditional or non-stratified societies, as a battle against the accumulation of wealth in a material and symbolic sense (power-prestige). It is catalyzed through celebrations and redistribution of valuables or roles. It is a time of the year when positions change and the wealthy or prestigious expend their resources to facilitate social equilibrium and resolve conflicts:

There you will see a courtly gentleman partnered with a cute little seamstress with pretty hands; Louis XV with a Puchuncaví villager; Pope Leo X with the most humble nun; a sun-tanned miner with the Queen of England and you will see a friendly consortium of the bonnet and the waistcoat, of the garment of the coarsest wool and the *frac*, of the cloak and the pancho, of the finest suit and the neckerchief, of the straw hat and the top hat in fellowship and sweet fraternity.

In short, Carnaval is a license we give each other to make ourselves equals through costume and for serious and proper people to play crazy and become the laughing stock of the children; it is a festivity of costumes where everyone shows off their moral merchandise. ("El Carnaval," *El Derecho*, February 9, 1888)

La Chaya was recognized as a principal and characteristic activity during Carnaval. Its importance displaced that of other activities such as the dance of masks, the *vidalay* dance, and horse racing, among others:

But the most characteristic aspect of Carnaval is La Chaya. This consists of both sexes lavishing upon one another plenty of water and minute fragments of paper, powder, and starch.

Señorita, may I cast a bit of powder upon you?

If you, sir, permit me to put my dampened sponge upon you, I
accept.
I know you have a little something hidden.
Not I, I don't have a thing.
How so?! Not a little packet of powder?
Alright then, I'll give you a little dusting.

And then erupts a confused disorder, tussles, wrestling, shouting,
and the taking of certain licenses permitted only during these days. And
at last, after a long contest, the contenders part ways, tired and deliri-
ous. ("El Carnaval," *El Derecho*, February 9, 1888)

An Ancient Custom

If our grandparents have passed along to us a custom that their ancestors also transmitted to them, let us welcome this custom, but let us
not adorn their temples with the rough trinkets that in that epoch once
served this purpose. Let us receive it, as it has been handed down to
us, but characterize it fittingly in the present time.

What would be said of us if by deference to the custom we would
slip back some twenty years or so, back to the time when debasing
ourselves was an obligatory game of Carnaval?

What if in the public square circles were to be formed for dancing
the vidalay, that demon-possessed dance that does not end until fa-
tigue debilitates the strength of those taking part?

By God, do not long for that time, but on the contrary, in view of the
discomforts arising from la Chaya, considering all the drawbacks related to the interruptions of all sorts of labors, the diversion must
be constrained until it can be suspended if possible, as it has been almost completely suspended in the capital and in Valparaiso. ("Después
de Carnaval," *El Huasquino*, February 25, 1857)

Custom is tradition; tradition is ancient; ancient is Indigenous; Indigenous is barbarian; barbarian is diabolical. These imaginaries have endured for centuries and are still present in our society in the dichotomy
between civilization and barbarism.[8] The prohibition of custom has been
guided by the Catholic Church through processes such as extirpation of
idolatry, the Inquisition, social control by Christian doctrine, and in this
case, during the formative period of the Chilean Republic. La Chaya was
recognized as an old Carnaval custom in Chilean society, like the dev-
ilish vidalay dance, or the *hondearse* slingshot game. These Indigenous
traditions, re-created in the Christian festival, were to be adapted to
present times, or to simply be eliminated, according to the example set by
the modern cities of Santiago and Valparaiso.

A mounting campaign to malign La Chaya, founded in the moralist
thinking of regional elites, can be observed in the regional newspapers.
Editorials put pressure on authorities to restrain and punish participation in the festivity. Elite imaginaries, evident in the regional press, associated the festivity with stereotypes and preconceptions constructed
during colonization. The writers distanced themselves from the festivity
and situated La Chaya in the realm of the common people. They wished
to restrain the happy, rampant, lusty, dangerous, and horrible ensembles
of urban plebeians and laborers in rural areas:

> Tomorrow is the first day of the popular diversion much embraced by
> the common people, which is called La Chaya; three days of raging folly
> and indulgence, including much that is detrimental to public health,
> and that, given the longevity in their minds of the disgusting customs,
> will likely not be forgotten except by civilization. ("Chaya," *La Unión
> Liberal*, February 18, 1882)

The old ways, barbarisms inherited from ancestors, were to be eradicated as soon as societies became civilized. This imaginary, outlined in
colonial newspaper columns, comes from a Eurocentric viewpoint. Histo-
ricity, culture, civilization, Christianity, and correctness are passed along
from the countries of Europe.

This reflexive axis has shaped the formation of the thoughts of our ar-
istocracies and Creole bourgeoisie, social groups that have exercised power
and inspired historical interpretations of the nineteenth and twentieth
centuries. It has influenced our interpretation of the political and military
moves of the Chilean state at the end of the nineteenth century, those
that enabled the occupation and forced eradication of Mapuche populations in the Araucanía. This large territory, occupied by savage, un-
tamed, barbarous Indians, should have been civilized and, rather than
being useless land, been used for the progress of the nation. Its colonization by men more fit and trained for this purpose was undertaken, and
the Chilean government brought German, Swiss, and Italian colonists
from Europe who, under contract, settled the lands of Gulu Mapu.[9] The
corollary had been established during the colonial period. Spaniards
constantly requested grants to occupy the lands that had been surveyed
and granted to Indigenous communities, always claiming abandonment
and lack of use of "vacant wastelands."[10]

> Now the last three days of Carnaval have arrived. As of tomorrow
> begins the ridiculous La Chaya diversion, fleeting days of debauch-
> ery, of worldly immoralities and liberties that the society must
> banish.
>   In every cultured town, we abstain from this annual devilry, which
> not only jeopardizes the health of people of both sexes, but which also

compromises morality—this habitual farce and the dirty and indecent words. ("La Chaya," *La Descentralización*, February 6, 1875)

The denunciations were expressed repeatedly, and the hegemonic, moralistic discourse gained strength. A festivity with a long tradition, fostering syncretism of Indigenous ceremonies with pagan expressions of the European burgers and purified by its inclusion in the Roman Catholic calendar, was to be banished from educated, modern, civilized communities.

Licentiousness, Immorality and Diversion

Finally, do not forget, fathers who have daughters, their chastity is endangered by a variety of means, which, since this publication is available to all, we will not specify here; and we say this in light of all that we have witnessed. ("Chaya," *La Unión Liberal*, February 18, 1882)

Carnaval and La Chaya made evident the more primordial tastes of society, the tastes for licentiousness, for immorality, for diversion, things that were increasingly uncomfortable for and persecuted by the local elite, who were not reflecting on the European origin of the licentious festivity. It would appear that during colonial times, discernment was greater, or at least, coercion was less. Colonial society coexisted with these festivities, and despite the punitive oversight of the Catholic Church, royalist authorities did not ban these collective expressions.

Punitive action by the state begins to emerge in the nineteenth century, led by a secular oligarchy, the persecuted becoming the celebratory "masses," the licentious, and the lustful:

It has yet still another little ugly secret. Take note, and do not pout, those of you who might oppose what we say. Any sly trickster, and even the man who is not, thinks he has the right to fondle the made-up girls, and, as custom has sanctioned these takings of liberty, no one dares punish the bold rascal.

The mysterious allure of la Chaya consists of the little squeezes, of the bare legs that permit themselves to be seen, and of the shapely forms outlined through wet clothing. Do you not believe that men would take pleasure in mistreating poor girls, wetting them down, exposing them to diseases, and to a thousand unpleasantries for no good reason? ("Chaya," *La Acción*, February 22, 1879)

Joy in La Chaya was expressed in the freedom of the body and the collective amusement of using perfumed and colored water and physical attraction to balance social and gender differences. The republican elite sought to sanction and prohibit these irrational unleashings of a society in the process of modernization and of cultural ascension by repressing the masses, imposing penalties and fines, and exaggerating the differences between out-of-control common people and the oligarchic class in control of their appetites.

In these excerpts, one can perceive various imaginaries related to bestiality or the animal nature of people, of individuals who are not capable of controlling their appetites and give themselves over to carnal desires beyond the bounds of morality, out of control, in complete abandon. In colonial-era writings one already perceives the imaginaries associated with celebrations, or heresies, of the Indians. Common to the narrative is the bacchanalian community wherein, like animals, the Indians conclude their festivals with collective sex scenes, a carnival of drunkenness and demonic dances (*taki onqoy*).[11]

The bourgeois elite began to bring together their moralistic, hegemonic, and conservative thinking, distancing themselves from these collective expressions to protect the honor and good name of their (unmarried) women. The catalyzing role of the festivity was weakened by its increasingly extreme alienation by groups in power. Men, the common people, and the beasts became a danger, a threat to good manners, and they began to be transformed into scapegoats in elite ways of thinking and exercising power.

> Yet [King] Momo cannot complain of his worshipers. The enthusiasm has been progressive. Sunday was muted by cold weather, on Monday it began to come together, and yesterday became frantic, outrageous, strident: cries of joy mingled with the noise made by the agile horses' hooves on the pavement of our streets. The water cast from the wineskins drew a circle in space, and would fall on the unsuspecting passerby, on the ground made wet from the continuous outpourings. ("Después de Carnaval," *El Huasquino*, February 25, 1857)

The entertainment, enjoyment, raucousness, noise, and shouting were smothered by authoritarianism imposed by a ruling class whose primary response to these expressions was punitive action.

This imaginary, developed during the colonial period and embraced by the elite as the republic emerged, reappears in another Chilean national historical context, with devastating effects. In this context, we can also recognize the call to order and social control made by the political center and right and the upper social classes. During his presidency, as leader of the Popular Unity coalition, Salvador Allende Gossens was generating social chaos, disorganization in administration, and loss of respect for the private properties of the landowning and industrial classes. It became necessary to contain the popular government. The image of President Allende as a debaucher conforms to the construction of a conservative discourse that even justified the action of the armed forces in the dictatorship period, permitting human rights abuses and atrocities committed by the state under the rule of General Augusto Pinochet.

Such arguments have been used more than a few times in Chilean history to justify offensives by the state's police apparatus to repress common people who demand their rights. The common working man is typically portrayed as an idle, easily distracted loafer (cf. Araya 1999).

From the City to the Slums

Carnaval, or rather the rude game of La Chaya, has declined this year. From the city it has fled to the slums, and only at these sites has it prevailed, its adherents having to seek it there.

Infinitely grotesque figures, which provoke hilarity, corpulent youths, soaked with water and with their faces covered in flour, with handlebar moustaches, dressed up like grandfathers and riding astride their horses; beautiful equestriennes riding Spanish style, the [male] riders ready to obey them and hoping for even the slightest insinuation, take note that this is what was seen again and again passing from one street to another, from this to that bureau, from Nueva Freirina to los Cachos.

In private without a doubt another kind of battle must break out, certainly not just of water, but between craving stomachs and tasty pastries and well-seasoned casseroles, gluttony has triumphed. ("Después de Carnaval," *El Huasquino*, February 25, 1857)

The rude game of La Chaya vacates the space of civility and stagnates in slums and rural areas. It follows that the common people, the masses, the plebeians will be the ones who keep alive this historical festivity.

New imaginaries of those who enjoy Carnaval are drawn in the writings of the columnists: the figure of the grotesque, the horrific, the monstrous. Overeating, gluttony, and battles of the bellies are be associated with the celebrants of La Chaya. Another feature of the imaginary is the unrest that occurs in the rural areas far from the control of the urban authorities. Because of this, Carnaval and La Chaya in the interior departments is even more unrestrained. Drunkenness, laziness, and refusal to work are readily apparent:

Huasco Alto. From Valle del Tránsito comes to us the following:
Dear Editor: Carnaval has been celebrated here with drunken binges because the deputy permitted the *chinganas*, despite having received orders from the government not to permit them.

I need not tell you, Señor Editor, that given the long duration of these whirlwinds of corruption, protected by the authorities, owners of rural estates have suffered serious damages during harvest, for lack of laborers, as these have been drunk or become ill due to drunkenness. ("Huasco Alto," *El Derecho*, February 25, 1888)

In the Huasco Alto, and specifically in the Valle del Tránsito (also known as the Valle de los Naturales), Carnaval was celebrated with appalling drunkenness in the lairs of corruption known as chinganas, resulting in laziness, vagrancy, lack of control, and therefore, losses to landowners because of the shortage of labor to work their farms.

If La Chaya and Carnaval celebrated in the cities were considered entertainment, what happened in the villages of the interior was lacking entirely in rationality and abounded in excess. The oppositional relationship established between the city of Vallenar and the Valle del Tránsito permitted the validation of an imposed Indigenous identity in that territory. The "huascoaltino" is the imaginary of the Indian of the cordillera: mangy, dark skinned, crude, lazy, drunk, elusive, uncontrolled.

Passing through the small town of Freirina during his exploration of the Capote mine, Ignacio Domeyko wrote in 1840:

In the mountains, a continental rift remains that belonged to pre-Columbian times in the Indian stronghold of the Guasco Alto, whose inhabitants even now retain the color and features of primitive Americans, although they have by now forgotten their language and ancestral customs. (Domeyko 1978, 49–50)

The population located in central cities of the valley came to understand that in the interior of the Andean Cordillera the Indians of the Huasco Alto lived on.

Class and Constructed Meanings

Imaginaries here describe the class that embodies and maintains La Chaya, the licentiousness, lust, grotesqueness, and gluttony. The identities of the common people are constructed through these hegemonic discursivities, transforming the plebeian subject into an object of repression to be civilized, cultivated, harnessed, and controlled:

Carnaval is now approaching and it is becoming almost impossible to walk the streets for fear that one will look like a Punchinello drenched in flour, water and paper which is recklessly thrown at us when we least expect it.
   The habits of celebrating la Chaya, perverse for the most part, make for a nasty custom that often has fatal consequences.
   The authorities, seriously and circumspectly, must use the law, to strictly forbid la Chaya, even more now that we are under threat of cholera. ("La Chaya," *El Derecho*, February 22, 1888)

The call for order becomes louder every year and the arguments are innumerable. Added to immorality, licentiousness, and the annoying nature and irrationality of this ancient custom were dangers to public health. This allegation was based in elite social meanings and notions of modernity. Threats posed by epidemics were ongoing in this period. Diphtheria, smallpox, and cholera haunted cities and rural areas. Medical specialists, dental surgeons, miracle ointments, and bloodletting were remedies for this new social preoccupation:

> Enthusiasm for this damned game grows from day to day. We say damned (and forgive us readers, in this sense we also are guilty), because everywhere one might look one finds nothing but bad consequences.
>
> Among the hazards to health that often result from this kind of rough diversion are scalp wounds, cuts to the arms from sharp implements, scrapes and all manner of wounds. ("Chaya," *La Acción*, February 22, 1879)

Causes of social problems have been interpreted using similar stereotypes throughout Chilean history. Indeed, they can still be observed in contemporary politics.[12]

Prohibition

Ultimately, the outcries were heeded by authorities, and in 1881, a proclamation was issued banning La Chaya in Vallenar. Imaginaries of the local elite were given life, and the authorities decreed sanctions for infractions of laws that would be enforced by police:

> Edict: Juan de Dios Fontecilla, Governor and Commander of Arms of the Department
>
> Whereas dated yesterday this government has decreed as follows:
>
> CONSIDERING:
>
> 1. That it is indispensable to strictly comply with the requirements of the Police Ordinance, especially articles 2, 3 and 6, and
> 2. Given the games and lack of restraint to which the people surrender themselves during the days of Carnaval, as occurs with the game called "chaya" and with horse racing, it is common to violate those provisions, to the detriment of private interests and public health, and potentially the lives of individuals,
>
> IT IS THEREFORE DECREED:
>
> 1. It is prohibited especially during the days of Carnaval, to gallop and run a horse within town limits, under penalty of two

pesos or four days in jail, in the first instance, and four pesos fine or eight days in prison, in the second, carriage drivers being included in this ban.

2. Likewise prohibited in the streets and public places of the same premises, is the game called "chaya," incurring the penalty of two pesos or four days in prison any person that might throw water or who is professed to throw it at pedestrians from any door, window or any other place elected for this purpose.

    The owner of any house that might be involved unawares in the commission of these acts will be liable for the penalty or the delivery of the offender;

3. To the same penalty imposed by the preceding article shall be subject the so-called "Masks" that violate the provisions of Article 3 of the cited Ordinance, and

4. The police commander is responsible for enforcing all parts of this Decree.

And because it is necessary that this provision inform all; therefore, it must be pronounced as edict in accustomed places, noted in the public record and filed.

Issued in the Chamber of Governance in Vallenar on the 13th day of February 1881.

Juan de Dios Fontecilla ("Bando," *El Huasco,* February 13, 1881)

The edict, pronounced and posted in accustomed places, decreed prohibition of the misconduct, frenzy, and licenses of Carnaval. An attack was mounted against the beasts and wet bodies, sensuality, the tastes for racing horses and perfumed and colored water, and the liberation of passion: manifestations of the culture of the common people.

The local elite imposed hegemonic moralist views and transformed the model for being and living in the city. The authorities and their instruments of repression (police, courts) were poised to protect the position of the oligarchy. The festivities of Carnaval and La Chaya were prohibited at the end of the nineteenth century, according to the path set by the modern central cities, which had managed earlier on to exterminate the ancient custom of backward and barely civilized societies:[13]

It is well known to the aficionados of this pernicious and immoral entertainment, that it is forbidden in public under severe penalty; and the same honor has also been accorded to those that like to work up a sweat in the saddles of their worthless horses. What good measures, many are the mishaps that will be prevented! It is not possible that in a civilized population such as ours such an abhorrent custom might prevail though everywhere else it has been abolished by proper civilization. ("La Chaya," *El Comercio de Vallenar,* January 31, 1883)

By the end of the nineteenth century, the century of the formation of the nation, the governing class and the emerging bourgeoisie had posited a country without joy, a country that was controlled, measured, and disciplined, without La Chaya, without lust, gluttony, cheering, or festivities. Through the course of time, these imaginaries become the foundation of what is today called the Chilean character: deferential, silent, depressive, cold, timid.

A Romantic View

In the twentieth century, dissident and remerging positive views of La Chaya are found in the newspaper columns. The recreational and beneficial aspects of a festivity rooted in joy and happiness are revisited and the long-lived celebration is validated:

Once again, dear readers, the time of the entertaining and popular game of la chaya is upon us.

I see them running about now, dodging little buckets of water. I remember seeing some young girls, friends, much entertained, and I believe that these days of Carnaval will be the only days that I see them fully possessed by their joy.

I think though the most extensive space possible be allowed me in this weekly newspaper, I could not express the great affection in my heart these days for this much appealing game.

May these four lines, dear readers, suffice to convey the joy and marked jubilation of the attraction to la chaya that possesses my soul during these days of tradition that bring indescribable joy to all.

I hope my dear readers that you might play, wander and enjoy to the greatest extent possible . . . during these days of happiness and general contentment. ("Deseos de Chaya," *La Aurora,* February 10, 1909)

The imaginary presented here is completely contrary to the lines penned by the bourgeois elite. Here La Chaya is for enjoyment and entertainment. The culture of the common people allows distraction for a few days and surrender to the pleasures of diversion. One need not be concerned with irrationality, licentiousness, and excess. On the contrary, the people engaged in the pleasures of this lively holiday.

Carnaval has always been a pleasant and beautiful festival, from the earliest times.

It has been, is, and will be, without doubt, the most enjoyable and decent diversion.

There is no person who has not felt that through that pleasing entertainment, his heart is made glad, his soul, his body, every part of him, becomes a happy and blissful being, lavishly enjoying the sweet caresses and fleeting laughter it brings, forgetting momentarily the worries and sufferings of this harsh struggle for existence.

That is why everyone rejoices, all enjoy la chaya, watching wisps of paper dance, and glide, twist and fall . . . fall to the breast of a dear friend or some nice person. ("Carnaval," *El Pololo*, 1917)

This image is entirely unlike that presented in previously analyzed newspapers: it is the world in reverse. In the discourse of ongoing resistance, in the commoner's world, ongoing struggle, suffering, and inquietudes could give way and free rein be given to ecstasy and happiness. The festivities could balance the heavy burden of living in a world full of injustice and sacrifice.

Memories

The final images here are presented by people presently living in the Valley del Tránsito, recounting their own memories of La Chaya:

La Chaya, it's been years since anyone's played the game of la chaya . . . since I was no more than a little boy, now no one plays la Chaya, they have forgotten la Chaya, who knows why, and before it was a big thing . . . the faces of the old ladies would be rosy and they would play the game with the confetti, the old men with confetti on their faces . . . until the chicha was all gone. (Pedro Alquinta, interview by the author, Chollay, Huasco Alto, February 12, 2005)

The oral testimonies of the inhabitants of Malaguin, Chollay, Conay, and other towns of the valley recall their homelands filled with fragrance, laughter, happiness amongst the *"viejas,"*[14] and certainly good drinking in the summer heat:

We did it . . . I got the chance to play La Chaya . . . the old people all covered in powder, confetti cut out of paper of all colors and mixed with water, basil water, the old ladies all cheering, everyone was happy . . . now all of that has been lost, it doesn't happen anymore . . . they would throw basil water at you, it was fragrant, and the old ladies would plant basil for that, to have for La Chaya, of course . . . they threw powder, and for Ash Wednesday, I think it was, they put ashes on their faces . . . it was lost . . . I managed to see it before, but when I came back it no longer existed . . . yes there was drinking, that's never lost. (Norberto Guanchicay, interview by the author, Malaguin, Huasco Alto, February 12, 2005)

La Chaya remained alive through the decades of the 1950s and 1960s. These years brought strong pressures to bear on the local populations. Ultimately, what was intended to be eradicated by means of force lost strength through the depopulation of rural areas. The difficulty of life in the Huasco River valley, magnified by drought and low crop productivity, pressures imposed by privatization trends on commons holders, and the ongoing demand for labor in the mines led to an exodus of young people and families seeking their fortunes in the Norte Grande. These phenomena, provoking diaspora in Chile and all of Latin America, are effects of the globalization of incipient capitalist economic development of the mid-twentieth century:

I got the chance to play, but I didn't like it, because I found it to be a coarse game . . . they fished water out of the canals in pails, they got entirely wet, and after that came along with flour used to make bread, and threw it in one another's faces, shouting loudly . . . Chaya!!! Those from the upper and lower parts [of the village][15] were shouting back and forth to one another "chaya más chaya, sin ovejita, sin sur y malaya,"[16] and *huasos* went galloping by . . . that tradition was lost by about 1968, that was more or less when the last chaya was celebrated. (Ricardo Escobar, interview by the author, Conay, Huasco Alto, March 6, 2007)

La Chaya faded into history as participation declined. Without *chaye-ros*, there would be no more La Chaya.

Conclusions

Imaginaries were configured in colonial times and then re-created by elites using the media to clarify and disseminate their ways of thinking. Imaginaries of the ancient, of Indigenous customs, debauchery, freedom, bodily lust, wickedness, crudity, and gluttony would later become dangerous, a threat, unhealthy—those unacceptable things that made the celebration inappropriate for civilization and modern times.

Chile has been portrayed as a country without mestizaje, as the whitest or most European: one people, one nation, and one language, as the constitution established during the Pinochet dictatorship still boasts. Reports and chronicles in the press at the dawn of the republican era show this principal imaginary undermined by the raucous scenes of Carnaval and festivities of La Chaya. In the case of La Chaya in Vallenar, the analysis of regional press in the nineteenth and early twentieth centuries reveals the presence of other imaginaries in Carnaval and, in particular, in La Chaya. The imaginary of ethnic purity descended from Europe has no place in reality at that time, neither in regional villages nor in small mining towns nor in the capital. We see instead a mixture of European tradition, Indigenous ceremony, and music and dance of Africa as well. We see a motley crew of bodies, mentalities, desires, and amusements.

The aristocratic class distanced itself from spaces where these celebrations took place and identified them with common people. Decrees and edicts of prohibition were the characteristic dynamics of this process at the end of the nineteenth century, and the forced eradication of the disagreeable celebration was presumed complete.

But dissident voices had a place in the press, and they reveal the presence of discursivities opposed to hegemony and a romantic view of La Chaya. From this perspective, La Chaya is entertainment that is decent and even beautiful. The forced eradication of the festivity is also called into question by memories and narratives of present-day inhabitants of the Huasco Alto, who, in interviews, recall and share anecdotes of childhood and adolescence portraying the joy of the viejas engaged in the revelry.

Mestizaje and globalization are the axes of the evolution of La Chaya. With Indigenous roots, La Chaya was mestizoised or syncretized in the colonial period and then gave way under impacts of a globalizing capitalist economic system in the twentieth century. In the end, what punitive and restrictive measures could not achieve was accomplished by the decline of participation in the festivity with the intensification of out-migration of the inhabitants of rural areas.

Notes

1. These newspapers are archived at the Chilean National Library. Transcripts of the Spanish-language quotations taken from newspapers are available upon request from the author.

2. Vallenar was named for Ballynary, his birthplace in Ireland, by Ambrosio O'Higgins, Spanish military governor of Chile and father of Chile's national hero and liberator, Bernardo O'Higgins Riquelme.

3. Note that the flour produced by the Indigenes before the arrival of the Spaniards in northern Chile was made with the seeds of the *algarrobo* and *chañar* trees endemic to arid and semi-arid climates. Wheat was introduced to America by the Spaniards.

4. Guazos (or "huasos") are Chilean horsemen, sometimes called "cowboys."

5. La vara is a contest of strength for horses that involves pushing against a long wooden rod, the "vara."

6. Choclo (or "pastel de choclo") is a traditional Chilean meat and creamed corn casserole.

7. Humitas are a traditional food in the Andes made with *masa harina*, corn, and other ingredients wrapped in corn husks for cooking and are somewhat akin to tamales.

8. In modern times, we observe the use of similar sanctioning discursivities to do away with visions opposed to social models sanctioned by elites. The concept of *social imaginary* is used here to refer to discursivities that enable collectivities to consider and construct themselves as societies subjected to a particular time and way of thinking. (See Anderson 1993; Castoriadis 1975; Durand 1994.)

9. Contemporary nationalist movements of the Mapuche have incorporated the concepts of Gulu Mapu to refer to the historic territory of Araucanía and Puel Mapu to refer to the historic territory of Patagonia, Argentina, which together make up Wallmapu, that is, all the land or all the territory.

10. *"Tierras baldías y vacas"*

11. Taki onqoy, or dancing sickness, was one of the first rituals persecuted by the religious congregations in the Peruvian Andes in the late 1500s. This apostasy, as it was called by the extirpators of idolatry (cf. Estensoro 2003; Millones 2007; Ramos 1992), was a movement in response to the call of the *huacas* (spirits) to the Indigenes to distance themselves from everything Christian and return to their autochthonous religions. This first millennial movement, as it has been called, has modern reinterpretations and a presence in contemporary Indigenous resistance.

12. As an example, the Transantiago Plan was implemented in 2005 during Michelle Bachelet's first presidency to renovate the public transportation system of Santiago. It has been plagued by serious and persistent difficulties. In the opinion of members of the ruling class, including Michelle Bachelet, the difficulties can be attributed to the "culture of the users" of public transport, i.e., the common people of Santiago who cannot fully comprehend modern systems of public transport. It was never about problems with planning or technical errors, but rather a difficult process of adapting Santiago savages to these electronic gadgets.

13. The celebration of Carnaval was prohibited in Chile's capital city in February 1821 (Godoy Orellana 2007). Thereupon, similar decrees were issued in the towns and cities of the interior.

14. "Vieja" is a popular term designating a woman, especially one's wife—the "old lady."

15. The geography of the Valle del Tránsito and the prevailing underlying influence of the concepts of hanan and hurin resulted in the designation of "upper" and "lower" settlement areas.

16. This refrain is a play on words that employs allusions to opposites and picaresque humor. It contrasts the horses used in La Chaya with sheep, the dry climate of the north with rain in the south, and *malaya*, commonly eaten by the poor, with meat consumed by the upper class. It would appear to be a call to everyone, however poor, to celebrate and take part in La Chaya.

PART TWO

Barriers to Empowerment Through Identity

CHAPTER FOUR

Born Indigenous,
Growing Up Mestizos

Schooling and Youth in Arequipa, Peru

MARIELLA I. ARREDONDO

The city of Arequipa, Peru's second largest, has experienced rapid growth due to migration from surrounding rural highland areas. In the past thirty years, Arequipa has seen its population increase by over four hundred thousand inhabitants. Recent population shifts are changing the perception long-time Arequipeños have of their city. Throughout Peru's republican history, the city has long been represented, from within and without, as a place of diverse racial and ethnic mixing, and it has been characterized as possessing a strong regionalist and unique mestizo culture. Mestizo refers to racial/ethnic/cultural mixing as a category of identity which can refer both to "the outcome of an individual or collective shift away from strong self-identification with indigenous culture, and to the myth of cultural homogeneity which elites imposed from above as a standard part of their repertoire of nation-building (Gould, Hale, and Smith 1994, cited in Gould 1998, 10). *Mestizaje* in Arequipa is conceptualized locally as the outcome of a blending (a process) of various ethnic, racial, and cultural mixtures (heterogeneous Europeans mixing with heterogeneous Indigenes) that resulted or produced one particular culture, the Arequipeño culture. For example, according to Peruvian historian Eusebio Quiroz Paz Soldán, "The singular physiognomy of Arequipa and its historical consciousness is based firmly on cultural identity, and at the heart of it, we can objectively recognize that it [Arequipa] is truly mestiza"

(1991, 674).[1] Understanding what mestiza means in Arequipa requires an interrogation into the different categories of identity that are used to define and organize the city and its inhabitants.

This chapter examines the hierarchical relationships among different ethnic, cultural, and social groups in the city of Arequipa through the analysis of young people's perceptions of the intersections among ethnicity,[2] race,[3] class,[4] and culture. I argue that Arequipa's perceived cultural identity as "truly" mestiza supports an ideology held among the dominant non-migrant urban residents that enables discrimination against rural-urban newcomers of Indigenous descent by disguising racial and ethnic prejudice as cultural differentiation. How deep this ideology has been internalized is made visible by the perspectives of young Arequipeños.

This study is informed by semi-structured interviews and surveys of students enrolled at three of the most elite private institutions in Arequipa that I carried out in 2007.[5] To provide anonymity, I call the two elite schools the Peruvian-German School and the Peruvian-U.S. American School. The third school is identified as the All-Girls French Catholic School.

The surveys consisted of a "free-thinking"[6] exercise, where students were given the opportunity to respond anonymously and in whatever manner they wanted (e.g., one-word responses, entire sentences, string of words tied together) to different word prompts that were flashed in front of them, such as mestizo, indigenous, racism, democracy, cholo, white, etc.

Separation and Domination: Race, Class, and Culture in Arequipa

The poverty gap between Peru's rural (53 percent) and urban (17 percent) areas is wide (World Bank 2013). Rural-urban migration represents a search for upward social mobility. In Arequipa, the dominant academic and romanticized perspective is that Andean and Hispanic cultures blended together at contact, resulting in idiosyncratic cultural, artistic, and linguistic[7] expressions to create a unique regional mestizaje that is particularly Arequipeño. Some believe the intense rural-urban migration of the past thirty years is mutating Arequipa's mestizaje into a blend that contains more Andean (Indigenous) influences than Western (non-Indigenous), thereby jeopardizing Arequipa's historical and cultural mestizo identity (Carpio Muñoz 1996). Native Arequipeño intellectuals urge native Arequipeños "to help them [Indigenous newcomers] get to know the city (because no one can love what they do not know) we have to show them our mestizo being (instead of discriminating against them; they [newcomers] can after all erase our cultural identity)" (Carpio Muñoz 1996, 679). This excerpt displays a type of regionalism based on safeguarding a cultural identity from corruption or change while at the same time attempting to advocate for the indoctrination of Indigenous newcomers into mestizo culture as a way to keep alive that mythical Arequipeño mestizo identity. Similarly, Weismantel (2001) reports that well-to-do Bolivians fear the capital city of La Paz might be "taken over" by "Indians." White Limeños lament the expansion of "their" city through the precariously constructed dwellings springing up in the outskirts and forming "young towns."

Peruvian society features a high degree of social stratification that has been legitimized, reproduced, and reformulated throughout its past through different political struggles. Different struggles at different times enabled multifarious forms of discrimination based on agreed-upon constructions of race, ethnicity, class, and mestizaje. More recently, the legitimation of class hierarchies has been reinforced by a form of discrimination being referred to as "silent racism" (de la Cadena 1998) or "racism without race" (Bonilla-Silva 2006) where the "haves" of "culture" are placed above the "have nots" of culture in the class hierarchy. Culture in this context refers to the cultural products and capital associated with Western (i.e., European/non-Indigenous) values, tastes, and lifestyle: a concept often referred to as "high culture" (Arnold 1869) or as the accumulation of cultural capital (Bourdieu and Passeron 1977), whereby one's access to dominant social networks and access to social and material resources brings power and success. In the Peruvian context, how one ends up possessing "culture" continues to depend on a person's place of birth (urban vs. rural, coast vs. highland, national vs. international, etc.), race and ethnicity, and education. In the city of Arequipa, surnames also play a role in situating people in the class hierarchy.

Marisol de la Cadena (2001a) presents an analysis of genealogical concepts of mestizo and mestizaje and examines Peru's historical construction of race, highlighting the importance that race, ethnicity, morality, and education play in the ongoing construction of class hierarchy in Peru. Changing ideas of race, ethnicity, culture, and class in the high Andean region (particularly in Cusco) in twentieth-century Peru eventually yielded a "culturalist" definition of race (de la Cadena 1998, 2000, 2001a). People claim to not be racist but admit to being prejudiced against people whose cultures are different from their own, at the same time maintaining a paternalistic attitude towards Indigenous people who live in remote communities. The notion of "race as culture" helps explain the seeming contradiction between the profound endurance of racism and the historical tendency to downplay the importance of race in Peru.

The asymmetry among Peru's different social/ethnic/groups is built on an historical ideological discourse that consolidated social domination by legitimating the existence of races and a hierarchical relationship among these. Alberto Flores Galindo, one of Peru's most influential historians and intellectuals in the 1980s, wrote about racism in Peru, asserting that racist discourse was first built around the relationship between European whites and Indigenous populations and then extended to other social groups. During Peru's colonial period, the use of the category of "Indian" served as a way to homogenize the defeated Indigenous population and reduce its cultural expressions into a "subculture of dependency," a term coined by Henri Favre (Flores Galindo 1988).

Until the 1940s, racism in Peru was validated by accepted scientific theories of the times and presented to students through history and geography texts. After 1940, race ceased to be used as an official classification on Peruvian identity documents, and the census of 1940 was the last to use race as a category of identity (Portocarrero 2007). It was after the fall of the Nazi regime at the end of World War II that racist doctrines lost scientific credibility in Peru (Portocarrero 2007).

Racism does not rely on official use of racial categories to survive as a practice of discrimination. Racism in Peru manifests in discriminatory practices that are legitimated by society through several mechanisms, one of which is a discourse that centers on "cultural differences" (Bruce 2007; de la Cadena 2000, 2001a; Hale 2006; Portocarrero 2007; Quijano 1980).

The centrality assigned to culture in articulating discriminatory ideas and practices may seem parallel to "racism without race" or what Bonilla-Silva (2006) calls "racism without racists" to refer to current forms of cultural discrimination no longer rooted in biologically defined race. Moreover, Stuart Hall (2000) contends that race and culture are so entangled and mutually reinforcing that distinguishing between forms of racism that highlight race or culture is unimportant. In a study of Guatemalan *ladinos*[8] published in 2006, Charles Hale argues that the anti-racist discourse of ladinos, while it represents a step away from the classic racism of previous times against Indigenous Guatemalans, serves to reconstitute the racial hierarchy by producing subtle and more enduring grounds for keeping the Indigenous population at the bottom of this hierarchy. Racial ambivalence seems to exemplify a desire of ladinos, in the Guatemalan case, to be free of racism without ceasing to benefit from the deep-rooted privilege that has positioned them since time of the Spanish Conquest at the top of the race and class hierarchies.

In Peru, social class, cultural identity, and race are inseparable; one's approximation to a Western (i.e., non-Indigenous) cultural lifestyle can place one higher up on the class hierarchy. If people suffer discrimination based on class, chances are that they also suffer discrimination because they are of Indigenous descent, or African descent. According to Bonilla-Silva, in Latin American nations like Peru, systems of racial stratification are highly complex, as "color" includes skin tone, phenotype, hair texture, and eye color; culture and education; and social class. This phenomenon is known as "pigmentocracy or colorism" (2006, 182). He further asserts that in this time and age "cultural racism" has become the articulating principle of racist thought and practice. This is occurring in Arequipa.

Dialogue about discrimination or differentiation appears to be based not on race but on differences in "culture." This is evident in the discourse of elite private school students, as the following example indicates.

Celia, a sixteen-year-old who attends Arequipa's elite Peruvian-German School, comments on groups of people who do not possess her culture. Her comments are part of a response to a question about whether one is discriminated against in Peru based on economics. "Well, at least speaking for myself, I don't consider myself a racist, but sometimes what I think bothers me is the type of culture of the people, because one can be of low economic means, of very humble origins, but sometimes it is the culture that one possesses that is different and that makes a difference" (interview by the author, Arequipa, 2007). Although I didn't mention race in my question, she mentions race explicitly. Her response suggests that, in her mind, race and class are firmly linked to culture, and if the culture is of a certain type, then it may be the justification to position that person lower in the economic hierarchy.

Although she does not consider herself to be a racist, she points out that Indigenous cultures are very different from her own. She associates those "others with different cultures" with people coming to Arequipa from the highlands. Difference appears to be something negative, and she uses the differences between her culture and that of Indigenous peoples to validate her prejudices.

Nonetheless, according to Celia, not all Indigenous people are bad people. She likes those who live in remote rural communities that she has visited during school trips, those that conform to the idea she has of Peru's Indigenous peoples—those who descend from the Incas, live far away, are poor but grateful for the charity they receive from people like her, and who must be helped, at least once a year (interview by the author, Arequipa, 2007).

Celia further asserts that, once in the city, these same people turn aggressive because of resentment they feel about the discrimination they face in these urban spaces. Then they are no longer Indigenous but become cholos. She continues:

> I have visited several villages and there you meet such wonderful people who are very grateful . . . [they are] beautiful people that are worth more than any of the people that live here in the city. Right? But the main difference I think is cultural because sometimes their culture, I don't know if it's because they [Indigenous people who migrate to the city] feel resentment or why, but it's much more aggressive.

Celia's reasoning seems in tune with the dichotomous society that surrounds her and the prejudice that exists. It's acceptable to like Indigenous people, but not when those same Indigenous people come to the city and adopt mestizo traditions and customs and become cholos because they are aggressive. She believes their aggression stems from the prejudice they endure.

The term cholo has a long history in Peruvian identity politics and has meant different things at different times. According to Pajuelo Tevez (2002), it wasn't until the mid-1960s, when Peruvian sociologist Aníbal Quijano wrote a monograph about the emergence of this group and its implications in Peruvian society, that the term was extensively examined. Quijano's work elaborates an interpretive frame to explain the new social and cultural sector in Peruvian society denominated "cholo" (see Quijano 1980). According to Quijano (1980), during colonial times, the term was used to describe a group of mestizos whose physical traits were predominantly "Indian" and who, even though they would adopt elements of Western culture, found it impossible to enjoy the privileges of the criollo[9] ruling caste because of their racial closeness to Indigenous people. Quijano points to the statement of the Spanish chronicler Garcilaso de la Vega, "El Inca," at the beginning of the seventeenth century that the offspring of a black man and an "Indian" woman were called mulatto or mulatta, while their offspring were called cholos, a word from the Islands of Barlovento (Canary Islands, Spain), which meant dog or wild dog (Quijano 1980).

The term, however, can also have positive connotations: one may call him/herself a cholo/a as a way to display one's pride in his/her identity as Peruvian, or it may be used by friends and family as a term of endearment. Cholo/a can be an insult or a term of endearment depending on the context and the participants. In the in-between cultural setting of urbanized Indigenous people, identifying as a cholo/a becomes linked to identifying as Peruvian. When the identity of cholo/a is adopted, the process of nationalization from Indigenous to mestizo seems to be complete. Although the discrimination persists, the Peruvian nowadays has the self-confidence and power (monetary and cultural) to push back.

Marta, a fifteen-year-old who attends the All-Girls French Catholic School, identifies as a "normal Peruvian." (When I tried to get her to explain to me what she meant by "normal," she couldn't; she just said, "People like me.") She asserted that even a cholo with money would not necessarily be allowed in her school because the school "reserves the right of admission" because not everyone possesses "culture." She seemed to be implying that her culture, that which a certain amount of sociocultural capital enables her to have, is the right culture. In contrast, the culture of the cholo lacks important components that prevent it from being considered "culture." More explicitly, what seems to be at stake here are not only the dichotomies of "low" vs. "high" or "popular" vs. "elite"—and thereby "Indigenous" vs. "Western"—but also a particular notion of "less/uncivilized" vs. "civilized," a remnant of colonial times and an inherited mind-set that continues to dominate in middle- and upper-class Peruvians.

Additionally, by disclosing that her school will not accept just any-body, she is doing two things: first, she is representing herself as some-one privileged; second, she validates the prejudices that she may possess by connecting them to systems in Arequipeño institutions that discrimi-nate by choosing to accept only people with a certain type of cultural, economic, and social capital.

You're a Cholo, But I'm Not: Cholo as a Peruvian Category of Identity

The validation of class hierarchies in Peruvian society through a cultur-alist interpretation of different social identities is not a new phenome-non. According to de la Cadena (2001a), turn-of-the-century Peruvian intellectuals, including Jorge Basadre, even though he was denouncing racism during the mid-twentieth century, retained a "culturalist" inter-pretation by validating social hierarchies based on race and ethnicity, thereby legitimating discrimination and exclusion.

Today, Peru's controversial Indigenous and, more recently, Afro-Peruvian identity politics, coupled with the implementation of assimila-tionist national language and cultural policies,[10] have left Peruvians in an in-between state regarding their social identity. Many Peruvians ide-alize their Indigenous heritage. They are proud of Machu Picchu and the architectural and cultural legacy left by Inca and pre-Inca civilizations, but people who have Quechua or Aymara surnames, or are born in the highlands or the jungle, or are employed as agricultural workers have an inferior status and are subjected to discrimination and marginalization.

Peru's in-between identity stems from its historical memory as a Eu-ropean colony and the mentality of domination and cultural conflict that this past created. Quijano (1980) asserts that in these types of "transi-tory societies" multiple sociocultural elements of diverse historical origin compete for control on an uneven playing field where social-class hierar-chies are validated and deemed natural. In the city of Arequipa, it is com-mon to hear young people of class privilege talk about Peru's "others" and their subjection to discrimination. Young people find it easy to validate the prejudices or biases they have because the society around them vali-dates them. For example, Diana, a sixteen-year-old student at the Peru-vian-US American School, discussed racism and discrimination in the city of Arequipa:

Author: And in Arequipa, do you see problems with racism or discrimi-nation?

Diana: Yes, not so strong, but yes, there are some.

Author: Against whom, mainly?

Diana: Well, one hears expressions such as "yuck I am not going to go to such and such place because it will be full of people from the *cerros* (hills); or, "now that Plaza Vea [a mega store] is here, it's a disaster trying to go there." One cannot get close, not even by chance, because there are lines and lines to get in, and there are several people who angrily told me, "Darn, all the cholos were there and they stunk," and so on. But, things aren't like that either. They [the people perceived as cholos] are also in their right to be there, I say to them, "You [her friends who were in line to go into the store] also are a cholo for standing up there in line with them."

Diana is very careful not to adhere to the comments that are made by her friends, in particular, towards the group of Peruvians depicted as cholos. She first tells me that her friends complain about cholos, but afterward defends cholos, as they have the right to go to the new store. She then labels her friends who complained about the Indigenous-origin cholos being at the store in the first place as cholos—occupying the same space as the other supposed cholos. In short, everyone has the right to go wherever they want, but if one goes where the masses go, one is tainted with *choloness*. Interestingly, the store in question offers patrons visiting by car and making use of the store's parking lot the possibility of avoiding the lines altogether, simultaneously enforcing the privilege of wealthier Arequipeños and underscoring the condition of those unable to take advantage of that "service." The policy clearly demonstrates that these stores also understand the social-class hierarchy in place in Arequipa and the potential danger of not shielding their wealthier customers from the possibility of discrimination by association with cholos, even the sort of accidental association implicit in standing in line in a public shopping space. This is also an illustration of the sort of voluntary segregation that occurs among middle-and upper-class people in Arequipeño society and the institutions that facilitate it by validating class hierarchy.

In the following exchange, Marta (the fifteen-year-old who attends the All-Girls French Catholic School) defines and characterizes a person who would be considered a cholo:

Author: Regarding race, do you think that in Peru there are different races?

Marta: Races? No. But it's always the case of seeing a specific person, someone who is "typical" [and saying] "he is a cholo, but I am not."

Author: What is a cholo like?

Marta: In my view, they are those people that you meet that are un-educated, that talk back, that are ignorant, litter the streets, and do whatever they want. They don't have education, or culture.

Author: So, I see, it's not based on their physical characteristics. In that case, if a person who is a *gringuita*[11] does all that you mentioned, would that person be a cholo?

Marta: No, obviously not. I don't know what they would call that person, but, well, I guess, yes, the color of the skin or physical characteristics do make a difference. So, when you say cholo it is something similar to an Inca (she laughs), to put it one way, with their big Indigenous nose.

It is interesting to note that at first Marta only speaks of behavioral traits associated with being a cholo. Cholos are perceived as "typical Peruvians." With further questioning, she comments about physical characteristics that might determine who would be a cholo. In Marta's view, cholos don't have culture. By "culture," she is referring to non-Indigenous values, tastes, and traditions. When Marta speaks of the cholo, she specifically refers to the masculine representation of the concept.[12]

Free-Thinking Exercise: Analysis of Findings

In this section, I analyze the results of the free-thinking exercise survey, which provide yet more insight into how different concepts associated with oppression and differentiation are being conceived by Arequipa's middle- and upper-class youth. Students attending the Peruvian-U.S. American School were surveyed. Eighty-eight seventh-grade students were given a blank sheet of paper and asked to note their responses to various prompts flashed in front of them on a large piece of white cardboard. Total anonymity was guaranteed, except for sex, grade level, and place of birth of students and their parents. The survey was administered by the students' social studies teacher. Here I focus on four prompts out of a total of fourteen: indigenous, mestizo, racism, and cholo. The responses are particularly illustrative because of their anonymity. Student respondents had no incentive to be dishonest and could say whatever they wanted, even if they knew their answers might not be "politically correct."

Responding to the prompt "Indigenous," almost half of the students surveyed (forty-one) considered Indigenous people to be those people who lived in the past, before or during the conquest. They linked the term/concept to the Incas and their Tawantinsuyu Empire, thereby making the thousands of contemporary Peruvians who self-identify as "Indigenous" invisible. According to Greene (2005), this find should not be all that surprising since in Peruvian society there is plenty of evidence of an ongoing Andean hegemony. Even prior to colonization by the Europeans, there was a hierarchy in place wherein the highland Inca ruled over lowland (Amazonian) Indigenous populations. This hierarchy has continued into present time. Elite society experiences a deep admiration for their Andean/Inca past but only when it is convenient, for example, in tourism or bonding with a decolonized national pride. Greene notes that over time, "repeated elitist appropriations of the Inca image have had considerable impact on actual Andeans. In a country where the elite have effectively already appropriated the Inca 'essence' and yet continue to degrade everyday 'common' Andean Indians, outwardly self-identifying as indigenous doesn't necessarily look so attractive" (2005, 29). The invisibility only seems to apply in the urban context. In contrast, within the bounds of their communities, Indigenous people are perceived by the elite as humble, poor, and organized but needing help.

When they migrate to the city, they are no longer Indigenous. Any attempt by Indigenous people to leave their rural context disrupts the urban middle- and upper-class model of society, and the presence of Indigenous people in the cities then shifts into something else altogether different. These people become urbanized Indigenes or aggressive cholos as they go through the process of becoming Peruvians.

In the city of Arequipa, it is very common to encounter people who self-identify as Indigenous. Many women (not usually men) wear traditional attire and speak Quechua or Aymara on the streets or in places of business. Sixteen students associated the term "Indigenous" with people in subservient social roles, such as servants, peons, agricultural workers, or even slaves. Two students wrote "my maid" (*mi empleada*). The third-largest group (twelve students) associated the term with class ("poor").

Five students responded with negative stereotypes. These included references to people with very little or with no education, expressed in words such as "illiterate" or "ignorant." A few students associated the term with people lacking "culture" or not having a very advanced one. Three students perceived Indigenous people as "the other," expressed in sentences such as "very different from us" or "not us." It is interesting to note that in all these negative associations, not one student wrote anything explicitly positive. No one was able to talk about Indigenous peoples' continued struggles for justice, either in Peru or in other parts of the world. The negative responses (illiterate, no culture or education, low social class, etc.) allow us to see how Indigenous Peruvians continue to be perceived by these middle- and upper-class students. Thinking about them in racist terms, portraying them in a negative way, and acknowledging them only in a specific context is how these young people attempt to make sense of the issue.

The second prompt was "racism." Most of the students responded by defining it as some type of discrimination based on skin color and social class. This supports the existing literature on the complex intersection between race and class in Peru. Thirty-one students associated racism with black people or with Africans, even though the Afro-Peruvian population is small in the city of Arequipa. This suggests that, to many students, racism occurs elsewhere and only against people of African descent and therefore not often in their city. Students recognize that racism exists, and they seem to understand how it works but don't seem to recognize it when it exists in their immediate context. Other students merely wrote the word "cholos" after the prompt racism. This response is rather ambiguous as it can either mean that cholos are the ones discriminating or that cholos are the target of racial discrimination. Only one student applied a discussion of discrimination to Indigenous people.

For the prompt "mestizo," almost all of the students gave me what is considered a Peruvian textbook definition of the concept in gendered terms: the racial mix of a Spaniard male and an Indigenous female. In Weismantel's (2001) examination of the different social and geographical spaces that the chola occupies, she describes the chola as being both idealized and taken advantage of, and as living in a limiting domain where there are few public spaces in which she can assert herself. At home and as a domestic worker, the chola oftentimes is both depended on and abused emotionally, physically, and/or sexually. This rendered description of mestizaje alludes to acknowledging the force that many times was involved in these early "unions" between colonizer men and Native women. Mestizo is also a fluid and relational term because youth of affluence often auto-identify as "white," even if their skin does not appear to be fair but rather resembles that of their Indigenous compatriots. Europeanized ideals of appearance may explain middle- and upper-class students' choices to avoid mestizo as an identifier and be the reason some think of Indigenous people as mestizos. Identifying as a mestizo could potentially lower their status, and it would be avoided if they are insecure about their social-class standing.

What the survey reveals supports findings of others who have studied race in Peru. Ripley and Saga Falabella, the two biggest department stores in Peru, only use Europeanized models who resemble a minority of Peru's population to advertise their products. The models tend to be fair skinned, tall, with light brown or blond hair, and light-colored eyes. The marketing strategy of these two big department stores plays on the assumption that Peruvians aspire to look European (Bruce 2007). Since the conquest, whiteness has been associated with privilege and power, and it has become synonymous with success, beauty, professionalism, wealth, and anything foreign. Mestizo or cholo, on the other hand, are synonymous with ugly, failure, poverty, sadness, and the highlands (Bruce 2007; Portocarrero 2007). Only state-sponsored ads or those advertising social services use models that resemble a more accurate cross section of the population.

The cholo prompt was by far the one that elicited the most varied answers. Most of the students connected the term with the highlands or highlanders (*serranos*), or with people who live in the hills on the outskirts of the city. In Peruvian society and in Arequipa, being from the highlands, or living in the city's surrounding hills, is a demarcation of lower social status and linkage to the rural. Surviving as an Indigenous farmer from the highlands or an Indian from the jungle is difficult. The possibility of climbing the social-class ladder resides in leaving one's Indigenousness behind by moving into urban centers.

Given the association of the cholo with migrants of Indigenous descent, it is not surprising to find that some students believe "cholo" means people with an accent (because their first language is not Spanish but Quechua or Aymara or any of the languages spoken in the Amazon) or describe cholos as people without culture and education, as hypocrites and thieves, or as "the other."

The concept of cholo has also become a symbol of national identity. This is reflected in the survey by a group of students who responded to the prompt by writing "Peruvian." The twist, however, is that the majority of those students also inserted comments indicating that cholo does not apply to all Peruvians, but only to those Peruvians who lack something (i.e., culture, education, social standing, etc.). For example, some responses included "a cholo is a Peruvian who is a thief" or "a cholo is a Peruvian without culture."

In her study of the perception of cholo in the capital city of Lima among young people of middle and popular classes, Cosamalón (1993) found that the word had derogatory, deprecating, and racist connotations for most students in the sample. If the term was associated with social characteristics—such as highlander, Indian, mestizo, poor, farmer, Andean music, etc.—those characteristics were followed by negative qualifiers such as ugly, inferior, animal, brute. Within the range of samples representing popular classes, Cosamalón found that the term generated an increasingly personal and internalized reaction for some interviewees. The more economically marginalized the subjects, the more likely the term evoked strong reactions to the point of impeding an articulation of a response and creating blockage, insecurity, or evasion. The author identified this reaction as common among youth who were ethnically "cholos" and of low economic status (Cosamalón 1993).

My findings here suggest that the concept of cholo, though more negative than positive among youth, can be appropriated and linked to national identity (not ethnic or social or racial identity). One can admit to being cholo because one is indeed Peruvian. It becomes a source of pride.

Conclusion

Arequipeño society is structured hierarchically, and institutions, in some cases, perpetuate a social-class hierarchy based on race, ethnicity, and class. In other cases, they continue to deny access to sectors of the population using culturalist interpretations to validate discrimination. When Indigenous people migrate to cities, they become cholos. This subjects them to numerous forms of discrimination: class, race, and culture are intertwined. Although the guiding principle of the importance of education convinces people that it is a mechanism that may be used as a stepping-stone to liberation from oppression and economic advancement, schools like those attended by Celia, Marta, and Diana are reproducing social hierarchies, keeping people of Indigenous descent separate.

This study suggests young people's experiences (in schools, with advertising, and even going shopping) influence identity formation and reinforce discrimination. The data indicates that students' thoughts about race, class, and ethnicity are influenced by the premise that rural-to-urban migration is challenging the conceptualization of Arequipa as mestiza. An internalized colonialism makes denigration of Indigenous migrants to the city common and accepted in the name of protecting Arequipa's unique mestiza identity. Mestizaje is understood to be the result of hundreds of years of diverse encounters and intermarriages, but the fear of well-to-do mestizos of the loss of Arequipeño culture through the recent vast migration of people from the highlands to the city suggests that acknowledging mestizaje as a hybrid between different cultures is acceptable as long as the urban Indigenous component of this hybridization does not stand out.

How deeply this ideology has been internalized is made visible by the perspectives of young Arequipeños. Arequipeño youth know the limits of integration and rejection of newcomers. Interactions between different social sectors continue to be mediated by a well-known script. When students refer to culture, many refer to international cultures or notions of high (i.e., non-Indigenous) culture that carry a special prestige even beyond that of the culture of the Peruvian elite in some cases. Boundaries of class roles are not clearly articulated, but rather disguised as differences in culture. Afro-Peruvians are acknowledged when recognizing different types of music or dance, but they are not recognized as Peruvian citizens with a distinct history, culture, and social reality. Indigenous, highlander, Andean, and Amazonian realities are still interpreted in schools as archaic and romanticized. The understanding of who is Indigenous is very much attached to perceptions of people living isolated in rural geographic spaces. This rural-urban contradiction in the perspectives of middle- and upper-class youth makes it acceptable to acknowledge and empathize with Indigenous people only in their rural contexts. As long as they remain there, they pose no threat to Arequipa's unique regional mestizo identity. Their movement into the city initiates for Indigenous migrants a complex process that begins with rejection and disapproval of their culture, identity, and history and may end with a shift in lifestyle and appropriation of cholo as a symbol of national identity.

Indigenous ways of knowing and believing are not recognized or inserted into the grand epistemological repertoire of educational institutions. Students are not being afforded the right to identify with them, learn from them, and feel a sense of commitment towards them. Because of the increase in rural-urban migration, it is particularly important not only to educate the urban population about the newcomers' realities, histories, and cultural traditions outside of folklore but also to validate the experiences and cultures of newcomers in the larger national context. In order for a multicultural nation like Peru to advance towards inclusion of its diverse cultural and ethnic social groups, it is important to provide spaces for dialogue between different sectors of society and for intra- and inter-group reflection. In spaces of transition (rural), as well as spaces of permanence (urban), Peruvians would benefit from an intercultural education aimed at constructing a just and inclusive society.

Acknowledgments

I would like to acknowledge Alfio Saitta for his analysis of this chapter. Also, thank you to Bradley Levinson, Shane L. Greene, and the four anonymous reviewers for constructive criticism of earlier drafts.

Notes

1. "La fisonomía singular de Arequipa y su conciencia histórica, se asientan firmemente sobre su identidad cultural, y en el fondo de la misma podemos reconocer objetivamente que es mestiza." All translations in this chapter are by Arredondo.

2. "Ethnic groups" are groups of people who perceive that they share common background, historical, and mythical memories; cultural and linguistic knowledge systems; and behavioral, and/or religious characteristics and beliefs. Ethnic groups do not need to share a history of oppression.

3. The concept of race is problematic. Science has demonstrated that biologically and genetically races do not exist. Despite its uncertainties and ambiguities, race continues to play a key role in structuring and representing the social world.

4. The definition of class in this chapter is linked to socioeconomic position in life, particularly as it refers to wealth, income, profession, and level of education. It also recognizes the power in controlling one's own work and the power found in controlling the work of other people.

5. Out of the three private schools represented in this chapter, two are categorized as very exclusive co-ed schools due to competitive admittance, the expense associated with enrolling in the school, and monthly tuition costs. The third is also considered prestigious, but as a Catholic school, it is more accessible to middle- and lower-middle-class families. The tuition and fees in this school are about half that of the other two schools.

6. I borrowed and adapted this method from oral historian Alfio S. Saitta because it offered the opportunity to obtain students' perceptions without any inhibitions on their part because of the anonymity of their responses.

7. Arequipeño lexicon includes borrowings from the Quechua, Aymara, Puquina, and Castilian (Spanish) languages; hence, Arequipa Spanish is a distinct dialect.

8. A ladino is a Europeanized Central American person of predominantly Spanish origin.

9. Criollo, in this context, means direct descendants of Europeans born in the Americas.

10. Although Peru has had, in theory, a very progressive bilingual intercultural education policy in place since 2003 supposedly geared towards all Peruvians, it continues to be geared only towards the Indigenous population living in rural areas.

11. A gringuita is someone with European (Anglo) physical characteristics.

12. Here I don't examine gendered differences, but I believe that men and women identified as cholos have different experiences. The young women interviewed for this study perceive the cholo (male) as a threat, whereas the chola (female) is not mentioned. For a detailed and thorough analysis of the role of the chola in Andean spaces, see Mary Weismantel (2001).

CHAPTER FIVE

Questioning the Nation

Affirmative Action and Racial Quotas
in Brazilian Universities

PAULO ALBERTO DOS SANTOS VIEIRA

Introduction: Racial Democracy
and *Mestizaje* as Myth

Affirmative action policies have existed in Brazil for some time. Between the 1940s and 1980s, Brazilian society tolerated policies of this nature, including a quota system, without major criticism. National legislation promulgated affirmative action policies which extended to the labor market and public universities.[1] From this perspective, there is nothing new in the use of mechanisms that promote equality. However, the situation changed when these policies were specifically extended to the black population. Since its implementation in 2002 in the public universities of Rio de Janeiro state, the system of quotas for black students has been heavily criticized vis-à-vis the validity of the racial criterion for the formulation of contemporary affirmative action policies.

This is relevant for the social sciences, as they are faced with controversies surrounding the formulation of public policies and their relationships to the race theme in a society that, until recently, claimed to have solved the racial issue through an ideology consecrated as a racial democracy.[2] The pillars of this myth are being eroded by contemporary policies of affirmative action.

Built on the proposition that there would be no real distinctions among different racial groups, the myth of racial democracy has sought to con-

92

ceal the fact that the supposed cultural synthesis hides social hierarchies and new forms of racial discrimination.[3] Therefore, quotas for black students in contemporary Brazil that seek to democratize access for this group at Brazilian universities challenge the previously established order within which the black population has always been perceived as inferior.

The current debate in Brazil about affirmative action policies, particularly those concerning racial quotas, has resulted in heated controversy, reaching all the way to the highest court in the nation. In March 2010, the Supreme Federal Court held public hearings to gather information to decide on the constitutionality of racial quotas in affirmative action policies. The debate is fruitful because it has resulted in profound reflection on the national pact established in 1930.

As a nation, Brazil emerged in the early decades of the twentieth century by making *mestizaje* one of its most prominent symbols. Mestizaje is anchored in the myth of racial democracy, which was based on alleged equal opportunities among different social groups. This myth, constructed in the 1930s, was hegemonic until the 1970s, when its influence began to decline. Brazilian society is engaged in "a transition from a monocultural representation built and secured by elites . . . to a social representation that unfolds daily and deeply in a dynamic and multicultural way. The Constitution of 1988, if superficially, expresses this change in the representation of most Brazilians" (Silvério 2005b, 91). Ongoing debates about affirmative action policies based on ethnic-racial divisions have laid bare deep asymmetries between different racial groups. Examining race and public policies confirms the existence of significant inequalities between the white and black populations that have been perpetuated for decades.

Using racial quotas in public universities has the potential to fulfill the constitutional principle of substantive or material equality and, at the same time, uphold the black population's rights in the public sphere. In this sense, racial quotas do have the potential to challenge the foundations upon which interpretations of Brazilian society were erected. It is important to point out that the significance of the debate on affirmative action goes beyond the problem of the absence of black students in public universities in Brazil. It reveals that Brazilian society is plural in its configuration. Racial diversity profoundly impacts the macro social structure. The current debate is indicative of the strong tensions around the classical interpretation in this country of an identity based in one territory, one language, and one people, thus attributing homogeneity to the Brazilian nation.

It is crucial that elimination of inequality be combined with the recognition of difference (Piovesan 2008; Silvério 2006). According to Alves dos Santos (2006), systems of inequality and exclusion in contemporary societies indicate that anti-difference universalisms seriously oversimplify the complex relationship between identity and equality, and inequality and difference. Assimilationist or redistributive policies produce fictitious cultural homogeneity that subordinates all otherness. This subordination, responsible for the creation of asymmetry, denies cultural, ethnic, racial, and sexual differences in favor of the national mega-identity.

Affirmative Action and Recognition of Difference

Policies formulated in recent decades designed to ensure a network of guarantees to heretofore disadvantaged social groups represent an attempt to redress historical inequalities and recognize difference. Today in Brazil, affirmative action policies span a wide range of public institutions of higher education. Nearly one hundred higher education institutions have adopted policies of this nature. It is very important that we have black students in university courses in the face of overwhelming evidence that, until recently, black students were excluded from the population on college campuses. The arguments and the statistical treatment by Henriques (2001) regarding the evolution of educational attainment for the Brazilian population between the mid-1910s and the 1980s and in subsequent generations are illustrative of the problem. In his study, Henriques demonstrates that there have been advances in the education of all people over nearly seven decades. Nonetheless, average schooling in Brazil does not exceed eight years, which is a reflection of serious social, economic, and labor problems. When the data are disaggregated by color/race, the level of education of the black population is on average two years less than the white population. This two-year gap is the same as that at the beginning of the twentieth century.

Affirmative action based on the difference between races in educational attainment can lead to new social arrangements so that such disparities are not consolidated into the social fabric as perennial disadvantages, as has occurred in secular social relations of Brazilian society to the detriment of blacks. This is well captured by Silvério (2005a), who shows that affirmative action recognizes existing social obstacles for African descendants in Brazil, who have repeatedly been denied the right to live and act as full-fledged citizens, but addresses this at the expense of black people themselves. He concludes that "a program of affirmative action is therefore needed that recognizes the ethnic and racial diversity of the Brazilian population; that restores relations among blacks, whites, indigenous peoples, and Asians in new ways; that corrects distortions of exclusionary treatment of blacks; that recognizes the sufferings to which they have been subjected not as a problem exclusively theirs but of Brazilian society in general" (Silvério 2005a, 146–47).

Recognition of diversity includes adoption of the race category as a factor guiding public policies that are designed on the one hand to overcome inequality and promote equality and on the other hand to reevaluate the contributions made by the black population in building this nation. During the administration of President Luiz Inácio Lula da Silva (2003–2010), federal law 10.639 of 2003 (which modifies law 9.394, the Law of National Education Directives and Bases (LDB) of 1996) made it compulsory in basic education (primary and secondary schools, both public and private) to teach Afro-Brazilian and African history and culture (Brazil. Ministério da Educação 2004). Making compulsory these inclusions in curricula in history, culture, literature, the Afro-Brazilian Arts, and the African diaspora (Brazil. Ministério da Educação 2004) seems to be a necessary challenge for Brazilian society at the beginning of this century to address deep inequalities between social groups, found in particular between whites and blacks. This is a challenge that, in addition to promoting equality, demands recognition of difference.

Debate about racial quotas reveals the formation of a theoretical framework that differs from interpretations based on purported racial democracy. This framework, still under construction, relies on the sociological concept of race to both provide an understanding of actual social relations and reinterpret social relations in Brazilian society to make race one of the structural elements of these relations. This is the backdrop for the public hearing held by the Supreme Federal Court in 2010.

The Controversy over Affirmative Action

There are few examples of topics discussed within the academic community that have such intense political and social repercussions as affirmative action policies. The first experiments in affirmative action policies implemented in public higher education were carried out in the public universities of Rio de Janeiro in 2002. Since then, the debate about affirmative action has expanded so that it is no longer restricted to academic settings but rather considers all institutions of Brazilian society.

Medeiros (2009) claims that the first demonstrations against the policies of affirmative action and racial quotas took place in 2002 at the State University of Rio de Janeiro (Universidade do Estado do Rio de Janeiro, UERJ). Several candidates who considered themselves "wronged" sought appropriate adjustments in their evaluations through legal action. Concurrently, various personalities (researchers, intellectuals, artists, journalists, etc.) became involved in the debate, explicitly positioning themselves against affirmative action. They claimed that affirmative action policies were alien to Brazil and were an anachronism for a society that had achieved, in a totally creative manner, a harmonious structure of ethnic and race relations. They did recognize inequality and racist practices, but attributed these evils to specific situations or other causes that do not characterize Brazilian society. At the World Conference Against

Racism, Racial Discrimination, Xenophobia, and Related Intolerance held in Durban, South Africa, in 2001, Fry and Maggie (2002), two of the most articulate researchers of this position on affirmative action policies, sought to characterize the position of the Brazilian delegation present as something novel and surprising. They contended that more traditional approaches to racial equality, forged in the early decades of the twentieth century, had never been held in check. These authors also praised racial democracy, in spite of the fact that since the 1970s, it has been losing effectiveness as a way to explain race relations in Brazil.

Asymmetries in social and economic indicators reveal how far from reality the premises of the racial democracy thesis are. The aims of the black movement in Brazil, articulated comprehensively at the conference in Durban, also undermine that thesis. These included challenging racist and discriminatory practices, acting in support of affirmative action policies, and claiming collective rights (as in the case of *quilombola*[4] recognition).

One must consider that it is unusual for social criticism of constructed ethno-racial hierarchies to be made explicit. In Brazil, the twentieth century was marked by successive regimes that conceived policy from the "top down," whether wrapped in the robes of democracy or emergency rule. Brazil has endured multiple experiences of the silencing of criticism and banning of dissent. We must consider the Old Republic and its bestialities, such as the agreements of agrarian and coffee elites responsible for the Encilhamento[5] crisis, the failure of the national banking system in 1891, and the "1930 Revolution." Under the New State, we experienced the internationalization of the Brazilian economy under the leadership of foreign capital and the military dictatorship (that took power in 1964) with a "love it or leave it" mentality. The New Republic and its transition away from the dictatorial period brought us the brief, emblematic presidency of Fernando Collor de Mello (Haddad and Schwarz 1998).

So, one can observe, from colonial times into the twentieth century, the construction of a paradigm and a society that held that individuals marked by stigmatizing racial differences could transition between classes, or not even consider them.[6] Thus, a set of arguments against the policies of affirmative action and racial quotas became part of discussions that were increasingly heated and intense.

Several arguments were used in a vain attempt to obstruct the adoption and implementation of affirmative action policies in public institutions of higher education. Most imposed a false dichotomy between policies and the quality and diversity of public education. Some claimed the impossibility of identifying blacks because of extensive miscegenation, while others foretold the decline in the quality of education from the black presence in institutions of higher education. Another argument was to defend the principle of individual merit in university entrance exams and hold that the rejection of meritocracy with the admission of students from affirmative action programs would lower the quality of education. Some argued that racism would intensify, and others that affirmative action measures were unconstitutional. These and other arguments emerged in interviews, articles, and debates about the use of the principle of equality (J. Gomes 2003).

Many contend that the debate about affirmative action started with the implementation of measures aimed at combating the historical exclusion of blacks from state and federal universities: UERJ, State University of Norte Fluminense (Universidade Estadual do Norte Fluminense, UENF), the Federal University of Bahia (Universidade Federal da Bahia, UFBA), and the University of Brasília (Universidade de Brasília, UnB).[7] However, the current debate on the validity of policies promoting racial equality has its origins in previous decades, in social movements resisting the military dictatorship that unconstitutionally took power in 1964 and the democratic movements that have worked for amnesty (broad, general, and unrestricted) and for the return to democratic normality in Brazilian society.

It is also necessary to consider the importance, particularly since 1978, of the creation of the Unified Black Movement (Alves dos Santos 2006). The struggle for racial equality was renewed in the 1970s, with political support from entities and associations that made up, and still make up, the black movement. It was a coalescence of various political agendas: to propose strategies that go beyond alleging racism, to re-evaluate the participation of blacks in Brazilian history and of mechanisms anchored in the principle of equal opportunity (or material equality), and to consider the struggle against racism as a precondition for re-democratization. This set of demands re-shaped initiatives to combat racism and promote racial equality. The idea of displacement (Hall 2006) inherent in changes promoted by the black movement suggests a shift from notions of democracy and a racially mestizo nation to the perspective of a multiracial nation. This involves, on one hand, the need to recognize ethnic-racial differences and, on the other, to re-examine citizenship in economic, legal, and political contexts (innate or constructed) that provoke discrimination, which, in turn, causes both material and symbolic injustice.

The promotion of affirmative action policies derives from the historical, political, and social contexts built by the black movement and by all who are engaged in the anti-racism battle in Brazil, notwithstanding criticism directed at supporters of affirmative action that characterizes their demands for recognition as an "importation" of foreign ideas. In fact, the successful strategy of politicizing the sociological category of race (N. Gomes 2005; Guimarães 2003) has made it possible to illuminate hitherto hidden aspects of Brazilian social relations. The political arrangements established between the 1970s and 1990s were beneficial to anti-racist activists primarily because a wedge was driven into the hermetic understanding of inequalities that had existed until then. Interpretations based solely on the socioeconomic dimension and race relations lost ground, explanatory power, and prestige in the face of the existing reality (Jaccoud 2008).

At the same time, arguments critical of affirmative action policies were countered with data produced by official agencies responsible for national research to guide public policy. Studies conducted by the federal government, for example by the Instituto de Pesquisa Econômica Aplicada (Institute for Applied Economic Research, IPEA), have shown that existing inequalities between social groups that make up the Brazilian population have a high degree of correlation with markers of difference. [8] Race and gender are the markers that show that inequality is not solely of an economic and social nature (Henriques 2001; Pinheiro et al. 2008). It appears that economic, social, educational, regional, age, and gender inequalities are tied to the race issue. Past decades saw policy implementation that was insensitive to race—despite stigmatization, marginalization, and hierarchical constraints—and the result has been an enormous asymmetry in Brazilian society between the white and non-white groups that compose it.

It began to become more evident, contrary to the alarmist and fatalistic projections of its opponents, that affirmative action might reduce imbalance and help to overcome the disastrous inequalities that beset the nation's population, giving one racial group—whites—access to material and symbolic assets, while others—the non-white population—still suffer exclusion. Quickly and readily various authors entered the debate and could demonstrate that the arguments of critics of affirmative action were weak and inconsistent and that they could not sustain the myth of racial democracy.[9]

Some critics have constructed a fallacious approach to strengthen arguments claiming the existence of a racial democracy. When they argue that mestizaje is a value of Brazilian society, they overlook the fact that the miscegenation responsible for the racial diversity of the population is linked with violent sexual encounters between European settlers and Indigenous peoples and the enslaved African population. Mestizaje is also an expression of racial inequality in society.

Mestizaje, when understood as the establishment of aesthetic and cultural values and moral standards, also tended over several decades to subordinate non-white groups and individuals. Failing to examine critically miscegenation and mestizaje, critics of affirmative action position themselves against racial quotas and insist on the existence of a racially one-dimensional Brazilian society. This view has been questioned in contemporary times because the latest research and official statistics produced by government agencies show that Brazil is an absolutely unequal society in racial terms.

Using powerful methodological resources to produce theory, proponents of affirmative action completely changed the landscape of debate.

Prominent critics have begun to publicly concede the importance of affirmative action policies as the idea of a harmonic, monocultural mestizo nation is replaced by recognition of a diverse, conflicted, and multiracial nation. This position has become prevalent in some media of national circulation (Cruz 2006; Moya 2009). The ongoing refusal to acknowledge racial criteria by some sectors of Brazilian society (most significantly the mass media and high-profile intellectuals) explains major tensions within the society, particularly with regard to the category of "race" and the sociological use of this concept.

On the one hand, there is now a widespread acceptance of affirmative action policies, including quotas; on the other, there remains strong opposition in some sectors of society, as could be observed during the public hearings held by the Supreme Federal Court. In any case, the current debate about affirmative action and racial quotas seems to indicate that the supposed racial democracy and the alleged cultural synthesis of mestizaje are no longer accepted by broad consensus.

The controversy over the use of the sociological category of race in the quota systems of Brazilian universities (and in public policies more generally) affects the whole society and its key institutions. Identities based in "race," gender, sexuality, and disability cut across class membership. It is an ongoing historical possibility that social groups on the margins of welfare rights may themselves be the protagonists of their emancipation. And the heated disputes over whether affirmative action policies should favor the black population constrain the power exercised by a monocultural elite in a society that presents itself, unlike before, as multiethnic, pluralistic, and diverse.

If social markers of difference such as gender and disability are used in Brazil, how can we explain the rejection of the principle when turned toward other social markers of difference, as in the case of race (Paixão 2008)? If we consider that public policy since the beginning of the twentieth century has been aimed at specific groups—in employment and education—what motives exist for hampering such mechanisms in the case of affirmative action and racial quotas in public universities in Brazil? These questions allow us to reflect on another dimension of the debate about the implementation of affirmative action in contemporary Brazil until now little explored. Laws such as the Child and Adolescent Statute and the Elderly Statute (age), constitutional provisions for people with disabilities, and the reservation of seats for women in political parties (gender) illustrate that Brazilian society accepts affirmative action and group rights without opposition as vehement as that observed when the issues are affirmative action and racial quotas in public higher education and the labor market.

Roots of the Controversy

Tackling inequality demands that we consider the influences of discriminatory economic development that has intensified since the 1950s and the cultural matrix formulated since the early decades of the twentieth century. Race theories of the late nineteenth and early twentieth centuries claimed that the presence of mixed races implied the degeneration of society. In the 1930s, Gilberto Freyre elaborated on the idea that the cultural synthesis of mestizaje inaugurated a new civilization within which all races would live in harmony (Freyre, Cardoso, and Nery da Fonseca 2006). These theories were based on the belief that races were biological categories. As Costa (2007) points out, Brazilian thinkers had basically agreed that humanity consists of biological races and believed that these races formed a hierarchy with whites at the top. Biology would provide a foundation for culture.

One of the serious problems arising from this vision is that mestizaje did not break patterns and social norms that define some racial groups as inferior and force them to occupy predetermined social spaces, almost always those of lesser prestige, recognition, and social value. The refusal to use the race category for the implementation of affirmative action seems to have close ties with this ambiguity about the hegemonic nature of mestizaje that has had a presence in Brazilian social thought for many decades. The implementation of race-based affirmative action policies reintroduces into contemporary political debate the fragility of theses wherein racial difference is eclipsed by the mythical mantle of professed racial democracy.

Criticisms of interpretations of race reflect the political environment of Brazilian society over the past forty years. The mobilization of social actors and their respective demands related to contemporary public policy occur in the context of the re-democratization of Brazilian society. In this context, with the emergence of social movements, including the resurgence of the black movement, the use of the race category enters the debate (Bernardino 2004). Dissent exists not because of particularistic affirmative action policies but because, since at least the 1930s, Brazilian society has lived with these policy instruments without associating them with race. Tension exists at this time because those who benefit by affirmative action now identify themselves as blacks. This is the real enigma.

Emphasizing that dissent does not stem from objections to affirmative action itself, but from the use of the sociological category of race, Bernardino (2004) and other analysts redefine the issue of inequality. Inequality is not a function of discriminatory development from the perspective of regional economics and international finance. It is based on unequal distribution of national wealth according to racial affiliations in Brazilian society (Soares 2008). Since the late nineteenth century, when the liberated and free black population sought to incorporate itself into the social fabric, this population has experienced living with difference represented by race.

Race influences the standard of living of blacks, and they, in any given occupation, have greater difficulties realizing the benefits of occupational achievement (Silva 2000). Relinquishing racial difference as an analytical category (Costa 2007) obscures social phenomena important to understanding complex relationships that have existed in Brazil in the past and continue to exist today. Decades of intense economic growth, upward mobility of certain racial groups, and indicators for the black population in education and the labor market undermine the characterization of Brazilian society as a "racial paradise." Data in tables 5.1 and 5.2 illustrate this.

The issue here is the politicization of race. With the initiative of the black movement in the late 1970s, the use of the race category seems to open a new strategy to combat the practice of racial discrimination. Affirmative action policies based on perceptions of difference and the debate generated by the strategy of combating racial discrimination show that difference has greater importance than that assigned by its critics. Concomitantly, among large sectors of society, support for policies based on race has grown and intensified.

Table 5.1. Percent of economically active population employed by industry group, by race, and by sex, 2006

Industry	White		Black and Mulatto		
	Men	Women	Men	Women	Total
Agriculture	25.1	13.2	41.8	19.5	99.5
General industrial	43.6	9.1	42.3	4.4	99.5
Manufacturing	34.6	21.7	27.8	15.0	99.1
Construction	39.4	1.9	57.1	1.0	99.4
Commerce and repair	32.6	22.6	27.7	16.0	99.0
Accommodation and food	24.5	26.1	23.0	25.6	99.2
Transport, storage, and communication	46.3	8.3	40.1	4.7	99.4
Public administration	32.9	22.1	28.6	15.7	99.3
Education, and health and social services	13.3	46.8	8.6	30.3	99.0
Domestic services	2.4	37.6	3.9	55.5	99.4
Other community, social, and personal services	21.3	32.0	19.0	26.7	98.9
Other activities	37.1	25.2	24.6	12.0	98.9
Undefined or undeclared	25.1	4.1	66.6	3.8	99.6

SOURCE: Brazilian Institute of Geography and Statistics, in Paixão and Carvano (2008, 100)
NOTE: The difference between the total for these groups and 100 percent corresponds to missing data for Asian and Indigenous people.

Table 5.2. Average years of schooling of the resident population by selected age groups, by race, and by sex

		1988				1998				2008			
Age		15+	25+	40+	65+	15+	25+	40+	65+	15+	25+	40+	65+
White	Men	5.2	5.0	4.0	2.8	6.8	6.6	5.8	3.8	8.2	7.9	7.1	5.0
	Women	5.2	4.7	3.6	2.4	6.8	6.5	5.3	3.4	8.3	8.0	6.9	4.3
	Total	5.2	4.9	3.8	2.6	6.8	6.5	5.6	3.6	8.3	8.0	7.0	4.6
Black	Men	3.5	3.1	2.2	1.0	4.5	4.2	3.3	1.6	6.3	5.8	4.8	2.6
and	Women	3.6	3.1	1.9	0.8	4.9	4.3	3.1	1.3	6.7	6.2	4.9	2.3
Mulatto	Total	3.6	3.1	2.0	0.9	4.7	4.3	3.2	1.4	6.5	6.0	4.9	2.4
Total	Men	4.5	4.2	3.3	2.1	5.8	5.6	4.8	3.0	7.2	6.9	6.0	3.9
	Women	4.5	4.1	3.0	1.8	6.0	5.6	4.5	2.6	7.5	7.1	6.0	3.5
	Total	4.5	4.2	3.1	2.0	5.9	5.6	4.6	2.8	7.4	7.0	6.0	3.7

SOURCE: Brazilian Institute of Geography and Statistics, in Paixão et al. (2010, 218)

We now have historical, theoretical, and political backgrounds to understand how processes and alternative projects in society since the early twentieth century have transformed racial difference into structural inequality, and see it confirmed by the recent data from the IPEA and the Brazilian Institute of Geography and Statistics (Instituto Brasileiro de Geografia e Estatística, IBGE).[10]

Race Challenges the Nation

The debate over affirmative action in public higher education presented in Brazilian literature has been shaped by concerns for equality and social justice (Medeiros 2009), principles born of bourgeois revolutions. Such principles influence a significant proportion of the defenders of affirmative action policies in Brazilian universities who see in affirmative action policies the means by which racial diversity can become central in formulating educational policy, and public policy as a whole.

The dimension of equality competes for space both in theory and within social movements. According to Feres Júnior and Zoninsein (2008) and others, the normative core of affirmative action is substantive (or material) equality, and the purpose of any political-legal system is to promote substantive equality among its members.

There are different perspectives with regard to diversity, understood here as the foundation of affirmative action. When referring to diversity in an official document, the Ministry of Education discusses three approaches. The first is based on binary inclusion/exclusion, which seeks to incorporate excluded people in order to set up a model socioeconomic policy with no regard for their specific identities. The second approach is based on affirmative action (or positive discrimination). In this approach, the understanding is that poverty and/or social inequality is problematic for certain social groups such as blacks, Indigenous peoples, or women, and it cannot be attributed exclusively to an individual's experience. In the third approach, diversity is treated as the "politics of difference" and distinguished from social-inclusion policies by the demand for recognition of the rights of different cultures to express themselves and act in the public sphere (Brasil 2008). These perspectives on diversity offer different conceptions about the significance of affirmative action policies.

Many of the sectors that were opposed to affirmative action are today showing themselves to be "friendly" to initiatives that have as their targets the disabled, women, Indigenous peoples, and so on. Blunt criticisms are directed only at those programs in public universities that persist in addressing the racial dimension of rights and affirmative action policies. Analyzing a large segment of the national media, particularly newspapers and magazines of national circulation, Moya (2009) asserts that over time it became clear that the media were driven by an exclusive focus on racial affirmative action proposals. They softened their position on quotas when race was not the criterion used and began to consider the possibility of such policies being applied using socioeconomic criteria.[11] The *Folha de São Paulo* newspaper has advocated replacing the racial criterion with an economic one in university affirmative action policies and has also expressed opposition to the law that established racial quotas in all federal institutions of higher education in the nation.

Such positions reveal that the nerve center of the debate is no longer the implementation of affirmative action policies. A consensus on the validity of affirmative action seems to have been reached, including in sectors that once reacted negatively. The disagreement seems to be about the ethnic and racial contours of such policies, as evidenced by debates surrounding the adoption of the Racial Equality Statute, eventually enacted in 2010. Its final version makes reference to racial quotas, which are still strongly condemned by some social sectors.

What is the basis for opposition to racial and ethnic affirmative action policies in law? Affirmative action recognizes the importance of race in a society like that of Brazil, which is marked by significant inequalities. Contesting political spaces in Brazilian society was a project that began to consolidate in the 1970s with the resurgence of the black movement.

Law 10.639 emphasizes that, in addition to guaranteeing seats for blacks at schools, it is necessary to properly appreciate their history and culture in order to repair damages to their identities and rights, ongoing in Brazil for five centuries. The law is not just about adding new curricular content. It is important to emphasize that this is not a move away from an ethnocentric focus markedly European in origin toward an African one in education, but a broadening of the focus of school curricula to promote Brazilian cultural, racial, social, and economic diversity. By requiring inclusion of new perspectives on identity, it may influence a rethinking of ethnic-racial, social, and educational relations, teaching and learning practices, and tacit and explicit goals of education.

In spite of the widening of the consensus around the adoption of affirmative action policies, the adoption of the Racial Equality Statute, and the public hearings at the Supreme Federal Court, much still remains to be done. What we can infer in the face of contemporary reality is that in Brazil today, affirmative action policies can move us beyond equality and enable us to configure a rich debate about the social indicators of difference that persist in being interpreted as substrates of inequality. Thinking about affirmative action policies and racial quotas in the context of difference can increase the presence of blacks in Brazilian universities, as well as allow for questioning of the social contract upon which the nation has been built. In so doing, it can open the door to new ways of treating the social differences that characterize Brazilian society.

Conclusion

The debate over affirmative action with racial criteria addresses issues and aims that are much deeper and more comprehensive than the definition of the percentages and criteria for quota systems. What is at stake today is the capacity to redefine the values, goals, and characteristics of Brazilian society.

In contrast to what had been predicted by some Brazilian authors, racial inequalities were not overcome by the process of capitalist development in Brazil. The social dynamics of race and class should not be confused even though they may be complementary. Racial-ethnic belonging has structured, and continues to structure, inequality in a society like Brazil, marked by rigid hierarchies responsible for the exclusion of blacks and Indigenous people in various aspects of social life.

The idea that racial mixing in Brazil could be responsible for a supposed integration is false. Undeniable miscegenation in Brazilian society led some interpreters to conclude that racial mixing would be enough to overcome discrimination. The social construction of mestizaje held that racial mixing would reach its fullness through a heralded equality between the races. It was based on the myth of racial democracy, which for forty years has been gradually eroded by mobilization of the black movement. Official statistics show that the black population occupies the worst position in Brazilian society by most measures and reveal an absence of black people in positions of power, prestige, and visibility in universities and the organizational structure of the state, for example.

The contemporary policies of affirmative action have transformative potential in a system that prevents certain subaltern social groups from accessing spaces of power and prestige in society. Affirmative action policies are political, arising from an analytic understanding that access to power and recognition of difference have been limited. Affirmative action policies are criticized as paradoxical. The paradox lies not in the policies, but in a society that favors some and marginalizes others. The ongoing debate demonstrates that the fight against racism has achieved new heights in Brazil. Contemporary affirmative action policies ensure the entry and permanence of black students in Brazilian universities and reveal that racial-ethnic differences and resulting social inequalities have been the basis of the construction of a nation.

Notes

1. Article 352 of the Consolidation of Labor Laws (Law 5.452 of 1943) and Law 5.465 of 1968 dealt with the use of affirmative action policies. These policies do not seem to have met with any disapproval in the press, specialized literature, or even within Brazilian society. The black movement's demands assume this historical fact to question the construction of inequalities on the basis of racial belonging.

2. All of the more than one hundred affirmative action programs that exist today in public universities in Brazil are based on race as a sociological concept, thus ruling out a possible biological interpretation of the concept. As is now generally accepted, there are no biological "races" among humans. The notion of biological race should not be confused with the classification of human beings into different races in social hierarchies.

3. Considering race relations in Brazil, a range of interpreters mistakenly conclude that the black population is at the core of the race issue. Nothing could be more misleading. When the subject is race relations, the principle is that all groups are racialized. What one finds in Brazil is that this racialization impacts different groups differently; for some groups, the racialization tends to perpetuate inequalities, setting limitations on access to symbolic and material goods, and for others, it consolidates the exact opposite (dos Santos Vieira 2012).

4. Quilombolas were historically communities formed by escaped slaves. Today, their inhabitants include blacks, mestizos, and Indigenes.

5. The Encilhamento was a rapid monetary and stock market expansion that began in 1889.

6. We can, in general, indicate that a shift in epistemological terms begins in the 1950s with studies of norms and standards for addressing difference. Authors linked to the Chicago School and so-called cultural studies are crucial. See, for example, Fanon (1983) and Miskolci (2005).

7. What occurred in 1999 at the University of Brasília is worthy of mention. The "Ari case" triggered the adoption, after intense debate, of affirmative action policies, making UnB the first university in the federal system of higher education to do so. A doctoral student of social anthropology was shown to have failed because of racial discrimination (Lima 2001), and the case exemplifies that race is not just some kind of a biological difference (Guimarães 2008; Hofbauer 2004), but is at the core of public policy.

8. The IPEA is a federal public foundation linked to the Strategic Affairs Secretariat of the Presidency. For more, see http://www.ipea.gov.br/portal/.

9. Bento (2005), Brandão (2007), Carvalho (2005), Duarte et al. (2008), and dos Santos Vieira and Medeiros (2008), among others, have demonstrated exhaustively the misconceptions that led to premature criticism of affirmative action.

10. The IBGE conducts the census in Brazil every ten years. See http://www .ibge.gov.br/home/.

11. In 2006, for example, an editorial in a prominent national newspaper defended the use of affirmative action policies, while maintaining its position of condemnation of racial quotas and other measures to be implemented based on ethno-racial classification.

CHAPTER SIX

Political Subjectification, *Mestizaje*, and Globalization

Constructing Citizenship in Aid and Development Programs in the Peruvian Andes

JORGE LEGOAS P. AND FABRIZIO ARENAS BARCHI

Introduction

Mestizaje is a complex and nuanced ideology. Of the notions that the social sciences treat, mestizaje is perhaps one of the more opaque—and loaded. The notion itself encompasses other ideas such as "race," "culture," "identity," and "ethnicity" in fabricating its multiple applications in everyday social, political, and academic settings. These applications overlap each other, producing successive interpretations of what it may be that is being mixed in the mestizaje. These overlapping applications of mestizaje in everyday life all seem to be interwoven with the same thread: the different ways of dealing with diversity.

The most common idea of mestizaje pretends that dissolving all differences in a universal egalitarianism is a neutral position. However, the "equality" it claims has a discriminatory subtext, which points to otherness as something that must disappear in favor of the nation, development, and social peace projects, among other things. Thus, from the oldest nation-state projects encouraged by imaginaries like the one mestizo race for building a new universal civilization (José Vasconcelos in 1925 [Vasconcelos 1997]), to academic interpretations of the synthesis of imaginaries and cultures after the colonization of the Americas (Gruzinski 1999) and the most recent works on how actors re-weave popular discourses of mestizaje to use them to exercise power (Chaves and Zambrano 2006; Cornejo Polar 1983; de la Cadena 2000, 2001a; Wade 2003), we perceive the great difficulty of finding a place for cultural diversity in social, political, and academic imaginaries, and the institutional architectures seeking to adopt it.

How far removed are we today from the Peru that so expressly claimed the value of Indian and mestizo identities for building a nation? In the mid-1940s, Luis Valcárcel, who claimed that mixing races only causes deformities and moral degeneration (de la Cadena 2001b), undertook policymaking from the Ministry of Education to strengthen Indigenous identity. Meanwhile, Luis Alberto Sánchez pushed his thesis of a "Peruanismo Totalista" ("Total Peruvianness"), as a mixture, "ideally equal," of Hispanic and Indian sides of nationality (Cornejo Polar 1983). However, the form of power now exercised by the state and international policies seems to no longer require explicit discourses that claim the value of specific groups. As we shall see, policies and actions characterized by a failure to identify their instrumental goals are served by the notion of one mestizo or culturally homogeneous Peru.

This chapter explores uniformity in the mestizaje imaginary present in the ideologies of the Peruvian state and non-governmental organizations (NGOs). Both employ "cultural diversity" as a variable in their discourse. We will look at some devices used to produce participatory citizen-subjects in the current framework of neoliberal globalization in which the Peruvian state finds itself embedded. These devices are used in development projects that conceive Andean rural society homogeneously as "poor" and neglect cultural traits (Quechua in this case) of the groups with whom they work. To illustrate this, we will use examples of private intervention in NGO development and government assistance. We seek to contribute to current thought on the production of political subjectification, on how "culturally" defined subjectivities are addressed by citizenship creation projects, and on necessary state reforms in Peru. This chapter focuses on hegemonizing state and NGO discourses and institutional mechanisms in Peru related to development and social egalitarianism to show how these systematically reproduce cultural and ethnic marginalization.

Neoliberalism, Globalization, and the National Project

Globalized politics in Peru and a national project entirely committed to a neoliberal world order characterize the national context in which these cases take shape. Although it is difficult to speak of a particular "project," and even more so of a "national" project, we find a trend that influences the past governments that have set the country's course. In 1990, after the absolute bankruptcy of the last remnants of the populist national project in the late 1980s, Peru entered a new period dominated by the logic of liberalization and structural reform of the economy. Among other changes, this meant that the state should assume responsibility for the country's growth and the stability of macroeconomic indicators as its main role. Through the promotion of investment by private capital (transnational or national), the state became a primary manager of national "economic success." The most well-positioned global market actors were directly assisted by the growth model, and these, in the case of Peru, were the ones heavily invested in extractive industries (mainly mining and hydrocarbons) and agricultural exports. Andean peasant (campesino) populations, particularly those in Comunidades Campesinas (Campesino Communities)[1] and the highlands of Peru (characterized by their great eco-climatic diversity and fragility of the soil) were incorporated in a subordinate position in the extractivist globalized economy, live at the margins of current market expansion (Gonzales de Olarte 1994), and are reduced to objects of state social assistance (Eguren 2006b).

The process of the socioeconomic and legal-political transformation of Peru began under Alberto Fujimori. Upon the collapse of Fujimori's corrupt government, the new governments that came into being (those of Valentín Paniagua and Alejandro Toledo) initiated a series of democratic political reforms. However, they did not change the economic project initiated by Fujimori, and they even promoted it with renewed vigor. The political reforms initiated during the "post-Fujimori period" were designed as "second-generation reforms" to sustain the neoliberal project. It is important to note that this process was promoted by the International Monetary Fund (IMF) and the World Bank, within the spirit of the Washington Consensus, guided by impulses of market liberalization and the prevalence of privatization and social individualization (Gonzales de Olarte 2006).

One of the major political reforms after the collapse of the Fujimori regime was decentralization of the state. It was President Alejandro Toledo, during his inauguration speech (July 2002), who called for, as a matter of urgency, the initiation of decentralizing reforms in the country and for local and regional elections that year. There are at least two elements central to this process of state reform: increased budget allocation for regional and local governments, and the establishment of a number of mechanisms for citizen participation that would align management and budgets of local and regional governments with citizen decision-making.

The purpose of these reforms, within the framework of an economy characterized by liberalization policies, was to overcome socioeconomic gaps and social conflicts arising from them by employing mechanisms that redistribute resources and are "closer" to the public. Using such mechanisms, the social actors involved in the process could represent the state and its institutions more meaningfully as their own, as citizens, and avoid being seen as agents with outside interests. To this resource-redistribution process, generated by economic growth through government decentralization and the co-management of resources at the local and regional levels, are added poverty-relief programs.

Several years after the enactment of these reforms and from the time that the Public Defender's Office began keeping track of social conflict, conflicts have multiplied (Peru. Defensoría del Pueblo 2005, 2007). These conflicts are basically of two types: conflicts between mining companies and communities, and conflicts between communities and authorities of local and regional governments (Peru. Defensoría del Pueblo 2005, 2007). The sharp increase in social conflict is explained by a number of factors: the main ones are inherent to the neoliberal model and its particular forms of implementation in Peru.

Efforts to sustain economic growth in Peru have involved aggressive promotion of investment in mining and agricultural exports by the state. In a country where the rural population is approximately 24.1 percent of the total population (Peru. Instituto Nacional de Estadística e Informática 2008) and more than 5,818 Native and Campesino Communities hold 39.8 percent of the arable land (Grupo Allpa 2004, 80–81), and in a context in which the Peruvian government plays on the side of big business, Comunidades Campesinas get the impression that they are completely beyond the interests of the state (which is not far from the truth). Complaints, aggressive confrontations over mining, and disputes between businesses and the communities on issues related to ownership and use of natural resources have multiplied considerably. At the same time, in many Andean communities, forms of social, economic, and cultural organization sustained by non-mercantile exchange, communitarian cooperation, ritual practices, and traditional knowledge prevail (Gose 2004), but they are marginalized by the current capitalist expansion, which imposes an economic logic based in market-driven rationality and individual or private choice (Monroe 2008; Valdivia and Ricard 2009). In the context of capitalist expansion, the rural highlands are seen as resources that should fuel the growth of centers of production and accumulation of capital, which are mainly concentrated in coastal cities. Furthermore, Comunidades Campesinas of the highlands and their lifeways are identified with "poverty" and "ignorance," and therefore, there is a perceived need for their communities to develop, modernize, or even disappear as such through migration to cities.[2] Thus, the Andes have basically become a source of water, energy, and minerals. Maps of mining concessions in Peru show various Andean provinces having conceded more than 50 percent of their territory (cf. CooperAcción 2012). This essentially extractive relationship with the Andean regions of the country is illustrated by the fact that the rural highlands have been privileged by state poverty-assistance programs rather than investment in agriculture there (Eguren 2006a).

This chapter was initially written during the second presidency of Alan García. Since then, Peru has installed a new government headed by President Ollanta Humala, represented by the slogans "the big change" and "growth with social inclusion." Contrary to the first claim, so far the Humala government continues to follow the extractive neoliberal model. Economic and bureaucratic measures are taken to boost mining investment, undermining the exercise of Indigenous collective rights. Regarding the second slogan, the idea of "social inclusion" is still framed as the implementation of emergency programs needed to compensate for the poor economic status of those excluded by the model. Paradoxically, this "inclusion" ends up legitimizing exclusion. Indigenous communities continue to be marginalized.

State Intervention for Poverty Relief: JUNTOS

In April 2005, the Peruvian government began to implement a conditional cash transfer program (CCT),[3] the National Program of Direct Assistance to the Poorest (Programa Nacional de Apoyo Directo a los Más Pobres, JUNTOS).[4] It aimed to replace poverty assistance with joint action of recipients and the state and targeted public investment to improve living conditions of children and adolescents to break intergenerational poverty transmission. Since August 2011, it has been administered by the Humala government's Ministry of Development and Social Inclusion.

Like other CCT programs, the JUNTOS program has two main objectives: in the short term, it aims to improve the living conditions of beneficiary families, helping them to overcome extreme poverty; in the long run, it attempts to stop the intergenerational transmission of poverty through "human capital" development for the next generation. To achieve these objectives, the program provides a monthly distribution of one hundred soles (approximately 35 U.S. dollars) for a period of four years to extremely poor households that have among their members pregnant mothers, parents, widows, elderly people, or those entrusted with the care of children fourteen years of age or younger. The money is given to the mother or, in her absence, to widowed fathers. At the end of this period, there is an assessment of the recipient families to determine whether or not they have overcome the condition of extreme poverty. If they have not achieved this goal, they continue to receive a transfer that is 20 percent less than the initial amount. The beneficiary families have to meet certain commitments to improve their levels of education, health, and nutrition; otherwise, transfers are suspended. Most importantly, the mission of the program is to contribute to the consolidation of democracy and the full exercise of citizenship for the beneficiary subjects through the development of human capital. For JUNTOS, this development consists of educating children of beneficiary families in the skills needed to better position themselves in the market and, therefore, national society.

In 2005, JUNTOS was implemented in four regions of the country: Huánuco in the north-central Andes, Ayacucho and Huacavelica in the south-central Andes, and Apurimac in the southern Andes. By now, the program has been implemented in fourteen regions of the country. The selection process, conducted by the JUNTOS program itself, has been carried out in three stages: geographic targeting,[5] household targeting via a survey designed and implemented by Peru's National Institute of Statistics and Informatics (Peru. Instituto Nacional de Estadística e Informática 2008), and community validation. In addition, program benefits have been directed at areas most affected by political violence between the 1980s and early 1990s (Instituto de Estudios Peruanos 2009).

Community validation involves communities directly in implementing the program by having them compile the list of beneficiaries, so that it becomes an expression of community choice and deliberation. This process is intended to accord necessary legitimacy to the program, especially considering the potential conflicts arising from the culling processes of beneficiary families. Deciding on beneficiaries would prove to be a result of community assembly deliberation and not actions of outside actors or processes alien to community decision-making practices.

Recent research carried out on the implementation of this program examines the relationship between program design (objectives, enforcement mechanisms, etc.) and realities of implementation (Díaz et al. 2009; Huber et al. 2009; Instituto de Estudios Peruanos 2009). These investigations highlight the potential of the program but also identify reasons why this potential is not realized. Factors addressed by the research include communication problems or ineffective transmission of information from implementers and promoters of the program to the target population. As evidenced by these studies, the target population, non-beneficiaries, and even program promoters themselves find it difficult to fully understand the program's objectives and nature. In particular, this is reflected in the fact that many people (mostly non-beneficiaries) don't understand which program criteria are used to define who will be beneficiaries and who will not (Huber et al. 2009).

The case of Pomacocha (a rural district of the Andahuaylas Province) is particularly illustrative of the weaknesses of communication between JUNTOS staff and the rural communities. According to Ludwig Huber and his research team (2009), dialogue with the community was only a briefing act. Pomacocha's community members and authorities were just informed that some had been selected by the program as beneficiaries. Most regrettable about this episode was that the Pomacocha authorities did not react, but simply accepted the decision. It was only after the meeting with the staff of JUNTOS that the people of Pomacocha tried to react in order to change the decisions taken by the program, but it was too late (Huber et al. 2009). Clearly, "dialogue" with rural communities in the Pomacocha case was used by JUNTOS to validate the beneficiary list defined by the Instituto Nacional de Estadística e Informática (INEI), rather than to facilitate real participation (Huber et al. 2009, 46). Dialogue between the program staff and the rural communities—a key element of the JUNTOS strategy—tends to be distorted. It confuses the population and becomes a mere formality to legitimate the official process.

The communications problems of JUNTOS are reflected in the development of feelings of confusion and dissatisfaction among the local people of many rural areas in the program (Huber et al. 2009; Instituto de Estudios Peruanos 2009). This is reflected in a number of myths and rumors about the program, mainly created by non-beneficiary families and by the population above the extreme poverty line (Huber et al. 2009; Instituto de Estudios Peruanos 2009).

Finally, although a goal of the program is to break the chain of intergenerational transmission of poverty through the development of human capital, health and educational services offered by the state have considerable shortcomings. It is therefore doubtful that the program can provide what is necessary for people to gain skills that would take them out of socioeconomic marginalization (Instituto de Estudios Peruanos 2009).

To interpret more coherently recent research and the apparent meaning of the program, we need to understand it within the context of neoliberal trends described earlier. JUNTOS faces two sets of major problems. First, it aims to break the intergenerational transfer of poverty by building human capital for the next generation, but it does not provide follow-up to allow families and children to sustain their battle against poverty (Instituto de Estudios Peruanos 2009). Moreover, because the highlands and the Amazon forests are seen as arenas for private investment in extractive activities, and the lifeways and systems of production and community organization are beyond the interests of the state, a better route to success for the program's intended beneficiaries, it seems, would be for them to leave and emigrate to cities.[6]

Second is the problematic issue of the relationship between culture[7] and citizenship, illustrated in the program's lack of a comprehensive view of the scenario that produces the extreme poverty of these populations. These populations are identified as poor not because their lifeways are inherently poor but because their lifeways and knowledge have no value in the context of neoliberal globalization. For example, traditional patterns of rural management of fragile lands and agricultural biodiversity are not considered significant to any state project or development plan.

What we want to emphasize here is that in spite of some recognition of ethnic difference (such as the use of language interpreters with beneficiaries) and although it is acknowledged as a key factor in building citizenship, cultural difference is interpreted as an attribute of poverty, making the development of human capital the focus of the program. Given the development schemes and the policies promoted by recent governments that continue neoliberal policies initiated in the 1990s, the peasant villagers, Quechua or Aymara, and the Indigenous people of the Amazon are represented as poor Peruvians in public discourse and by actions and designs of the state. In other words, as part of the project for overcoming poverty in Peru, these people must gradually abandon their lifeways.

Citizenship and Participation in NGO Development Projects

The cases here illustrate how citizenship is conceived through NGO development projects, intended more or less directly to shape the political subjectification of Indigenous peasants as they exercise citizenship. First, we include a national consortium of non-governmental development organizations (NGDOs), private Peruvian organizations acting as local administrators of international development cooperation networks; and second, we include the Cusco section of the United Nations Children's Fund (UNICEF) because, as a multilateral institution, UNICEF is dedicated to promoting social development, but not as a project of any government. The first example will serve primarily as a means to facilitate better understanding of the conceptual framework within which the second example is set.

The Grupo Propuesta Ciudadana and the Promotion of the Exercise of Citizenship

The Grupo Propuesta Ciudadana (Citizen's Proposal Group, GPC) is a national consortium that includes the most well-known NGOs working to promote the exercise of citizenship in Peru. An analysis of discourses (in publications including newsletters, web pages, documents, and social policy analyses) involving eleven partner NGOs providing guidance or conceptual support to projects aimed primarily at increasing citizen participation illustrates the main trend of this work (Legoas 2007).

When these publications refer to "citizen participation," it is mainly associated with the idea of "vigilance." Citizen vigilance is the activity of social control by which the actors in a democratic political process will carefully monitor compliance with commitments and transparency of management by authorities. For example, in the newsletter "Participate Peru" ("Participa Perú"), used by GPC to promote citizen participation, only 10 percent of the articles are dedicated to issues of participation, while 80 percent are primarily concerned with political and administrative aspects of regionalization and decentralization of the state. Another 10 percent are devoted to the subject of oversight of local governments and other local and regional authorities as well. Also, in some of GPC's "Analysis Notes" ("Notas de Análisis"), the association between participation and anti-corruption objectives is used to promote "participatory" mechanisms to remove existing elected officials from office. In another of its publications entitled "Citizen Proposal" ("Propuesta Ciudadana"), nine of the fourteen issues available online through 2007 addressed questions of social control, watchdog groups, accountability, and related topics. Finally, on GPC's "Participa Perú" website, the "Be Vigilant Peru" ("Vigila Perú") program, designed to promote citizens' watch actions, is accorded the most abundant and systematic treatment. The GPC argues that there is a need to create an overall culture of vigilance.

Excerpts from GPC articles help illustrate this idea of citizenship as participation in social control and oversight. These references to "vigilance" are made precisely in texts intended to define or give substance to the idea of "participation," suggesting that participation ends up being subsumed by the idea of vigilance:

> The Peruvian government has taken important steps toward generating the rules and tools to facilitate community access to public information. Similarly, we believe that much remains to be done in building a culture of transparency and vigilance. (GPC in Legoas 2007, 26; authors' translation)
>
> We believe in monitoring, and therefore, in the vigilant person. (SEPAR and GPC in Legoas 2007, 26; authors' translation)

We see here the construction of a policed vision of citizenship, in which the citizen is understood as instrument and object of social control. In the current neoliberal context, where the orderly management of local and regional finances appears to possess outstanding merit, cultivating vigilant citizenries is an achievement. We find there is at least a narrowing of the political dimensions of participation and citizen as a participating subject, if not an impoverishment of meaning and scope of power.

UNICEF Action Strategies in Marcapata

If the search for concerted participation of the population in the design of local policies is a sign of action in the strengthening of citizenship, our next example, UNICEF, is a clear demonstration of some of the ways these citizen-ization efforts occur. This organization works to promote better living conditions for children worldwide, particularly in countries with fewer financial resources. It focuses on the fields of health, education, and rights, and it also has special concerns for women. To this end, it performs or promotes a series of development projects, which are supposed to have an immediate effect on children of the places where it intervenes. The work of UNICEF resembles that of a number of local NGDOs also concerned with education, health, and living conditions of women.

The Marcapata district comprises a rural peasant-Indigenous population that speaks mainly Quechua. It is located on the eastern slopes of the Andes from Cusco between approximately 2,500 and 5,000 meters above sea level. Since approximately 2006, after improvement of the access road, UNICEF has increased its intervention there. It has made agreements with the Municipality of Marcapata and other local authorities to produce educational materials, organize training workshops, and support the Marcapata Health Center. Its most recent commitment was to sponsor the participatory elaboration of a development plan for the district, which incorporated the municipality's leadership in its intervention strategy.

In terms of handling international financing and technical staffing according to imposed standards, methodologies (focused on strategic planning, planning by objectives, logical frameworks, etc.), and strategies for outreach and contact with beneficiaries, UNICEF acts as any other development operator in the district. These approaches are supposedly different from those of the state and allegedly more horizontal and participatory. Since indirect assistance is thought to promote agreements and projects that address children's health and education, UNICEF's intervention had become increasingly indirect, i.e., seeking to improve the living conditions of children through aid (technical or inputs) to local health centers, schools, health management and education systems, municipalities, NGOs, community-based organizations, etc.

Promotion of the implementation of a comprehensive development plan in Marcapata seemed certain. Ultimately, the results of development planning would indirectly, but significantly, support UNICEF's goals. The UNICEF promoter formulated part of the work strategy in the following way:

In order to provide resources to the municipality and in order to support municipal management, we need to plan our activities around children and youth issues. Once we plan, we will know what else we will need, what activities we will do and what resources we can . . . uh . . . what resources we need. And when we face this situation, everyone will say: "I will contribute with this or that, sign me up for this or that."[8]

After the signing of an agreement between UNICEF and the Municipality of Marcapata, which aimed to strengthen the latter as UNICEF's strategic ally, meetings were held between the two parties. The goal was to get the municipality to assume and become familiar with its role as leader of the planning process. UNICEF requested an initial meeting with local actors to hold a brief exchange that would lay some groundwork for future implementation of the planning process. It was not to be very official or definitive, just something to allow UNICEF to take a first step in preparing to support the budding process. In attendance were Marcapata teachers and nurses, the governor,[9] district representatives, municipal employees, and district radio journalists.

The meeting was led by a UNICEF staff member who, standing at the head of the room and facing all attendees, began with a quasi-monologue about UNICEF's priorities and objectives and the need to improve the living conditions of children in Marcapata. He then began discussing the best way to start the participatory planning process:

But how are we going to work this? This is where perhaps we can establish working groups, roundtables, or "forums." That is, we have to build the so-called "consensus-building local roundtables." What are those roundtables? They are specialized meetings where institutions, the governor, the police, the health sector, education sector, the little town school and all of them . . . have to get together to discuss the implementation of a work plan . . . Get it? And all this led by the Municipality. Who presides over this dialogue space? The District Municipality. Now . . . What name can we give this space? . . . And who will choose the name for it? All of you, of course.

We do not bring any preset agenda . . . We are not NGOs: we do not say "this must be done." What we do is help these issues become visible, so that the municipality may allocate funds to them . . . So our proposal is to help you prepare this concerted development plan; help you write the participatory budgeting; help what all of a sudden is project formulation; in improving staff skills, etc. There are so many things that can be done . . . Now who is going to decide this? Obviously, all of you.

The UNICEF agent clearly presented a series of principles that UNICEF's intervention in the Marcapata area would respect and promote. The Marcapata Plan would be a product resulting from a comprehensive process; local actors themselves would discuss it; it would originate from issues defined by local actors; and local actors would make the systematic decisions, committed to working on the various proposals that emerged from the plan.

However, immediately after saying that local actors define the issues, the UNICEF agent began to express his own views on children's issues, leaving no space for discussion rooted in the views of local actors: "For the Peruvian case, we [UNICEF] believe that childhood is about three major themes: health, education, and rights issues." To those of us present as outside observers, this appeared to be an out-of-place re- mark, but it was immediately followed by others similar in nature. It was the UNICEF agent himself who immediately went on to give a name to the consensus-building roundtable: "What can we call the dis- trict coordination space here?" He himself answered "'DDC' . . . okay?" While repeating this, he wrote the name on the board, thereby reaffirming the idea of naming it "District Development Committee of Marcapata."

In essence, the meeting marked the beginning of a process that devi- ated from the original purpose, which had been to lay the groundwork for a future plan established by local actors. This discursive strategy eventually put local actors in a position opposed to the ideals of partici- pation and focused on the needs of the population defined at the begin- ning of the UNICEF agent's presentation. The agent demonstrated a persuasive ability to lead the attendees to focus more on points he was raising than on needs or motivations they themselves might have. He would say, for example: "What would you say for example if we did . . ." and then immediately suggest something specific. He would say, "I will tell you the story of what they did in the neighboring province" or "Wouldn't it be nice if, for example, we did . . ." and continue with a pro- posal to implement a particular activity. This turned the meeting into a briefing on the ideas and priorities of UNICEF, followed by details on what would be needed in Marcapata. The UNICEF agent ended up determining—sometimes subtly, sometimes blatantly—almost all the is- sues related to a local plan for children.

He defined not only the "what" but also the "who," "when," and "how." He continued:

> Then all our support will be focused on strengthening municipal man- agement, but why, to what purpose? So that the support goes from the municipality to all sectors in need of support. That is, the municipality has to reinforce the work done by the health sector, that of the educa- tion sector, the work done by the Ombudsman, or the Governorate, and police, etc.
>
> For example, educational training for teachers, so that they learn to detect cases of violence against children in their classroom. That is a subject that interests us greatly. And another subject of interest, and I

do not know if that happens around here, is sexual abuse. And if it doesn't happen it is good to prevent it from happening. We are also interested in work related to child labor. Work per se is not bad at all, but there are jobs that are forced, jobs that require children to drop out of school and stop studying. That is one other thing that we have to incorporate in the plan.

You know . . . every family has twelve children. Girls even fifteen years old have a partner and carry their pregnancies to term when they are still teenagers. What does this mean? . . . It means that they will be unemployed and that they will have children like rabbits. That mother during pregnancy needs attention . . . that means they have to come here to the district to get ready [to give birth] or at least receive care from the health center. And where can she stay . . . where? . . . Where else better than in a "Maternity Waiting Home." So, what can we do there, for example? Can the Municipality contribute funds to build that home?"

The mayor, taken somewhat by surprise, responded right away by saying "Absolutely." Thus, the UNICEF agent went on to define almost every step of a plan (which was not drafted before we left the area the following year, in 2009). He went into even the minutest details, as follows:

The municipality can build such infrastructure. Okay, great, that's nice. The implementation . . . what would the implementation involve? Beds, for sure, right? Stoves, kitchen utensils, etc., that can be supplied by UNICEF, right? Then UNICEF was in charge of the implementation. Now, in the case of PRONOEI [Non-formal Programs for Early Childhood Education—Programa No Escolarizado de Educación Inicial], exactly the very same thing: the municipality can provide the infrastructure, we would provide the support for the implementation, and we would train PRONOEI teachers from the beginning, and the educational sector would take on the responsibility of providing the service.

Finally, the UNICEF agent highlighted the substantive meaning attributed to the participation of local actors in this coordination meeting: "If only we could work around at least four of these themes it would be good, right? Now . . . you prioritize it." Ultimately, his discursive performance led the audience to reduce citizen participation to a simple choice between proposals that he raised. The most "difficult" task for the attendees was to compile a comprehensive list of activities consistent with priorities introduced by the agent.

Local actors ended up adapting their own interpretations of the local reality of Marcapata to the interests of an external actor. We do not mean to rule on the relevance of the contents of the speech by the UNICEF agent on childhood problems or actions that might be taken by UNICEF. Although one may sense a critical tone in our narration, our objective is not to "criticize" the agent's work or UNICEF in particular. Nor do we want to make Manichean judgments about the actors, the legitimacy of their interests, or their exercise of power. In fact, we believe that the local actors enmeshed in these relations of power are ultimately responsible for outcomes whether due to their participation or lack of it. To any possible voice of "oppression," an act of actual or potential "liberation" may correspond, and both are expressions of power that may or may not be realized. The meeting described was not exempt from this relational logic. However, during the meeting only one person raised a critical voice that tried to bring the session back to the expected initial agenda. No others supported him. Toward the end of the meeting, one of the teachers made an unmistakable gesture of surprise and suspicion when it became obvious that decisions were being made at the meeting: "Is all of this valid?" he asked the agent. "Because . . . at the beginning of the meeting, we were told that to begin planning, various authorities and local representatives should be present." The agent replied, "Of course it's valid! Or do you think we're playing here?!" in an imposing but funny tone. "This is serious," he then remarked, inducing smiles, and the session continued on the same course.

In short, what concerns us directly is to show how a discursive strategy produces a local participationist counterpart that meets the NGO's priorities for action and fails to incorporate the principles highlighted by the UNICEF agent at the beginning of the meeting. We believe that the UNICEF representative employed a very specific discursive strategy. First, he encouraged attendees to see themselves as legitimate, empowered, and active actors. Second, he changed the objective of the meeting (which had been to lay the groundwork for engaging in long-term planning) and acted according to new objectives (to define right there and then an action plan in line with UNICEF's interests), without seeming to do so intentionally. Third, he himself answered the questions he asked about what the necessary courses of action would be while simultaneously seeking to convince local actors that what was being decided was what they wanted and needed. Fourth, he reduced the scope of action of local actors to simply prioritizing preestablished options provided by him.

Without doubt, this strategy established the role of participants as citizens diverted from the course of expressing and promoting their own interests in their own localities. Similar to the paradoxical mechanism of "inclusive otherness" (de la Cadena 2000), which constructs a discourse of difference while at the same time depriving the otherness of all its unique features, the strategies of UNICEF contribute to a discourse on participation that is robbed of its attributes of symmetry and plurality. This is a political exercise governed by the prevailing values and interests of external actors.

We suggest that discursive action by an agent (in this case a UNICEF staff member) should, at most, set a possible trend in the actions of local actors, not *determine* them automatically. This case shows precisely that local actors' reactions don't necessarily affect the vector of power exercised by external agents.

Conclusions

In Peru, the neoliberal project produces poor people to be served by programs such as JUNTOS. It also generates resources to be returned to local and regional governments that must be policed as proposed by the GPC. This, in turn, determines the nature of participatory local governance. In many cases, this takes place without consideration of local interests, as suggested by the UNICEF example. The effects of these interventions, intentional or incidental, is to establish participationist subjectification by means of a logic of action that conceives local actors as "poor" and makes the idea of participation synonymous with promoting interests of external actors.

In the various strategies, ideas, and approaches of these external actors, a more or less coherent idea of citizenship is outlined and characterized in at least three specific ways. First, local actors are pressured to give meaning to their political behavior as citizens who subjectify as deficient and backward, and therefore have an obligation to overcome this condition. Second, the broader vision of participation is that of the vigilant citizen. This type of local political behavior facilitates capitulation to the neoliberal model in which the Peruvian national project is subsumed. And finally, as they play their participatory roles, local actors are alienated from their own interests. This results in citizens operating as functional components of the neoliberal national project at the local level.

These roles and the representations of local actors through various relations of power comprise the ideal profile of the rural Andean citizen who, making formal concessions, denies his or her cultural subjectivity, interpreting it as simply an attribute of his or her own condition of poverty. For the current modernization project to succeed in Peru, it is presumed necessary that these citizens gradually abandon their cultural differences (language, rituals, bonds with their territory, and economies, among other things) in the "Fight Against Poverty" ("Lucha Contra la Pobreza"). The modernizing discourse, despite differences in tone or form, dictates through the use of the concept of citizenship that rural Andean communities, their members, and their Indigenous, peasant ways of life be transformed by development and assimilated. This is a "paradox of democracy" wherein equality amongst citizens leads to strengthening of established relations of power, reproducing preexisting patterns of oppression in society (I. Young 1995).

Symbolic and institutional environments establish the idea of a culturally homogeneous Peru as the most immediate background reference, appealing once again to the classic notion of mestizaje. This leads to "mestizo citizenship" of neoliberal making. Carol Smith (in Alonso 2004), not without reason, asserts that the *mesticista* strategy inherent in projects of the nation-state has not necessarily been as successful as expected, despite the different variations and popular reappropriations of the sense of mestizaje highlighted by de la Cadena (2001b) and Wade (2003). The notion of mestizo citizenship belies the stubborn persistence of the old, underlying homogenizing nationalist projects and exclusion of Indigenous populations.[10] The thread mentioned at the beginning of this chapter that interweaves overlapping social, political, and academic applications of "mestizaje" in everyday life to deal with culturally diverse realities manifests its most discriminatory expression here.

Implementing a political system capable of acknowledging and incorporating otherness in a citizenship project must go beyond the level of policies that aspire to enable minority integration into systems of modernity or modernization through affirmative action. This calls for a more open understanding of citizenship in Peru.

Interculturality appears to be a democratic strategy that motivates the construction of citizenship, but its recognition processes have been established by social and political agencies with specific modern and cultural views. A more open approach to citizenship must be expressed through political and social institutionalization of the rights of agents from different groups so that they may participate in public life by putting to use their own practical and semantic systems. Considering this challenge raises political questions: How might a social, cultural, economic, and political project (and related public policies) build a society that recognizes the value of cultural difference? Who might lead such a project?

It is impossible to answer these difficult questions here. However, one insight that supports the effort is that democracy, even as a modern system and despite its recognized limitations, is an institutional framework that allows, more than any other, for popular struggle to produce social, cultural, economic, and political transformation. Considering this, it seems that change in Peru must begin by rethinking current modernization processes and their contradictions, limits, and hegemonic expectations. This is prerequisite to defining a new social, cultural, and political project to reconstruct modern institutions and processes based in the democratic spirit of the recognition of difference. Each successful action taken in the construction of a new citizenship project must consider, recognize, and deal with cultural specificity and conflicts that arise between Indigenous culture and modernization, to allow "any man that is not shackled and brutalized by selfishness . . . to live happily in all homelands" (Arguedas 1971, 287).

Acknowledgments

Thank-yous to the Association of Graduate Students at Laval University (AELIÉS), the Wenner-Gren Foundation for Anthropological Research, the Research Group on Political Imaginaries in Latin America (GRIPAL, Montreal), and the Centro Bartolomé de las Casas (CBC, Cusco).

Notes

1. Comunidad Campesinas are rural institutions established by Peruvian law that organize rural populations around a collectively owned territory.

2. See "El síndrome del perro del hortelano" ("Dog in the Manger Syndrome") by former president Alan García Pérez, published in *El Comercio*, October 28, 2007.

3. The CCT programs have their origin in Mexico and Brazil. Around 1997, Mexico implemented Progresa, a program which later became Oportunidades. In Brazil, this took place at the municipal level through the social program Bolsa Escola, the predecessor of Bolsa Família. Today, with support from the World Bank and other multilateral organizations, CCTs are being implemented in twenty-six countries (Fiszbein, Schady et al. 2009).

4. See the JUNTOS program web portal at http://www.juntos.gob.pe.

5. Geographic areas with two or more unsatisfied basic needs (NBI), the highest poverty gaps, extreme poverty, and chronic child malnutrition (see http://www.juntos.gob.pe) were targeted. In addition to these, another selection criterion is the impact of political violence (Instituto de Estudios Peruanos 2009).

6. This is assuming that the markets in these cities have the capacity to "absorb" a new wave of mass migration into conditions other than marginality and urban poverty.

7. We understand culture to be more than a conglomeration of features and artifacts that can be put to use strategically; we view it instead as an ever-changing organizer of ways of being and thinking of social subjects that orient their forms of social and political agency.

8. The UNICEF interview data came from our field notes about Marcapata from 2007 (AU02-B70 2007_11_07) and 2008.

9. The *gobernador* (governor) in Peru is the district's direct representative of the central government and is an authority separate from the municipal power.

10. In the face of this, many insist on calling themselves Inkas or Runaes as a way of demonstrating resistance that is becoming a movement and a collective consciousness in the Peruvian Andes.

CHAPTER SEVEN

The Door to the Future

Cultural Change and the Cheyenne Sun Dance

JENNIFER WHITEMAN

> We have a responsibility for all of mankind, not just the Cheyenne. The
> Ceremony must continue in order for the world to survive. Regardless of
> external social pressures, we must perform the Sun Dance as directed by
> Sweet Medicine in order to maintain the health of the earth.
>
> —*Southern Cheyenne Sun Dancer, interview by the author,*
> *Concho, OK, April 25, 2011*

The Cheyenne Sun Dance is a time of personal, community, and earthly
renewal. It is a time of harmony and self-sacrifice. Each summer, hundreds of Cheyenne men and women take part in this very sacred and
ancient ceremony (fig. 7.1). Families come together and partake in communal living, and for a brief moment, time and space expand beyond the
limits of our reality. Ultimately, the Sun Dance is the constant that keeps
the Cheyenne tethered to the past, the present, and the future; indeed,
the Sun Dance is the door to adaptation and survival.

This chapter considers Marx's theory of objective historical materialism and the cultural concept of *mestizaje* as it explores the Cheyenne's
tenacity and resilience to change. This resilience relies on the Cheyenne's
flexibility in adapting their economic base. It then examines the dynamic
collision between the divergent European and Cheyenne superstructures

FIGURE 7.1. General view of the Sun Dance Lodge, 1903. By Carpenter, reproduced in Field Columbian Museum, Anthropology Series, Volume IX, "The Cheyenne" by G. A. Dorsey. Photo Lot 89–8, National Anthropological Archives, Smithsonian Institution.

and the role Cheyenne spirituality plays within that space. Laying this essential foundation propels my inquiry into the present day. In-depth interviews with Cheyenne ceremonial people and elders reveal that the Sun Dance is the grounding constant that connects the Cheyenne to the past, the present, and the future. As have others engaged in struggles inherent to mestizaje, the Cheyenne have transcended historical and political oppression common to subaltern societies. As many chapters in this volume illustrate, cultural mestizaje is an important form of political and social adaptation in Latin America. While the term is seldom, if ever, used with reference to cultural change and adaptation of Indigenous peoples north of the Mexican border, there are parallels in the historical processes that have shaped the adaptation and cultural survival of North American Indigenous peoples. This chapter provides an illustrative case.

Historical materialism may expose the expansive reach of the capitalist paradigm as it collides with Cheyenne culture and tradition, but it does not explain the unchanging constant of the Cheyenne Sun Dance and spirituality. The Cheyenne, like most Indigenous groups worldwide, have been forced to succumb to a free-market society through assimilative measures, ultimately in the act of survival. The Cheyenne people rely on the Sun Dance to articulate their subjective experience outside the dominant paradigm of the U.S. superstructure.

Historical materialism attempts to explain the various epochs of European development from slavery to feudalism to capitalism and focuses on the interrelationship between the superstructure and the economic base. In Marxist theory, the superstructure is comprised of culture, social, economic, political, legal, ritual, and other characteristics of a society. The economic base, or civil society, consists of all the productive relationships that people enter into. Marx (1904) believed that the real foundations of a society are those relationships, which we must enter into to survive. They enable the growth of a society's legal and political superstructure, from which a social consciousness emerges.

Although the United States is generally considered a mosaic of various divergent cultures, the predominant superstructure is still European based. As a result, the prevailing mores and values are not consistent with those of the Cheyenne.

Considering Cheyenne spirituality alone may yield a distorted perception or abstraction of reality (Lloyd 1983).[1] And failing to recognize a society's superstructure or economic base makes it difficult to perceive causal factors that generate change. Historical materialism is useful in interpreting cultural change, and I use it here in this way, though in a limited fashion. Marxist analysis sets the stage for understanding much about the experiences of the Cheyenne, but it does not emphasize spirituality or the unique status of Native people. Marxism sees advancement through technology and the liberation of humanity from the dominance of nature. However, without the Sun Dance, which embodies nature, the Cheyenne people would not have maintained the necessary link to the past, a link that connects history with the future.

Spirituality is the primary element in the Cheyenne superstructure. Cheyenne spirituality is not an oppressive force, as was religion in Marx's time. The Sun Dance provides the continuity through time that allows the Cheyenne to evolve and adapt to their changing surroundings. According to educator and Cheyenne spiritual leader Dr. Henrietta Mann, the Sun Dance has been, and continues to be, the door to the future, a door that permits the Cheyenne to remain connected to the past while simultaneously maintaining that critical social coexistence in the present-day Cheyenne superstructure and the American superstructure.

Using historical materialism, a Western objective theory, as a lens to examine the Cheyenne's subjective experience in the Sun Dance is, in effect, engaging in intellectual mestizaje. Mestizaje is typically understood as a mixing of races or cultures that results in something new. Gloria Anzaldúa describes mestizaje as a geographic space: "I stand at the edge where earth touches ocean / Where the two overlap / A gentle coming together / At other times and places a violent clash" (Anzaldúa 1987). She describes mestizaje as a space where cultures come together and occupy the same proximate location. In this complex space, there is a dichotomy of potential peaceful coexistence and disharmonious clashes. This resistance mestizaje rejects the notion of being defined by the ruling elite (Wade 2005).

Mestizaje is a lived process instead of an ideology or national identity. A lived process embodies ideology while maintaining "enduring spaces for racial-cultural differences alongside spaces of sameness and homogeneity" (Wade 2005, 240). In particular, instead of a culture dissolving and becoming homogenous, it retains the original elements in the imagination as a permanent space.

This maintained permanent space for the Cheyenne is the Sun Dance. As a lived process, it is the door to the future that helps the Cheyenne retain their culture. Cheyenne spirituality is all-encompassing. The prayers of the Sun Dancers create a ripple effect of blessings, beginning at the center pole of the Sun Dance arbor and rippling out to the dancer's family, to the surrounding community, and further to the nation and on outward to envelop the entire world. Wherever the touch of the sun's healing rays reach, Cheyenne thoughts and prayers are there as well. Tribal elders interviewed for this study believe the Sun Dance ceremony, family, and language are the necessary ingredients to cultural identity and survival. The Sun Dance is crucial to maintaining these key markers, which permits the Cheyenne to evolve and adapt over time. Constructs such as the Cheyenne tribal legal code, as set forth in *The Cheyenne Way* by Llewellyn and Hoebel (1941),[2] are not seen as keys to survival. Rather, the prophecies of Sweet Medicine and Erect Horns (discussed below) perpetuate the culture and dictate cultural norms. As one elder explained to me, the Sun Dance gives redemption and ultimately hope.

History of the Cheyenne

The Cheyenne consist of two bands, the Northern Cheyenne and the Southern Cheyenne; combined, the tribes have over thirty thousand tribal members. Even though they have lived apart for over one hundred years in very different geographic environments, they still share a common language, religious and ceremonial practices, and cultural heroes. Moreover, the familial connections between the North and South are still strong. The Cheyenne are not unique in being separated into Northern and Southern bands, as several tribes have similar divisions. However, unique to the Cheyenne are the vastly different settings they now inhabit.

The Northern Cheyenne are presently located on a reservation in Lame Deer, Montana, which is situated in a valley nestled in the Rocky Mountains. The Southern Cheyenne are not located on a "reservation,"[3] but inhabit a territory that spans from central to western Oklahoma. The cities most populated by Cheyenne people are Concho, El Reno, Kingfisher, Canton, Watonga, Thomas, Clinton, and Weatherford, spread over eleven counties. Whereas the Northern Cheyenne have limited integration with non-Native society, the Southern Cheyenne are completely interspersed among non-Natives.

The federal government combined the Southern Cheyenne and Southern Arapaho tribes in Oklahoma, making the unified Cheyenne and Arapaho Tribes. Of all Cheyenne and Arapaho tribal members, 8,594[4] of those members currently live in Oklahoma; however, nationwide the total membership is 12,430 (Cheyenne and Arapaho Planning and Development Department 2010). The actual numbers of tribal members who identify as Cheyenne alone is undocumented.

High incidences of social maladies such as addiction, domestic violence, abject poverty, and poor health are mirrored in both communities. A new theory evolving in the public health arena that attempts to explain this is the concept of historical trauma. This theory is premised on the idea that "populations historically subjected to long-term, mass trauma—colonialism, slavery, war, genocide—exhibit a higher prevalence of disease even several generations after the original trauma occurred" (Sotero 2006).

According to historian Thomas Weist, the name Cheyenne was derived from the Sioux word Sha hi'ye na, meaning "Red Talkers or the people who speak a foreign language" (Weist 1977). The French pronounced "Sha hi'ye na" as "Cheyenne," and this pronunciation has been used ever since. The Cheyenne people, as they exist today, consist of two groups: the Tsistsistas (the like-hearted people or the People) and the Suh'tah (thought to mean "the People left behind"). Cheyenne oral tradition claims the two groups first came in contact with each other prior to a battle. The story goes that the Suh'tah warriors were verbally volleying back and forth when the Tsistsistas heard the language and recognized it as their own. At that point, the Tsistsistas and the Suh'tah came together and found they had not only a similar language but also similar cultural beliefs. Cheyenne oral tradition holds that the two groups were originally one band, but were separated when an ice float they were traveling on broke apart, separating them.

The Tsistsistas tell of a time before they joined the Suh'tah. Their oral history relates four different times of the people; the Ancient Time, the Time of the Dogs, the Time of the Buffalo, and the present Time of the Horse. A brief description of this history will demonstrate the Cheyenne people's ability to adapt to change as each epoch overlaps the other.

The Ancient Time

Linguistic study and oral tradition suggest the Tsistsistas lived in the region of what is now called Ontario, Canada. Weist claims that when the old people would talk about this time they would generally begin with "before the Cheyenne had bows and arrows" (Weist 1977, 82). In this region of Canada, the Tsistsistas lived in permanent earthen lodges in small villages. They fished the great lake and hunted small game with spears and snares. However, oral history tells that the People were always hungry, which necessitated moving the village to find food. To the south of their village, the scouts found a land full of marshes and high reeds, but on the other side of the marsh was prairie land. The people moved there in their dugout canoes (Berthrong 1963; Grinnell 1972; Weist 1977). By the time the Sioux arrived in 1650, the Tsistsistas were well established in the upper Mississippi River region. This was the Time of the Dogs.

The Time of the Dogs

French fur traders documented the first recorded evidence of the Cheyenne in 1673 (Berthrong 1963; Grinnell 1972; Weist 1977). At this point, the Tsistsistas lived near the eastern bank of the Mississippi River and above the mouth of the Wisconsin River.

During the Time of the Dogs, the Tsistsistas adjusted their economic base to include dogs and corn, and they improved their defense tactics. Wild dogs were tamed to become beasts of burden, and with travois attached, the dogs carried supplies and small children. In addition, corn became a primary staple in the Tsistsistas diet, along with deer and fish procured from nearby prairies and lakes. As in the Ancient Time, the Tsistsistas lived in earthen lodges, but now in small villages on the highest point of a bluff overlooking the Sheyenne River in North Dakota. Fortifications were added to protect the village from its enemies, permitting the Tsistsistas to remain here for approximately ninety years.

Eventually the Tsistsistas were forced westward by their better-armed enemy, the Chippewa. The Chippewa traded furs and pelts with the British in return for muzzle-loading flintlock rifles, ammunition, beads, tomahawks, and steel knives. Similarly, the Tsistsistas established trade relations with the French at La Salle's fort near present-day Peoria, some three hundred miles from their village. Throughout the Time of the Dogs, the economic base of the Tsistsistas was greatly impacted by trade with Europeans. Weaponry became more advanced and life became more precarious.

The Time of the Buffalo

At the beginning of this era, the Tsistsistas were still living in the earthen-lodge village on the bluff in North Dakota and using dogs to carry heavy loads. They planted corn, beans, and squash in May and June, but during the summer months, they left the village in search of buffalo herds. In autumn the Tsistsistas came back for the fall harvest, but left again for the winter hunt on the prairie once the cold weather set in.

While on one of these buffalo hunts, the Tsistsistas met the Suh'tah near the Missouri River. Nearby, the Suh'tah were camped in portable buffalo-hide teepees. The Suh'tah no longer lived in a permanent earthen lodge village. Instead, they followed the buffalo. Once the two groups realized they spoke the same language, they joined together as the Tsistsistas, or as they are also commonly known, the Cheyenne. Sometime between 1770 and 1790, the Chippewa burned down the Cheyenne's last permanent village on the bluff.

Abandoning their way of life as agriculturalists in permanent villages, the Cheyenne moved to the Black Hills, in present-day southwestern South Dakota, to follow the abundant game that was found there. They became great horsemen. Their collective lives changed forever as they became nomadic plains hunters and followers of the buffalo.

After a time, the Cheyenne trade relations with the French were broken down by attacks from the Sioux and Chippewa, who were vying to dominate all trade in the region. The Cheyenne needed rifles and other European goods, but to obtain those items, buffalo robes and meat were required, which they did not have. Nonetheless, the Cheyenne managed to maintain trade with friendly tribes for vegetables, ending the need for a permanent village.

During this time the Cheyenne allied with the Arapaho to overcome shortages in their numbers (Moore 1992). The Cheyenne and Arapaho were attempting to gain entry in the north-south trade chain near the foot of the Rocky Mountains (Berthrong 1963; Grinnell 1962). The tribes were able to hold the Shoshone and Utes at bay in the mountainous regions while at the same time blockading the Kiowas from their "trading partners the Crow" (Berthrong 1963; Grinnell 1962; Mooney and Petter 1907). By 1840, the Cheyenne and the Arapaho Tribes were a force to be reckoned with both militarily and economically (Moore 1992).

The remainder of this era was also fraught with conflicts and wars with European invaders, who slowly encroached on the Cheyenne territory, pushing them ever farther westward. The Cheyenne attempted to avoid war, but time and again were forced to fight to survive.

The creation of the Santa Fe and Oregon Trails encouraged over "100,000 immigrants and their livestock" to enter the Tribes' territory, thereby decimating the landscape (Moore 1992, 96). The buffalo were driven away, while some of the most pristine traditional camping areas were overrun with immigrants. By 1860, the non-Indians, no longer wanting to trade with Indians, changed their focus to the acquisition of the tribe's land. About this same time the Cheyenne Dog Soldiers[5] began attacking settlers and immigrants entering their territory along the Platte

River. As tensions between the Indians and the whites grew, the men of the First and Third Regiments of the Colorado Calvary, led by Colonel John M. Chivington, attacked a peaceful Cheyenne village camped at Sand Creek.

The attack took place early in the morning while the camp slept. The Dog Soldiers were away hunting, leaving only women, children, and the elderly in camp. The men of the First and Third Regiments swooped into the camp, murdering, torturing, and dismembering the people of the tribe (Moore 1992). All the while, Peace Chief Black Kettle beckoned the people to come to his tipi, which waved the white flag of peace and the American flag, which was supposed to protect them. Instead, the blood-crazed soldiers continued their onslaught (Grinnell 1955). In fact, several of the men removed the female genital areas of many of the Cheyenne women and attached those parts to their saddle horns, displaying their trophies as they paraded through Denver (U.S. Senate 1867). In his testimony before Congress, Cavalryman James Cannon recounted:

> In going over the battleground the next day I did not see a body of a man, woman, or child but was scalped, and in many instances their bodies were mutilated in the most horrible manner—men, women, and children's privates cut out &c; I heard one man say that he had cut out a woman's private parts and had them for exhibition on a stick; I heard another man say that he had cut the finger off an Indian to get the rings on the hand; according to the best of my knowledge and belief these atrocities that were committed were with the knowledge of J. M. Chivington. (U.S. Senate, 1867)

The Massacre at Sand Creek incited a violent retaliation from all of the Plains tribes. Though shaken, the Cheyenne and Arapaho warriors were fierce and generally outnumbered the U.S. military forces, which had been reduced and diverted due to the Civil War. In an effort to stem the unrest in the Great Plains, the U.S. government signed a treaty with the Cheyenne and Arapahos. It was a prudent and strategic move. The treaty compensated the tribes for the atrocities that happened at Sand Creek; it also created a reservation that intersected the present-day border of Kansas and Oklahoma.

The Time of the Horse

The Time of the Horse marks the beginning of the reservation period, and it is the time we see the most change in the Cheyenne way of life. Life on the reservation forced the Cheyenne to adopt a capitalist economy, which replaced their traditional barter and trade economy. This was not a gradual adaptation, but an abrupt change that left the People reeling from its effects. Once again the Cheyenne found themselves divided into two bands. Their time living as a whole group is relatively short compared to the time in which they were not. Dull Knife took his followers north to the Tongue River Indian Reservation, now known as the Northern Cheyenne Indian Reservation, in Montana. To the south, Black Kettle and his followers came to dwell in the state of Oklahoma, in Indian Territory, as did many other tribes who experienced tragic Euro-American encounters. The U.S. federal government assigned agents to "introduce farming and, to a lesser degree, a wage economy" that would allow the Cheyenne to be more "self-sufficient" (Weist 1977, 164).

Typically, however, the foods and crops the agents provided for farming did not fare well in either the northern or the southern climates. To add insult to injury, the Southern Cheyenne were not permitted to leave the reservation, which hampered their ability to procure small or large game. Starvation and hunger were inevitable. In order to survive, the People acquiesced to new economic practices of the increasingly dominant culture (Mann 1997; Powell 1969; Weist 1977). As with shifting tectonic plates, the Euro-American superstructures collided with and buckled the Cheyenne superstructures, causing a vertical shift in the fabric of culture, identity, and language.

Resistance and Adaptation

Historical records show that by 1865 the Southern Cheyenne were already well on their way to evolving again to adapt to their new environment. George Bent, the son of white trader William Bent, and his Southern Cheyenne wife Owl Woman (Mis-stan-stur) described several Northern Cheyenne who visited their camp in February 1865:

> These northern kinsmen of ours were dressed very differently from us and looked strange to our eyes. Our southern Indians all wore cloth blankets, cloth leggings, and other things made by the whites, but these northern Indians all wore buffalo robes and buckskin leggings; they had their braided hair wrapped in strips of buckskin painted red, and they had crow feathers on their heads with the ends of the feathers cut off in a peculiar manner. They looked much wilder than any of the southern Indians, and kept up all the old customs, not having come much in contact with the whites. (Bent, in Weist 1977)

The changes that had shaped the lives of Bent and Owl Woman made the northerners seem "wilder" to them. It is clear the superstructures of the United States were influencing them to assimilate to the dominant society. The Southern Cheyenne acquiesced to the use of trade goods such as cloth and metal pots, replacing the labor-intensive buffalo-hide and -organ processing. In contrast, the Northern Cheyenne's reality was still defined by their relationship with the buffalo and nature. Although the superstructures are somewhat similar between the Cheyenne of the north and of the south, the change in the economic base of the south is evident in the disjuncture between the Northern Cheyenne's and Southern Cheyenne's modes of production: specifically, the acceptance of white trade goods in the south and adherence to the old ways in the north.

As endogenous structural changes took place, external conflicts with the dominant society's concepts of economy and culture (property, language, and religion, for example) intensified (A. Miller 1994). The demise of Cheyenne communal life began with the arrival of Europeans to their lands. Their norms were replaced by property ownership and other capitalist norms. They were also affected by disease and racial stratification. This new life was very different from what the Cheyenne were accustomed to: from the procurement of food and how they dressed—aspects of their economy—to how they spoke and how their children were disciplined. The Cheyenne were in a state of culture shock, experiencing a collective social trauma, precipitously near genocide. Evolution did not mean progress from some earlier disadvantaged state to a new and improved state. To the Cheyenne, the demise of the buffalo mirrored their own fate. How the Cheyenne deal with the newcomers determines their success at surviving the continual invasion. According to one Northern Cheyenne Elder informant, the prophet Sweet Medicine[6] warned the people about the coming of a man with stitches:[7]

> For me it goes way back, even before the white man set foot on this land, in this country, it goes back to Sweet Medicine. Everything we do now he talked about . . . . He didn't say a white man but he did say a man in stitches. When he enters your life, he's the one that is going to change your life; he is the one who is going to take you away from your Native foods . . . you['re going to] get lost in this life and that is what he talked about. If you look at it in terms of what he predicted and what he foresaw and all the changes that would come, and he talks about it, he talked about leaving our Native food and then the . . . [white] food would make us weaker and weaker. (Northern Cheyenne Elder 2, interview by the author, Lame Deer, MT, July 5, 2008)

As lived processes, Cheyenne spirituality and the Sun Dance provided coping mechanisms for the Cheyenne. Instead of Cheyenne culture dissolving and becoming homogenous with non-Native society, with the Sun Dance, they were able to retain the original elements of being Cheyenne in the imagination of the people as a permanent space. The forward motion of time could not be stopped, but by practicing spiritual and cultural rituals, the Cheyenne maintained these permanent geographic and cultural spaces.

A key mechanism of capitalist expansion that impacted the Cheyenne
was the introduction of a new commodity, cattle. According to Southern
Cheyenne Director of Culture and Heritage Gordon Yellowman,[8] when
speaking about cattle, Sweet Medicine said, "This hairy person (whiteman) will . . . bring a spotted animal with horns, with big eyes and a long
tail that will . . . touch the ground. This animal will live on dirt and eat
anything. If you take after it and eat it, you will also eat almost anything
else" (Wisdom of the Elders 2004). Although the Northern Cheyenne
were aware of this and other prophecies, they did not have much choice
and succumbed to change in an effort to survive in the new white man's
way.

One Northern Cheyenne Elder relates how their efforts to survive
were stymied:

> That's been happening [assimilation], it's been talked about . . . Dull
> Knife talked about [it and] we became farmers, we became successful
> ranchers, and then there was this one time Cheyenne ranchers had
> fifteen thousand head of cattle and six thousand head of horses but the
> government came in and said you gotta reduce your herd. You know
> we'll make them a tribal herd, and the calves will be replaced whenever
> the tribe [has excess] . . . the whole thing was successful, so they as-
> similated, that is a sign of successful assimilation. (Northern Chey-
> enne Elder 1, interview by the author, Lame Deer, MT, July 4, 2008)

And historians confirm this was in fact the case (see, for example, Grinnell 1972 and Weist 1977). In 1903, the federal government allocated
one thousand cows and forty bulls to interested tribal members. By 1912,
under Northern Cheyenne stewardship, the cattle herd had grown to
twelve thousand and received top dollar at the Chicago cattle market. By
1916, the federal government stepped in to manage the herd as a tribal
enterprise. The U.S. government implemented a plan to reduce the
Northern Cheyenne horse population, a main component of the Cheyenne traditional economy, in an effort to make way for more cattle, killing approximately one hundred horses per month (Weist 1977). Then,
because of poor management by the Bureau of Indian Affairs (BIA), the
tribe lost eight thousand of the twelve thousand cattle they owned. The
BIA insisted the cattle be grazed in an area to the far east of the Cheyenne settlement during the winter. Severe weather set in, killing thousands of cattle that were placed in this grazing area; those kept close to
camp survived. Many of the Cheyenne who resisted and kept their cattle
close at hand found themselves in jail for breaking the U.S. government's
law. According to BIA records: "In 12 years of Indian Bureau mismanagement, two-thirds of the Indian-owned cattle on the reservation had
been lost. . . . The tribe, as a whole, is charged with more than $130,000
debts run up for the tribal herd" (Weist 1977, 123). After the debacle of

mismanagement, the BIA took 143,000 acres of the best grazing land and leased them to white ranchers for ten cents an acre (Weist 1977).

Change

The effects of hegemony could no longer be resisted. Through the lens of historical materialism, we find the Cheyenne environment evolving as they adapted to a new economic base. Cheyenne superstructural changes have followed, in beliefs, teachings, and ceremonies.

One Northern Cheyenne Elder notes, "The question is, how much Cheyenne are we?" She continues, "How much have we gone into this new life? . . . I now talk English . . . I don't ride horses; I don't know how to ride horses, I drive a car. I live in the city, I use electricity. How much of it [far] have we gone into this life that Dull Knife talked about and that Sweet Medicine talked about?" She also asked, "If I am assimilating, what am I assimilating into—Irish, Scottish, German?" (Northern Cheyenne Elder 1, interview by the author, Lame Deer, MT, July 4, 2008). Her query demonstrates the complexity of social evolution: how much of what the Cheyenne were still exists in today's younger generations?

Most point to off-reservation boarding schools as the bludgeon that erased the collective memory of Native people. The schools were used as a tool to break down traditional Cheyenne superstructure. To ensure survival and enable them to cope with a new cultural environment, many parents were compelled to "voluntarily" send their children to attend the schools. The children learned how to speak English and how to make items needed in the dominant society's economy (such as wagons, shoes, and harnesses), but they did not know how to operate in Cheyenne communities once they returned home from the boarding schools. Most could not remember enough Cheyenne to communicate with their families. Although they had acquired new skills, the children who returned as young adults were not able to participate fully in the lifeways of their people (Henrietta Mann, interview by the author, Weatherford, OK, June 25, 2008).

Mann relates that her grandfather volunteered to go to boarding school and stayed for one year. He was taught English and industrial crafts, such as making shoes and harnesses. The girls who attended were taught white cooking skills, like how to use milk and churn butter (Mann 1997, 61). Along with acquiring "life" skills, the children were acculturated into Christianity to save them from pagan ideologies. Richard Henry Pratt, founder of the off-reservation Indian school model, declared that education will "kill the savage but save the man" (Mann 1997, 62).

A Southern Cheyenne Elder recalls her first day at the Concho Indian day school located in Concho, Oklahoma:

I started my schoolin' at quartermaster school. I could not speak English [and] I hoped that [I would understand]. The teacher used to sit
on the right-hand side of the god and that was some teaching to do by
the Indians. . . . They forced us with lye soap to speak English. We
were not allowed to speak our language. They forced us to take vita-
mins with cod liver oil . . . They would be waiting for us outside the
dining hall [with it]. (Southern Cheyenne Elder 1, interview by the
author, Weatherford, OK, June 23, 2008)

Today, as the Cheyenne continue to tell the stories conveyed in their
oral histories and continue the ceremonies of the old ways, they are pre-
serving an identity that has not been lost completely after the trauma
inflicted by the boarding schools.

Endogenous social change can be observed in social relations constructed on the reservations after the end of the Time of the Horse.
While the women learned canning and men learned farming techniques,
older Cheyenne, born prior to reservation days, practiced the old ways
and kept those traditions alive. A confluence of culture allowed the next
generation of Cheyenne to evolve into a hybrid of their earlier selves,
creating a new cultural synthesis—a kind of mestizaje. On one hand, the
Cheyenne resist the dominant superstructure and its capitalist economic
base by maintaining traditions and spiritual values, while on the other
hand, the Cheyenne meld and bend their mores and modes of production to the dominant society's superstructure and base. In this complex
space, the dichotomy of potential peaceful coexistence and disharmonious clashes is quelled by the Sun Dance.

Sun Dance

The Sun Dance is a ritual renewal given to the Cheyenne by the Suh'tah
prophet Erect Horns.[9] Incorporated into the Sun Dance is an annual
ceremony that includes Sweet Medicine's Arrow Renewal. Each year,
once the Arrows are renewed, the Arrow Keeper and the Sun Dance
Priests set the date of the next Sun Dance. In recent times the Sun
Dance has occurred in late July. The date of the Sun Dance has been
modified to accommodate the workweek and falls over a three-day
weekend.

Other modifications are incorporated into the Sun Dance as well. The
Cheyenne use pots that are covered in enamel to get around the metal
contamination Sweet Medicine spoke about in prophecies. Sweet Medicine taught the Cheyenne people that if they were to eat from the metal
cookware of the "hairy man" or "man with stitches," they would lose
their sacred way of life, so the enamelware is used for its protective coat-
ing over the metal.

Some modifications are cause for concern, such as concepts of propriety for women.[10] One Southern Cheyenne Sun Dance woman said, "The women, nowadays, are disrespectful in that they wear shorts and pants into the Sun Dance arbor." My informant and guide to the Cheyenne Sun Dance required the women in our camp to dress in handmade wing dresses, as is customary.

Prior to the dancers leaving their families for that sacred space, much preparation is required. A week before the Sun Dance, the dancer and his family begin to set up camp. Traditionally, the family erects a willow shade as shelter for the family to eat and gather together (fig. 7.2). More often than not, most camps will use the traditional structure. However, a few families will use modern shades that are less labor intensive to construct. Generally, these families are at the Sun Dance for blessings from the dancers, but do not have a dancer in the arbor.

One Southern Cheyenne Elder and Sun Dance participant explains how the Cheyenne are able to continue on as a collective, as a community, and not be assimilated into the dominant society:

> The Cheyenne are adaptable. Rituals may have changed but they are adapted to changing environments. Basically we have taken our time adapting on our own terms. . . . [I] cannot say that without Anglo contact [we would not have adapted nonetheless]. Instead of assimilation it is cultural adaptation. We can adapt to change . . . [that is] . . . all around us. We maintain the core of who we are. We still take that and it carries us into 2008. There are generations that will take the spiritual core. [For] example, in terms of a circle . . . [life is] all encompassing, everything in the universe. The Cheyenne do not have a closed circle but [one that] . . . opens to the east. [It] may not be completely round [and it] . . . has a door for women. Especially noticeable when we paint [in the Sun Dance].[11] The black paints around the ankles and wrists [representing trails] . . . never shuts them off. The road of the sun . . . [and of the] sacred hat . . . never close that door because it is always opens to the future. [The] door to the future . . . Allows flexibility to change with the times. (Southern Cheyenne Elder 2, interview by the author, Weatherford, OK, June 25, 2008)

What this Southern Cheyenne Elder means when she says the Sun Dance opens a door to the future is that, notwithstanding the pressures to embrace the dominant society's concepts of reality, the Sun Dance provides a shining path that makes it possible for all Cheyenne people to remain grounded in who they are as a people. The intricate ancient rituals I observed at the Southern Cheyenne Sun Dances from 2008–2011 are preserved through oral tradition, and they continually construct the Cheyenne cultural identity, part of the tribe's superstructure.

FIGURE 7.2. Cheyenne children with willow shade in background at Sun Dance in 2009. The girls are wearing traditional wing dresses.

The Cheyenne believe the Sun Dance is a time for sacrifice and redemption. One Southern Cheyenne participant put it this way:

> We have a responsibility for all of mankind, not just the Cheyenne. The Ceremony must continue in order for the world to survive. Regardless of external social pressures, we must perform the Sun Dance, as directed by Sweet Medicine, in order to maintain the health of the earth. The Sun Dance cleanses your pathologies. That's why we need four years to complete the ceremony. You can change your life with the Sun Dance, and the people will forgive you of your problems. When we dance we are blessed by our suffering.[12] (Southern Cheyenne Sun Dancer, interview by the author, Concho, OK, April, 25, 2011)

Three Northern Cheyenne participants express their understandings of how the Sun Dance is necessary for the retention of Cheyenne culture:

Northern Cheyenne Elder 2:
   Cheyenne culture, the way I believe it there is a lot of things to talk about like how to be a Cheyenne, and I believe in all cultural ways like Sun Dance and fasting and pow-wow and how you dress in the Indian way. It is really hard to be a Cheyenne Indian.

Northern Cheyenne participant:

I know he is going to pray for us [speaking of the Sun Dancer]. I know he is going to help us and that makes me feel good. You want to help him whether it is giving him material things or praying for him while he dances; it's just all part of being a Cheyenne. When you pray you think of him. You know you pray that they make it through and that everything works out well for him and you.

Northern Cheyenne Elder 1:

A sacred Sun Dance, that's what I mean about everything being interrelated into your tribe and into your family, your spiritual beliefs and that makes you a Cheyenne, but if one is missing and you don't have a family, then you are lost. The larger society, they want to be Cheyenne, but the one thing missing is the whole family, the whole tribe.

(Interviews by the author, Lame Deer, MT, July 4, 2008)

Conclusions

The concepts of economic base and superstructure can be applied to cultural adaptation and change because they enable us to understand the importance of modes of production in the evolution of a society. Marx holds that "it is not the consciousness of men that determines their existence, but on the contrary their social existence that determines their consciousness" (Marx 1904, 4). The meshing of the old traditions of the Cheyenne superstructure with the dominant society's superstructure conforms to the dynamics of historical evolution conveyed by Marxist theory. Berlin (1963) posits that new reforms must "ferment" in old traditions to gain footing. Analysis of the Cheyenne Sun Dance suggests that old traditions ferment and survive in new forms.

Ceremonial aspects have survived from ancient times with few changes, despite the fact that modes of production have changed. Such change is reflected in the Sun Dance: clothing has changed and the use of enamelware pots has been introduced, as has been the use of augers to dig postholes for the arbor. The teachings of the prophet Sweet Medicine in relation to the Sun Dance and the Arrow Renewal help preserve Cheyenne spirituality. Cheyenne kinship groups have remained strong instead of breaking up, disappearing, and relinquishing control of Cheyenne people to the dominant society. Cheyenne informants understand that a Cheyenne would not be Cheyenne without these things. Several informants stated that it is hard to be a Cheyenne, but they will maintain a collective identity.

Adaptation and change are necessary survival skills mastered by the Cheyenne people. Historical events are paramount in determining the means of production, and these influence the evolution of social relations. The Cheyenne modes of production evolved over time, as they evolved from settled horticulturalists to nomadic hunters of the plains. As their hunting economy was destroyed, the Cheyenne had to adapt from a nomadic existence to a sedentary life, rooted this time in a capitalist economy.

The Cheyenne resisted and adapted to the ruling class concept of society, but on their own terms. Putting to use the survival skills they had acquired on the plains, the Cheyenne retained aspects of their cultural practices as they constructed their new collective identity. They have demonstrated both flexibility and resilience throughout the course of the imposition of a divergent superstructure. The dominant society's modes of production and economic base exercise considerable influence, but have not severed the Cheyenne's ties to their unique identity, rooted in their collective memory. Community and familial ties and the fortifying nature of the Sun Dance ceremony strengthen Cheyenne identity.

Historical materialism suggests that Cheyenne identity emerges from changes in subsistence patterns and the imposition of institutions of the state, like boarding schools. Historical materialism, however, cannot explain cultural survival, how Cheyenne identity is passed down by families, and how ceremonies like the Sun Dance remain central to the survival of collective identity throughout the expansion of capitalism. It cannot reconcile the pervasive and primary dependence on spirituality and familial ties.

Mestizaje, a lived process, helps explain how the Sun Dance provides a coping mechanism for the Cheyenne. Cheyenne culture has not disappeared into the melting pot with non-Native society. The Sun Dance helps the Cheyenne retain the original elements of being Cheyenne in the imagination of the people as a permanent space. The Sun Dance has been the door to adaptation. The Sun Dance is the constant that keeps the Cheyenne tethered to the past, the present, and the future.

Notes

1. Elisabeth Lloyd, philosopher, views Marx's dialectic as more a "triadic dialectic." In it she finds three primary laws: "1) the transformation of quantity to quality [quantitative vs. qualitative]; 2) the unity of opposites; and 3) the negation of the negation [null hypothesis]."

2. *The Cheyenne Way* (Llewellyn and Hoebel 1941) attempts to describe the Cheyenne's manner of dealing with dispute resolution and disharmony. Although *The Cheyenne Way* is a very important text for most Cheyenne scholars, the majority of Cheyenne interviewed had never heard of it. Llewellyn and Hoebel chose the Cheyenne for their study because the tribe was known for having structured institutions. They found that the Cheyenne's methods of maintain-

ing order were aligned with what they envisioned as a primitive form of jurisprudence.

3. Arguably, the Cheyenne and Arapaho Tribes' Oklahoma reservation has never been disestablished. Only Congress has the ability to disestablish borders, and it has yet to do so. However, there is some disagreement as to a judicial decision that declared the reservation disestablished. For further reference see Moore (1992).

4. According to the Cheyenne and Arapaho Tribes Constitution, tribal membership is based on having at least 1/4 blood quantum. "Each person of 1/4, or more, degree of blood of the Cheyenne-Arapaho Tribes . . . , shall have membership in the Tribes." If we expand membership to individuals beyond the blood-quantum marker, the numbers are much higher: approximately 23,234 members in Oklahoma.

5. The Cheyenne Dog Soldiers is a warrior society of the Cheyenne.

6. Sweet Medicine, Tsistsistas prophet and medicine man, gave the Cheyenne the scared arrows and the Arrow Renewal ceremony. It is said Sweet Medicine lived in a cave in the Cheyenne sacred mountain Bear Butte (located in South Dakota near Sturgis) where he received special teachings and gifts from the spirits. He took these prophecies and religious ways back to the people, and they still live by his teachings today.

7. Cotton clothes sewn with stitches

8. Chief Yellowman is a respected Sun Dance Priest, artist, and activist of the Southern Cheyenne People.

9. Erect Horns is a Cheyenne cultural hero and prophet. Oral history tells of a time when the People were starving. Erect Horns was chosen to endeavor on a quest to find food. He and his wife journeyed and came upon the sacred mountains. There the Creator showed Erect Horns the construction of the Sun Dance Lodge and said that having the Sun Dance would ensure that the buffalo returned (Dorsey 1905).

Once the date is set for the Sun Dance, a male tribal member announces that he is organizing the ceremony. In the south this man is referred to as the pledger. He pledges his time and resources to sponsor the ritual. Four days prior to the Sun Dance the pledger and his wife enter into the Lone Teepee, which represents the sacred mountains, Bear Butte, and reenacts Erect Horns's quest (Dorsey 1905).

10. Women do participate in the Sun Dance. In fact, the ceremony cannot occur without a woman sponsor. The woman must pray the sun up so that when the rays hit the sun symbol painted on her chest the Sun Dance may begin for that day.

11. The Cheyenne dancer's body is painted with earth paints by his or her painter. The painter is a person who has completed a Sun Dance vow and who has been given instructions from his or her painter in the proper manner of applying the paints. The ceremony is handed down through the generations using this oral tradition. A dancer must commit to at least four years before being permitted to paint another. The dancer's family must cook for the painter's family and bring gifts after each application of paints. This happens twice on the second day and four times on the third.

12. In the summer of 2011, the suffering was intense for the dancers. We were experiencing unusually high temperatures. At the height of the ceremony, the heat was unbearable, reaching over 117°F. The heat of the sun and the heat of the campfires were intense. Great mental strength is needed to complete this ceremony. One cannot enter this sacred place without proper preparation. Taking no food and no water for three days and two nights is a very difficult spiritual path. It was not only difficult for the dancers but also for the families who supported their loved ones in the arbor.

PART THREE

Empowerment

CHAPTER EIGHT

From Mestizos to Mashikuna

Global Influences on Discursive, Spatial, and Performed Realizations of Indigeneity in Urban Quito

KATHLEEN S. FINE-DARE

Introduction

This chapter provides a brief study of how some working-class residents of Ecuador's capital city of Quito are currently (re)constructing aspects of Indigenous identity through strategies that once might have been labeled passive processes of acculturation (cultural borrowing) or *mestizaje* (race mixture). Through complex and often convergent mechanisms of discourse and urban sociality, indigeneity is today going through a process of redefinition in this part of the Andes, less through the application of criteria of race or language than through the following: participation in cultural performances such as music, dance, and private ceremonies; the deployment of new rhetoric that actively critiques the idea of *blanquea-miento* (whitening) even as it replicates many of the erasure-of-difference effects of such; and the activities of Indigenous organizations such as the Pueblo Kitu Kara, which tries to understand the role that a "new indigeneity" (Fine-Dare 2013b)—one influenced by global environmentalist, spiritualist, and Indigenous activist trends—is playing in both realizing and frustrating their organizational ends.

By considering the intersection of various key discussions and performances regarding identity, recognition, and territorial rights over community green spaces that have been taking place since around 2001, this chapter focuses on ways that descendants of former hacienda workers, urban Indigenous migrants, and *mashikuna* (comrades) of both Indigenous and non-Indigenous ancestry look for representational space in national and municipal government offices (including those of the national Indigenous federation, Confederation of Indigenous Nationalities of Ecuador [La Confederación de Nacionalidades Indígenas del Ecuador, CONAIE]); local political, environmental, and cultural organizations; and other venues, including social media posts.

Although this complex case study (only a very brief account of which can be presented here) is a microanalysis of cooperation as well as schisms and disagreements over issues of identity and cultural property, these phenomena must be situated within the increasingly globalized environment of the Ecuadorian Andes. There, a push for generating real and symbolic capital derived from eco- and cultural tourism has contributed materially and symbolically to a focus on indigeneity as the most highly marked component of a "mestizaje" undergoing a great deal of reformulation.

Background

Nestled in the Guayllabamba River basin on the eastern flank of the Andes mountain chain, Quito, the capital city of Ecuador, stretches nearly twenty-five miles long but is only three miles wide. Quito is the largest of eight cantons comprising Pichincha Province, with a total population of 2,239,191 as of the 2010 census.[1] Quito is considered, as Norman E. Whitten (2003) describes, the "head, heart, and soul" of the nation and is the embodiment of state, ecclesiastical, economic, and social power. It is here that the Ecuadorian national imaginary (including some views emanating from the Indigenous movement) continues to convey a stereotype of the disappearing and essential Native person by identifying rural isolation, agropastoralism, Indigenous language use, and anti-modernity as factors key to "being Indian."

My research is located in a sector of northwestern Quito called Cotocollao,[2] which is the largest urban parish in the Pichincha Province, registering a population of 87,064 residents in the 2001 census (Ecuador. Instituto Nacional de Estadística y Censos 2002). Due to its ease of access and productive, well-watered lands, much of the area was awarded as encomiendas during the Spanish colonial period, and a great deal of doctrinal education was imposed and labor exploited by various orders of the Catholic Church. The Jesuit order maintains a presence through its internationally regarded archive, library, and museum—the Biblioteca Ecuatoriana Aurelio Espinosa Pólit—which is located right where buses curve to head upwards towards the many working-class neighborhoods that lie on the outskirts of Cotocollao. At least twenty other buildings in the sector have been registered as National Cultural Patrimony, one of which, La Delicia, was the house of the Marquesa de Solanda, the wife of the revolutionary hero Antonio José de Sucre. La Delicia was renovated between 1992 and 1996, and today it functions as the northernmost administrative seat of the Municipality of Quito (see "Cotocollao es el barrio favorito en la campaña en Quito," *Hoy*, August 21, 2004).

The sector—known for decades as *"el barrio de los indios"*—has always embodied a great many deep social contradictions, ranging from the homeless who sleep in doorways to those who live in luxury condominiums and are members of nearby exclusive clubs such as Quito Tennis and El Condado. When the first agrarian reform law was passed in 1964, at least 85 percent of the Indigenous population of Cotocollao worked in various types of labor relations for the many haciendas in the area (Borchart de Moreno 1981, 259). Although the reform did away with certain of these exploitative labor arrangements, it created new forms of dependency, many stemming from the fact that most of the Indigenous exworkers sold their awarded holdings for extremely low prices, which often plunged them into homeless poverty (see Blankstein and Zuvekas 1973). Some Indigenous and mestizo residents had to seek employment in Quito for low wages, while others sold charcoal, which contributed to area deforestation. Some landholders, anticipating the reform, sold their lands to speculators, which accelerated the urbanization process and the erosion of recognizable Indigenous presence in the area.

Pueblo Kitu Kara

The multifaceted Indigenous movement in Ecuador is a result of protests and resistance efforts that began in the colonial period, picked up steam in tandem with early twentieth-century labor struggles, and took on a national and even international presence in the 1980s (Becker 2008, 2011). By the twenty-first century, the divisions of the Ecuadorian populace into simplistic "white," "black," "mestizo," and other race-based categories had blossomed into a host of nationalities and "pueblos" ("peoples" with less juridical recognition than "nations"). The Ecuadorian government agency that oversees ethnic affairs, the Development Council of Indigenous Nations and Peoples of Ecuador (Consejo de Desarrollo de las Nacionalidades y Pueblos del Ecuador, CODENPE), recognizes the congeries of Indigenous peoples living in and around the Quito basin of Pichincha Province (sometimes known as the Quito Kichwa) as the Pueblo Kitu Kara, which is part of the overall Nacionalidad Kichwa del Ecuador (Ecuadorian Kichwa Nation). Although Pueblo Kitu Kara is loosely affiliated with a network of Indigenous groups that fall under the umbrella of the CONAIE, it receives no direct funding from them (Gómez Murillo 2007).

The Pueblo Kitu Kara is sometimes called the Pueblo Originario Kitu Kara (the autochthonous Kitu Kara community), the Étnia Kitu Kara (the Kitu Kara ethnic group), or the Nación Kitu Kara (the Kitu Kara nation). The name confusion reflects the historical complexity of the region and the ways that culture, politics, and spirituality are linked. The Pueblo Kitu Kara has a governing council (*consejo de gobierno*) that chooses one representative to serve as a liaison to the Ecuadorian government via CODENPE. In 2008, the Ecuadorian government approved the unprecedented creation of a judicial office (*fiscalía*) to centralize and coordinate claims to land, water, and property for communities affiliated with (or seeking help from) the Pueblo Kitu Kara organization (Fine-Dare 2010; Williams and Fine-Dare 2008, 18).

International funding from non-governmental organizations (NGOs) and the World Bank are channeled by CODENPE into local educational and infrastructural projects proposed by local Pueblo Kitu Kara organizations. The relationship between CODENPE and Indigenous interests is seen by many to be contradictory, however, particularly as it calls for a certain homogenization of beliefs, practices, and diverse cultural markers, for example, in the implementation of programs in health and intercultural education. To counteract this bureaucratizing contradiction, some urban residents (many of whom self-identify using the Quito term for Indigenous person, *runa*, or persons, *runakuna*) have created independent local organizations to highlight issues of ancestry, culture, and territoriality while maintaining a tentative relationship with the Pueblo Kitu Kara organization. In the remainder of this chapter, I turn to two important local expressions of Indigenous identity in northwestern Quito, the Yumbada and the Rosela/Quema de Chamiza dances.

Yumbada Dancing Across the Quito Basin

The Yumbada, or dance of the Yumbos,[3] represents lowland trader-shamans who exchange wisdom, healing, and commodities with highlanders (fig. 8.1). This dance complex—which features three different types of *danzantes* colorfully costumed with gourd capes, satin dresses and pants, feathered crowns, palmwood lances, and seeded bandoliers, while a fourth danzante dressed as a monkey serves as a trickster-protector—took powerful hold sometime in the early twentieth century in the rural/urban interface of the Quito area. Tied symbolically to the power of deer (*taruka*), the sun (*inti*), the lowlands (*yungas*), and, most importantly, the mountain peaks (to which some dancers refer by using the southern Quechua term *wamani*), the Yumbada provides, to use Frank Salomon's (1981) imagery, a kind of "switchboard" connecting ex-

FIGURE 8.1. Three generations of Cotocollao Yumbada danzantes in the Quito office of the Ecuadorian Ministry of Culture (left to right, Christian Valencia, Enrique Romero, and Miguel Simbaña). Note significant symbolic differences between the "Yumbo Mate" costume on left and that of the "Yumba" on right. "Mono—Monkey—Martín" poses with the mamaco's flute (*pingullo*) and drum (*tambor*). June 21, 2008.

periences of Quito basin residents that cross time and space (see also Whitten, Whitten, and Chango 2003). Nonetheless, the costuming, timing, and meaning of the dance vary in ways that reflect the cultural diversity found in the Quito basin, ranging from independent familial support and financing to performances in San Isidro del Inca that still pay a tithe to the parish priest (Borja 2009; Fine 1991; Fine-Dare 2007; Williams 2007).

The Cotocollao Yumbada that took place for decades in northwestern Quito was suspended for a few years in the late 1990s due to an economic recession. Its reemergence in 2003 was due to the influence of a wide variety of locally situated and globally related factors, both direct and indirect. Although the Yumbada was reconstituted with a longstanding drum and flute player,[4] the leadership was criticized by some for including new practices that were not considered "traditional" by some of the danzantes. For instance, persons of non-Indigenous background and/or who had no rightful legacy were allowed to dance, and the scene

was made much more open to women danzantes. In addition, funding
for certain aspects of the Yumbada was provided by the municipality,
which opened the family organizers up to charges of not only creating a
folkloric "spectacle" but also working in the interest of personal gain.

Religious tensions also exist, as dancers adhere to a wide variety of belief systems, ranging from evangelical Christian to Catholic to what some
might call "New Age"–inspired shamanic beliefs. The dance is a product
of complex religious histories as well. Unlike the Yumbada performances
that take place in surrounding communities in the Quito basin, the
Cotocollao Yumbada traditionally took place around the time of the spring
equinox and precisely during the week of Corpus Christi when the Holy
Host is commemorated. As in the Corpus Christi processions in Spain
that represent the distance from holiness to savagery (Dean 1999), the
Cotocollao Yumbo dancers always brought up the rear in the Cotocollao
Corpus Christi procession. In 2007, however, the symbolic tensions between the powers emanating from the mountains and those from inside
the Catholic establishment came to a decisive head. The parish priest
overturned a bucket of corn beer (chicha) outside the church door (an
act seen as extraordinarily disrespectful, particularly to the women who
labor for days making what is viewed as a type of sacrament), stomped
up to the altar in front of the packed church with a Yumbo lance snatched
from its owner, and declared: "I have the power of the Yumbos up here
with me, but it is nothing compared to the power in the body and blood
of Christ." The congregation cheered.

This priest told me later that while he tolerated the recognition of a
community's cultural heritage, he could not abide the "drinking, eating,
and pissing" that he claimed went on unchecked in the plaza and demeaned
the sanctity of Catholicism's most holy celebration. He disapproved of the
Yumbada's veneration of the image of Saint Sebastian, who is kept in the
house of a former hacienda owner's family and who carries rich symbolic
meanings that go beyond Catholic hagiography. Using language that sings
a centuries-old familiar tune, the priest viewed himself and his congregation as engaged in a battle against the forces of uncultured paganism. The
year 2007 would be the last that the Yumbada was to associate itself with
the Corpus Christi procession. By 2012, the decision had been made to
hold the public Yumbada one week following Corpus Christi and to publicly characterize the performance as the "dance of the mountains," rather
than as an event that was connected to the Catholic liturgical calendar.

Despite the priest's unintended confirmation of the power of the Yumbada, some of the dancers and their family members continue to worry
that the media attention and partial municipal underwriting is turning
the dance into mere spectacle. But many who participate do so in the
hope that the act of dancing and learning about the history of the event
will clarify questions they have about their own identity. "Are we Indi-

ans, Kitu Karas, Yumbos, or simply natives of this place?" one of them posed rhetorically to me in 2006 (Fine-Dare 2007, 68), echoing the kinds of inquiries Zoila Mendoza found circulating among dancers in Cuzco who explore the ambiguities of an urban Indigenous existence (Mendoza 1999, 87–88). David Guss has noted this ambiguity in the motivating forces behind the Gran Poder dances in La Paz, Bolivia (Guss 2006), citing Salomon's view that the dances "reflect the contradiction and tragedy of 'group[s]' poised in the space between two cultures—neither rural nor urban, tradition nor modern, Indian nor mestizo" (Guss 2006, 318, citing Salomon 1981, 164; see Stutzman 1981, 80).

This ambiguity, however, need not be viewed as "tragic." Perhaps it might be considered a dialectical collapse of the "hermeneutic arc" described by the philosopher Paul Ricoeur, who envisioned one side of the arc as the "understanding" those standing on the outside of a ritual wished to learn and interpret, while on the other side lie the "explanations" provided by those in the know (Ricoeur 1991, cited in Howard-Malverde 1997, 8). When rituals take place in places as historically and culturally diverse as Cotocollao and Velasco, it is not surprising that events such as the Yumbada require of all participants both understanding and explanation, or that the "same" dance takes dramatically different forms in different locales.

The Velasco Rosela Dancers

The barrio San Enrique de Velasco is one of twenty-one neighborhoods (barrios) located in the urban parish of El Condado, which was carved out of and lies just to the north of Cotocollao. Velasco is sandwiched between new, state-built condominiums that have replaced a section of the "protected" but rapidly diminishing forest that rings Quito and an elite, gated community and its private country club, El Condado, which prohibits Velasco residents from gaining access to a freshwater spring to which they claim ancestral rights. Once a privately owned hacienda, Velasco became an independent community after the agrarian reform of 1964. In 2006, a population of 2,478 was reported, comprised of Indigenous inhabitants who are native to the area or who are rural immigrants, especially from Cotopaxi Province (Taller Cultural Kinde 2007).

My research focus since 2005 has been on the activities of three related families headed by former *huasipungueros* (permanently indentured laborers) from the Velasco hacienda. One of these families created the Kinde (or Kindi, "hummingbird" in Kichwa) Cultural Center in their home in 2001, now called Casa Kinde. For many years the centerpiece of Casa Kinde was a private elementary school, the pedagogy of which reflected in some ways that of Ecuador's Indigenous university, Amawtay Wasi ("house of wisdom," now defunct as a result of a government mandate), which linked instruction to practical activities, spiritual understandings, and interpersonal respect. Casa Kinde's goal was to create an "experimental education" center that recognized and promoted an indigeneity that neither conformed to the canons of strict and highly bureaucratized Kichwa bilingual instruction nor accepted the idea that Indigenous identity could be imposed by anyone but themselves, including other Indigenous organizations. Although the teachers taught the children rudiments of the Kichwa language, the fact that none of them spoke the language or had received prior instruction in it presented a major obstacle to their achieving recognition as a center for Indigenous—defined by the state as "bilingual"—education.

Despite the fact that the school, called Mensajero del Saber (messenger of wisdom, one mythical characteristic of the hummingbird) failed to receive approval from the Ministry of Education, they were able to link the final year of instruction to a certified bilingual education center in the south of Quito, under whose authority the students eventually graduated. Because the school instructors—all of whom were female but one—believed a hallmark of true indigeneity to be gender equity and peaceful homes free of the violence, especially that which is alcohol fueled, that plagues the neighborhood, Casa Kinde continues to offer culturally and agriculturally focused after-school programs. It might well be argued that the centerpiece of the "neo-indigenist" project of Casa Kinde was as much the modeling of the ethos of a globalized feminism that prioritizes human rights and gender parity as it was instruction in the collective rights characteristic of global Indigenous struggles.

An outgrowth of the school's hands-on education focused on local realities was the construction of an instructional organic greenhouse fed directly by water that comes from a source they carefully manage high up in the mountain by means of a yearly collective work party, or *minga*. After the school closed, two more greenhouses were built with the assistance of an engineer employed by the municipality. Every Friday morning two Casa Kinde members go down to the municipality's La Delicia patio to sell Kinde greenhouse produce as well as cleaned, plucked, and packaged corn-fed chickens raised in carefully tended coops located next to the greenhouses. The Friday market is part of an urban agriculture program disseminated throughout Quito by the Ministry of Agriculture, which requires and provides prior training in produce and poultry management, sanitation practices, and customer relations.

In addition to their agricultural and poultry enterprises, Casa Kinde has conducted a great deal of ethnographic, genealogical, videographic, and oral history work to recover what they call the "ancestral Andean rhythms" of music and dance. Since 2001, friends, relatives, and neighbors have been interviewed regarding the form and meanings of the dances and music that once characterized the culture of Velasco and other nearby haciendas in the early twentieth century. In 2006, I attended a rehearsal associated with the observances of the days of Saint John (San Juan) and Saint Peter (San Pedro), also known as the Rosela dance. An elderly uncle and ex-huasipunguero, whip in hand, put a line of novices ranging from tiny tots to adults of both sexes gently through their paces on what were then still dirt roads, marked with the in-time affirmation "Hu-ha-hai." In order to re-create appropriately styled costumes, they consulted their closets and memories and looked at photographs I had taken in the 1980s of San Juan and San Pedro dancers who danced in front of the church portico in Cotocollao.

The Festival Quema de Chamiza has several components, both public and private. These elements range from the ceremonial gathering of brush for the bonfire from areas of the sacred geography surrounding the neighborhood; to coordinated public-wall painting, where the themes "we are a people in motion" and "we dance with purpose" are repeated; on through the Friday evening snaking (*culebrilla*) dance that joins family and friends throughout households in the neighborhood. The Rosela group, accompanied by other danzantes, dances around the bonfire one evening and also performs during the day on a stage located centrally in

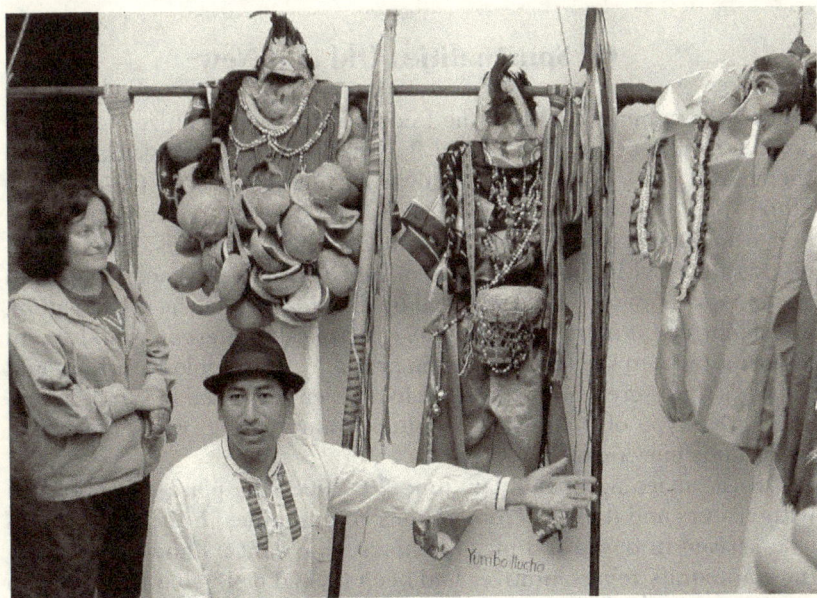

FIGURE 8.2. The Director of Casa Kinde, Pablo Gómez Semanate, explains the significance of Yumbo and other dance costumes to visitors during an open house. Barrio San Enrique de Velasco, Quito, June 2007.

the neighborhood from which banners denoting the Pueblo Kitu Kara
and Corporación Kinde are hung. While home-prepared chicha is served
to an audience seated in bleachers, Kinde members explain the purpose
of their performances and introduce performers contracted from other
areas of Ecuador.

Because several aspects of the Festival Quema de Chamiza are funded
by Ecuador's Ministry of Culture and other governmental entities, the
staged public aspect is a necessity. But this has opened up the festival to
criticisms of being "folkloric," a negative term that strongly connotes that
indigeneity is merely performed rather than lived. The fact that three
Kinde members also participate in the Yumbada of Cotocollao has also
brought criticism from those who see them as newcomers who want to
change the essence of the dance, for instance, by deemphasizing the role
played by the consumption of alcohol other than chicha. One year, the
display of their own Yumbo dance costumes in the Kinde center for an
open house (fig. 8.2) angered the Yumbo dance boss, because he did not
give the permission that the Velasco dancers did not believe was his to
grant. The sectarian oppositions that unfold during these times of festival illustrate contrastructural elements that keep indigeneity alive, if
complex. One good illustration of this was the participation of the San
Enrique de Velasco Roselas in the 2008 Inti Raymi festivities.

Of Spiritualities Old and New

During the summer of 2008, the Pueblo Kitu Kara organized and sponsored a formal celebration of Inti Raymi, or the Festival of the Sun, in
the central plaza of Tumbaco, a town located just east of Quito. Since
2002, the Pueblo Kitu Kara has (re)claimed over eighty thousand members who pertain to sixty-four "marginalized" communities in the northern highlands of Pichincha Province. When I attended a meeting of Kitu
Kara in downtown Quito, I was told by the president of the organization,
a resident of Lumbisí, that the *toma* (plaza-taking) event would be an
important way to see the variety comprised by the Pueblo Kitu Kara and
the ways they were coming together in an event designed to symbolize an
alternative type of political and cultural power tied to the Ecuadorian
Indigenous movement.

On the morning of Sunday, June 29, 2008, the plaza quickly filled
with visitors and dancers from various communities in the Quito basin
who arrived in buses and pickup trucks. The dancers and accompanying community representatives had been invited by Pueblo Kitu Kara to
participate in the first annual taking of the Tumbaco Plaza, an act that
would affirm that all groups who participated in reclaiming their Indigenous heritage in this public space would triumph. Dancers from Velasco
arrived early, wearing their newly sewn clothing and commandeering a

spot in the center of the plaza (fig. 8.3). The entire event took about a half hour, as very animated and organized groups made their way from a public into a semi-private area where they could take a rest to eat lunch with their families and regroup for a collective ceremony to take place in the courtyard later in the afternoon focused on human and cosmic harmony.

The event was, in the end, scarcely a "takeover" of the plaza in the old sense of Andean *tinkuy*, or ritual battle. Much about it was difficult to interpret, ranging from the curious fact that no group appeared representing nearby Lumbisí (including the Lumbiseña Kitu Kara president) to the culminating ritual that combined pan-Andean and New Age universalistic ritual and symbol within the confines of the Catholic Church patio area. For one member of the Quito elite to whom I recounted this story, the closing events symbolized nothing less than a farcical attempt to invent Indigenous identity out of whole cloth. To some of the Velasco participants, however, the event was not a farce but rather a less-than-perfectly organized venue that offered them the possibility to perfect their

FIGURE 8.3. Velasco Rosela group led by its Gallo Capitán, Manuel Gómez Semanate, takes the Tumbaco plaza during an Inti Raymi event organized by the Pueblo Kitu Kara indigenous organization. Manuel's sister, videographer Roció Gómez Semanate, dances to his direct left. June 29, 2008.

public performance skills and, most importantly, interact with neighbors
who had some common motivations and reactions. Some of them admit
that they are struggling with the right way to reclaim something they believe to be truly theirs but have nearly lost. It troubles Velasco residents
that, unlike those inhabitants of Lumbisí and more rural areas, none of
them speaks Kichwa any longer, which puts them into a gray area in the
eyes of the state, other Indigenous peoples, and the general populace
regarding just "who" they are.

Inherent to identity politics is facing criticism that one's intentions,
methods, practices, and even one's accepted history are fabricated, de-
rivative, corrupted, acculturated, assimilated, and otherwise non-authentic
or non-traditional. The man who had assumed leadership since 2003 of
the Cotocollao Yumbada (and who passed away in 2012 at the age of
fifty-four, leaving his legacy to one of his daughters in a highly controversial move) liked to talk much more about "tranquil" living, world
peace, and fixing a filthy environment than he did about "Indigenous
identity" per se. During one of our last visits with him and his wife, my
husband and I spoke briefly with his extremely ill father, Pedro Morales
Sr., whose entire life had been reduced to the mementos on the wall next
to his tiny bed. He mostly talked in tears, responding less to my few
questions than to what my presence evidently evoked: travel to distant
places, youth, good health, and life outside his urban concrete walls.
"Oh, your grace [su mercé]," he reminisced, "what a time it was, that
time I went to the montaña, what a distance I traveled, meeting the un-
baptized Jívaros, how beautiful it was." He held his hands, crippled with
arthritis, in front of his thin, ragged face, pointing them towards the image of the Virgin of Quinche next to his bed. "I don't know how to read
or write, but my heart is with them, all the little saints, and with my little
Father in the sky."

I looked above his soiled knitted cap and saw parts of his old Yumbada
dance costume on the wall, feathers attached to a spear that he may well
have gotten from his sojourn "to the beautiful Oriente, to 'Archirona'
[Archidona]." He spoke of his time as a young man working on the hacienda, where he said he got along with the boss, who treated him well,
like a son. The old man's son listened patiently to his father's jumbled,
rambling memories about Yumbo dancers who had already died, the illness in his stomach, his days working as a young man, how much cheaper
food used to be and how much better it tasted, how he drank very little
in the old days, how the people cried to see him sing and dance, and how
the devil tempted him with silver.

For his son, these oppressive days of the hacienda were, thankfully,
long gone. But he also doubted that the "escape" from these miseries to
an urban lifestyle was much of an improvement. After working more
than fifteen years in a factory, he and his wife struggled another decade
to make a living repairing dirty electrical equipment in a phone booth–

sized shop into which diesel fumes belched from the busy street. What would be the point of recuperating an "Indigenous" past if life in the end would be little better than this one? What the junior Morales and his wife dreamed of was clean air, green pastures, blue skies, and travel to beautiful places. Yumbo dancing was important to Morales because it immersed him in spiritual thoughts, wrapped him in beautiful fabrics, and introduced him to new young people with whom to converse about the world.

One in particular, a sociology student who had struggled to find work as an artist and in community theater projects, had been admitted into the Yumbo dance group, although some of the other dancers whose role was assured through inheritance grumbled about it. "Who is that person?" they asked, not mentioning Indigenous ancestry but implying its marked absence. The integration of the young man and two of his friends into the group and the changes they suggested to the dance format and the costuming were viewed as impositions. "What does that guy know?" a son of one of the best-known *mamaco*s of the Cotocollao Yumbada asked bitterly, shortly after his father's death (fig. 8.4):

He shows up on the television dancing the Yumbada; he speaks to the press; he's everywhere! But he doesn't know anything about the true Yumbada, or the true faith. Why, it's crazy to say the Yumbada is about Inti Raymi or the Pachamama ["earth goddess"] or any of that nonsense. It's about San Sebastián! He's the real heart of the Yumbada; my dad knew it and was inspired by the saint to compose his tunes. Why, the saint is so powerful, so holy, that the real one isn't brought out for the dance—the one you see is a replica. The real San Sebastián has a face that tells you if he's mad at you or pleased. He can trick you, get angry. It's for him that we dance. How can they say he's the Pachamama?

The disagreement over the locally indigenized Catholic Saint Sebastian versus the pan-Andean, neo-spiritualized Pachamama perhaps symbolizes better than anything the nature of current changes in the name of indigeneity that have come to a world long characterized by mestizaje. If "acculturation" is taking place, it is through its original sense, which denotes not assimilation and loss but the sharing and accrual of elements in rich, often dialectical, fashion. Global exchanges of information are accelerating this bricolage, as the Municipality of Quito's mandate to develop cultural and ecological tourism intersects with eclectic spirituality, both of which have appropriated archaeological finds into their claims over historical and physical landscapes. *Yumbo danzantes* are commonly invited to appear at events that take place at an archaeological site with a museum that highlights ancestral Yumbo culture. Some of the newer additions to the group claim that the traditional gathering up of the

FIGURE 8.4. Family members of the late Pingullero mayor of the Yumbada of Cotocollao (José Benjamín Simbaña Simbaña, known affectionately and respectfully as "Papa Mín"). His grandson, Paul Alexander Simbaña Janeta, also a tambonero mamaco, holds Papa Mín's drum and flute. The family claims to be the true tambonero descendants, and several members continue to dance in the Yumbada tradition. Barrio Mena del Hierro, Quito, June 27, 2008.

Yumbo dance troupe should begin at this site, located in the piedmont some thirty-five miles away, and be focused on the non-Kichwa elements of this Indigenous ancestry.

Other spiritual elements related to indigeneity go out to the rest of the world in the form of blogs, Facebook, and other social media sites where information, misinformation, and personal views are disseminated freely. A few years ago, I met a young woman from Cotocollao who was on a college graduation trip to the United States with the aim of "distributing messages from the elders" to Indigenous people. By the time Carla Badillo arrived on my campus, she had already made her way to San Francisco, Phoenix (where she stayed with a family friend who had migrated to the United States many years ago), Taos, and Albuquerque, everywhere identifying herself as a member of the "Pueblo Kitu Kara" and blogging her experiences daily, posting dozens of photos (fig. 8.5). She greeted people with the Kichwa term *mashi* (friend, comrade) and thanked them using

FIGURE 8.5. Quito poet and journalist Carla Badillo Coronado videotapes Native American dancers at Fort Lewis College in Durango, Colorado. September 26, 2008.

the Kichwa term *yupaychani*, although nothing in her ancestry linked her "organically" to a Kichwa lineage.

Students at my college were fascinated by her. She read her extraordinary poetry at the college's Hispanic cultural center and spoke to the class I taught on Native peoples of the Andes. One of the students in the class was Michael Joseph, a member of the Confederated Tribes of the Colville Reservation from Washington State. He requested that I bring Carla that evening to a powwow he had organized on the Southern Ute reservation where he worked in behavioral health. She was introduced as a respected visitor and invited to come to the microphone, where she eloquently discussed universal Indigenous rights and the importance of communicating across the globe. When I asked Michael if it mattered that Carla was not "really" an Indian but instead the English-speaking daughter of a well-off "white" South American attorney, he replied no: it was her heart that mattered, her perceived knowledge of Andean indigeneity, her participation in spiritual activities with a variety of Indigenous groups, her willingness to learn and to share, and her basic charm and goodness. She connected him to a world from which he, as a North

American Native person, had always felt artificially barred: an entire Native hemisphere lying south of the Rio Grande.

Conclusion

In 1975, Judith Friedlander published a controversial book, *Being Indian in Hueyapan*, that examined the ascription of Indian identity onto residents of a Mexican community in Morelos whose culture "like the Aztec pyramid in the Plaza of the Three Cultures . . . is in ruins." According to Friedlander, the only reason that Hueyapanos identified as Indians was because outsiders designated them as such, as "a reflection of the culture of a highly stratified contemporary society" (Friedlander 1975, xv).

The reverse of this situation obtains in Quito today. Although one might argue that the Indigenous cultures of the Quito basin have similarly been in ruins since, especially, the urban aftermath of agrarian reform, the indigeneity of residents is largely self- rather than outsider-imposed. As much as this circumstance might be desired in terms of the greater agency it affords residents, it has also created a new kind of invisibility and even competition for the right to assume the Indigenous mantle. For instance, many of those who talk about indigeneity most freely in Quito are not themselves Indigenous, but rather middle-class Ecuadorians who selectively identify with aspects of Indigenous culture for a variety of reasons ranging from existential to economic, and who collaborate with Quito Indigenes in ways ranging from sincerely kin-like to admiringly wannabe to exploitatively clientelistic.

What a growing number of scholars argue is that political, economic, and global circumstances that once maintained a distinction between persons Indigenous and those who were not have changed dramatically, not only facilitating Indigenous organization but also swelling the ranks of Indigenous persons demographically as the paradigm of interculturality (*interculturalidad*) informs Indigenous coalition-building throughout the Americas.[5]

The authors of a 2008 article focused on Brazil see this process happening throughout Latin America and suggest that elevated Indigenous population growth can be traced not only to lower mortality rates and migratory influx but also to the ways that twenty-first-century "identity politics have prompted ostensibly non-Indigenous people to reclassify their race-ethnicity and self-identity as Indigenous" (Perz, Warren, and Kennedy 2008, 8). This includes people of Indigenous ancestry themselves, who demonstrate in some very interesting ways basic principles of broadly conceived Andean socio-symbolic and spiritual organization that continue to inform responses to often drastic changes.

Many researchers in urban environments in the Quito basin, in addition to witnessing public ritual performances and private educational, organizational, and pedagogical events, have seen recognition of local ancestral power embodied in saints who reside in homes rather than in the church and in the dead who lie in the cemeteries and outlying graves. We have heard people evoke with respect the chthonic power of nearby mountain peaks that link the forces of sky, water, fire, wind, and stone. These are not the acts and beliefs of people who are lost in the gray areas of their in-between-ness, but rather place-based evocations of shape-shifting identities that reflect, contribute to, and push back against the forces coming from times past, times to come, and the times in which they live. Indigenous peoples have built and lived in urban and other constructed settlements for centuries. We need to develop alternative views for recognizing the complexity, innovation, and fundamental inter-culturality in the ways this is and always has been done, not only in the Quito basin but also across the hemisphere.

Acknowledgments

I must first give collective thanks to many residents of Cotocollao, El Condado, Carretas, and other locations in northwestern Quito who have endured my presence and prying for many years with much patience and graciousness. I am particularly grateful to the *mamas* and *taitas* involved in the Rosela, San Juan, and Yumbada dances, who allowed me to be an inquisitive spectator. I specifically thank Andrés Andrango, Carla Badillo, Karina Borja, Francisco Chiliquinga, Jacqueline Chiliquinga, Lupe Chingo, Carlos Cornejo, Guido Díaz, Pascuala Farinango, Raúl Fuentes, Alicia Gómez, Manuel Gómez, Miguel Gómez, Pablo Gómez, Ricardo Gómez Murillo, Rocío Gómez, Tatiana Gómez, Javier Herrera, Alexandra Martínez, Fannylu Morales, the late Miriam Morales, Nancy Morales, the late Pedro Morales, Alexandra Ribadeneira, Enrique Romero, Ernesto Salazar, Augustina Semanate, Daniel Semanate, Francisco Semanate, the late Luz María Semanate, Manuela Semanate, Padre Froilán Serrano, Freddy Simbaña, María Inés Simbaña, the family of the late José Benjamín Simbaña (including Marcelo Simbaña and Paul Simbaña), Enrique Tasiguano, Mauricio Ushiña, Christian Valencia, Santiago Velasco, Norman E. Whitten Jr., Julie Williams, José Yánez, and the staff of Susana Dávila, who at this time of this research was the head of the cultural center of the "La Delicia" Ecuatorial Zone office of the city of Quito (Administración Zona Equinoccial La Delicia, Municipio del Distrito Metropolitano de Quito). I am very grateful to Stefanie Wickstrom, who organized the session for the Fifty-Third International Congress of Americanists (Mexico City, 2009) in which an earlier version of this chapter first appeared, and to the late Phil Young, who, along with Stefanie, helped edit this chapter to intelligibility and who, unfortunately, I never got the chance to meet in person. My deepest gratitude goes to Byron Dare, who has shared these experiences in Ecuador with patience and a better eye than mine for seeing the world as it is rather than how I might like it to be. Finally, I am very grateful for the funding I received to carry out this work, which came primarily from the U.S. Fulbright Commission and the following Fort Lewis College sources: the Department of Anthropology; the Office of the Dean of the School of Natural and Behavioral Sciences; the fund for faculty grants administered through the office of the provost; and the Fort Lewis College Foundation. I am grateful for the careful work of the Institutional Review Board of Fort Lewis College and for the Fort Lewis College Library, which has graciously put on exhibit several masks and other instructional materials regarding the important traditions of festival and danzante performances in the Ecuadorian Andes.

Notes

1. http://www.inec.gob.ec/cpv/descargables/fasciculos_provinciales/pichincha.pdf

2. I was attracted to Cotocollao because of its archaeological and other cultural and historical significance (Villalba 1988), and I first began working there in 1980, a key year for the florescence of the Indigenous movement in Ecuador. After a hiatus of more than a decade, I returned in 2000 to begin a study of the effects of large migratory movements of people into Quito from countries such as Colombia and Peru, and of workers allied with international organizations that flooded Ecuador as neoliberal economic practices opened the door for volunteerism and other non-governmental activities to fill gaps in the provision of health, education, and welfare services. The effects of these human movements in response to global economic factors cannot be underestimated, particularly as they have affected the transformations to and the power of Indigenous identity.

3. The designation of Yumbo has many meanings in Ecuador, ranging from a now-extinct Chibchan-speaking people who lived on the western piedmont of the Andes "downslope" from Quito to modern Kichwa-speaking Indigenous residents of the eastern slope of the Andes in the Napo-Baeza-Archidona region. Because trade took place in an arc that linked valuable goods from the Pacific Ocean, obsidian and other valuables from the Sierra, and the wealth of the eastern tropical forest, the term "Yumbo" came to be applied to traders who made their way across this vast region. A feminine version, "Yumba," applies not only to Yumbada *danzantes* who costume in long dresses, often taking the name of female mountain spirits, but also to the chthonic spirit of springs, waterfalls, and other natural features who is said to be particularly protective of women who are mistreated by men (Fine-Dare 2013a).

4. The *mamaco* or *tambonero* is the person (always male, but symbolically gendered as female) who provides both the drumbeat and flute melodies to the

dance. He is characterized as the heartbeat of the performance, without whom it could not take place at all.

5. Joanne Rappaport defines interculturality as "the selective appropriation of concepts across cultures in the interests of building a pluralistic dialogue among equals . . . which has been harnessed as a vehicle for connecting such domains as Indigenous bilingual education to the political objectives of the Native rights movement." Three "interwoven threads" make up interculturality. First, it is "a method for appropriating external ideas, connecting the diverse network of activists, *colaboradores*, and occasional supporters of the Indigenous movement into a common sphere of interaction." Second, it offers "a utopian political philosophy aimed at achieving interethnic dialogue based on relations of equivalence and at constructing a particular mode of Indigenous citizenship in a plural nation." Finally, "it poses a challenge to traditional forms of ethnographic research, replacing classic thick description with engaged conversation and collaboration" (Rappaport 2005, 5–7). Because, according to Rappaport, interculturality ranges from the political to the pedagogical (often used as a gloss for "bilingual education"), it is important to realize that it can look very different in distinct sectors of the Americas.

CHAPTER NINE

Indigenous Peoples as a New Category of Transnational Social Actors

An Analysis Based on the Case of Argentina

SABINE KRADOLFER

Mexicans descended from the Aztecs;
Peruvians descended from the Incas;
Argentines descended from the boats.

Introduction

On May 20, 2010, days before the bicentenary of the May Revolution, marking the day that opened the way for Argentina's independence, thousands of Indigenous people participating in the Marcha de los Pueblos Originarios walked through the center of the city of Buenos Aires to converge in Plaza de Mayo, the very heart of the political power of the state.[1] This mass of people (more than twenty thousand, according to the organizers) was formed of three columns of demonstrators who had started marching some days earlier, on May 12, in the peripheral regions of the northeast (provinces of Formosa, Misiones, Corrientes, and Chaco, with representatives of the Toba, Wichí, Mocoví, and Guaraní peoples), the northwest (provinces of Jujuy, Salta, Tucumán, Catamarca, and Santiago, with representatives of the Diaguita, Kolla, Atacama, Aymara, Wichí, and Guaraní peoples), and the south (provinces of Río Negro, Neuquén, and Mendoza, with representatives of the Mapuche and Huarpe peoples). In the late afternoon, delegations from more than thirty Indigenous nations had a meeting with President Cristina Fernández de Kirchner.

The slogan of the march, *"Marcha por el camino de la verdad, hacia un estado plurinacional"* ("March for the way of truth, toward a plurinational state"), breaks with the monolithic vision of the Argentine state—even though this nation was constructed as a melting pot (*crisol de razas*) of European immigrants, Indigenous people, and descendants of Africans—and suggests thinking about national identity in the plural. Something that struck me as I started my anthropological research in the northern Patagonian province of Neuquén in the mid-1990s was that many of the non-Indigenous people I had met there answered the question, "Where are you from?" with a detailed explanation of their origins: "I arrived from Córdoba in the 1970s, but I'm a grandson of Italians." The reference to European origins and identification with categories that seemed very distant from those of a "pure" Argentine heritage did not seem to bother them when, at the same time, they spoke of their actual national identity. When we talked about the Mapuches, the Indigenous people who live there, things turned more radical: "They say they are Mapuche Indians, but you know, when you look at ancient photographs, and you compare them to people you meet in the countryside, you see that the Mapuches do not dress typically anymore, they have lost a lot of their culture—for me, they are not 'pure' Mapuches anymore," or, "You know, they are not originally from Argentina, they crossed over from Chile some centuries ago, so they are not 'true' Argentines. They are invaders because they occupied the territories of the Tehuelche people, and they killed them."

Such essentializing discourses on the ethnic identity of "others" have been made possible by a century of invisibilization processes that led to the idea that the Indigenous part of the population had been integrated into an Argentine society represented as culturally monolithic. If the habitants of Neuquén were aware of the presence of the Mapuche population, which composes a large part of the poorest social class and is therefore a cheap labor force with which they interact daily, they did not see the Mapuche as a people with another culture, but as "black heads" (*cabecitas negras*), that is, as people belonging to the lowest class of unskilled workers. The national integration model successfully removed all traces of indigeneity from the population.

The aim of my chapter is to illustrate how processes of change have been ongoing in Argentina for more than thirty years, giving more and more visibility and voice to Indigenes and inscribing their struggles in the larger frame of the transnationalization of Indigenous movements and claims. What is particularly interesting to note in the context of this book on *mestizaje* is that in almost all moments of Argentine history, social categorizations have avoided the notion of mestizaje and that it is unthinkable to imagine that out of the mix of Europeans and Indigenes could emerge a new intermediate category. Thus, we are in a completely different situation from that in, for example, Mexico—with José Vasconcelos's *The Cosmic Race* (1925 [1997])—where a plaque in Mexico City memorializes the battle of Tlatelolco and the defeat of the Aztecs in 1521: "Neither a victory nor a defeat, but the painful moment of birth of today's Mexico, of a race of mestizos."[2] This paradox will be the leading point of my argument.

This chapter is based on anthropological research on Mapuche communities and organizations in the Argentine Patagonia and in some bodies of the United Nations (UN) working with Indigenous peoples. I wish to show how the local definition of ethnic identity by Mapuches themselves, as well as by non-Mapuches, is shaped by decisions made at the international level on the question of indigeneity and how people apply it to defining themselves, directly or indirectly.

Far from seeing indigeneity as a static and substantial type of identification, I will show how this socially constructed category is dynamic and how processes of Indigenous self-adscription (now recognized by international organizations and states) demonstrate fluidity and flexibility. In America, indigeneity is conceptually associated with belonging (or relating) to one of the peoples who inhabited this continent prior to the European invasions starting in the fifteenth century. Even if Indigenous peoples are undergoing processes of "ethnical do-it-yourself" (Morin and Saladin d'Anglure 1995), these types of (re)identifications are not mere strategic choices (Spivak 1988), but should be seen as dynamic intents of (re)articulating ethnical belongings which are co-constructed by actors and institutional legal frames. Being Indigenous has to be seen as an "incessant [movement] of differentiation, not a massive state of pre-existing stabilized 'difference,' namely an identity" (Viveiros de Castro 2006, 2).

Therefore, I begin by analyzing how the international legal context that defines who is Indigenous and who can benefit from collective rights has modified the relations between Indigenous peoples and the state. Next, I discuss the specific case of the Argentine way of dealing with autochthony since the final annexing of the last free Indigenous territories at the end of the nineteenth century to show how, after more than one hundred years of invisibilization of Indigenous peoples, the constitutional reform of 1994, encouraged by previous international conventions, laws, or treaties, led to reaffirmation of the specific identity of an important and unexpected part of the population. The aim of the republican state was to integrate the Indigenous population into Argentine society and transform them into proper citizens through assimilation. They were supposed to forget their original cultures and languages and integrate into a melting pot. Paradoxically, immigrants were not expected to leave

their roots behind; on the contrary, the introduction of external European cultural elements into Argentine society was valued and fostered.
In this particular context, miscegenation evolved in a fundamentally different dimension compared with other Latin American countries.

(Re)constructing Indigeneity:
When the Local Meets the Global

The movement toward re-ethnification we can observe in Argentina, as
well as in all of Latin America (Bengoa 2000), has led in this particular
context to the rebirth of some peoples—like the Huarpe, the Ona, the
Quilmes, etc.—who were believed extinguished for several centuries.
Others, like the Mapuches (people of the land; from *mapu*, land, and
che, people), historically known as one of the most important groups in
this area, are now strongly increasing demographically because the new
generations of Mapuches who were raised in the cities have inverted the
tendency of their parents and grandparents who tried to conceal their
cultural differences in order to integrate into Argentine society. The aim
of Indigenous organizations is not only to make their struggles and claims
visible but also to draw attention to their mere existence and to the fact
that they haven't disappeared. With the Marcha de los Pueblos Originarios, we are witnessing a gradual breakdown in the dynamics of invisibility, marginalization, and negation of Amerindian populations once
perpetuated by the state.

The political processes that have elaborated new definitions of indigeneity and redrawn specific boundaries to differentiate "Indians" from
"whites" twist various legal components at international, regional, national, and local levels. The end of the Argentine dictatorship in 1983
occurred at a moment when, at the international level, the problems of
Indigenous peoples around the world, in their relationships with states
as well as with non-Indigenous populations, had begun to gain the attention of human rights organizations, institutes, and studies. In 1982, the
first organization dedicated solely to the concerns of Indigenous peoples,
the Working Group on Indigenous Populations (WGIP) of the Sub-
Commission on the Promotion and Protection of Human Rights (then
called the Sub-Commission on Prevention of Discrimination and Protection of Minorities), was established by a decision of the UN's Economic
and Social Council. Twenty years later, in 2002, the UN Permanent Forum of Indigenous Peoples was launched. In 1989, the Convention Concerning Indigenous and Tribal Peoples in Independent Countries was
adopted by the General Conference of the International Labour Organization (ILO Convention No. 169). On September 13, 2007, the Declaration on the Rights of Indigenous Peoples (the "Declaration") was
approved by the UN General Assembly after more than twenty years of

work that began with the drafting of the Declaration of the WGIP in 1985, which was completed in 1993 and reviewed between 1995 and 2006 by another ad hoc working group.[3]

Specifically, for this period in Argentina, there are three major legal milestones to bear in mind. First, in 1985, Federal Law 23.302, "Protection and support of Indigenous communities" (which was enforced only belatedly), adopted a certain number of measures for protecting Indigenous people, provided, however, that they lived in "communities."

Second, Indigenous peoples were officially recognized on August 11, 1994, with the adoption of a new federal constitution. Until that moment, the constitution of 1853 had specified in Article 67, Paragraph 15 that the national congress should "see to the safety of the borders, maintain peaceful relations with the Indians and facilitate their conversion to Catholicism" (Falaschi 1996, 237). In contrast, the new text specifies, in Article 75, Paragraph 17, that the national congress should

> recognize the ethnic and cultural pre-existence of Indigenous peoples in Argentina; guarantee respect for their identity and the right to a bilingual and intercultural education; recognize the legal status of Indigenous communities, the possession and communal ownership of the lands they traditionally occupy . . . while regulating the transfer of other land suitable and sufficient for human development; no land may be alienable, transferable or susceptible of being charged or seized. Ensure their participation in managing natural resources and other issues that concern them. The provinces may exercise these powers simultaneously.

Third was the ratification, on September 3, 2000, of ILO Convention No. 169, which had been adopted almost ten years before, in 1992.

These fundamental changes in the relationship between the state and Indigenous peoples and the proliferation of human rights organizations and international organizations dealing with Indigenous issues had very important impacts in Argentina. A dictatorship had been replaced by a democratic government, and multiculturalism recognized rights to racial, ethnic, and cultural differences, and acknowledged and conformed to international laws and conventions. Grassroots human rights organizations occupied an important place in the rise of social movements, and at the end the 1980s, they participated in the debates about planned festivities for the five hundredth anniversary of the "discovery" of America by Columbus. Indigenous voices emerged from these organizations, and new pressure groups formed by Indigenous peoples were created that gained important support from existing human rights associations. They strongly criticized the fact that Latin American states wanted to celebrate and commemorate an event that represented the beginning of a long-time process of dismembering Indigenous societies.

The Historical Processes of Invisibilization of Indigenous Peoples in Patagonia

"There are no more Indigenous peoples in the land" was a commonly held Argentine belief that testified to the efficacy of the invisibilization of the autochthonous societies after the last war against Indigenous groups in the Chaco and in Pampa-Patagonia at the end of the nineteenth century. This process goes back even earlier in time, when the need to build the Argentine identity of a white nation with ethnic, linguistic, and religious unity increased after the country's fight for independence in 1816, and this invisibilization was pretty much achieved by the end of the nineteenth century with the annexation, after years of bloody wars, of the last remaining free Indigenous territories in the south (Pampa-Patagonia) and the north (Chaco) to ensure total control by the state of its territories. At this time, and because of the slower penetration of European populations into these huge frontier territories, which stayed longer under Indigenous administration, the Indigenes did not have to undergo the important processes of racial intermingling well known in Mesoamerica, Brazil, and the Andes as mestizaje. Indigenes resisted the foreign armies and entered into peace treaties first with the Spanish Crown and later, after national independence, with representatives of the Argentine and Chilean states to maintain control of their territories. From here on, I will focus on the Indigenous Mapuche inhabitants of the Pampa and Patagonia to analyze their relationships with the authorities of the new Argentine nation,[4] created in 1810, and based on the division between Indian and "white" populations, to study how societies can become established on both sides of a border, a division still in force. White refers to the distinction made as well by the Mapuches between themselves and the *huinca*—a word that has multiple meanings of white, thief, and foreigner—and to the distinction (Indian vs. white) currently made in Argentina to separate Indigenous people from the non-Indigenous immigrant population.

In the last quarter of the nineteenth century—under pressure for land on behalf of the *estancieros*[5] and for food commodities from international markets because of the international economic crisis—the government of President Nicolás Avellaneda (1874–1880) made the decision to conquer the free Indigenous territories of the Pampa. Adolfo Alsina, Avellaneda's minister of war and navy, put an end to the traditionally peaceful relations with the Indigenous peoples and, with the assistance of new technological resources like the Remington rifle and the telegraph, planned and carried out the first invasion of the territories of the Pampa. After Alsina's death, Julio Argentino Roca (1878–1880) succeeded him and directed the Campaña al Desierto (Desert Campaign)[6] in a joint action with the Chilean government, which was also conducting a military operation to annex the Mapuche territories west of the Andean Cordillera. This campaign, conducted in 1879, pushed the southern border of Argentina back to the rivers of Neuquén and Negro, where Patagonia starts. It resulted in a significant relocation of Indigenous populations and established the necessary bases for colonization of the river valleys north of Patagonia. Roca was elected president (1880–1886) after his triumphal return to Buenos Aires. He continued the conquest of Patagonia between 1881 and 1883 with the Campaña del Nahuel Huapi (Nahuel Huapi Campaign) and the Campaña de los Andes (Andean Campaign), during which the persecution of the Indigenous populations continued until the surrender of their last headmen in 1885. Given the damages caused by these military operations, they can be considered "genocide" (Delrio et al. 2010; Navarro Floria 1999, 104–6).

The processes of invisibilization of the Indians started before their military submission, as indicated by the term "desert," which qualifies the territories of the Pampa and Patagonia for conquest. The Conquista del Desierto in the official historiography presents a double problem in the use of the term "desert." The first lies in the use of the term itself; the second lies in the use that the nineteenth-century *conquistadores* made of it. Indeed, the territories to which this term referred did not actually suffer from dryness—or in any case, the majority of them did not, as only some areas of Patagonia can be regarded as semiarid. On this subject, it is interesting to note that the idea of "desert" at this time in Argentina applied equally to arid regions and tropical forests, since it referred to spaces empty of "Western civilization": namely, to territories propitious for the expansion of "civilization" and "progress." This reference to a lack of population relates, obviously, only to the "civilized" white people. The principal objective of the campaigns directed by General Roca was the occupancy of new territories with the aim of exploiting their resources, and regarding them as deserts became an effective argument justifying their occupation (see Kradolfer and Navarro Floria 2006). The ideal of the "white," Christian, "civilized" nation of Argentina in the nineteenth century could be realized only by making the Indian populations disappear—physically and symbolically (Delrio 2005). During the military campaigns, the Indigenous peoples who did not perish in armed struggles and raids against civilian populations (the Argentine army also attacked settlements where women and children remained) were deported as prisoners to Buenos Aires, then divided into various urban centers of the country. Families were separated. Men were employed as bonded workers in the construction of railroads, in the *estancias* located in the center of the country, and on sugarcane plantations in the area of Tucumán. Some were forced to enlist in the army and navy, and thousands were exiled to the prison of Martín García's Island. Women and children, meanwhile, were distributed among the wealthy families of Buenos Aires who needed servants (Varela and Font 1995, 178–79). The populations that escaped death and exile remain, at this moment, small groups of isolated inhabitants or wandering tribes deprived of lands and means of subsistence, witnessing the systematic destruction of their society.

Constructing a "White" and "Civilized" Nation

As shown by Pantin Guerra (2007), when intellectuals think about national identity, as did Ernesto Sábato in *La cultura en la encrucijada nacional* (1973), they imagine Argentina as a melting pot of different immigrant populations, and this mixture is interpreted as representing a national hybrid:

> Those who reject the European component should be reminded that each culture is hybrid and that the idea of something platonically American is ingenuous (Sábato 1973, 24–25);

and before:

> To deny the Argentineness (*argentinidad*) of tango is such a pathetically suicidal act as to abolish the existence of Buenos Aires, a quintessential hybrid city, typically breeding the immigrant alluvium in the mother earth who received him, and therefore painfully representative of the nation we now have. (Sábato 1973, 11–12; cited by Pantin Guerra 2007, 107–8)

Contrary to what we observe in Mexico, for example, Argentine miscegenation resulted from mixing peoples of different European origins, while Indigenous as well as black components of society were negated. This also contributed to invisibilization by colonial domination of the first inhabitants of this land. Buenos Aires and tango are therefore presented as emblematic of this "national" mixture process. The focus on the capital city in defining argentinidad and national identity is emblematic of a vision of this region as the central point of the entire land, regarding the rest of the country, the provinces, in a pejorative way as *el interior*, that is to say, as remote and sometimes wild regions that must be civilized. And even when we look deeply into these other areas where the Indigenous presence has always been important, we notice that their existence has been invisibilized and negated to the point that Lazzari (2009), for example, speaks of an Indigenous ghost (*indio fantasma*) that he defines as a "negative Other who is vanishing" to illustrate the actual situation of the Indigenous populations settled in the province of La Pampa. As with the tango, the Pampa can also be seen as a mythical reference to the Argentine national identity, as both are considered the core of Creole (criollo) and gaucho cultures. But even there, the Indigenes are mostly absent in the construction of a rural identity.

> Pampeanity (*la pampeanidad*) is defined as an original form of the national Creole. Creole suggests the native or the nativized, a fundamental element in any discourse on the nation. The Pampean Creole is represented in the figure of the gaucho and frontier soldier, first in his

victorious fight against the Indians, then in his noble withdrawal before the advance of the foreign or gringo pioneer. The Creole spirit embodied in the gaucho absorbs both the Indian and the gringo, the historic paradigms of indigeneity and civilization, respectively. When the historic substance of the Creole vanishes with the "disappearance" of the gaucho and the Indian, the Creole spirit is being reincarnated in a paradigmatic population: the creolized gringo immigrant. (Lazzari 2009, 10)

As Lazzari points out, and as I observed during my fieldwork in Patagonia, many euphemistic categories are used to speak of indigeneity in alternative ways. Instead of naming themselves "*indígenas*," "*indios*," or using the name of their nation (Mapuche, Ona, Wichí, etc.), Indigenes prefer to call themselves—and are called by "whites"—paisanos (peasants), *descendientes* (descendants, meaning "descendants of Indigenous people"), *pobladores* (settlers), and *puesteros* (habitants of a *puesto*, a very small ranch). Only rarely is the category of mestizo used to designate a mixed-blood person of Indigenous and criollo origins, but it would never be used in the common sense to denominate a criollo person descended from European immigrants. According to Briones, the "moral elites of Argentina have constructed the 'mestizo' as an undervalued category, a stigmatized mark always closer to the 'Indigenous' component than to the 'non-Indigenous element' taken as the metonymic operator of the 'typical Argentine' mark" (2002a, 69). This explanation makes clearer why the passionate plea for hybridism and mestizaje by Sábato sounded so provocative in 1973 after more than 150 years of nation-building.

Under the impetus of the Enlightenment philosophy, which inspired the creation of the new independent nation of Argentina in 1810, there was a strong willingness to integrate the Indians into the structures of the new state and to recognize them as free and equal citizens. As stated in the preamble of its constitution, Argentina is a land opened to "all men of the world who wish to dwell on Argentine soil," but only a few years after its foundation, privileged inhabitants were those coming from Europe, as specified in Chapter 1, Section 25 of the constitution of 1853: "The Federal Government shall foster European immigration." During the process of consolidation of the nation, the reference to heroic times was not taken from the Indigenous past, as it was in Mexico and Peru; thus, no reference to "national" Indigenes is made in the hymn *Marcha Patriótica* (*Patriotic March*), adopted during the time of independence (Briones 2004). The only reference to the Indigenous past is to the Inca: "The dead Incas' graves are shaken, and in their bones is restored the ardor which bestows upon the children of the Motherland the ancient splendor." I fully agree with Briones when she notes that

instead of mentioning local groups, a mark of distant and prestigious indigeneity is selected—the invoked "Inca"—to confine it to such a remote time that it has died, as the only thing this mark can do is be moved into their graves, while the patriots—its Creole "sons"—renew an already "ancient" splendor. (2004, 77)

Surely, the lack of culture similar to those of the Aztec, Maya, or Inca Empires, which can be highly regarded as other forms of "great civilizations," and the proximity of violent military conflicts opposing the new independent nation (and not the Spanish conquerors) by vivid Indigenes demonstrating no interest in being integrated into the national melting pot were elements contributing to the construction of discourses opposing "white civilization" against "Indian barbarism." The possible contagion of barbarism in the ideals and values of the new white nation made it unrealistic to tolerate interior borders in the federal territory and the autonomous development of separate Indigenous societies.

(Re)articulating Indigenous Communities and Identities

Mapuches nowadays are scattered among the Patagonian provinces of Neuquén, Río Negro, Chubut, and Santa Cruz, and in the provinces of La Pampa and Buenos Aires, while the largest part of this population lives on the other side of the Andes, in Chile. Despite their self-identification as the same Indigenous people, Mapuche societies on both sides of the Andes, as well as in different provinces in Argentina, have different social and communitarian organizational structures. Some small differences also exist in their language (Mapudungun), but we must consider that a substantial number of those who self-identify as Mapuche have nowadays lost their Indigenous language or are more fluent in Spanish than in Mapudungun. In Argentina, variations at the social and organizational levels are related to the federal political system and disparities in the regulation of Indigenous questions by the provinces in which Mapuche groups are situated (Briones 2005). Until the creation of the provinces on June 15, 1955, by Law 14.408, the Patagonian territories (Neuquén, Río Negro, Chubut, and Santa Cruz) were directly administrated by the federal state. The headmen of the remaining *lof* (communities) were obligated, by this time, to negotiate occupational land rights directly with the federal authorities in Buenos Aires, more than one thousand kilometers away from their settlements. After 1955, relations between the provinces and the Indigenous peoples gave evidence of new trends as each new entity created a new juridical and political framework. In the last forty years, Neuquén, for example, is illustrative of several examples of recognition of the Mapuche lof that are linked

to the provincial style of constructing hegemonies, consisting of the parallel operations of confrontation with the federal level (denounced for "centralism") and of the province's construction through political and development strategies of sociocultural integration, accompanied by a strong state welfarism. (Falaschi et al. 2005, 179)

This is the reason the province began recognizing eighteen "reservations" or "*agrupaciones*" ("groupings") in 1964, as the lof were called at that time, in Decree 737: "Land reserves for Indigenous groupings." Affirming "the historical importance of the Mapuche in the formation of the regional society and identity" (Briones and Díaz 1997, 16) permitted early recognition of the Indigenous presence in this province while others began taking the communities into account only later, as with Río Negro in 1980 and Chubut in 1990.

Over the years, and despite substantial migration from rural areas to urban areas, particularly to the city of Neuquén, the center of provincial support to the Mapuche remained concentrated in the communities, which increased through their recognition in several other provincial decrees, from eighteen in 1964 to thirty-eight in 1998.[7] The focus on communities defining indigeneity was supported by national context and by Federal Law 23.302. It applied, however, only to people who live within legally recognized communities, as suggested by the law's name: "Protection and support of Indigenous communities." As a consequence, they leave dispersed rural Mapuche settlers, as well as urban Mapuches, out of this definition of "mapucheness." This situation has tended to create the idea that the communities were the prototype of the "only authentic Mapuche lifestyle," as they were the only structure for which a particular legal framework existed.

The shaping of indigeneity through law has been called by Briones (2002a) the "legalization" of indigeniety (*la "juridización" de lo indígena*) and defined as the penetration of new dimensions or aspects of the "living world" into and for the legal system (Cohen and Arato 1992). In the case of Indigenous people, for example, this refers to "the processes that manage group membership, converting to a question of rights to be legally specified and specifiable" (Briones 2002a, 79).

The importance of the legal system in defining ethnic identity inspired French to develop her theoretical model of "legalizing identity" in which

there must first be a particular law that has come into existence for the purpose of protecting or regulating the rights of specific groups to maintain ethnoracial and cultural differences. (2009, 5)

For French, it is important to consider how:

the legalizing identity framework . . . influences officials responsible for the law and its interpretation, as well as those who disseminate it through political practice and organization. (2009, 12)

In Argentina, as a result of the legal recognition of indigeneity, and even if Law 23.302 came very slowly into force, many Indigenous communities appeared in the late 1980s, and their number increased even more after constitutional reform. The National Institute of Indigenous Affairs (Instituto Nacional de Asuntos Indígenas, INAI) runs the National Register of Indigenous Communities (Registro Nacional de Comunidades Indígenas, RENACI). This register allows communities to be recognized officially at the federal level even when local authorities are reluctant to do so.

In Patagonia, the process of rearticulation of Indigenous communities is particularly interesting since it strongly calls into question the idea that the Indians would have completely disappeared. Until about twenty-five years ago, the Argentine ethnic panorama could have given the impression that the goal of the Conquista was reached: "civilization" had gotten the upper hand on "barbarity." But, as noted before, in the mid-1980s this image changed, and the fact that the number of Indigenous communities has been increasing all over the country since then testifies to the determination of Indian populations to maintain their specific cultures, societies, and ways of life. If, during more than a century, they maintained their customs in a hidden way to outwardly comply with the state's ideology, since the federal and provincial states have recognized their existence, they are now on the political stage to reassert publicly their identity and to claim their rights. A large number of Indigenous communities (and sometimes entire peoples) have begun to re-emerge because the state now allows them to exist.

From Communities to Mapunkies: A Plea for an Identity Kaleidoscope

After the new federal constitution came into force in 1994, the next census, in 2001 (National Census on Population, Households and Settlements), took into account, for the first time, ethnic belonging based on self-identification. The results were surprising because they showed a strong presence of the Indigenous population throughout the whole federal territory as well as the public resurgence of people claiming to belong to Indigenous groups considered extinct for decades or even centuries, including the Huarpe, Ona, Charrúa, Quilmes, etc.

Before this survey, the Argentine state had renounced taking into account the ethnic variable in the general census and did not distinguish Indigenous people from the rest of the population. Only the censuses of 1869, 1895, and 1914, and the last census dedicated to the Indigenous population (Censo Indígena Nacional [Indigenous National Census, CIN]), conducted in 1966–1968 (Argentina. Ministerio del Interior 1966–1968), give information on Indigenes. The latter identified slightly fewer than 29,000 Mapuches in the Patagonian provinces, but these data were incomplete (Radovich and Balazote 1992, 164).

According to the 2001 census, in the Patagonian provinces of Neuquén, Río Negro, Chubut, and Santa Cruz, no fewer than 76,606 people claimed to be Mapuche. It is estimated that 71 percent of this population is settled in urban areas. Communities that are seen as embodying the archetypal essence of the Mapuche lifestyle make up only 60 percent of the Mapuche population in rural areas (13,195 individuals representing 17 percent of the total Mapuche population), with the remaining 40 percent of rural Mapuches dispersed throughout the territory (Argentina. Instituto Nacional de Estadística y Censos 2001). This last category of small goat and sheep breeders, who are not officially regrouped in communities, do not benefit from social and development projects directed by the state for Indigenous people nor do urban Mapuche populations, even though a large number of them are nowadays living in cities where they have created Indigenous associations that claim special social, political, cultural, and economic rights.

The urban associations of mainly young Mapuche people defining themselves as Mapurbe—urban Mapuche—started appearing after the nation's return to democracy in 1983. The young people who formed them are descended from rural populations, but their fathers and mothers migrated to the cities in 1950–1960, seeking work and better living conditions. In the movements for internationalization of Indigenous claims in the late 1980s, the Mapuche leaders contacted other Indigenous organizations and non-governmental organizations (NGOs). Some were able to get logistical, technical, and financial support from outside, and they became active in defense of Indigenous rights. These leaders can be defined as "cultural brokers" (Bierschenk et al. 2000), as they are Indigenous people who have acquired a detailed knowledge of the dominant "white" social and political system of the Argentine state, and they are therefore able to mediate the relationship between Indigenous societies and national or international organizations.

From the beginning, these urban organizations in Neuquén chose to work in strict collaboration with the rural population to legitimize their actions because the "true" Mapuches are located, in the eyes of the state—and in many cases for the NGOs as well—in the communities. To challenge the state, they assert the image of the community as the "only true" lifestyle of the Mapuches. In this way, they contribute to the construction of an idealized and romantic image of the community's everyday life presented as radically different from that of other small rural non-Indigenous stockbreeders. In doing so, the Mapuche organizations foster a discourse on the essentialization of Indigenous societies by the Argentine state since its creation.

As provinces establish their own Indigenous policies, there are important differences in the treatment of the Indigenous question around the country. Mapuche identity has been impacted by important variations inherent in local historical processes as well as in diverse provincial politics (Briones 2005). In Neuquén, a focus on indigeneity was already present in its first provincial constitution of 1957 (Article 239, Paragraph d): "The Indigenous reserves and concessions will be maintained and even enlarged. Technical and economic help will be provided to these groups so as to stimulate them to instruct themselves and to make rational use of the allocated lands to improve the living conditions of its settlers" (Varela 1981, 96). This legalization of indigeneity explains why this provincial government went on to create a large range of paternalistic and integrative sociocultural policies as well as development strategies and assistance measures addressed to Indigenous communities that would have an important impact on their social structures. Because of this, Neuquén would appear to be a province with an important Indigenous component while others that also count a significant Mapuche population, e.g., Río Negro and Chubut, started to legislate later and therefore appear "less Indigenous" than Neuquén. It is interesting to note that the agenda of one of the most important Indigenous organizations of Río Negro, the Consejo Asesor Indígena (Indigenous Assessment Council), guided its actions toward class-oriented politics that articulated Indigenous claims with those of peasants and small producers, describing "economic exploitation and political domination before cultural discrimination and oppression" (Briones 2002b, 105). Chubut was the last province to take the Indigenous question into account, as the first programs and laws were set up only in the 1990s.

To summarize, the Mapuche identity and the Wallmapu—the traditional territory—are marked by divisions between not only urban and rural dwellers but also provincial and federal governments that implement different public policies and consider ethnic claims based on their unique treatment of the Indigenous question. Nowadays, to affirm a Mapuche identity no longer refers to a unique, fixed, and timeless culture but to several characters that are flexible, changing, fluid, and highly dependent upon the contexts in which they have been shaped. Claims of Mapurbe that have been articulated since the beginning of the twenty-first century demonstrate that, despite the communal uprooting that affected this part of the Indigenous population in the twentieth century, the feeling of belonging to a particular culture is still very strong in the minds of many people. It is interesting to note that some of claims of groups of young Mapuches are very different from those we might expect from Indigenous people. For example, they express themselves through musical creations by retaking punk, heavy metal, and rap rhythms to express Mapuche identity in the music of the "Mapunkies" or "Mapuheavies" (Ferrari 2005; Kropff 2005).

Conclusion

In this historical and geographical examination of domination and Mapuche identity, I draw attention to the particular treatment of indigeneity in
Argentina in the absence of an ideology of mestizaje in this country.
Both assertions—"there are no Indians anymore in this country" and
"we, Argentines, came off the ships"—perfectly reflect the attitudes of
the country before new external politics and new international Indigenous rights movements, coupled with internal human rights movements
and Indigenous mobilizations, compelled the state to take multiculturalism into account. Because of negation of the autochthonous origins of
the country, processes of mestizaje made it de facto impossible to mingle
these populations with imported ones, who were therefore seen as forming the core of national identity.

> By saying that the "Argentine" emerged mainly as non-Indigenous and
> non-mestizo, we refer to the fact that the composite that would have
> resulted under the supervision of the moral elites in the local racial
> melting pot operated as a signifier of a silenced and pure whiteness. It
> is presumed that "we, Argentines, came off the ships" through West-
> ern European immigration at the end of the nineteenth century and
> beginning of the twentieth century—not by land, as do immigrants
> from neighboring countries, and not by plane, as most Asian and more
> recent immigrants from Western Europe do. This implies that mes-
> tizaje and national identity are mutually incompatible terms. (Briones
> 2002a, 71)

To survive the effects of the Conquista del Desierto, the Indigenous
people of Argentina had to conform to the state's liberal republican ideology and occlude their cultural differences. In contemporary times, however, addressing federal and provincial administrations, the Mapuche
people appear very modern and traditional at the same time. Their claims
in the name of indigeneity, and international regulations in this field,
give them the authority to speak and take part in political processes.
They are now active social subjects with political clout, sometimes addressing the state as the Mapuche Nation—with a huge traditional territory, the Wallmapu, which extends through part of Argentina and
Chile. New definitions of their culture have been elaborated, and nowadays they address claims of collective rights that accommodate their
social organization better than individual rights. At the same time,
however, colonial processes and power relations shaped this people in
very different ways in different local contexts. Even if the claims are often
made in the name of all the Mapuche people, we have to bear in mind
that the Mapuche identity comprises a wide range of sub-identities.

Acknowledgments

This research was realized partly through the support of the Swiss National Science Foundation.

Notes

1. For more information, see the blog of the march, http://marchanaciona lindigena.blogspot.com (accessed July 14, 2013) and the Mapuche journal *Azkintue* (no. 42 [May–June 2010]), http://www.azkintuwe.org/azkintuwe_42. pdf (accessed July 14, 2013).

2. All translations are mine.

3. More than a few sectors of the most important international organizations are involved in situations affecting Indigenous peoples: intercultural health care in the World Health Organization (WHO); conferences on the environment and biodiversity in UNESCO; traditional knowledge and traditional cultural expressions in the World Intellectual Property Organization (WIPO), etc.

4. Actual and past Mapuche populations are settled on both sides of the Andean Cordillera in territories that since the nineteenth century have been under Chilean administration on the west side and under Argentine administration on the east side. The fact that Mapuches have been dominated for more than a century by two different nation-states led to the strengthening of local particularities, making a unified analysis of the whole Mapuche people quite difficult to conduct (for some attempts, see Hernández 2003 and Ray 2007).

5. Extensive cattle-raising ranches—*latifundia*—are called *estancias*, and their owners are called estancieros in Argentina.

6. This campaign gave its name to the whole conquest of the Pampa and Patagonia (1875–1885), which is known as the Conquista del Desierto (Desert Conquest). The term "desert," which is very problematic, will be reconsidered later in this chapter.

7. Since the middle of the 1990s, other communities have formed. Many are not recognized by the provincial authorities, but rather by national authorities once their inscription in the National Register of Indigenous Communities is complete. For a detailed analysis of these strategies, see Kradolfer (2011).

CHAPTER TEN

Divine Design

Crafting and Consuming the Sacred in Afro-Brazilian Candomblé

ANGELA CASTAÑEDA

Scene One: The Encounter

In the summer of 2005, I found myself in the quiet resort town of Armação de Búzios—roughly one hundred miles northeast of Rio de Janeiro.
It is a beautiful space with breathtaking ocean views and picturesque
streets lined with restaurants and boutiques. The timing of my visit,
winter in Brazil, meant the streets, restaurants, and shops were mostly
empty, but for a handful of tourists. One night as I strolled down the
main *rua das pedras* (street of stones), the bright lights of small boutiques
casting a warm glow through their elaborate storefront windows, I was
glancing down periodically, careful not to lose my footing on the dark
cobblestone streets. Then, out of the corner of my eye, I saw it. I stopped
to peer more intently through the large display window and then quickly
made my way inside. There it was—an *orixá*, or its image, for sale.

Just as I was drawn to the rhythms of the *atabaques* (ritual drums)·
during my first fieldwork experience in a Candomblé house of worship in
São Paulo some ten years earlier, I felt captivated by the crafting of orixá
imagery. As the symbols drew me nearer, I felt heightened awareness of
my own multiple identities: Latina, anthropologist, consumer, and
tourist. With perspectives from each of these identities, I could see
these symbols not only reveal images of the divine but also offer em-

bodied interpretations of race and a window to the commercialization of Candomblé.

This chapter highlights the cultural complexities of commercialization, focusing on relationships we have with the world of things. It focuses on material culture by emphasizing the context of producers' everyday lives via empirically grounded ethnographic work that traces the importance of "possession" in both its sacred and secular interpretations. This chapter portrays globalization as a process still ongoing and draws attention to complex local responses. It addresses Deborah Kapchan's question, "How do aesthetic styles associated with the sacred inhabit new, nonsacred contexts, and what does this amalgam produce in the global circulation of meanings?" (2007, 2). I consider the role of *mestizaje*[1] as lived experience in the representation of Candomblé religious symbols.

My research is grounded in reflexivity and the importance of context and the ethnographer's voice in the research process. I am a Latina of Mexican ancestry raised in a middle-class Catholic family. I found the ritual and symbolism of Candomblé familiar and comfortable. During my fieldwork, I encountered Candomblé worshipers suspicious of my role as an anthropologist, but most often the reaction from locals was a sense of camaraderie with my Mexican heritage. I include the context for the "encounters" with Candomblé to emphasize the ways in which ethnographic objects are crafted by the ethnographer. As Barbara Kirshenblatt-Gimblett notes:

> Ethnographic objects are made, not found, despite claims to the contrary. They did not begin their lives as ethnographic objects. They became ethnographic through processes of detachment and contextualization. Whether in that process objects cease to be what they once were, is an open and important question. That question speaks to the relationship of source and destination, to the political economy of display. (1998, 3)

The concept of the political economy of display is tied to multiple notions of culture, which include "culture as lived practice, culture as heritage, and the culture industry" (Kirshenblatt-Gimblett 1998, 144). My research further explores the concept of the political economy of display and illustrates these three areas of culture by recognizing Candomblé as a lived practice in the bodily possession of its devotees, as heritage in its folk interpretation, and finally, as industry as it enters the global marketplace.

Scene Two: The Stage

The word Candomblé refers to a religious tradition of African origin established in Brazil. It reflects influences from a diverse range of communities. It is important to note that globalization has impacted and continues to impact Candomblé. Candomblé was born as a direct result of expanding capitalistic global economic systems, which brought slaves from Africa to Brazil. This led to confrontations between groups with distinct cultural and spiritual backgrounds: Portuguese colonists who were Catholics; slaves from areas, including Angola, Congo, Nigeria, and Benin, who brought multiple African-based belief systems; and Indigenous peoples. Ethnic groups representing Bantu, Yoruban, and Fon communities made especially important contributions to the religious beliefs and cultural practices in Brazil (Lopes 2004).

From their initial "discovery" of Brazil in 1500 until the abolition of slavery in 1888, Portuguese colonists worked to meet the global demand for sugarcane production by participation in the transatlantic slave trade. The majority of African slaves arrived at ports in northeastern Brazil, principally Salvador de Bahia, but the impact of the slave trade is evident throughout the country. Thus, Candomblé was established in Brazil as a direct result of the expansion of the global economy. It continues to adapt to global economic forces involved in the commercialization of its symbols.

Candomblé is ultimately a religion of survival. Enslaved Africans, dislocated from their homeland and stripped of their family ties, called upon their ancestral spirits to help maintain a sense of identity and cultivate a new religious family in the Americas. Once rooted in Brazil, Candomblé worship traveled with migrants from northeastern territories to southern industrial cities such as São Paulo and Rio de Janeiro. In these new urban environments, Candomblé once again fostered creation of a familiar space and "mutual aid society" (Murphy 1994). Joseph Murphy, religious scholar of the African diaspora, notes that the word Candomblé invokes many meanings in Brazil, citing its references to a religion, a space, a spirit, and a community. Those who participate in Candomblé help relocate the cultural, historical, and traditional ties that link Brazil to Africa (Murphy 1994).

In addition, the need for alternative spaces for black identity was met through participation in Candomblé, which brought together various African ethnic groups (Bantu, Yoruban, and Fon) and created a space where "the sense of African ethnic identity was both heightened and reconfigured toward a more pan-African meaning of being black in Brazil" (Harding 2000, 5). In this sense, mestizaje, in its most basic conceptualization as "mixing," is inherent in Candomblé's formation.

Mestizaje is often identified as a nation-building ideology, which makes it seem inclusive. Ronald Stutzman (1981) characterized mestizaje as an "all-inclusive ideology of exclusion." In Brazil we find the concept of mestizaje "connected historically to hegemonic constructions of Brazilianness" (Muteba Rahier 2003, 46). Recent scholarship has begun to challenge interpretations of mestizaje-ness as rooted in nation-building ideology. A focus on an embodied notion of the lived experience has been introduced as an alternative understanding of the concept. In particular, Peter Wade's work on Afro-Colombian communities (2005) deconstructs the use of mestizaje-ness as nation-building by emphasizing that mestizaje should be looked at as a lived process, focusing on how people deal with racial-cultural mixture on a daily basis. Ultimately, Wade proposes an image of mestizaje that includes

> a mosaic, made up of different elements and processes, which can be manifest within the body and the family, as well as the nation. Seen in this way, mestizaje has spaces for many different possible elements, including black and Indigenous ones, which are more than merely possible candidates for future mixture. (2005, 254)

Using a contemporary embodied interpretation of the mestizaje concept, we are able to identify different types of "knowledge" and make a shift from the ideological to embodied and performed culture. In Candomblé, this transfer of embodied knowledge takes place through the vital role of possession or spiritual communion with the orixá. Worship focuses on harnessing blessings, power, energy, or knowledge, also known as *axé*, from the orixá and establishing a mutual relationship between these spirits and the human experience through practices that include initiation, possession, and animal sacrifice. Maintaining a strong relationship with one's guardian orixá is an integral component of Candomblé worship and requires proper training and appreciation of the complexity of each orixá. Sheila Walker describes this relationship:

> Each Orisha[2] also has an energetic relationship with specific colors, foods, animals, minerals, and days of the week as well as with natural phenomena. Thus, in identifying one's guardian Orisha, and in knowing him or her increasingly well as a result of the progressive process of initiation, an individual learns how to relate properly to these elements and to harness their energy, their manifestations of the spiritual force of the Orishas, to direct one's life more successfully. (1990, 119)

Ossaim and Omolú are just two of many orixá I encountered doing research. The image of Ossaim on the bag in Armação de Búzios is the first of two examples I discuss here. Ossaim controls medicine with his expertise on plant and herbal remedies, and his colors are green and white. While each orixá has designated plants in its repertoire, only Ossaim is said to know all plants' secrets.

Omolú holds the earth as his natural element. His colors are black, white, and red, and he governs issues of health, illness, and disease. Omolú is always depicted covered in raffia to disguise his face and most of his body. His image is depicted in the handcrafted doll, the second example discussed here.

The crafting of the orixá images of Omolú and Ossaim in commercialized form demonstrates the multivocality of these Candomblé symbols.

It can be seen as a survival tactic in a globalized marketplace. From the very beginning of Candomblé worship in Brazil, the orixá and their followers have been forced to make changes and craft new interpretations of orixá worship to foster their own survival and that of their religion. This is most evident in the use of Catholic saints to mask orixá, leading to what some scholars refer to as syncretism. Today, for some Candomblé followers and admirers, the economic pull to secularize these deities is a product of the needs for financial survival and the continued development of a sacred belief system.

Today, evidence of Candomblé's presence is visible in many aspects of life in Brazil, but throughout much of the country's history, persecution and marginalization by state and Church authorities compelled secrecy. In the 1930s, state officials began to "reimagine" the Brazilian nation with an appreciation for its mixture of Indigenous, African, and European cultures, which led to a greater appreciation of not only Candomblé but also other Afro-Brazilian cultural practices such as samba and capoeira. Its public image continued to expand in the 1970s with the growth of the tourist industry in key Candomblé centers such as Bahia (Van de Port 2006). In Salvador de Bahia, "due to this new public role, candomblé has become a veritable 'symbol bank,' serving a highly diversified clientele . . . who have taken up candomblé symbols to communicate" (Van de Port 2007, 181). Walker (1990) also documents this new use of Candomblé symbols, noting that Afro-Brazilian culture is recognized worldwide in a predominantly folklorized and commercialized form.

I visited the Museu do Folclore Edison Carneiro (Folklore Museum) in Rio de Janeiro, where an entire section of the upper floor of the museum is dedicated to Candomblé. There, I found ritual objects, photographs of houses of worship, and mannequins adorned from head to toe in beautiful orixá ceremonial dress. All of this was presented with minimal lighting, which appeared to have been done purposefully to craft a more mysterious aura to Candomblé's mystique as an "other" and "exotic" form of Brazilian folklore.

Walker and Van de Port raise questions about the political implications of categorizing Candomblé as religion or as folklore. Katherine Hagedorn notes in her work on Cuban Santería that defining Candomblé as folklore is disempowering "because those religious traditions were categorized by nonpractitioners not as divinely potent modes of communication between deities and mortals, but rather as 'folk traditions,' objectified and reconstructed without consideration for their contemporary religious context" (2001, 4). Hagedorn identifies a historicized process she calls "folkloricization" in which "an inward-directed, noncommodified religious tradition becomes outward-directed, commodified, staged, and secularized" (2001, 9). As Candomblé symbols are commercially crafted, the process of recontextualizing continues, and it is further exaggerated when these material objects enter the global marketplace.

It is important to note that recontextualization and commercialization are not new challenges to Candomblé, but in their current form, they spark new interest as the boundaries of insider/outsider are increasingly expanded. In addition, any analysis of commercial exchange in orixá worship should take into consideration the transactions inherent in Candomblé, which include charging for rituals performed and the purchase of necessary articles (animals, cloth, candles, etc.) for rituals.

Scene Three: *Feito a Mão*[3]

Let's now return to the original "sighting" of that bag in Búzios. It was a white canvas tote bag with the image of Ossaim, orixá of the forest, plants, and herbs, outlined in gray on one side and his name on the other (fig. 10.1). It was adorned with thin silk ribbons of various green tones that dangled from one of the handles. Attached to the ribbons was a small tag with the designer's logo and price on one side and a brief explanation of the orixá's characteristics on the other. Having recovered from the initial shock of making this discovery, I was surprised again by the bag's price—150 reais,[4] or approximately 75 U.S. dollars! It was the last one left in the store.

What I found most interesting about this piece of material culture was the use of the orixá image and its corresponding characteristics or "powers" to market what was basically a simple canvas tote bag. The design of the bag included a key textual element—the description of the orixá—used to lend credibility to the mediated message. The tag also suggested that the target consumer audience would include individuals lacking the religious competence in Candomblé to fully appreciate the bag's imagery without the description. It also alluded to the space where the bag would be marketed, a setting void of religious context or explanation.

It was years after this initial encounter before I could reach the designer for an interview. A failed e-mail attempt followed by the discovery of an abandoned storefront on my second attempt led me to my third attempt in 2009, when I finally found myself sitting across from Priscilla,[5] the designer of the bag from Búzios. The sweet smell of freshly baked pastries and strong aromatic coffee swirled around us, accompanied by a symphony of sounds from the upscale café where we conducted the interview.

Priscilla arrived early. She was a very young woman with a slender build, blond hair, fair complexion, and bright blue eyes. Her English was impeccable, with just a slight hint of an accent. She proceeded to tell me her story. She was an upper-middle-class Brazilian with a degree in design from the Pontifical Catholic University of Rio de Janeiro (Pontifícia Universidade Católica do Rio de Janeiro, PUC–RIO), the pricey Catholic university in Rio. She had several internships at upscale boutiques in

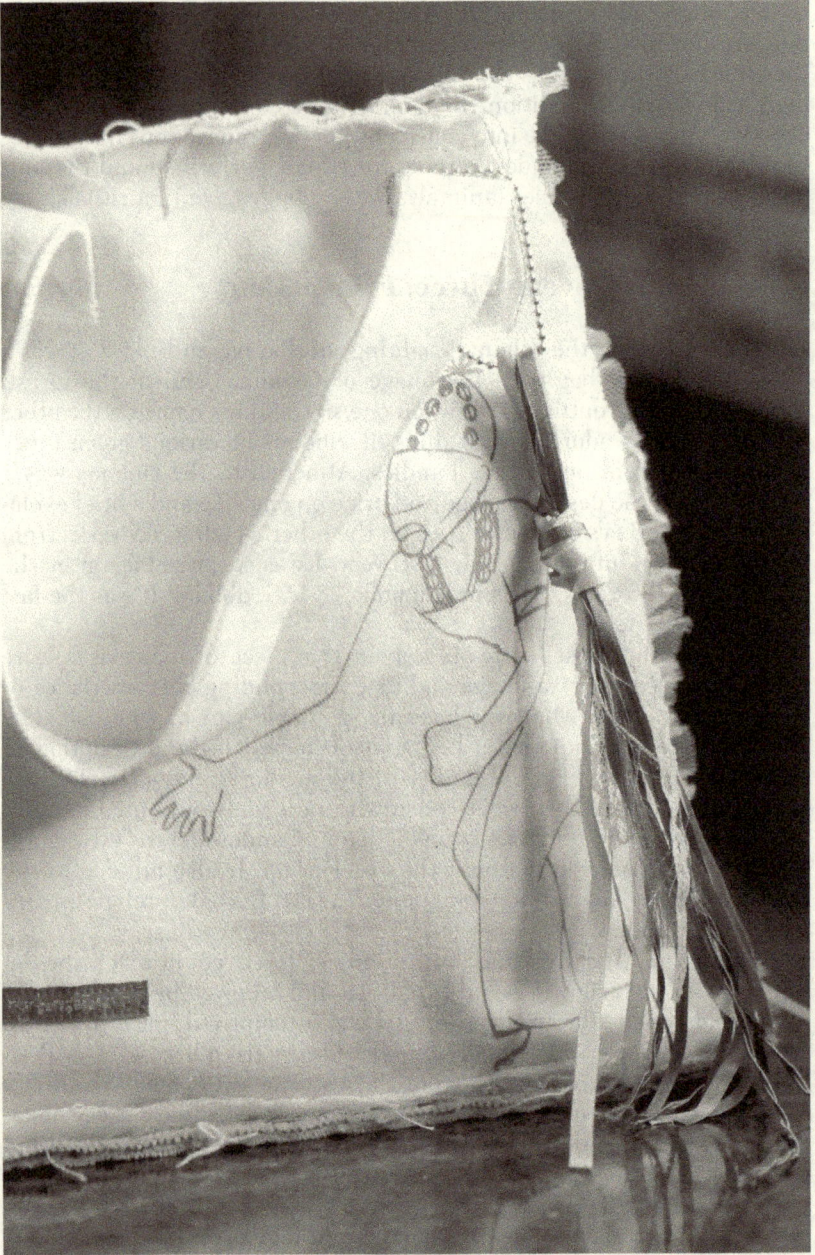

FIGURE 10.1. Canvas tote bag depicting Ossaim, a Candomblé spirit who controls medicine with plant and herbal remedies.

and around Rio. Then in 2002 her life changed. She was involved in a terrible car accident while traveling from Búzios to Rio, which left her hospitalized for months and using crutches for over a year. During her recovery, Priscilla was unable to return to her work as a design consultant in Rio, and it was during this period of reflection that she transformed her talent for marketing and design into a career selling designer handbags.

During our interview, Priscilla explained that she starts with an idea, concept, or design which she then captures in a model bag, in very rough form. She then passes models with instructions and drawings to her seamstress, who makes prototypes. With Priscilla's approval, she sends materials and information for the collection to be made at a factory in the interior of Rio.

While Priscilla admits to having no personal experience with the religion, she described being drawn to the orixá imagery through a friend who was involved in Candomblé worship. After deciding to use her friend's drawings of the orixá on her bags, Priscilla felt obligated to research each deity to provide what she termed was a "proper representation." Her research included asking for advice about and overall approval for each orixá bag she designed from friends who were Candomblé practitioners.

Priscilla made only a handful of bags representing each orixá and commented that the most popular design was of Iemanjá—the motherly figure and goddess of the ocean—the most widely worshipped deity in Rio de Janeiro. As to her clientele, Priscilla noted that consumers of her bags mostly include people who are attracted to the aesthetic and not those with any religious competency in Candomblé. This is what led Priscilla to place particular importance on the descriptive tag attached to each bag. This key component provides consumers with information on the orixá's characteristics that might entice consumers who want to harness that energy or feel an affiliation with that deity. Priscilla further contextualized the religious roots of her work by constructing a mini-altar to display her bags, complete with herbs, fruits, foods, and colors associated with each deity. This "folkloricization" further highlights how the sacred and secular merge in this form of material culture.

Another example of the commercialization of Candomblé is captured in beautifully handcrafted dolls. Adalena, a community activist and artist, crafts orixá from scraps of fabric. She shared her story with me during an interview conducted at her home and studio in the quiet neighborhood of Santa Teresa in Rio de Janeiro.

My journey to Adalena's home took me across town on bus, metro, and trolley rides until I finally arrived at the steep, cobblestoned street where she lived. There was a large metal door surrounded by a stone wall covered in velvety green moss. I used the buzzer to gain access and quickly stepped through the door looking for Casa 10. I found Adalena's home, her door wide open, soothing samba music playing inside and colorful

flags dancing in the breeze above her doorway—signaling the June celebration of the *festas juninhas*. Adalena welcomed me into her home. A
strong-looking woman in her early sixties, she had tightly curled hair
peppered with gray; soft, light brown skin; and bright green eyes. I commented on the beautiful view of the Corcovado, Rio's famous Christ
statue, from her balcony, and Adalena smiled in agreement. But she
quickly made mention that everything is not as peaceful as it seems, as
she pointed to the three favelas (slums) also in view.

Adalena's story begins with her childhood. She described vivid memories of her mother working long hours as a seamstress. With little extra
money for toys, her mother would use scraps of fabric to make dolls for
Adalena. These dolls—lovingly crafted by her mother's hands without glue
or stitches, each knot representing the love and dreams she had for her
daughter—fostered Adalena's creativity and imagination.

In the 1990s, Adalena harnessed her creativity and founded a cooperative with the goal of supporting women artists, celebrating Afro-Brazilian
culture, and bridging popular culture with education by working in some
of Rio's poorest favelas. The cooperative focused on fabricating faceless
black dolls just as Lena's mother had done, without any glue or stitches
(fig. 10.2). Adalena describes her work as creating a visual language in the
dolls based on faith and the power of images such as those of the orixá
deities. Adalena, a Candomblé follower, says that each doll speaks to people independently but that they all transmit "something," and what that
might be depends on each consumer.

Adalena explains that some people buy the orixá dolls because they
"know" about the religion and others buy them just for their aesthetic appeal. Adalena notes that Omolú, for example, is popular with tourists who
are attracted to its "primitive" visual aesthetic, but she believes something
more is transmitted in the exchange. While what is being transmitted var-
ies for each person, Adalena firmly believes that the process of handcraft-
ing each doll creates a transfer from the artist to the doll and ultimately to
the consumer. Adalena spends precious time crafting each doll lovingly
with her own hands—transferring her thoughts, hopes, dreams, and intentions to the doll. The power for this transmission is found in symbolic
elements—poses, colors, and shapes—of each handmade doll. Adalena
hopes these will cause consumers to appreciate and reflect on what each
doll represents, thus further reinforcing this creative process.

Like Priscilla, Adalena is also concerned with the art of displaying
her work. However, she adamantly disagrees with the use of her dolls as
fetishes for bringing good luck or harnessing axé. She recalled one instance where she demanded that her dolls be moved away from other
"good luck" objects for sale at a local artisanal shop. Adalena believes
that crafting these orixá does not interfere with Candomblé worship.
She believes that people are eager to recover it from its secretive past and
that she is furthering its legitimization through the creation of her dolls.

FIGURE 10.2. Handcrafted doll depicting Omolú, the Candomblé spiritual entity governing health, illness, and disease.

These two examples provide us with a window into the processes of production and consumption of material culture. At first glance, we find women entrepreneurs with creative and artistic talents who recognize the value of symbolic meaning when marketing their products. However, the differences in their lived experiences form part of the material culture they create. Priscilla's private-school training and readily apparent European ancestry contrast with Adalena's humble upbringing and Afro-Brazilian heritage. These marked differences in lived experience and different levels of religious engagement with Candomblé characterize the racial-cultural mixture that ultimately influences each woman's artistic process and product.

Scene Four: No Gift Wrap Necessary

Globalization includes the ebbs and flows of exchange of spiritual elements. "Religion is a lens—a privileged one at that—for getting at the globalizing late capitalist world's intersections of power, money, cultural practices and repertoires" (Gálvez 2007, 6). Globalizing forces the recontextualization of Candomblé symbols. From the very beginning, newly arrived African slaves were forced to meld their spiritual deities with Catholic saints in an attempt to survive.

This process of mixing and mestizaje-ness continues as Candomblé symbols are reconfigured on a global stage for consumption. How is the intended meaning behind the use of these orixá interpreted? Can the product's meaning be subverted or resisted by consumers? Or does there have to be some basic "system of recognition" (Jackson 1999) or shared meaning? Jackson writes, "The intentionality of the producer can often only be inferred, and consumer creativity is such that a product's range of meanings will always exceed the attempt to impose a single reading" (1999, 105).

Erik Cohen (1989) asks us to consider the "source of initiative" for commercialization. He identifies two forms of initiative: spontaneous and sponsored. The main difference is found in insider/local versus outsider/external status. In the examples here, Candomblé competency and membership are the guiding factors in defining insider or outsider status. While both Priscilla and Adalena are insiders as Brazilians brought together under the nation-building concept of mestizaje-ness, their lived experiences and embodied practices, particularly with Candomblé, mark Adalena as an insider and Priscilla as an external agent using the orixá for purely commercial reasons.

The two examples of Candomblé used here also represent past and present forms of the political economy of display. Priscilla's bags extract Candomblé symbolism from its context of origin and carry a neatly summarized description reminiscent of a museum tag, which adds a look of authenticity to each piece. This stands in contrast to Adalena's dolls, which represent an assertion of her own political identity as an Afro-Brazilian and Candomblé worshipper. The differences illustrated by these examples suggest a possible change in the political economy of display. Display once sought to emphasize the exotic-ness of "others," with little to no response expected from their communities. Today, these communities have a voice in this representation, which means having to decide about their own participation in the politics of display. Indeed, Adalena reflects this lived experience. Her participation as an orixá worshiper on both sacred and secular levels marks her attempt to maintain control over the commercialization process. In fact, Adalena consciously chooses to limit any deliberate interpretation of Candomblé meaning on her part as the producer, instead leaving this translation in the hands of the consumer.

The politics of representation are evident in Adalena's work, which is grounded in deeper political and educational objectives. Adalena seeks to empower Afro-Brazilians, while Priscilla's bags reflect a superficial attempt at educating others about something she has limited knowledge of and experience with. Adalena explained that she initially began making dolls with children in the favelas, or shantytowns, near her neighborhood as part of an effort to bridge popular culture and education. In this way, Adalena worked to provide positive images of Afro-Brazilians in the form of dolls. Her dolls are made with very basic black material, with no eyes or mouth. This is to encourage the imagination of each child or consumer, specifically so that the children might see themselves reflected in the dolls. Adelena referred to this time in her life as a rebirth of her own, more politically motivated, Afro-Brazilian identity.

Robin Sheriff's work on the construction of mestizaje-ness in Rio de Janeiro (2001, 2003) provides rich ethnographic detail on how poor Brazilians of color assert their membership in the *raça negra*. Adelena uses her self-identification with the raça negra in an attempt to reappropriate this negative term, and she emphasizes this pride in her African heritage by crafting the Candomblé orixá dolls. Their distinct *tipos* (characteristics) mark the raça negra, and they are symbols of Brazilian national folklore.

The end result of my encounters with both the bags and dolls described here was their purchase and subsequent placement in my black carry-on bag (which was, coincidentally, lined with material stamped "smuggler"). I was reminded of my role in this process, in the commercialization of Candomblé, and I reflected on my participation in this chain of events linked by transfers of money and control.

"Religious practices in candomblé have always privileged the human body as the prime site of . . . the appearance of the sacred" (Van de Port 2006, 445). The ultimate form of communion with an orixá is spirit possession, where one embodies the spirit, offering their own body to be used as a vessel for spirit manifestation. The verb "to possess" can be used in two ways. A spirit may possess another, or an exchange may result in possession of an object. "Possession implies not a lack of control, but a transfer of control to another entity" (Kapchan 2007, 60). Utilizing this dual application of "possession" enables us to recognize the multivocality of Candomblé symbols. There are multiple ways of knowing embodied in them, just as a contemporary, embodied interpretation of mestizaje includes both embodied and performed culture. What, exactly, is being exchanged?

Commercialization is a multilayered process that is closely intertwined with the lived experience of both producers and consumers. Emphasis on lived experience also illustrates multivocality and the politics of representation found in Candomblé, as well as the complex ways in which racial identity is constructed.

More reflection is needed on the continuum of mestizaje-ness as lived experience and its connections to the flow of culture that is both material and spiritual, from production to consumption. The items of material culture turned ethnographic fragments discussed here are now found occupying bookshelves in my living room. Kirshenblatt-Gimblett notes that "like the ruin, the ethnographic fragment is informed by a poetics of detachment" (1998, 18). In my possession, these ethnographic fragments prove I was "there" and bridge "the mundane, ordinary and profane bounds of home, and the extraordinary 'sacred' places and 'other' times associated with [my] travels" (Swanson and Dallen 2012, 492). At the same time, they add another "link to the commodification chain" (Hagedorn 2001, 226). Perched high above and out of reach of curious hands, these orixá once worshipped for their power to possess others have now themselves become mere possessions. In essence, these craftings of Candomblé symbols are a continuation of the possession at the heart of orixá worship. Commercial possession, rather than bodily possession, is a vehicle for communication shared with a larger community, simultaneously secular, sacred, and global.

Acknowledgments

This research was supported by professional development funds from DePauw University.

Notes

1. In Portuguese the word is *mestiçagem*.
2. Alternative spellings for orixá include *orisha* and *orisa*.
3. Handmade.
4. All monetary conversions are based on an approximate exchange rate of two reais to one U.S. dollar.
5. Names have been changed to protect the identities of those involved with this study.

CHAPTER ELEVEN

Women's Roles and Responses to Globalization in Ngäbe Communities

PHILIP D. YOUNG

Introduction

In this chapter, I discuss four major variables that have contributed to significant changes in the roles of Ngäbe women and their relationships to men since the 1960s: religion, wage labor, education, and development projects. Given my research experience and my relationships with Ngäbe people, here I examine and understand women's roles in their relationships with men as they have changed in contexts related to globalization.[1] In 1964, I observed that women seemed to be passive observers of male decision-making in the public arena. Less than fifty years later, in 2011, Silvia Carrera, a forty-two-year-old single mother, was elected as the first female general *cacica* (chief) of the Ngäbe-Buglé Comarca since its establishment in March 1997.

I conducted doctoral dissertation research among the Ngäbe in Chiriquí Province in 1964–1965 (P. Young 1968) and have returned for research visits many times since. My network analysis of data on 254 marriages spanning four generations collected in 1965 showed how these marriages linked kin groups in different communities. These data served as the basis for my generalizations about exchange marriage, polygyny, and postmarital residence (P. Young 1971, chaps. 5, 7). Qualitative data based on conversations with both women and men during subsequent visits provide

193

the basis for assessing changes in women's roles, as well as the major factors influencing these changes. Women and men with whom I spoke from the 1960s into the present ranged in age from teenagers to elderly adults in their seventies and older. In the 1960s, I needed the permission of male kin to address women directly. This is no longer the case. By now I have known some individuals since they were infants and have elicited their views on many occasions over the years.

In addition to my own work, I have consulted Marianella Martinelli's report on Ngäbe women (1994), done as part of the Ngöbe Agroforestry Project (Proyecto Agroforestal Ngöbe, PAN) sponsored by the German Development Agency (Deutsche Gesellschaft für Technische Zusammenarbeit, GTZ). Martinelli spent one month collecting interview data in four Ngäbe communities, all four of which are now within the boundaries of the comarca.[2] I have spent time in three of these communities. Martinelli and I differ on some points. This is not surprising because we visited these communities at different periods of time. It appears that Martinelli accepted at face value everything that all of her interviewees said. This has led to what I consider some questionable interpretations. However, in a positive sense, the statements of Martinelli's collaborators present a wide range of views and thus display both the variation and the complexity of the changing roles of women in Ngäbe society.

Corroboration on some points has been provided by anthropologist John Bort, who has also worked with the Ngäbe for many years. He and I have conducted most of our research among the Ngäbe in the Nidrini region of the comarca, formerly a part of Chiriquí Province. Additional comments on the status of Ngäbe women have been provided by Lucia Lasso, Andrea Martinsen, and Bethany Ojalehto. All three have worked in Ngäbe communities in the Ñö Kribo region, formerly a part of Bocas del Toro Province. I suggest that the observations and interpretations in this chapter apply in considerable measure to Ngäbe in all three regions of the comarca: Kädriri (formerly part of Veraguas), Nidrini, and Ñö Kribo.

Background

The Ngäbe are the largest Indigenous group in Panama, in 2010 numbering over 260,000. About 140,000 Ngäbe (54 percent of the total), as well as 9,178 Buglé, live within the Ngäbe-Buglé Comarca (Republic of Panama 2010).[3] The comarca was established by Law 10 of March 7, 1997, and the *carta orgánica* (administrative charter) was approved by Executive Decree 194 of August 25, 1999 (Coordinadora Nacional de Pastoral Indígena et al. 2003). The comarca is a contiguous area of about 2,500 square miles (6,500 square kilometers) carved from the provinces of Bocas del Toro, Chiriquí, and Veraguas. Most Ngäbe communities (*caserios*) are small hamlets rather than towns and are highly dispersed throughout the territory. Dispersal coupled with the greater isolation and remoteness of some communities has had a noticeable impact on rates and acceptance of change. The Ngäbe population has increased over seven-fold from 35,867 in 1960 to 260,058 in 2010 (Republic of Panama 1960, 2010). Several thousand Ngäbe have migrated permanently to the towns and cities of Chiriquí and Bocas del Toro Provinces, and a few thousand to other locations in Panama.

During the period from the 1960s to the present, the Ngäbe have been subjected to increased pressures from external social, political, economic, and developmental forces. In the 1960s, Ngäbe who left their traditional territory soon identified as mestizos, a necessary coping strategy at the time, but over time, most have come to reject *mestizaje* and continue to identify as Ngäbe. Gender roles change in tandem as both women and men respond to the impact on Ngäbe society and culture as a whole of the changing and accelerating contact with the outside world, that is, the complexly interrelated set of processes referred to as globalization (see introduction in this volume).

Gender Roles and Division of Labor in the 1960s

A summary of the way things were in the 1960s (see P. Young 1971) will set the scene for a discussion of changes that have taken place since that time in gender relations and women's roles. In the 1960s, the Ngäbe conformed to the pattern of other Central American subsistence-based Indigenous groups who practiced slash-and-burn agriculture. That is, both men and women traditionally performed necessary agricultural tasks, but there was a sexual division of labor, the norm in subsistence-based, nonindustrial societies. Women's tasks in the 1960s can be described as different from those of men, but equally important. The complementarity between women's and men's tasks was necessary for survival. Necessity can motivate the division of tasks and in turn shape cultural values and ideals about what should be women's work and what should be men's. For the Ngäbe in the 1960s, ideals occasionally gave way to needs; today, this is more frequently the case (see below).

Ngäbe men cleared land of trees and brush and burned the slash. Men and women participated equally in planting. Weeding the fields was predominantly men's work, but women helped when there was a pressing need to complete the task rapidly and it was not possible to organize a cooperative labor force of male kinsmen. During major harvest periods, women did slightly more harvesting than men, but men also participated frequently. Harvesting of bananas, plantains, root crops, squashes, and new corn on a day-to-day basis was almost exclusively women's work. Men occasionally brought back to the house a stem of green bananas or a few tubers to replenish the larder, if they passed by their fields on the way home and were not otherwise burdened with firewood or game from a successful hunt. In general, this division of labor is still perceived as the way things ought to be.

However, even in the 1960s, women were becoming increasingly responsible for more aspects of agricultural production. I attributed this shift to an increase in cattle raising and the gradually increasing need for wage labor to meet household needs, both of which placed additional heavy demands on men's time. In the 1960s, it was already evident as well that the rapid increase in the Ngäbe population had resulted in a scarcity of suitable agricultural land and yields were declining due to the need to shorten the fallow intervals before replanting fields.

Domestic tasks were divided, some being considered exclusively the domain of women and others of men. Ideals do not always match realities, and expediency frequently blurs the boundaries. Thus, one sometimes found men building a fire, cooking, sweeping the house, and caring for children, normally the tasks of women. When necessary, women performed some of the tasks of men, such as chopping firewood, sharpening machetes, and weeding fields. Both men and women fished. Women, however, with very rare exceptions, never hunted, cleared forest, or cared for cattle. Women did (and still do) own cattle, but these were cared for by husbands, fathers, or brothers. People did not necessarily enjoy performing tasks that were culturally assigned to the opposite sex and often complained. Very young boys imitated work tasks of men, and girls imitated women (and both genders still do).

Children gradually became full participants in adult labor, but there was no specific age at which this occurred. They normally began to assist their parents with adult tasks at the age of about eight, sometimes earlier. Girls cared for younger siblings, including infants, from a very young age (sometimes as young as four or five, based on my observations).

At first menses, girls went through a four-day ritual, nearly universal in the 1960s and still common today, the main purpose of which was instruction by elder women in proper behavior and demeanor toward others, especially men, and household duties and responsibilities. A traditional ritual for boys that represented their passage into full adulthood at about age fifteen with the assumption of full male duties and responsibilities was no longer practiced in the region in which I was conducting research in 1964–1965. By that time, wage work of a few weeks or months on farms and plantations outside the Ngäbe territory appeared to be serving as the functional equivalent of the traditional initiation into full adulthood, which included the right to marry.

Marriage in Ngäbe society was not simply the union of man and woman; it was also the basis of alliance between kin groups. In the 1960s, exchange marriages between kin groups were still very common, as was polygyny. Child betrothal, while still practiced, was rare. Exchange marriages in the 1960s were considered the ideal. They were described by men as an exchange of sisters, but structurally they involved symmetrical exchange of women and men between two kin groups. In 1965, exchange marriages made up 42 percent of a sample of 254 marriages spanning four generations, and there was no significant difference in frequency between generations. Fathers, with some input from mothers, made the arrangements for their sons and daughters. Even then, some young people resisted arranged marriages. Elopements did occur, and elders lamented that the younger generation did not respect the old customs. Marital histories of 121 men spanning three generations yielded a frequency of polygyny of 59.5 percent.[4] Traditional marriage customs were still alive and well in the 1960s despite the contrary perceptions of the elder generation (P. Young 1971, 185ff.).

Post-marital residence was ideally virilocal, that is, residence with the husband's kin.[5] In 1965, out of a sample of 242 married women spanning four generations, 51 percent were residing virilocally. Bilocality, shifting residence between the husband's kin group and the wife's, a frequent choice during the early years of marriage that usually shifted later on to virilocality, accounted for an additional 26 percent.[6] Post-marital residence isolated a great many women to varying degrees (depending on distance) from their consanguineal kin.

In terms of decision-making at the household level and beyond, women were clearly subordinate. In public discussions and decision-making, whether at the kin-group or community level (often the same thing, as many communities consisted of single kin groups of males and in-married females), or the inter-community level, women rarely spoke. When this did happen, only elderly, highly respected women spoke. Men dominated the public sphere and women were relegated to the domestic sphere. However, men acknowledged privately that their own publicly expressed views were often influenced by household conversations with the women in their lives—mothers, wives, elder sisters, adult daughters.

In the mid-1960s, very few schools existed within the Ngäbe territory, and most of these were primary schools offering only three grades. In 1965, I was told that there were only twelve schools in Ngäbe territory in Chiriquí Province and that only four of these schools were functioning. Girls were rarely sent to school. Most fathers did not believe their daughters needed any formal schooling. Boys were often sent to live with Latino[7] families in the Panamanian towns surrounding the Ngäbe territory with the expectation that in exchange for household work they would be sent to school. These expectations were not always fulfilled. In the mid-1960s, there were no development projects sponsored by agencies of the Panamanian government or any international organizations.

I conducted all of the above research within the context of an autochthonous religious movement (see below) which was at its height of popularity in 1964–1965. It spawned political activity that eventually became more important for the Ngäbe in achieving some of their goals than the religious movement itself.

Since the 1960s, numerous changes have precipitated adaptation in Ngäbe women's lives. I believe four changes have been the most significant: the Mama Chi religion;[8] increasing dependence on wage labor in a changing market (P. Young and Bort 1999, 125–26); educational opportunities (P. Young and Bort 1999, 130–31); and development projects.

Mama Chi Religious Movement

The religion of Mama Chi (Little Mother), also called the religion of Mama Tada (Mother Father, referring to the Virgin Mary and Jesus), began with the appearance of heavenly Christian personalities to a young Ngäbe woman in September of either 1961 or 1962.[9] This religion-based social movement was both revitalistic and transformative. It represented simultaneously a rebellion against problems thought to result from increasing contact with the Latino world and against certain traditional rituals and customs, including male domination and abusive treatment of women by some men. How widespread the latter was before Mama Chi is unknown. The fact that Mama Chi admonished men to cease abuse of wives and daughters is a clear indication that such abuse was occurring, but no data exist that give any indication of how frequent or widespread it was. This religious movement initiated and stimulated over a period of years a reorientation of attitudes and practices that have significantly altered the lives of Ngäbe women.

During my stay in the field in 1964–1965, I saw little evidence of physical abuse of women or children, but the possibility exists that such abuse was at an extremely low point precisely because of the teachings of Mama Chi. She prohibited the consumption of alcohol and the main traditional rituals at which strong alcoholic beverages were consumed—*balsería* and *chichería*—and this prohibition was observed by almost everyone. This is significant because Martinelli (1994) noted that most reported incidents of abuse among women in her four sample communities were related to alcohol consumption. My own data confirm this. (Martinelli also comments that physical abuse of women by men is higher in the Panamanian population than among the Ngäbe.)

It is reasonable to conclude that the Mama Chi religion did improve the situation of women by reducing the frequency of physical abuse before it gradually lost its force as a major driver of social transformation. There is no evidence that the movement engendered any significant changes in the traditional division of labor or in the incidence of arranged marriages and polygyny. What the Mama Chi movement did accomplish, however, had important consequences for the future course of events that have impacted Ngäbe women's roles.

The movement had at least four positive outcomes (P. Young 1976, 1978). First, there developed a new vision of solidarity as a people, a sense of ethnic pride, and a rejection of derogatory stereotypes held by Panamanians of them, their language, and their culture. This sense of ethnic identity was further strengthened with the establishment of the comarca in 1997.

Second, while at first many parents adhered to Mama Chi's order that children not be sent to the Panamanian schools, somewhat paradoxically there emerged among many of Mama Chi's followers a heightened awareness of the positive value of formal education, especially literacy in Spanish, as a powerful means of defending their interests in dealing with government agencies, as well as outside institutions and Panamanians in general.[10] This led to increased attendance at schools within Ngäbe territory.

Third, the Ngäbe came to see more clearly the extent of their dependence on the cash economy of the outside world and began experimenting with alternative means of engaging with the cash economy. These alternatives included an increase in small-scale entrepreneurship and experimentation with cooperative ventures (Bort 1976; P. Young and Bort 1999). Knowledge gained served as a precursor to the later formation of women's organizations, which were also helped along by development projects.

Fourth, intensified political activism developed as an offshoot of the religious movement. The resulting process of politicization led to recognition "of the possibilities of using political means to achieve socioeconomic ends" (P. Young and Bort 1999, 118). After three decades of political action, in March 1997, the Ngäbe and neighboring Buglé finally received legal recognition of much—but not all—of their traditional homeland as the Ngäbe-Buglé Comarca.

What I did not recognize at the time is that the Mama Chi movement also served as the foundation for improving women's lives, a process that is still ongoing and incomplete. The Mama Chi religion was not the singular cause of this process. In historical perspective, numerous factors contribute to such processes. The religious movement itself was a reaction to a number of events over the course of time that did not sit well with the Ngäbe, including social, economic, and political oppression from the outside and, from the inside, the failure of some traditional practices to cope with the altered cultural milieu. It also set in motion a re-thinking of the role and value of women that has continued as the Ngäbe confront and attempt to adjust to the intrusive impacts of the late twentieth- and early twenty-first-century wave of globalization. Paradoxically, many women and girls of the post-1970s generations know little or nothing of Mama Chi herself and her early influence on the beginnings of greater independence and better treatment of women, although they may know something of the religion in Ngäbe communities where it is still active.

Increasing Dependence on Wage Labor in a Changing Market

For many decades the Ngäbe economy had been predominantly subsistence based. By the 1960s, it was clearly in the midst of a substantial shift from a still-heavy reliance on subsistence agriculture and animal husbandry, supplemented by hunting, fishing, and gathering, to increasing reliance on wage labor to provide the cash necessary to purchase manufactured goods and some foodstuffs. Population growth was seriously straining the available land base, creating a situation in which fallow cycles were shortened, precipitating a decline in yields. Outside goods, once considered desirable luxuries, such as radios, sugar, kerosene, flashlights, and aluminum cooking pots, had come to be seen as necessities. In the 1960s, permanent out-migration to the towns and cities of greater Panama increased, as did some emigration to Costa Rica.

With the shift to increasing wage labor, many men were away from home for long stretches of time, from several weeks to several months. Lacking sufficient help from close male kin, women had to assume a greater share of agricultural labor. This led to more control over the disposition of household resources. This was important in that it gave many women new decision-making experiences. In the 1980s, as the labor market became increasingly saturated in Panama, Ngäbe participation in the coffee harvest in Costa Rica increased. Often entire families traveled to Costa Rica for the coffee harvest. This has continued to the present. Coffee harvesting is paid according to the quantity individuals pick, and some women earn more than men at this endeavor, perhaps because of more precise manual dexterity developed over the course of years of making net bags (John R. Bort, personal communications, April, May, and June 2009). Increased exposure to the outside world and cash income, coupled with education and the resulting Spanish-language ability (see below), have broadened women's horizons, given them a greater sense of security and independence, and have thereby lessened the extent to which they are willing or obliged to submit to domination by men.

In the 1980s, the labor market shifted to predominantly short-term and contract work. In the 2000s, it has shifted back to considerable long-term employment, and while some men take their families with them (where permitted), others leave their families in the comarca. Once again, women exercise greater household responsibilities and bear a heavier work burden. Improved transportation both within and outside the comarca has made it possible for those engaged in long-term stints of wage labor to visit their families more often, at least for short visits. While this may keep the social linkages stronger than in the past, it does not necessarily relieve the burden on women.

An ongoing government program, the Red de Oportunidades (Network of Opportunities),[11] administered by the Ministry for Social Development (Ministerio de Desarrollo Social, MIDES), began in 2006 to provide Ngäbe women who have children with vouchers worth $35 per month (distributed bimonthly) for the purchase of basic foodstuffs. In 2010, this was increased to $50 per month. This has helped to alleviate poverty resulting from overpopulation, land scarcity, and long absences of men (not all of whom are faithful about sending money home), who can no longer assist women in producing enough subsistence crops to feed their families adequately. The vouchers are provided directly to women, enhancing their control over household resources. The vouchers can only be exchanged for basic staple foodstuffs and soap, and purchases must be made at stores within the comarca that have been certified by the program. This has led to a proliferation of small stores, both co-op and family owned, within the comarca.

Education

As the number of schools within the Ngäbe territory gradually increased from the 1970s on, more parents began to send their daughters as well as their sons to school. The substantial increase in schools made education the most important of the forces driving changes in women's roles and gender relations, and remarkably, it occurred within a single generation. In the 1960s, Ngäbe girls rarely received any formal education at all, and even moderate fluency in Spanish was exceedingly unusual among women. In the mid-1970s, during the course of the first substantial development project for the Ngäbe—Plan Guaymí—it was still difficult to find even a few women in Chiriquí and Veraguas Provinces who were sufficiently literate in Spanish to qualify for project training programs. By the 1980s, the Panamanian Ministry of Education had increased the number of schools in Ngäbe communities, but almost all were still primary schools offering only three to six grades.[12] By the turn of the twenty-first century, the number of primary schools had further increased, and now there are several secondary schools within the comarca. Dropout rates are still high across the board, but greater convenience of schools and a change in attitude among some fathers about the value of education—or at least the value of being able to speak Spanish—for daughters have resulted in more girls receiving at least some primary education. Currently, there are some women with secondary education (and the number is increasing) and a few with college degrees (Andrea Martinsen, personal communication, December 2010).

In the social learning that takes place through formal education, Ngäbe do not learn about the history, values, ideals, and customs of their own culture (the Ngäbe model), but about those of the Hispanic-mestizo Panamanian culture (the Latino model), standardized and, of course, partly mythologized. This is an experience common to Indigenous peoples in the Americas and, more generally, in colonial settings worldwide. At home they learn their own history, values, and customs. The disparity between two sets of values and customary practices results in cognitive conflict, which is resolved in three different ways, from least to most common:

- wholesale acceptance of the Latino model and rejection of the Ngäbe model—uncommon within the comarca but formerly common among those who permanently out-migrated prior to the 1990s: classic mestizaje;
- wholesale rejection of the Latino model—very uncommon, particularly among younger women within the comarca and permanent out-migrants;
- acceptance of selected features of the Latino model but continued adherence to many features of the Ngäbe model and continued self-identification as Ngäbe—most common among both women and men, both within the comarca and among out-migrants since the late 1990s.

Exposure to Latino social and moral ideals taught in school has altered attitudes toward polygyny and arranged marriages, especially among women. Women with some formal education resist entering into polygynous relationships or marriages arranged by their parents and are inclined to demand greater respect from their spouses. As with past innovations, over the course of two or three generations, as those with living memory of the differences pass on, features which originate externally come to be seen as part of Ngäbe tradition.[13] Currently, the traditional Ngäbe ideal of polygyny is giving way to monogamy—perhaps better described as serial polygamy because both many men and many women have a series of partners. Arranged marriage is rapidly giving way to choosing one's own spouse. (As noted above, even in the 1960s, there was already some resistance by young adults of both sexes to arranged marriages.) Like women, many young men are not enthusiastic about arranged marriages, but they continue to favor polygyny. Although analytically (or etically) these changes can be viewed as part of a process of becoming culturally more mestizo, it is important to emphasize that these changes in attitudes toward traditional marriage practices are not seen by the majority of younger Ngäbe as diminishing their cultural identity and causing them to become more mestizo. Ngäbe in their late forties and older, mostly men, often do lament the greatly reduced incidence of exchange marriage and polygyny. During my recent visits to several Ngäbe communities, both men and women told me that exchange marriage has virtually disappeared, although some said that there may still be some cases in remote, isolated communities.

Martinelli (1994) noted what she interpreted to be the beginnings of a class system in some communities, observing that educated women and those married to schoolteachers or other salaried employees did not want to associate with women who had little education or spoke little or no Spanish. I suggest that there may be alternate interpretations for Martinelli's observations, e.g., that some or all of these women were strangers to the community, or that, as is traditional among the Ngäbe, women (and men) tend to associate most frequently with kin. While some individual wealth differences are evident, during my visits to Ngäbe communities since 1997, I did not observe any behavior that I could, as a cultural anthropologist, interpret as the beginnings of class distinctions.

Development Projects

Plan Guaymí was, so far as I know, the first long-term development project for the Ngäbe sponsored by an outside agency; it lasted for three years from 1975 to 1978. It was carried out by the Interamerican Development Institute, a U.S.-based non-governmental organization (NGO), in collaboration with the Panamanian Ministry of Education. Subsequent development projects for the Ngäbe sponsored by outside agencies have also been carried out in collaboration with a government ministry or other government agency or a licensed Panamanian NGO. Plan Guaymí was not obliged to incorporate women in the project, but every effort was made to do so. However, as noted above, due to insufficient literacy in Spanish, very few women were able to qualify for the training programs. While this project did have some positive outcomes, it had no discernible impact on Ngäbe women's roles or gender relations.

By the 1980s, the Ngäbe had become the intended beneficiaries of many development projects. Most, if not all, required that women be incorporated in some way in project activities. By this time literacy was already increasing among Ngäbe women. Project activities were usually directed at teaching women managerial skills and guiding them in the formation of women's organizations, which often took the form of co-ops for the production and sale of arts and crafts. Determining whether women's organizations were completely absent prior to the influx of external projects is problematic. Men's cooperatives existed since at least the early 1960s and thus provided an internal model. In any case, the activities of various projects certainly fostered a proliferation of Ngäbe women's organizations, not all of which were geared toward craft production.

The greatest success was achieved by PAN, which began implementation activities in 1994 (after a year of background data collection) and continued for eleven years through 2004 (Arosemena 2004; Mendoza B. et al. n.d.). The German development agency GTZ funded and provided technical support for the project. It was implemented jointly by GTZ and the National Environmental Authority (Autoridad Nacional del Ambiente, ANAM) of Panama.[14] It had its base of operations in San Félix and carried out project activities in Ngäbe communities in three districts of Chiriquí: Remedios, San Félix, and San Lorenzo (Nole Düima, Mironó, and Besikó, respectively, after the creation of the comarca). Among its various activities, relevant here is that the project trained women in basic agronomy and agroforestry skills and as community organizers (*promotores sociales*), helped them form organizations, and provided technical assistance to extant women's organizations. Without minimizing the accomplishments of the project, it bears repeating that by the mid-1990s many more Ngäbe women had received some formal education and thus had the basic skills necessary to participate in the GTZ's training activities. And, because they were bilingual, they could train women who were monolingual.

The GTZ personnel found that women's organizations for the production and sale of Ngäbe arts and crafts already existed in several of their target communities. Their production consisted of colorful and utilitarian net bags, beaded collars, baskets, women's dresses, and straw hats (the latter made by men). However, these loose-knit co-ops were not well organized, they lacked clear leadership, and their products varied in quality. They often sold their wares at extremely low prices because they were in competition with one another, or simply because the customer base was small and unstable. Educated Ngäbe women already trained by the GTZ helped train the women in these nascent organizations in administrative skills, simple accounting, public relations, formulation of projects, and also self-esteem. In addition, elderly experienced women were sought out to share their repertoire of designs for the net bags and to help the less skilled improve the quality of their products. The result was that these groups "went from simple groups that were only dedicated to the sale of their products to small community enterprises . . . with a desire to benefit all members, families and neighbors" (Mendoza B. et al. n.d., 7). The end result of these efforts was the formation of an umbrella organization to represent all of the arts and crafts organizations of the comarca that wished to join. The Federation of Ngäbe-Buglé Artisanal Organizations (Federación de Organizaciones Artesanales Ngäbe-Buglé, FORANB) was established in December 2003 with twenty-one organizations and eventually grew to over forty-seven organizations totaling over one thousand members, mostly women (B. Gomez 2004; Mendoza B. et al. n.d.). It established a retail outlet near the town of San Félix. The retail store has since closed due to internal problems. Among the Ngäbe that I know, rumor has it that FORANB became dysfunctional due to internal bickering.

Finally, it is worth mentioning that since the first unpaved road penetrated Ngäbe territory in Chiriquí Province in 1978, the Panamanian government has extended several roads to Ngäbe communities throughout the comarca, some of them paved or partially paved. Buses and pickup trucks now run on a regular basis from Panamanian towns bordering the comarca, and some run from the main bus terminal in Chiriquí to or near various comarca communities. This has greatly facilitated Ngäbe travel in and out of the comarca, making it much easier for both men and women to buy and sell goods and seek short-term employment. Although Martinelli (1994) noted that most men would not permit their wives to travel alone, not even to other Ngäbe communities for meetings, there appears to have been a change in attitude in many men and an increase in the independence of women, judging by the vast sea of Ngäbe women, many of them unaccompanied by men, wearing the traditional *nagua*[15] in the main bus terminal in the city of David on any day of the week. My notes from 2010 indicate that some men, while permitting their wives to travel alone to nearby Ngäbe communities, remain resistant to allowing their wives to travel alone to workshops outside the comarca, for example, to Coclé Province. In 2010–2012, I saw many women traveling alone within the comarca and in San Félix, some on horseback. In the 1960s, this was a very rare sight: women seldom traveled alone, men rode the horses, and women walked.

Conversations and Observations, 1997–2013

In the 1960s, when a tradition of male dominance was still strong, a non-kin male could not converse with a woman without the permission of her father or older brother if unmarried, or her husband if married. This custom was followed rather strictly, but did not apply to prepubescent girls and elderly women. In recent years many women, both married and unmarried, have conversed with me without hesitation, itself an indication of the greater independence of women. In 1997, an educated woman, twenty-two years of age, from Caserio A[16] told me that her husband had beat her once when he was drinking. She warned him the next day that if it ever happened again, she would leave him.

In 2010, another woman had returned from several years of living in town with her Ngäbe husband to live with her aging parents in Caserio A. I had known her since she was a toddler. In 1997, when she was still living in town, I saw physical evidence of her husband's abuse. Her children were still young then. She told me in 2010 of her husband's frequent abuse and how she had stayed with him until the children were all in their teens or older. She said that now she had left her husband permanently.

I was introduced in 2010 to a middle-aged woman from Caserio B by a young Ngäbe male friend who told her that I was interested in knowing if things had changed for women in recent years. She immediately told me that women are now more liberated. She said that, in her own case, she suffered physical abuse in the past, but no more. She added that in the past if a man saw a woman working, he was too "macho" (her word) to help, but now some men help.

A middle-aged woman from Caserio C who is now living permanently in town told me she had been physically abused several times by her husband over the years and finally left him when most of her several children were grown. Her teenage daughter and her youngest, a seven-year-old girl, live with her.

In addition to the fact that I had conversations with women who apparently no longer believe they need a significant male's permission to speak with a non-kin male (although I should note that, by adoption, I am kin to some of these women), conversations and observations since 2010 substantiate the claim of women to greater independence. In the 1960s, even if women were willing to have their pictures taken, I needed the permission of the male head of their household to do so. During my 1997 visit, many men and women asked me to take their pictures, the women without consulting males first. In 2010, I was quite surprised when, unlike in earlier years, many married women and unmarried young ladies asked to have their pictures taken with me, and some even put their arm around me while the picture was being taken! This was something entirely new. No women had ever asked this before, and it is clearly an indicator of the greater independence of women.

Beyond the Comarca

While my focus has been on women in Ngäbe communities within the Ngäbe-Buglé Comarca, some mention should be made of those who leave the comarca, with their husbands and children, with only their children, or alone, due to lack of agricultural land or other means of support in the comarca. Some of these women end up begging on the streets; others become prostitutes. The more fortunate find low-paying jobs as housekeeping, maintenance, or kitchen staff in hotels and boarding houses (*pensiones*) or as housekeepers or nannies for Latino families. While a few are able to earn enough for a relatively comfortable existence, most, to their dismay, find that they have simply exchanged the rural poverty of the comarca for the urban poverty of the city, which is often more severe.

Discussion and Conclusions

Partly as a result of the Mama Chi movement and the accompanying process of politicization, there slowly emerged a strong sense of ethnic pride among the Ngäbe. A politics of identity was solidified with the granting by the government of comarca status in 1997. While it has not resulted in a wholesale return to traditional beliefs and practices, it has resulted in a strong sense of pride of heritage among both men and women, of self-identification as Ngäbe, and of corresponding resistance to being identified as mestizo.

Mama Chi and the religion she founded represented a reaction to decades of recent oppression and provided a framework to the Ngäbe for a collective reassessment of their situation in the face of increasing involvement with Panamanian national culture and forces of globalization. She also precipitated changes in the relationships between Ngäbe men and women. In the face of recent large-scale challenges to their territory, their livelihood, and their rights as Indigenous people by extensive mining exploration and hydroelectric projects (approved by the government without their consent and in some cases without even the consultation required by Law 10 that established the comarca), there is some evidence of a reawakening of the religion.

It is unclear how widespread the mistreatment of women by men was prior to this religious movement, but the prohibition of such mistreatment is a strong indication that it was not uncommon. The movement, although it dwindled as a significant social force in the 1970s, does appear to have had a consciousness-raising impact on women and at least some men. Domestic violence was evident in the 1990s and continues, but several women with whom I have spoken in Ngäbe communities in the Nidrini region of the comarca who were married after 1972 have since left their husbands and told me they did so because of physical abuse. Others have told me of physical abuse but remain married (though not necessarily living with their husbands).

In 1992, psychologist Barbara Smuts, based on selected cross-cultural data, presented five general hypotheses concerning conditions that (collectively) would increase the likelihood of domestic violence against women. Paraphrased here (and not in the order she presented them), these are (1) weak female alliances, (2) strong male alliances, (3) weak or lack of support from consanguineal kin, (4) male control of resources, and (5) less egalitarian relationships among men (1992, 13–15, 19, 22). The Ngäbe were not included in her data set, but considering the situation of Ngäbe women in historical perspective, I would say conditions 1, 2, 3, and 4 generally prevailed in the 1960s and earlier.

In the 1960s, non-kin-based female alliances were weak or nonexistent, and male alliances were strong. Ngäbe women did not completely lack kin support, but the amount they got from kin—especially male kin—varied. Traditionally, they got less support if the marriage was an exchange than if it was one-way. Virilocal or patrilocal residence reduced potential support, and according to some women, they were under the domination of their mother-in-law or, in the cases of polygyny, the senior

wife. With respect to condition 5, relationships among men in the 1960s
were generally egalitarian. Again, it is likely that the apparent low incidence of domestic violence in the 1960s was due to the teachings of
Mama Chi. This speculation is strengthened by the fact that domestic violence became more evident with the waning of the religious movement.

By the end of the twentieth century, numerous non-kin-based female
alliances existed, kin support of women was much more in evidence, polygyny was rapidly disappearing, and post-marital residence was becoming
more a matter of choice. Better transportation and the use of cell phones
had greatly facilitated female communication with distant kin. Female
control of economic resources had increased substantially since the 1960s.
Relationships among men were somewhat less egalitarian by the end of
the century, but this does not appear yet to have affected the vulnerability
of women to physical abuse. Overall, Ngäbe women are, as they themselves claim, much more independent than in the past, and while not immune to physical abuse, they are now better able to obtain the support of
kin and other women. With their increased control of economic resources,
the choice is now available to many to leave their abusers.

Insofar as decision-making is concerned, women, young and old, always had some input in household decisions and behind-the-scenes influence in the public decisions of men—sometimes considerable in the view
of males with whom I have spoken. Education and some independent income have given some women a new sense of self-assurance and independence and greater assertiveness in household decision-making. Likewise,
there has been a shift from overwhelming male dominance in public
decision-making to some public participation by women. While respected
elderly women have always, on occasion, voiced their opinions in public
gatherings, especially when they did not like what they were hearing
from the men, younger women remained silent and literally peripheral
in a spatial sense, hovering around the edges of male gatherings. Now
some younger women participate in public community discussions and
decision-making. A few have been elected to public office, as was Silvia
Carrera, the first female general cacica of the Ngäbe-Buglé Comarca.
Nonetheless, as John Bort, Lucia Lasso, and I have observed, the election of even educated women is still rare. At a community gathering I
attended in January 2008, after several men had voiced their views, the
Ngäbe male facilitator asked if there were any women who wished to
speak. He repeated this invitation several times, but no woman spoke,
even though this meeting was to present personal testimony, not to
make decisions.

Polygyny has decreased greatly since the 1960s, although it has not
completely disappeared. Some men attribute this to the more difficult
economic circumstances in today's world, making it hard for a man to support more than one wife. This may be partially true, but the argument of

women is that education (which, in Panama, involves teaching the Christian moral ideal of monogamy) has been the predominant factor in changing women's views about the advantages and disadvantages of polygyny. This is well illustrated by two educated daughters who have repeatedly questioned their mother, an elderly woman I have known for over forty years, about why she put up with their father having multiple wives. Her response is always the same: "You girls just think differently than I do." Education and changing economic circumstances are also the two factors most likely responsible for the considerable decline in arranged marriages since the 1960s, although, as noted, there was resistance among young people to this practice even in the 1960s.

Development projects, such as the Ngöbe Agroforestry Project, have both enhanced the self-confidence of women and increased the number and efficiency of women's organizations within the comarca. In large part, this has been possible only because of the educational opportunities that were available to the current generation of young adult women. Two very recent developments are adding to the self-confidence, independence, and connectedness of some young women, and these developments are likely to spread: computer use and cell phones. A school in Soloy is equipped with dozens of solar-powered computers, which are used at least as much by women as men, and a woman supervises their use.

Cell phones are becoming increasingly common, and many women have them. They are inexpensive: calling cards sell for as little as two dollars, and one only pays for outgoing calls. The cards are valid for a year, and one can receive calls even if there are no minutes left on the card. The use of cell phones has dramatically enhanced rapid communication. Family members and friends, both within and outside the comarca, can now stay in contact more frequently, travel itineraries can be exchanged, and information about scheduled community events and job opportunities can be rapidly transmitted.[17] The literacy and numeracy of younger generations of Ngäbe women have facilitated their use of computers and cell phones. There is no doubt that Ngäbe have access to, and are adopting, the latest technological innovations more rapidly than in the past.

Since the 1960s, over the course of several decades of increasingly accelerated and varied social, economic, and political interaction with government institutions and non-Indigenous Panamanians (and a few foreigners), changes in women's roles and gender relations have been gradual and quite varied from one community to the next. Change has depended, among other things, on the relative degree of isolation of communities, the degree of education of women, the extent to which women have a source of independent income, and the extent to which the men in their lives accept the greater independence and assertiveness of women. But there is no doubt that Ngäbe women today are more independent and more assertive, as they themselves claim to be.

Acknowledgments

I gratefully acknowledge the comments of John Bort, with whom I have collaborated over the years in research on Ngäbe society and culture, and the collaboration of all those Ngäbe women and men who befriended me and shared their knowledge and insights about their culture and changes that have taken place over the years. I also thank Lucia Lasso, Andrea Martinsen, and Bethany Ojalehto, who commented on earlier drafts of this chapter and provided information on women's roles in contemporary Ngäbe communities in Bocas del Toro Province and the Ñö Kribo part of the comarca. Four anonymous reviewers offered insightful suggestions, not all of which I could address due to space limitations. I take full responsibility for any errors that appear here.

Notes

1. The relationship of women to their children is also important, but it is beyond the scope of this chapter.

2. A comarca is approximately the equivalent of an Indian reservation in the United States.

3. The Buglé, although culturally very similar to the Ngäbe, insist on their distinct cultural identity. Brief published descriptions (Herrera and González 1964; P. Young 1995) picture the Buglé as generally more traditional than the Ngäbe, and certainly less well known.

4. The youngest (fourth) generation consisted of only four married men, none of whom were polygynists. All had been recently married.

5. Patrilocality, living in the husband's father's house after marriage, is a subtype of virilocality.

6. See P. Young 1971, 125–40, for a detailed discussion of post-marital residence.

7. Latino is the term Ngäbe use to refer to Panamanians and is equivalent to ladino in Guatemala and mestizo elsewhere.

8. For accounts of the Mama Chi religion and its social consequences, see P. Young 1971, 212–24; P. Young 1976; P. Young 1978; P. Young and Bort 1999, 116–18; Guionneau 1988; and Sieiro de Noriega 1980, 60–65.

9. Both Sieiro de Noriega (1980) and Guionneau (1988) give September 1962 as the date when Mama Chi saw the vision. During my field research in 1964–1965, my Ngäbe collaborators consistently gave the date as September 1961.

10. There is much more to this story then can be told here.

11. For more details on the Red de Oportunidades program, see the MIDES website, http://www.mides.gob.pa/?s=Red+de+Oportunidades. The MIDES program is not limited to comarcas.

12. As late as the 1990s, parents who wished their children to receive a secondary school education had to send them to schools in Panamanian towns

bordering the territory, which meant they had to find Panamanian families willing to provide them with room and board. The exception was a secondary school established in the early 1990s by Jesuits in San Félix, specifically for Ngäbe girls and boys, with facilities for room and board. Many of the women that John Bort and I know attended this school, although not all of them completed the full course of study.

13. This phenomenon has been referred to in the literature as "invented tradition." Of course, in the sense that all traditions are cultural constructs, all traditions are "invented."

14. After the establishment of the Ngäbe-Buglé Comarca in 1997, ANAM created a regional administration within the comarca administered by the Ngäbe, which then became the GTZ counterpart in the project.

15. The nagua, a colorful, short-sleeved, free-flowing dress that covers the body from neck to ankles, is clearly a very public marker of Ngäbe identity for women in Chiriquí. While women in Bocas del Toro are almost never seen in a nagua in public and often do not wear them in their own communities, they do still self-identify as Ngäbe and still speak their own language in the household. The term nagua is apparently derived from the Spanish *enaguas* (petticoats).

16. Alphabetic labels for the communities are used here to conceal location to protect the identity of the respondents. *Caserío* is the Spanish term used to refer to Ngäbe communities that were hamlets, but some are now large enough to qualify as towns.

17. My thanks to John Bort for these observations about the use of cell phones.

CHAPTER TWELVE

Politicizing Ethnicity

Strategies in Panama and Ecuador

VÍCTOR BRETÓN SOLO DE ZALDÍVAR
AND MÒNICA MARTÍNEZ MAURI
TRANSLATED BY PHILIP D. YOUNG
AND STEFANIE WICKSTROM

The theme of the emergence of ethnicity in Latin America and its crystallization into organized pluriethnic platforms that empower political actors at the national and international levels has been gaining prominence in the social sciences in recent decades. Without doubt spurred by the visibility that Indigenous movements have achieved in settings such as southeastern Mexico, post-war Guatemala, and Ecuador during the Indigenous "uprisings" of the 1990s, and with the ascendency of Evo Morales to the presidency of Bolivia, the research agendas of anthropologists, sociologists, and political scientists have focused attention on trying to explain the "resurgence" of the "Indian question."

An "ethnic fever" has characterized some social movements articulated around the right to difference. What are the factors, situational and structural, that enable us to recognize it? How far can movements get in questioning monoethnic and monolingual foundations of nation-states constructed on mestizo ideologies? Approaching these questions comparatively reveals a direct connection between articulation of these new forms of conveying the collective action of an important segment of subaltern sectors with disintegration of the national development models of yesteryear and consolidation of neoliberalism. This transition sig-

212

naled the collapse of the myth of well-being and social inclusion in a "national mestizo society" in corporatist nation-states. In Ecuador and Panama, the earlier trend of "becoming mestizo" has given way to explicit assertions of Indigenous ethnicity. In this historical framework, conditions were generated that made possible the configuration of "new social movements" that, through a curious combination of classic demands with others of a cultural-identity type, gave them a formidable capacity to appeal to public authorities.

Beyond these considerations, however, there are two inescapable questions. First, why has ethnicity united social responses of subaltern groups in some contexts and not in others? Second, how do we explain the existence of nationwide organizing platforms, as in Ecuador, while in other countries, as in Panama, certain ethnic groups have achieved greater measures of autonomy, control of resources, and visibility in the national and international arenas without joining other collectives in formal organizations of this type? In this chapter we address these questions by comparing historical and ethnographic data obtained over the course of more than a decade of fieldwork on cultural mediation, development policies, and the configuration of Indigenous movements in Panama (especially in the Kuna Yala Comarca) and Ecuador (especially in the Andes).

The Framework of Comparison

As we address the final question posed above, it seems appropriate to mention the analytic proposal of Deborah Yashar (2005, 2007) who attempts to delimit the principal variables that politicize ethnicity in Latin America. She begins with the premise that ethnicity is politicized within the framework of profound change of "regimes of citizenship": the change from a corporatist regime to one of neoliberal character that would endanger enclaves of local autonomy, which would, in turn, motivate ethnic emergence.[1] However, this change, per se, does not account for the emergence of Indigenous movements. According to Yashar, it is also necessary to analyze the interaction of two other variables: the existence of an associated political space that offers real political opportunity to organize and the existence of inter-community networks that enable transcendence of the local and addressing of the state's development apparatus.

Corporatist regimes in diverse political guises (democratic or authoritarian) were characterized by the implementation of a group of inclusive policies. Corporatist regimes assimilated "Indigenes" as "peasants" by means of agrarian reform programs of rural development or investment in social policies. Redistributing land and securing it against seizure facilitated the consolidation of spaces of local autonomy within which Indigenous culture could be reproduced and upon which the impact of the state was relative (Yashar 2005). Neoliberal regimes, on the other hand, reduced local autonomy and access to state resources and dismantled the protective corporatist apparatus. As a consequence, they established the bases for a politicization of ethnicity, given that corporatist development could no longer mediate class conflict. Overall, for the ethnic movements to emerge and become politicized, the existence of inter-community networks that permitted the transcendence of local identities and the construction of imaginary collectives of an Indigenous "we" was necessary. The state, churches, non-governmental organizations (NGOs), and other actors have played fundamental roles in consolidating these networks. Finally, Yashar concludes that the existence of a political context that would facilitate associations was indispensable.

Although thought-provoking, Yashar's model leaves aside a combination of important variables that might explain, on the one hand, the emergence or not of ethnicity as a vector of politicization for certain subaltern sectors and, on the other, why in some contexts politicization crystallizes in the public sphere. The cases of Ecuador and Panama suggest the necessity of inclusion of the consideration of vectors of politicization from a comparative perspective. The object of this work is, then, to explore the tension between *mestizaje* politics and Indigenous political strategies in debates about ethnicity. In both countries the emergence and visibility of Indigenous populations extend from the national level to the highest spheres of the development system and multilateral development organizations. In Panama the politicization of ethnicity has been conveyed by means of mono-ethnic organizing platforms. The historical experience of the Kuna is one example. In Ecuador the strategy has been the constitution of a nationwide confederation of ethnic organizations, Confederation of Indigenous Nationalities of Ecuador (La Confederación de Nacionalidades Indígenas del Ecuador, CONAIE). Our analysis is focused on contextual and structural elements that have directed parallel, but not necessarily convergent, strategies. The organizing experiences of Panamanian and Ecuadorian Indigenes enable reflection on dynamics of political identity in recent years.

As a first approximation to this complex reality, we emphasize the impact of demography and distribution of the Indigenous population, forms of dialogue or relations of racialized subaltern groups with the state, opportunities for articulation with other networks (leftist political parties, churches, etc.) and general synergies of articulations, and changes in regimes of citizenship and dialectical relations established between Indigenous peoples and the development establishment.

Ecuador Set Against Panama or the "Ecuadorian Model" as a Reference Point

Ethnic movements in Panama and Ecuador are considered to be among the most successful on national political playing fields. The emergence of autonomous Indigenous territorial regimes in Panama is a reference point and a pioneering example. The Indigenous population, despite being only 12 percent of the total population, has achieved a high level of political autonomy with respect to the nation-state through the formation of comarcas. According to the national census of 2010, 48 percent of Panama's Indigenous population lives in comarcas, Indigenous territories with semi-autonomous political organizations under the jurisdiction of the national government (Herlihy 1995). The comarca is a political-administrative entity that depends ultimately on the state, which can establish political-administrative regimes to limit the effective exercise of recognized rights or exploit natural resources in Indigenous territories by invoking the public interest (Wickstrom 2003).

González Pérez (2010) identifies some common characteristics among functioning autonomies in Colombia, Panama, and Nicaragua. As does Díaz Polanco (1997), González Pérez highlights transference of decision-making and administrative authority to democratically elected officials, recognition by the state of political structures of self-governance, and demarcation of a territory wherein collective rights over land and natural resources are exercised. Van Cott (2001) points out two other factors applicable to the Panama case: access of Indigenous sectors to decision-making and alliances with agents that support their demands for autonomy.

According to González Pérez, Van Cott (2000), and Roldán Ortega (2000), what accounts for the autonomy processes in Panama, Nicaragua, and Colombia is the context in which they are produced, one framed by the multicultural paradigm and policies of recognition intended to modify historical relationships of the state with Indigenous peoples. The Panamanian case, however, cannot be explained by focusing on structures of political opportunities. The creation of autonomous political territories there did not take place in wider fora of negotiation establishing the country's political system. Panamanian Indigenous organizations never acted together to reclaim Indigenous autonomy nor was Indigenous autonomy approved during times of change of the political system (Martínez Mauri 2011).

. Some comparative works conclude that Panama is a pioneer in Latin America in inaugurating a system of autonomous Indigenous territories (in 1938) but has not responded equally to all demands for autonomy. While the Kuna Yala Comarca has achieved a relatively high level of cultural control and consolidated self-governing structures (Assies 2005), assessment of other comarcas is less optimistic (González Pérez 2010). Following the thread of this argument, and considering the suffering of the 52 percent of Indigenous Panamanians who live outside of comarcas (Leis 2003), as well as that of inhabitants of the Ngäbe-Buglé Comarca, Jordán Ramos (2010a) asserts that, despite the existence of a system of autonomous Indigenous territories, the Panamanian state excludes Indigenous peoples from the processes of political negotiation and decision-making.

Indigenous peoples in Ecuador, on the other hand, are famous for their unity and considerable capacity for national mobilization and for having sustained a political alternative to the traditional left for many years (at least from the end of the 1980s through the beginning of the twenty-first century). In contrast to Panama, the Ecuadorian Indigenous movement has a pyramidal structure characterized by the autonomy of each of its levels and the organizations of which it is composed. Its foundations are made up of a dense web of local organizations—designated "first-tier" or "base"—that extend throughout the territory (communities, cooperatives, and associations). From this base emerge "second-tier" federations (OSGs),[2] each of which consists of a large grouping of base groups. Higher up we find a third level, federations of OSG federations, encompassing entire provinces. From these emerge three large groupings that correspond to the three ecoregions of the country: Confederation of Peoples of Kichwa Nationality (Confederación de Pueblos de la Nacionalidad Kichwa del Ecuador, ECUARUNARI) in the Andean Sierra; Confederation of Indigenous Nationalities of the Ecuadorian Amazon (La Confederación de las Nacionalidades Indígenas de la Amazonia Ecuatoriana, CONFENIAE) in the eastern Amazon; and Confederation of Indigenous Nationalities of the Ecuadorian Coast (Confederación de Nacionalidades Indígenas de la Costa Ecuatoriana, CONAICE) on the coast. In 1986, an alliance of these formed CONAIE, which is perhaps the most recognized but not the only organization of this type. Others are the National Federation of Peasant, Indigenous, and Black Organizations (Federación Nacional de Organizaciones Campesinas, Indígenas y Negras, FENOCIN), which has established a more class-based dialogue than CONAIE, and the Ecuadorian Federation of Evangelical Indians (Federación Ecuatoriana de Indígenas Evangélicos, FEINE).

The organization of CONAIE is not hierarchical, as is a typical political party. Each organization that makes up the movement is autonomous. The pyramidal structure is a conglomeration of institutions potentially in conflict and competition with one another. Temporary alliances are established in the interest of mobilizing capacity and negotiating with authorities. The effectiveness of such a structure in Ecuadorian politics was manifested in significant Indigenous uprisings in 1990, 1994, 2000, and 2001, as well as in engagement in negotiation at the highest levels with the state.[3] Finally, and no less relevant, is the fact that this transformation has been accompanied by a dialogue revolving around ethnicity that generates a series of concrete objectives, notable among which are the formation of a plurinational state, the struggle for autonomy and access to land (mainly in the Andes), and the defense of conservation, control, and use rights of traditional resources and spaces in Indigenous territories of Amazonian peoples to guarantee continued survival and social reproduction.

For comparative analysis, it is important to understand how internal boundaries between Indigenous peoples and the rest of the collectives that make up respective "national societies" are constituted, as well as the temporary nature of alliances among Indigenous peoples themselves. In Panama, unlike in Ecuador, Indigenous peoples have always negotiated with the nation-state bilaterally, in the absence of a consolidated and unified national Indigenous organization. Nonetheless, some Indigenous leaders, especially Kuna, feel a great admiration for achievements of the Indigenous movement in Ecuador.[4] This illustrates pan-American orientations of Indigenous social movements.

Leaders from throughout Latin America have looked to the example of CONAIE for years. It has achieved the greatest capacity to influence the course of national policy of the Indigenous organizations in the region. We should remember, for example, the Indigenous uprising in January 2000 that, through alliance with middle ranks of the army, overthrew the country's president, Jamil Mahuad. One week after the Ecuadorian uprising, the president of the legislative assembly of Panama, Enrique Garrido, a Kuna, declared that the Natives of his country could also mutiny, given the marginalization and poverty in which they lived. Mobilizations by CONAIE had shown that "governments must understand that when a people are hurt and without recourse, they take such actions" ("Reaction to the Uprising in Ecuador: Central American Indigenes Sound the Alert," *El Mercurio* [Santiago, Chile], July 2, 2000, http://www.emol.com).

Demography of Indigenous Populations

Demography of the Indigenous population is, for a number of reasons, a key factor to consider in evaluating its political strategies. First, because in the actual context of implementation of policies of recognition, we must consider not just the mathematical question (how many they may be) but also the way in which states define the category "Indigenous." Second, we must evaluate the means that the state uses to obtain information and control the Indigenous population: censuses, statistical information gathered through programs to combat poverty, reports of multinational agencies, etc. Third, we should consider how the numbers make the Indigenes (in)visible and favor or inhibit their mobilization.

In Panama, analyses of census data show a change in understanding the Indian question during the twentieth century (Martínez Mauri 2012). In the first censuses of 1911, 1920, and 1930, the vast majority of the Indigenous population of the country was left out of the tally because census takers did not visit Indigenous communities due to transportation difficulties. It was not until 1940 that the Office of Statistics and Census began to work with the concept of "Indian tribes" (Heckadon 1982). Unlike earlier censuses, which addressed the "Indian race" or

"Indians" in general terms, the idea became established that the Indigenous population is that which had "retreated in large part to inaccessible mountain valleys and coastal islands" (Republic of Panama. Oficina del Censo 1943, 54). A distinction was then made between the civil population (groups within the sociopolitical structure of the republic) and the Indigenous population (people who lived in tribes with their own [primitive] social structures). In this way, the category "Indian" was transformed from a racial criterion into a "social" category: Indigenes who lived within the sociopolitical structure of the republic, spoke Spanish, and professed Catholicism were considered a part of the "civil population" and were called "cholos" (Republic of Panama. Oficina del Censo 1943). Indigenes who worked on banana plantations, in urban areas, or in the Canal Zone were counted as part of the civil population. Not surprisingly, on the basis of the census criteria, the Indigenous population of Panama only comprised 5 percent of the total. When it came to planning infrastructure and services, the state made decisions on the basis of this incomplete and biased information, justifying the lack of investment in Indigenous zones.

During the 1970s, after General Omar Torrijos came to power, the Indian question was thoroughly discussed by the assembly of *corregimiento* representatives in drafting a preliminary plan for the National Constitution of 1972. Discussion focused on Article 116 of Chapter VII, "About the Agrarian System," which stipulated that the state guarantees lands to the Indigenes in the form of collective property.[5] The necessity arose to determine precisely who the Indigenes were. After a time, in the 1980s, it was established that the Indigenous population was "that composed of inhabitants who live under a tribal organization, in populated places situated in regions inhabited by them and who speak a dialect and conserve their traditions" (Republic of Panama. Dirección de Estadística 1981). The criterion of self-identification was not considered until the 1990 census. Thanks to pressure from some anthropologists and the demands of Indigenous organizations, in the 1990 census Indigenes were "all who declared themselves as belonging to some aboriginal group, independently of where they are living. Accordingly, Indigenes can be found in any geographic area of the country." According to the 2010 census data, the Indigenous population had reached 12.26 percent of the national total (417,559 people) and was divided into eight large ethnic groups.[6]

In the Ecuadorian case, the juggling of numbers has also been considerable. Here we consider the censuses of 1950, 1990, 2001, and 2011. That of 1950 introduced the language criterion and registered 347,475 individuals who spoke an Indigenous language (10.9 percent of the national population at that time). In the 1990 census, the question, "What language do household members speak among themselves?" was included. The data were not convincing either to scholars or the Indigenous leadership "because the 362,500 persons who said they spoke an autochthonous language, and were therefore considered Indigenes, represented only 3.8 percent of the total (9,648,189 inhabitants)" (Chisaguano 2006, 18). The census of 2001 took self-identification into account for the first time, in the organization of the population by ethnic categories. That year, 830,418 people explicitly considered themselves Indigenes (6.8 percent of the total of 12,156,608 inhabitants). While the population of non-Indigenes increased by 22 percent in the inter-census period from 1990–2001, the Indigenous population increased (in absolute numbers) by 129.1 percent. The data from 2011 confirm this trend. Using the same criteria of self-definition as in 2001, Indigenes accounted for 7.03 percent of the population (1,018,176 out of 14,483,499 inhabitants of the country).

In addition to data from the censuses, Ecuador has data gathered in 2000 from the Survey of Medical Indicators of Children and Households (Encuesta de Medición de Indicadores de la Niñez y los Hogares, EMEDINHO), which includes questions such as language spoken by parents of interviewees and enables cross-referencing variables. The results make clear that, in reality, more than 14.3 percent of the population over fifteen years of age speaks an Indigenous language, self-identifies as Indigenous, and has parents that speak or spoke a Native language (León Guzmán 2003).

These data are not reflected in pamphlets of activists and Indigenous leaders claiming the Indigenous population in Ecuador approaches 50 percent of the total, but this should not lead us to believe they are mistaken. We must keep in mind that the Indigenous population is not evenly distributed throughout the national territory. The majority of the Indigenous population is concentrated in the Andes, which accounts for the emergence of ECUARUNARI there. This regional organization, given its high mobilization capacity (demographically and politically), was in a position to help determine the "necessary measures" (like the uprisings) taken by CONAIE during the 1990s and helped comprise the backbone of the Indigenous movement. Assuming that the entire Indigenous population is no more than 10–15 percent of the total, we can conclude that CONAIE's capacity to establish alliances with non-Indigenous social sectors must have been powerful in the decade of the great protest mobilizations (between 1993 and the downfall of the government in 2003). The real and operative possibility of paralyzing the neurological center of the country (the roads to Quito, capital of the republic) and the lack of conflicts of interest between the Amazonian and Andean organizing platforms (the former centered on the question of oil drilling and mining or territoriality in the eastern provinces and the latter historically centered on peasant demands such as recognition of local and regional powers and, recently, above all, control of mining activities, in particular enclaves at the base of the Andes) must also be taken into account in evaluating the success of multiethnic confederations like CONAIE.

Territorial Distribution

Comparing the Ecuadorian experience with that of Panama confirms that distribution of the Indigenous population is a factor determining articulation of pluriethnic organizing platforms. Indigenous populations of Panama (12 percent) and Ecuador (10–15 percent) are not very different. The difference is geographic dispersion. In Panama the eight Indigenous groups are located in peripheral areas difficult to access.

The Indigenous comarca of San Blas (established in 1938) is a coastal and island territory on Panama's Atlantic Ocean side, extending to the Colombian border. (It was called Kuna Yala beginning in 1990 and Guna Yala after April 2011.) Until the 1970s, there was no road to link this territory to the rest of the country, and until recently, the only means of getting there was by small plane from Panama City or by boat, launch, or dugout canoe from Colón or Colombia.

The comarca of the Emberá-Wounaan was created in 1983 in the Darien. The Darien gap is the only part of the American continents that the Pan-American Highway does not pass through. The Emberá-Wounaan Comarca is disconnected from urban centers and divided into two areas separated by several kilometers of forest and pasture. Area One in the district of Cémaco is located in the northeastern part of the country on the border with Colombia. Area Two is a zone close to the Pacific coast extending to the headwaters of the Sambu River. This comarca, in addition to being geographically divided, is also pluriethnic, with Emberá and Wounaan communities.

The Kuna Madungandí Comarca, established in 1996, has a border with Kuna Yala and is connected by road to the capital due to the Ascanio Villalaz Hydroelectric Center (which formed Lake Bayano). It was constructed on the Bayano River in the 1970s by the Torrijos government. The project inundated territory occupied by Kuna, Emberá, Afro-Panamanians, and peasants, creating poverty and heightening their marginality (Wali 1995).[7]

The Ngäbe-Buglé Comarca came into being in 1997. It is located in the western part of the country, bordering the banana plantations of Changuinola, more than eight hours by land from the capital. Two Indigenous groups live in this comarca: the Ngäbe and the Buglé. Finally, the Kuna Wargandí Comarca, established in 2000, abuts the other two Kuna comarcas and the Darien.

The Naso, Bokota, and Bri-Bri have not succeeded in negotiating for comarcas with the Panamanian state. They are groups with only a few hundred people who live in remote areas in the western part of the country.

The 52 percent of the Indigenous population not living in comarcas reside in nearby areas left out during the processes of delimitation; in other rural areas of the country; in the urban areas of Panama City, David,

Santiago de Veraguas, and Colón; on banana plantations, for example in the area surrounding Changuinola; or in tourist centers like Contadora Island, earning a living as salaried employees. These conditions are not conducive to establishing solidarity between Indigenous groups, in part because of the internal dynamics of each group. Kuna migrants in Panama City and Colón, for example, prefer to group together, founding neighborhoods on the edges of the city, reproducing their sociopolitical organizational model, naming authorities, and constructing congress houses. Groups are also influenced by the political strategies of external agents that undermine solidarity.[8]

In Panama, unlike Ecuador, the isolation and distribution of Indigenous populations throughout the national territory and economically precarious work situations in multiethnic urban and transnational contexts have conditioned their organizational dynamic.

State Relations with Racialized Subaltern Groups

Ecuador

Ecuador was constituted as an independent republic, as were the rest of the Latin American countries, on the basis of a citizenship discourse inspired by models such as that of the United States, the French Republic, and the Courts of Cádiz, all immersed in revolution. (For more on this in the United States and the French Republic, see chapter 1.) The great paradox of this process lies in the fact that the new Ecuadorian republic of free citizens treated certain social groups as "citizens" while others remained "subjects" of a political order "that makes them servants and that redefines ancient ethnic and racial hierarchies" (Guerrero 2000, 18). In this context, the "Indians" were officially invisible and deprived of their voice; their interaction with state authorities was carried out by others who "translated" their demands and aspirations into correct political language. This state of affairs lasted until the emergence of the Indigenous movement in the last two decades of the twentieth century (Guerrero 1997).

How was such a transcendental break possible? To answer this question we center our attention on Andean Indigenous populations. Throughout their prolonged contact with the state, they have always been subsumed as subaltern groups in the structure of domination. We also focus the analysis on processes unleashed by the agrarian reforms driving the country during the 1960s and 1970s (laws of 1964 and 1973). In the Ecuadorian Andes, in effect, ethnic platforms emerged in rural interstices and, therefore, are difficult to interpret without taking into consideration the profound significance of the agrarian reforms and the dynamics inherited from state-peasant relations.

Works available on the impact of the agrarian reform laws of 1964 and 1973 on the rural sectors of Ecuador are many (Barsky 1988). We will not elaborate on them here, except to recall that in 1954 on the threshold of the reforms, 2.1 percent of the farms (those with more than one hundred hectares) occupied 64.4 percent of the agricultural land, while units smaller than five hectares (73.1 percent of the total number of farms) occupied only 7.2 percent. The expansion of the agrarian frontier and, to a lesser extent, redistribution (confined to the Andean area) translated into a noticeable reduction in the index of concentration of property. This seemingly greater equity arises in large part, however, from putting into cultivation lands located in the subtropical and tropical lowlands that had not been agrarian lands before, and it is, therefore, more fiction than reality. The Ecuadorian Institute of Agrarian Reform and Colonization (Instituto Ecuatoriano de Reforma Agraria y Colonización, IERAC) demobilized the peasantry by encouraging colonization of the lowlands

From the Indigenous-peasant perspective, the reforms marked a growing deterioration in the quality of life of a large portion of supposed beneficiaries in the medium term. Among other things, it resulted in a significant contraction in demand for manual labor in Andean rural areas, due to mechanization of the surviving haciendas transformed into capitalistic units producing for the internal urban market or for export, and acceleration of the processes of internal differentiation of peasant economies. The redistribution of agricultural lands least suited to cultivation ushered in, over the course of time, a permanent process of reduction in size of landholdings and increasing insecurity of succeeding generations of former *huasipungueros* (tenant farmers on hacienda lands). Their only possibility of gaining access to a parcel was to break up lots apportioned by IERAC or to try to cultivate parcels at the highest elevations— the *páramos*, now significantly deteriorated. Given these conditions, seasonal migration of smallholder Indigenous peasants from the highlands to the lowlands intensified, influenced in part, as well, by the labor demand of the oil boom of the 1970s. The seasonal nature of these migratory flows facilitated maintenance of ties with communities of origin. This made local identities foundations upon which a new pan-Indigenous collective could be built.

The elimination of the *huasipungo* system and the end of hacienda domination did not put an end to racial hierarchies. The re-articulation of relations of production reorganized racialization of subaltern sectors (Pallares 2002). Agrarian reform marked a parting of the waters in the social evolution of Andean Ecuadorians, such that, thanks to the speeding up of integration of Indigenous communities to the market and the state, "the consciousness of belonging to a group 'us,' that was initially defined in the local milieu," transformed "into a feeling of belonging to a larger Indigenous community" (Lentz 2000, 226). The ethnic frontier was being reconstructed at the same time that a common identity and project for "Indigenous nationalities" was strengthened.

Another important factor is that the rural Indigenous population emigrated during agrarian reform less permanently than the white-mestizo population, with the result that many Andean parishes experienced an important process of indigenization between 1962 and 1990. This was also the source of an ethnic fever that ran from north to south through the Andean corridor at the beginning of the final stages of the struggle for the land (Carrasco 1993; Zamosc 1995).

The processes unleashed in the Indigene-peasant class as the large landowner regime was collapsing, the elimination of precarious relations of production, and the establishment of a new model of relations with the state marked a before and after that underlies the extensive redefinition of peasants as Indigenes and the consolidation of a solid organizational framework among the rural class. This framework was strengthened, a posteriori, in the 1980s and 1990s, by state and private (NGO) development agencies, as we shall see later.

Panama

Understanding how forms of the historical relations of the Panamanian state with the Indigenous groups that reside within its borders differ from those in Ecuador requires that we go back to times before Panama became a country in 1903, when it was a province of Gran Colombia, and then a region of the Republic of New Granada.

At the end of the nineteenth century, after four centuries of failed attempts at colonization, some of the zones inhabited by Indigenes were unattended and the people abandoned to their fate. The truth is that, during the republican period, when Panama was a part of Colombia, the Indian question did not occupy a prominent place in the political agenda of the state. Few of the numerous constitutions of that period lent any attention to the Indian question. The federalist constitution of 1863 made clear in Article 18.4 that Indigenous civilizations were under the jurisdiction of overall government, and the constitution of 1878 declared that territories occupied by tribes would be governed by special law. Only those considered civilized and that had a population greater than three thousand could send an emissary to the House of Representatives. The constitution of 1886 (in force in Colombia until 1991) broke with this federalist trend and returned to a unitary model, making no explicit references to Indigenous groups. The last Colombian law that affected the peoples of the isthmus that is today Panama was Law 89 of November 25, 1890, which regulated "the form in which the savages being reduced to civilized life would be governed" and organized Indigenous town councils.

Although no firm policy directed at Indigenous affairs was implemented, at times, as with the decree of April 19, 1826, the protection and civilizing of the Indigenes of the Darien were prioritized through commerce and missions. At other times measures were formulated that recognized rights of Indigenes to maintain, at least in part, their institutions and territorial spaces, as with the agreement that the Kuna signed with Colombia on January 10, 1871. Among other things, this agreement (formalized by decree of April 19, 1871) guaranteed Kuna access to education and natural resources of their territory, Tulenega. It also designated a national commissary charged with protecting the Indigenes and exploring possible routes for construction of roads across the isthmus. The agreement, although negotiated directly by Indigenous representatives, was never completely effective. However, it is a good example of how, in the nineteenth century, states like Ecuador maintained a "ventriloquist mode of relations" with the Indigenes, while others, like Colombia, clearly identified Indigenous societies as political subjects.

After 1903, with the birth of the Republic of Panama, policies toward Indigenous groups were marked by two contradictory tendencies. One was the desire of the state to civilize Indigenous societies (education, evangelization, integration into the electoral system, etc.). The other was a tendency to concede autonomy: recognition of Indigenous governments and territories. This came in response to the failure of economic and political measures to acculturate and integrate them into national development, as well as the presence of external actors.

The establishment of San Blas, the first Indigenous comarca, between 1925 and 1953 would substantially influence relations between the state and Indigenous groups in Panama. The Kuna case demonstrated the importance of taking advantage of historical circumstances, including their agreements with the government of Bogotá in 1871 and the United States's presence during the Tule revolution of 1925 and its negotiations with the Panamanian state. Geography—San Blas being a border zone—and sociopolitical variables, including the formation of a group of young Indigenous intellectuals with considerable diplomatic capacity and the unity of distinct Kuna factions through a legitimate and representative organization, the Kuna General Congress, also made the Kuna case an example to follow in Panama. Beginning in the 1970s, both Indigenous groups and government agencies in charge of their affairs would try to replicate Kuna organizational forms in the Ngäbe, Buglé, Emberá, and Wounaan cases.

Kuna chief Estanislao López, elevated to the position of national Indian chief,[9] was entrusted with visiting the communities of the larger Indigenous groups in Panama to convince them of the need to adopt the congress system as a model of sociopolitical organization and for interaction with the state. The General Congress of the Emberá-Wounaan Comarca was institutionalized according to this model in 1983, the General

Congress of the Kuna Madungandí Comarca in 1996, the General Congress of the Ngäbe-Buglé Comarca in 1999, and the General Congress of the Kuna Wargandí Comarca in 2000. The Naso, with great expectations for a comarca, despite having a political structure founded on the recognition of a king, also adopted the standardized model, creating the Naso Council at the end of the 1990s. However, they were never officially recognized by the Panamanian government.

In conclusion, it should also be noted that Panama, unlike many other Latin American countries, never ratified the International Labour Organization's Convention No. 169 nor did it adopt a new multicultural constitution. Because of this, changes in "regimes of citizenship" have been minimal. Even if we cannot document that existing Indigenous autonomy has decreased, we can identify retroaction in policies of recognition of Indigenous governments and territories. This is clearly exemplified in the failure to approve the preliminary plan for the Naso Comarca at the beginning of the 2000s and the approval in 2009 of Law 72. This law establishes procedures for a limited, administrative recognition of collective ownership of lands outside comarcas that fails to respond to demands for autonomy of the Indigenes without comarcas. Their resources and territories are not recognized as Indigenous, and their political organizations are not recognized as government.

Articulation with Other Networks and Synergies Unleashed

Ecuador

During the second half of the 1960s and the first half of the 1970s, in support of their struggles for land, the Catholic Church assumed a protagonist role favoring the peasants by channeling and resolving many of the conflicts unleashed in the Ecuadorian Andes. In this sense, the posture of the "Church of the Poor," then under the direction of Bishop Leónidas Proaño from the Diocese of Riobamba (in the Chimborazo Province, with the largest Indigenous population in the country) is significant. Also significant is establishment of a distinguished group of institutions, like the Ecuadorian Center for Agricultural Services (Central de Servicios Agrícolas del Ecuador, CESA), the Center for Studies and Social Action (Centro de Estudios y Acción Social, CEAS), and the Ecuadorian Popular Progressive Fund (FEPP). All of this was born out of the acceptance of agrarian reform by the Church, made explicit in a pronouncement of the Ecuadorian Episcopal Conference. This was reinforced by a progressive trend emerging from the Second Vatican Council (1963) and the Third General Conference of the Latin American Episcopate of Medellín (1968). In this context, laity and clergy committed to the cause of the peasants and Indigenes pledged to strengthen NGOs that, like those above, had a marked reformist character and could establish aid programs in response to demands of the popular sectors. Their work was key in shaping the Indigenous movement later in two ways. First, with this support, organizations established organizational frameworks that still guide their work today. Many took root while Proañista priests worked to strengthen associational structures of the Indigenous world as a tool for social change (Fondo Ecuatoriano Populorum Progressio 1987). Second, the establishment of the above-mentioned NGOs set a trend of rural development that pursues objectives of communities and federations of communities (second-tier federations, the OSGs).

As we consider the roles of actors from the progressive Church (reconciled priests, catechists, literacy tutors, and rural outreach workers), we should not forget that prominent leftist militants, through the Ecuadorian Federation of Indigenes (FEI)—created in 1944 by the Communist Party to stimulate unionism among the Indigenous population—had initiated the important work of training Indigenous organizers. Researchers have encountered people who lived during the time of the agrarian conflicts of the 1960s and 1970s who remember lawyers and activists of the FEI advising community members on the most efficient strategies for taking lands and assisting in the establishment of peasant unions also active in intervening on the margins of what was happening with the haciendas (Guerrero 1993).

What appears to be most remarkable of all is that, instead of dissolving identities, these experiences reinforced them; instead of strengthening the formation of an imagined national mestizo community, they unleashed processes of reaffirmation of Indigenous identity. This invites reflection on the importance that different models of intervention had in the shaping of genuine organic intellectuals (in the Gramscian sense of the term) in the Andean milieu, who came to play a key role in the struggle for land and collective action under the umbrella of *indianismo* ("Indianness"). They became the first organizers of unions, communes, and associations and arose as the mediators between the complex world of hacienda peons and that of their external allies against oligarchic landowners. As they established organizational links with Indigenous communities, Catholic outreach workers and FEI activists supported the dense fabric of existing domestic and communal solidarity and encouraged the support of traditional leaders for movement leaders.

Panama

The history of the articulation of the Panamanian Indigenous movement with other networks does not differ much from that of Ecuador. Although the Kuna had initiated transnational contacts with pan-indigenist organizations before the 1970s,[10] no movement with pretensions of breaking interethnic boundaries existed until then. As we consider the emergence of civil Indigenous organizations, we must take into account the military coup of General Torrijos in 1968 and the influence of liberation theology. The Torrijista anti-imperialist and revolutionary discourse, along with the agreement to return the Panama Canal, profoundly influenced the generation of young Indigenes who entered Panama's National Institute (Instituto Nacional de Panamá) and the University of Panama (Universidad de Panamá) at the end of the 1960s. Relations with the United States compelled the birth of new Indigenous organizations such as the Kuna Youth Movement, founded in 1972 to promote the political participation of young Kuna in Torrijismo. With the support of the military government, new organizations succeeded in attracting a considerable number of Indigenes studying or working in urban areas. Far from their communities of origin, this new generation of leaders was becoming conscious of problems facing the nation. Some joined the Communist Party and studied in countries, like the Soviet Union, friendly to the Torrijos regime. From Indigenous associations born in Panama City, young Ngäbe-Buglé, Kuna, and Emberá mobilized at the local and national levels, working with civic organizations as migrants, peasants, or students, but not as Indigenes.

The lack of unity of the Panamanian Indigenous movement is closely related to the ideological framework within which the first social movements in Panama arose. The Marxist ideology of the People's Party inhibited the emergence of an Indigenous movement based on demands adapted to the needs of the original peoples. At the beginning of the 1980s, a new generation of young Indigenes took the reins of the leftist social movements and began distancing themselves from communist ideology. Assistance and information from the new transnational Indigenous organizations forming in Central and South America inspired this distancing. Ideas circulating in the exterior contradicted the Marxist-Leninist orientation of the People's Party and corresponded to their own criticisms of communist ideology. They called into question the communist notion of homogeneity and referenced cultural diversity and common problems of Indigenous groups throughout the world. The young Indigenes allowed themselves to be seduced by this new doctrine and soon realized that "the Indigenous movement needed to be a movement completely separated from political affairs." Instead of continuing to propagate the unifying ideas of the People's Party, they proposed "to embrace the flag of Indianismo" (Marcial Arias, interview by the author, Panama, December 23, 2002).

A new generation of young urban Indigenes took on the transition from revolutionary movement to *indigenista* movement. Thanks to alliances that they were able to establish with Indigenous organizations and foreign NGOs, they soon founded the first Indigenous NGOs: organizations that provided information and advised those interested in the cause of Pana-

manian Indigenes. The cause was distant from daily concerns of communities, closer to international debates about Indigenous rights.

The Catholic Church also marked the path that the Panamanian Indigenous movements would follow, beginning in the 1970s. After a profound internal critique, youth, progressives, and occasionally Indigenes
in the Church pushed for change in the form of understanding the faith
and coexistence with Indigenous beliefs. Missionaries working with Indigenous groups, the majority Claretians and Jesuits, began a transition
from an indigenista mission—in which the Indigenes were only the object of evangelization—to an Indianist mission in which the Indigenes
became subjects. In this context, they helped incipient organizations of
young Indigenes and strengthened the traditional political structures of
their communities.

Indigenous Groups and Neoliberal Development

Liberalization and opening are two of the magic words of neoliberal or-
thodoxy. Neoliberalism has proceeded in all of Latin America to remove
protection from the internal markets of supply and production and to
consolidate a legal framework capable of guaranteeing the operation of a
capitalist property market. This was accompanied by an unprecedented
withdrawal of the state from the realm of development policy, facilitating the proliferation of new agents in the rural areas (NGOs, for example) that went about supplanting the state in some spheres of activity
neglected by governments. We have witnessed, in sum, a complete privatization of policies and initiatives in rural development. Data provided by
Jorge León (1998) for the Ecuadorian case are illustrative: nearly three-
quarters (72.5 percent) of the NGOs that made their appearance in Ecuador during the twentieth century (through 1995) were established
between 1981 and 1994. Structural adjustment policies were implemented
beginning in 1982.

In the Andean region, NGOs played a very active role in the articulation of the OSGs as counterparts to their projects. This is because these
platforms are manageable structures, apparently well matched to the
bases of which they are composed, that, to play a bit with the rhetoric of
their leaders, condense all the virtues emanating from communitarian-
ism (with which Andean peasants have so often been stereotyped from
idealist perspectives). In a previous investigation (Bretón 2001) about
NGOs and Indigenous organizational structures, on the basis of a sample of 170 organizations with a total of 405 active rural development
projects at the end of the 1990s, we were able to confirm a clear tendency to concentrate projects and investments in parishes in the Andes
with the most Indigenous populations. While rural poverty is found distributed throughout the inter-Andean corridor, it appears that, with

some exceptions, the predominantly Quichua rural areas were the principal beneficiaries of development cooperation. The effect of ethnicity, the concentration of NGO programming in predominantly Quichua zones, contributed to a rapid process of organizational strengthening in the rural milieu. That this process appeared to be a consequence of the operational tendencies of the development agencies suggested to some investigators affiliated with the World Bank that because one of the characteristics of the Indigenous peasants was their high density of social capital, one of the Bank's priorities should be to encourage "empowerment" and improvement of the quality of life of this ethnically differentiated rural population (Bebbington and Carroll 2000; Carroll 2002, 2003).

The reality, however, is quite distant from this sweetened image of operations of NGOs. More ethnographic work is needed on the nature of their work, on the complex bundle of relations that have been established between leaders and bases, and on the links between these leaders-mediators and development agencies. At the moment, however, we are in a position to conclude that 1) most NGOs have been established thanks to the promotion, assistance, and inducement of foreign institutions tied to development programs, meaning that the motivation for their existence is external; 2) OSGs compete amongst themselves to maintain and increase their "clientele" (bases), producing misunderstandings, disagreements, ruptures, divisions, and conflicts; and 3) their functional dependence on obtaining resources from the development apparatus has brought with it the substitution of an ideological Indigenous leadership identified with political protest for one of technocratic character, estranged from the old organic intellectuals and converted into a sector of professional mediators more interested in the characteristics and importance of projects to be implemented than in the scope of projects or the abandonment by the state of its social obligations. All this has exerted a powerful influence in channeling demands of the Indigenous movement into forms compatible with the hegemonic model.

Ethnicity has been converted into a pole of attraction for investments in development; made Indigenous organizations in Ecuador "priority subjects" of interventions of the development apparatus; facilitated the establishment of a sector of Indigenous leaders in positions of management and/or control of many of these resources; and actively contributed to removing class content of many of the historical demands of the Indigenous movement (which had no place on the playing field of "projectism"), ethnifying discourse, and confining the demands and achievements of CONAIE within the imaginary of the "permitted Indian" (Hale 2004).

In Panama, the effects of development policies on the organization and institutionalization of the national Indigenous movement have been similar. The transformation, at the end of the 1990s, of the only organization that has up to now achieved unification of all the Indigenous congresses, the National Coordinating Body of Indigenous Peoples in Panama (Coordinadora Nacional de Pueblos Indígenas de Panamá, COONAPIP), illustrates this process. This organization sprang up around a project of a creating a common future in the context marked by the United States's invasion of Panama in 1989 and the five-hundredth anniversary of the "discovery" of the Americas in 1992. Despite the fact that it was initially very active on the political scene (pressuring the legislative assembly in favor of initiatives of great significance for the Indigenous groups, such as the drafts of laws relating to the Wargandí and Ngäbe-Buglé Comarcas, Ley Fundamental of Kuna Yala, legalization of territories of Emberá communities that were outside the comarca proper, and ratification of international conventions), COONAPIP was quickly transformed into an agency more concerned with the management of international funds than with politics. This change coincided with the implementation of a program financed by the European Union for institution building called the Program of Assistance for the Indigenous Peoples of Central America (Proyecto de Apoyo a los Pueblos Indígenas de América Central, PAPICA). As soon as COONAPIP became its national counterpart, very significant divergences began to appear among the groups of which it was composed, to the point that the General Congress of the Kuna Yala Comarca left the organization. Although many thought that the departure of the Kuna General Congress would be the end of COONAPIP, the organization, though weakened, remains active, representing the Emberá Congress, the Kuna Congress of Madungandí, the Kuna of Wargandí and Takarkunyala, the Ngäbe-Buglé General Congress, and the Naso Council. Since 2009, there have been attempts to revitalize COONAPIP through the promotion of a change of leadership, the upgrading of technical equipment, and the reintroduction of the Kuna General Congress.

Projectism and the emergence of NGOs made up of Indigenous professionals have also given rise to new tensions between traditionalist sectors (local and general congresses) and those who are supposed to be the new Indigenous representatives. An example is the competition for political representation and funds between Kuna NGOs (numbering about ninety around 2005) and the General Congress of the Kuna Yala Comarca. This competition demonstrates to what extent the emergence of new agencies responds to factors like the changing role of the nation-state, the initiatives of some Kuna professionals to create new sources of work, and the presence of donor entities (international agencies, NGOs of countries of the north, etc.) (Martínez Mauri 2005).

Some Final Reflections

Although we recognize the historical importance to the Ecuadorian Indigenous movement of claims of Amazonian peoples (Martínez Novo 2007) and the adoption of the traditional Andean model of the "peasant commune" (recognized by the state since 1937) by coastal groups such as the Tsáchilas (Ventura 1996), it is certain that the organizational density of the Andean Quichua communities has been a key influence in shaping CONAIE. The concentration of the Quichua population along the inter-Andean corridor must be considered when identifying causes of the consolidation of a pluriethnic macrostructure. Posed counterfactually, if it had not been for this circumstance, it would be difficult to explain the emergence of CONAIE.

To explain the articulation of a collective "Indigenous" identity capable of converting itself into a political vector of the first order, we must consider the nature of the changing relation of the state with Andean groups, at least since their "liberation" from the state's administrative apparatus. In other words, how did they emerge from the state's system of private administration of haciendas into the national sphere and later become established political players? The agrarian reform played a key role, because it represented an acceleration of the processes of internal differentiation of the Indigenous peasantry and thus formed the bases for the shaping of a new mediator elite that later would consolidate its status by means of its dialogue with the development apparatus and with the agents of national political power. In this process, a whole cast of characters, from the Communist Party and the progressive Catholic Church initially, to a distinguished cluster of cooperators, trainers, and technicians in the golden age of NGOs, competed to build and reinforce a very peculiar organizational structure. Peculiar because, in reality, it was an ad hoc construct brought about by the modus operandi of the development apparatus: here, the practical sense of the leaders and Indigenous foot soldiers was praiseworthy, especially considering their majority condition as subalterns. It is precisely this condition as subalterns racialized as inferior by white-mestizo sectors that facilitated, given seasonal migration, mutual recognition as "Indigenes" and the possibility of emerging from the mountains and seeing themselves reflected in the faces of those who were equally humiliated and excluded in the lowlands as "Indians."

Comparing this situation with the Panamanian context, characterized by the marginalization of the Indigenous population both geographically and economically, we recognize the importance of addressing historical processes over the long term in order to understand the formation of pluri- and monoethnic platforms. Only from this perspective can we understand the history of Indigenous autonomies in Panama, influenced by the political trajectory of the Kuna since the nineteenth century, and the late emergence of an incipient national Indigenous movement characterized by Torrijismo, liberation theology, and last but not least, lack of legitimacy in the eyes of Indigenous political organizations (but not those of the development apparatus) of the only national Indigenous organization, COONAPIP.

Finally, we want to emphasize that neither the strategic yet conflictive alliances among Ecuadorian Indigenous peoples nor the more solitary struggles of the Indigenous peoples of Panama can be understood without looking beyond the influence of globalization to more local dynamics. To understand these complex historical processes, it is necessary to analyze multiple factors, among them relations with the state, interethnic borders, and the place that the Indian occupies in the national imaginary. In doing so, we find that, rather than dissolving identities and global politics of mestizaje, the experiences of Indigenous peoples in both countries reinforce the processes of political reaffirmation of Indigenous identities. Their struggles and visibility as political actors represent the crisis of the politics of mestizaje as hegemonic ideology.

Acknowledgments

Part of this investigation has been made possible by the Postdoctoral Program Juan de la Cierva (JCI-2011–09784) and the research project "Hegemony, Domination, and Administration of Populations in Latin America: Continuities and Changes" (CS02011–23521), both supported by the Spanish Ministry of Economy and Competitiveness.

Notes

1. A "regimen of citizenship," as used by Yashar, defines members of the political community, rights this conveys, and typical mechanisms of intermediation with the state. In a sense, this is akin to the "system of administration of populations" used by Andrés Guerrero (2010).

2. *Organizaciones de segundo grado.*

3. This capacity has produced a series of concessions unthinkable a few decades earlier and transformation of rubrics such as respect on the part of the non-Indigenous for the Indigenous, constitutional recognition (in 1998 and 2008) of a number of important historic demands of the Indigenous movement, the appearance of Indigenes on the national political scene as regular actors, and the questioning of international understandings of their "conquest."

4. For example, a distinguished Kuna intellectual and lawyer, a member of one of the first Kuna NGOs (Kunas United for Napguana) and, until recently, technical staff of the World Bank in Panama, believes that Ecuador, along with

Bolivia, has served as an example to follow in relation to access to government positions (Atencio López, interview by the author, Panama, March 30, 2003).

5. This article was transformed into the current Article 127, Chapter VIII: "The State will guarantee to Indigenous communities the reservation of necessary lands and collective ownership of the same to ensure economic and social well-being."

6. The Ngäbe are the largest group (62.38 percent of the total of Indigenes), followed by the Kuna (19.28 percent), Emberá (7.49 percent), Buglé (5.97 percent), Wounaan (1.74 percent), Naso (or Teribe; 0.97 percent), Bri-Bri (0.26 percent), and Bokota (0.23 percent).

7. Although this hydroelectric center was planned with the objective of satisfying the country's energy demands, the communities living in the vicinity still have no electricity.

8. One example is the situation of the Indigenes who worked and lived on the banana plantations. During the 1950s, the United Fruit Company established in Bocas del Toro negotiated the working conditions of workers coming from the comarca with Kuna authorities. An ethnic hierarchy was established that impeded horizontal relations among the Indigenes working for the international company—the great majority of them Kuna and Ngäbe. Instead of creating multiethnic organizations when fighting for their interests, the Indigenes opted for the creation of monoethnic organizations, like the Kuna Workers Union (UTRAKUNA), which was recognized by the Panamanian government in 1972. See Bourgeois (1988).

9. *Cacique nacional indígena.*

10. In the 1940s, the Kuna linked up with a pioneer pan-Indigenous movement, the League of Nations of North American Indians. See Crum (2006), Deloria (1969), and Martínez Mauri (2007).

CHAPTER THIRTEEN

Beyond *Mestizaje*

Andean Interculturality in Ecuador

JOHN STOLLE-MCALLISTER

On June 4, 1990, the majority white-mestizo residents of Quito found the highways leading to their city blocked and the central areas of the historic district occupied by Indigenous activists. What most surprised many Quiteños was not so much Indigenous demands for effective land reform and redress of a series of legal issues, but rather that they *still* existed at all. Despite the fact that some estimates put the Indigenous population as high as three million out of a total population of twelve million, for many Ecuadorians, Indigenous peoples remained invisible or folkloric relics of the past. Over the next two decades, Indigenous organizations not only positioned themselves as the most public and effective face of the country's popular movements but also led a national dialogue about ethnic identity and cross-cultural relations that has moved Ecuadorian public discourse, unevenly and haltingly, away from Ecuador as a "mestizo" nation and toward it as an "intercultural" one.

Ecuador's Indigenous peoples were largely invisible to many non-Indigenous, because two centuries of an official discourse of *mestizaje*, which posits a national identity based on the synthesis of European and Indigenous cultures, had systematically erased them. Since most official expressions of mestizaje are ultimately Eurocentric attempts to superficially suture asymmetrical social, cultural, and economic relationships, they leave little room for other types of cultural expression. Although this concept may offer vindication and inclusion for some ethnically marginalized groups by incorporating them into discourses of national iden-

234

tity, for many Indigenous and Afro-descendent populations, it is a tool in a nation-building project that explicitly excludes them. After all, if a nation is based on a singular synthesis of its multiple cultural legacies, how are those groups who have maintained different identities and different practices to be included?

To counter this elite-directed assimilationist strategy, Indigenous and other minority organizations and intellectuals have embarked on a sometimes problematic project of interculturality, based not on covering over differences but rather on dialogue and debate between cultural groups aimed at transforming social, economic, and political relationships. In the case of Ecuador, the Indigenous movement has not only attempted to gain better material and political opportunities for its constituencies but also, by promoting pride in and demanding recognition of Indigenous identities and cultural practices, offered an explicit critique of the notion of mestizaje. Speaking from the margins of the mestizo nation, Indigenous groups have connected their material inequality with their historic exclusion from the nation-building process. Since their languages, cultures, communities, and economic production fell outside of the mestizaje framework of national belonging, public discourse ignored them. Spanish literacy tests, for instance, disenfranchised Indigenous people until 1979, demonstrating the "mestizo" state's unwillingness or inability to recognize publicly many of its citizens because of cultural difference. The rise and success of the Indigenous movement in Ecuador, therefore, is in part due to its ability to challenge elite-controlled constructions of mestizaje and to force a reconsideration of what it means to be Ecuadorian.

Indigenous demands for participation in, but not assimilation into, public life represent a fundamental challenge to state construction of nationality. Instead of the homogeneity implied in nationalistic discourses, Indigenous organizations demand imagining the plural and accepting difference rather than eliding it. The 2008 constitution, for instance, recognizes the plurality of the Ecuadorian nation, leaving the framework for further deepening and institutionalization of those ideals. On a more concrete level, in the ethnically mixed (primarily between white-mestizo and Kichwa) municipality of Otavalo, Kichwa organizations have successfully leveraged their slight demographic majority into control of local government institutions. Because, however, it is governing multicultural communities, the administration of Mayor Mario Conejo (2000–2014) has necessarily needed to negotiate with multiple groups and develop policies and programs that adequately represent the diverse interests of its population.

Mestizaje and Interculturality

With their independence from Spain, leaders of the newly independent American states needed to imagine themselves as different from their former colonial rulers and simultaneously suture the many ethnic differences that existed in each country. Although they maintained their orientation toward European thought and political practices, they began articulating a discourse of national identity that often glorified an enlightened, "noble-savage" Indigenous past while casting their populations as ones of mixed Indigenous and European background. That is not, of course, to suggest that the new republics became egalitarian utopias of cultural diversity. Indeed, the white, European-descended criollo elite continued to occupy positions of economic, political, and cultural power. Indigenous communities lost what little protection they had from the Spanish Crown and found their lands encroached upon and their communities bonded in various sorts of debt peonage to increasingly large landholders. While mestizaje may have provided a means through which some mestizo individuals could advance socially, for the majority of Indigenous people, it represented an ironic contradiction: just as the nation-state acknowledged the importance of past Indigenous peoples, it relegated actual Indigenous peoples to the role of savages and hyperexploitable labor.

Although Latin American cultures are clearly marked by the continual exchange of different cultural groups, there remain inequalities in the relationships between those groups. Colonial and national elites historically attempted to appropriate parts of subaltern cultures, without giving up control over the ultimate meanings created through that process. The Indigenous movements of the past generation, however, have questioned both the underlying inequality of the political and economic system and the exclusionary nature of modern/liberal thought, including the predominant "mestizo equals nation" formula. They recognize that their national societies are multivoiced systems and propose that different groups maintain their relative autonomy while negotiating more equitable relationships. Intercultural solutions to the issues created by unequal multicultural societies represent attempts not only at rethinking the foundations of a shared culture but also at reorganizing social relationships. These intercultural proposals endeavor to recognize the connection between relative position, power, and cultural production. In the project of the region's Indigenous movements, therefore, interculturality is not just a new interpretation of the heteroglossic make-up of Latin American societies but rather represents a reassessment of the political and epistemological assumptions about the creation of knowledge and the reproduction of power. Interculturality's ultimate goal would be, as Catherine Walsh (2009) and Walter Mignolo (2011) use the term, a "decolonial" society, one freed of the unequal institutions and legacies left by European hegemony.

How is interculturality different from other models of explaining cultural mixing, such as neoliberal multiculturalism? To begin with, interculturality originates as a proposal from the region's marginalized populations. It is fundamentally a political project aimed at allowing subaltern groups to participate in national public life without having to sacrifice their cultural differences or be otherwise assimilated into the dominant culture. Rather, it proposes that different groups construct meaningful interactions and share experiences, perspectives, and practices to build a more equitable society. A truly intercultural society would embody the Indigenous movement's call for "unity within diversity," which implies collaboration through respecting difference and building on each group's strengths. Such a strategy would necessitate decolonizing both public institutions and individual minds, which have historically reinforced exclusionary policies. It also requires developing new forms of representation, as the universalizing discourses of national unity do not allow for other ways of thinking or being. Finally, it has at its root the elimination of the structural economic and social inequalities that parallel the country's "asymmetrical multiculturalism" (Ramón 2005, 53). As the word implies, intercultural refers to what happens "between" cultures, specifically the relationships and interactions that occur between different cultural groups. Interculturality, therefore, is not simply the juxtaposition of difference, but the active dialogue and debate between differences, which lead to the sharing and transformation of experiences, meanings, and practices.

Interculturality proposes to recognize differences and take concrete steps toward rectifying the inequalities inherent in them. It is neither recognizing difference for the sake of difference nor assuming that different cultural groups have systematically and equally shared their cultures with each other to produce a "new" one. It aims, instead, to "overcome the supremacy of cultural hegemony and epistemic 'truths' assumed as universally valid, through a cultural resignification that challenges power relations by 'putting into doubt' and questioning [those truths] from a position of subalternity" (Puente Hernández 2005, 47). Unlike the ways in which mestizaje has been used by elites, because interculturality originates from marginalized sectors, it aspires to the recognition and inclusion of those marginalized sectors by creating new epistemological, economic, and cultural foundations.

Like all terms and concepts, however, interculturality is not immune from appropriation by elites to describe projects of unequal inclusion and assimilation (Guerrero Arias 2011). The term interculturality has its genesis in education programs ostensibly designed to integrate Indigenous populations into mainstream, national-mestizo society. The phrase "bilingual, intercultural education" has been applied by state education systems to their programs for Indigenous communities. Notably, "bilingual and intercultural" only applies to the Indigenous system, whereas the majority mestizo students do not participate in these programs, which are often underfunded and tend to reproduce cultural inequalities rather than promote meaningful cross-cultural dialogue (Farfán 2006; Martínez Novo and de la Torre 2010). Fidel Tubino (2002) criticizes this approach to ethnic dialogue as "functional" interculturality, particularly

as it is applied to education, because it assumes certain superficial and
essentialist attributes of cultures, while ultimately aiming at assimilating minority cultures into the dominant group. It does not propose an
authentic dialogue between groups. Other critics denote such approaches
as neoliberal multiculturalism, particularly as practiced by international
organizations such as the World Bank, which recognize the importance
of cultural difference but seek to find ways to use those cultural differences to shore up and expand capitalist economies and liberal, modernist institutions. These approaches, while recognizing the existence of
cultural differences, seek not to construct new, democratic, and decolonial institutions but rather to seek ways to *include those minority groups*
into dominant cultural institutions and practices (Mignolo and Escobar
2010). Theorists and practitioners of decolonial interculturality, on the
other hand, do not seek the *inclusion* of peripheral cultural groups into
institutions and epistemologies that have historically and systematically oppressed them but rather hope to transform them into ones that
are capable of mediating cultural difference in the process of creating
social and cultural diversity as fundamental building blocks of national
projects.

In a colonial situation, such as the one in which Indigenous communities live, an obstacle to interculturality lies in valuing one's own cultural
heritage, because colonialism devalues and distorts the cultures of others.
Europeans came to bring civilization and salvation to the "savages" of the
Americas and the Africans they later brought as slaves. Despite changes
from colony to republic, those basic values never changed, and although
the colonial system has adapted to changing times, it continues to rule
through the division of its marginalized population. Whether the terms
used were civilization, Christianity, development, progress, or modernity,
Indigenous culture was always identified as "backward" and in need of
repair or replacement. Because ongoing and systematic assaults on Native
cultures have often led to the internalization of these negative assessments
and an all-too-common sense that Native languages and cultural practices
were inherently deficient and imperfect, intercultural processes begin
with the revalorization and reaffirmation of subaltern cultures. It is only
by being able to recognize oneself that one is able to recognize others and
thereby have an understanding of one's own culture and interests that
allow one to enter into a meaningful dialogue with others. In this sense,
Indigenous activists have avoided labels such as mestizo or hybrid to describe their cultures, precisely because such approaches devalue their
differences.

A second fundamental component of interculturality is recognition
and respect of others. While this, of course, occurs at the interpersonal
level, respect and recognition also challenge those entrenched colonial
cultural and institutional barriers that enforce inequality. Mutual respect requires not only that members of subaltern groups be open to

understanding others but also that members of dominant groups be willing to question their own deeply held cultural beliefs and practices. Indigenous activists, therefore, do not see interculturality as just their work but rather as a counterhegemonic civilizational project that involves liberating national society from its colonial legacy (Walsh 2009).

Interculturality, therefore, is not just an abstract ideal but rather the basis for orienting concrete political projects that seek the inclusion of marginalized sectors in an open system of dialogue and exchange. Interculturality ultimately frees groups and individuals from the restrictions of colonial institutions and allows them to seek out and "generate processes of autonomy for individual development . . . and to decide which elements of other cultures to incorporate and which to reject, depending on their concrete needs and realities" (de la Torre 2006, 79). In seeking the recognition of cultural pluralism, along with the transformation of group relationships which that recognition implies, advocates of interculturality are searching for ways in which members of cultural groups can not only make use of their own cultural repertoire but also be involved in an ongoing process of exchanging ideas, knowledge, and practices with other groups. Rather than seeking cultural isolation, the goal of interculturality is to find ways of cultural sharing. Social, cultural, political, and economic equality would allow traditionally marginalized groups, coming from a perspective of self-understanding, to decide what parts of other cultures are adequate for their own form of development and how they can best appropriate what is useful or good, as they contribute to forging viable national societies.

Under this vision of interculturality, Indigenous communities are able to work for their own development, while maintaining their identity (which, of course, is always in a process of change). Historically, the price of entrance into the benefits of the modern world has been the abandonment of one's cultural heritage, values, and identity. Interculturality, as a political project, moves beyond identity politics to create a new inclusive praxis whose goal is the liberation of all from the alienating pressures of colonialism or Eurocentric mestizaje.

Ecuador's Indigenous Challenge to Mestizaje

Since interculturality comes from historic political struggles, it is important to consider the specific context of Ecuador. Like those of other Latin American countries, Ecuador's history is marked by the colonial legacy of racial and ethnic hierarchies, resulting in widespread inequality. At the same time, the Ecuadorian state has, since independence, needed to develop and promote a national identity that elided those differences in the name of national unity, progress, and modernity. Mestizaje became the historic framework to articulate this project.

In his history of the construction of Ecuadorian national identity, Hugo Benavides (2004) argues that although Ecuador is undoubtedly a multicultural and multiethnic country, elites have persistently attempted to erase those differences in their efforts to construct a narrative supporting their economic and political control over the country, resulting in what he calls the "nation-state's fractured subjects" (23). Beginning with the colonial encounter, race became a means through which Europeans legitimized their domination of other peoples, insisting on their inherent biological and cultural superiority, and

> the contemporary racial makeup of the Ecuadorian nation corresponds to this initial establishment of the primary racial categories as white (Spanish), white/mestizo, Indian, [and] black (Afro-Ecuadorian). . . . All of these groups, however, are included in a larger racial ideology of mestizaje and *blanqueamiento* which establishes a racial ideology of whiteness as the highest ideal and symbol of civilization. (42)

These racial categories are also often articulated with socioeconomic and political status, further reinforcing their apparent legitimacy. That is not to say that there is neither considerable contention over the enforcement of racial boundaries nor acceptance by all people of the notion of "whiteness" as inherently superior but rather that discourses of race and ethnicity circulate around and correspond to the historic establishment of white domination.

Colonization established "race" as one of the cornerstones of social categorization in Ecuador. Although there was no singular cultural group of "Indigenous" people at the moment of the European invasion, Spanish racial sensibilities sought to homogenize the heterogeneous groups of original inhabitants as "Indians" in contrast to their "white" status. Later, "black" was added to the overall racial makeup as enslaved Africans were brought to the region. There was considerable biological and cultural mixing among these groups, resulting in what were referred to as *castas*, who were neither Indian nor white, but who were proscribed from participating in higher levels of society. As these mestizo people grew in number, they began to be considered their own racial group (Roitman 2009, 97). Mestizaje also began to be understood as not only the biological mixing of races but also the mutual cultural appropriations that were taking place among these communities. This cultural fluidity, along with the sometimes-porous borders between mestizo and Indigenous communities, allowed for "Indigenous people who adopted non-Indigenous identity markers . . . to claim a mestizo identity and its benefits: this laid the foundation for a growing perception of *mestizaje as a process of acculturation for Indigenous people*" (Roitman 2009, 97; italics in the original).

After independence, with the abolition of Indian tribute in the 1850s (and with it the main legal distinction of Indigenous people) and the

Liberal Revolution of the late nineteenth century, the Ecuadorian state increasingly placed mestizaje as the centerpiece of its nation-building strategies. It became not only a way of dealing with difference but also, because Ecuador's elites controlled who was considered a mestizo and what the mestizo nation was, a way of defining what it meant to be Ecuadorian. Roitman argues that like all discourses, mestizaje is not neutral, and the "elite's construction of mestizaje in Ecuador, significantly, reflected a preoccupation with incorporating the masses into the state project, by providing a strategy of integration for the Indigenous people of Ecuador, rather than an interest in questioning and rephrasing their own identity" (99). Mestizaje and accepting the norms dictated by elites, such as abandoning Indigenous practices, was the means through which Indigenous people could become fully part of the nation. It was decidedly not an inclusive multicultural project, and it is no accident that the majority of the Ecuadorian population today calls itself not mestizo, but *white*-mestizo.

Mestizaje, in this context, therefore, is not necessarily a way of accessing one's multiple ethnic heritages but rather a means of laying claim to one's whiteness and to belonging to the hierarchically superior group. In terms of national ideology, mestizaje is the means of erasing ethnic difference to belong to the nation. While discussing Ecuador's Indigenous ancestry, then military dictator General Guillermo Rodríguez Lara famously opined that there were "no more problems in reference to the Indians . . . we all become white when we accept the objectives of national culture" (Whitten 1984, 167, quoted in Benavides 2004, 45). As late as the 1970s, therefore, the president of Ecuador could state that to be Ecuadorian one had to adopt the national, mestizo culture and thereby become "white."

This ideal is obviously fraught with contradictions. Throughout the nation-building enterprise of mestizaje, whiteness is held up as the ultimate goal of civilization, thereby eliminating the "Indian problem," while it simultaneously glorifies an Indigenous past as a cornerstone of Ecuadorian national identity. Benavides (2004) argues that

> more than a literal reality, the mestizaje ideology is an ideal, a wish, and a rhetorical recourse for covering up any difference (racial, ethnic, economic, religious, sexual, etc.) in the country. Difference is seen as dangerous; therefore, its mere presence brings into question and threatens the construction of a national identity. In Ecuador, a mestizo ideology has traditionally been employed by the elite to maintain power over the Indigenous population and other national groups. It is as if, through the invention of a national Ecuadorian identity, the elite is attempting to homogenize and hide the "other." Up to now, the country has been based on the exclusion of difference. (47)

Mestizaje serves, therefore, not as a liberationist gesture toward respecting cultural diversity but as a means through which that diversity is
managed and stamped with the values and characteristics of dominant
white, European culture.

Imagining and Building an Intercultural State

For many Indigenous and Afro-Ecuadorians, national identity, as espoused
through mestizaje, necessarily excludes them, unless they are willing (and
able) to change who they are and accept the imposition of colonial identities. Beginning in the 1960s, as ethnicity became more politicized, subaltern groups began to question more systematically the bases upon which
their relationship with the state and with the majority culture were constructed. By June 1990, the country's national Indigenous organization,
the Confederation of Indigenous Nationalities of Ecuador (La Confederación de Nacionalidades Indígenas del Ecuador, CONAIE) was prepared
to lead its first national protest, which occupied Quito and paralyzed
most of the country. The Levantamiento (Uprising) represented the most
visible presence of an Indigenous movement that now had a national
reach and rejected not only economic inequality but also the cultural inequality implied by a universalizing mestizaje. The surprise of many
non-Indigenous people demonstrated that many of them did not realize
there were many Indigenous people left in the country nor that "their
Indians" would revolt in such a way, which suggests the degree to which
the trope "mestizaje equals nation" dominated the majority's thinking on
ethnic issues.

The Indigenous movement's strength, cohesion, and success represented an ongoing process of organizing and of building self-identity that
has its contemporary roots in the early twentieth century, when Socialist
and Communist parties activists began working with Sierra Kichwa
communities. It is important to note that those early organizers, in particular, operated in conjunction with community leaders, respecting and
promoting cultural and linguistic differences (Becker 2008). Over time,
the leftist parties became more focused on class issues (essentially repeating the same mestizaje argument of their elite opponents), leading to
a break with the newly assertive Kichwa organizations in the 1970s. In
1980, Kichwa communities of the highlands formed a regional organization, Ecuador Runakunapak Rikcharimuy (Confederation of Peoples of
Kichwa Nationality [Confederación de Pueblos de la Nacionalidad Kichwa
del Ecuador, ECUARUNARI]), and actively participated in the foundation of CONAIE in 1986. Besides class concerns (land reform, in particular), the movement also framed its arguments in terms of nationalities,
as opposed to ethnicity, and sought such rights as bilingual education,
local autonomy, and traditional forms of justice.

Through a series of uprisings throughout the 1990s, CONAIE positioned itself as the voice of not only Indigenous peoples but also the broader popular movement by simultaneously advocating for far-reaching economic change as well as recognition of specific ethnic demands (Albó 2008; Gerlach 2003; Sawyer 2004). Their intercultural project of resistance to neoliberalism and their critique of undemocratic state structures contributed to weakening the commonsense acceptance of mestizaje. Their protests made explicit links between an economic elite that benefitted from widespread inequality and the systematic suppression of difference. If mestizaje serves to suture over differences, as Roitman and Benavides argue, then the Indigenous movements and their linkages with non-Indigenous groups with common issues challenged the notion that Ecuador was a singular people. They sought to participate in public life by speaking for themselves and their own interests while finding common cause with other exploited groups. They refused to accept assimilation into a national project that denied their existence by proposing instead that Ecuador reorganize itself as a pluricultural and plurinational state.

One of CONAIE's central arguments is that the Ecuadorian state needs to recognize its Indigenous inhabitants not as contributors to the mestizo nation but rather as distinct nationalities unto themselves. Along with that recognition would come local autonomy within territories under Indigenous control as well as the reformulation of the state to allow for Indigenous participation without demanding their assimilation. This challenge to the predominant modernist linkage of nations and states could lead to what Deborah Yashar (2005) has denominated a "postliberal" state, based on plurality, which cuts to the heart of mestizaje by insisting on cooperation among different groups rather than the forging together of differences to create a new homogenous whole. To effect the kinds of dramatic changes that the Indigenous movement has long advocated has required a multi-tiered strategy not only to reposition Indigenous peoples in the national imaginary but also to re-found the state itself, both nationally and locally.

The movement has become an important political presence. The political movement Pachakutik was founded by CONAIE in 1996, and it has consistently won representation in the National Assembly and, as a main partner in the 2002 presidential coalition with Lucio Gutíerrez, held several cabinet positions. Its national political success, however, has been mixed at best. Pachakutik/CONAIE's short-lived alliance with Gutíerrez proved disastrous and demonstrated internal leadership divisions, which have been exploited by political rivals since then (Becker 2011; Mijeski and Beck 2011; Ramírez Gallegos 2009). Although CONAIE has won important concessions from the state, such as the right to bilingual education and control over some development funds, which have contributed to pluralizing the state, it has not been able to sustain its political momentum from the 1990s.

One of the most important contributions to re-founding the Ecuadorian state, however, comes from its undeniable influence in framing the 2008 constitution. Although the writing process was at times contentious, and Indigenous organizations were not completely satisfied with its outcome, the constitution, as the organizing document of the Ecuadorian state, acknowledges the plurality of the country's population. The preamble, for instance, reads:

> WE (*nosotras y nosotros*), the sovereign people of Ecuador
> RECOGNIZING our millenarian roots, forged by women and men from different peoples
> CELEBRATING nature, the Pacha Mama, of which we are part and which is vital to our existence,
> INVOKING the name of God and recognizing our different forms of religiosity and spirituality
> APPEALING to the wisdom of all the cultures that enrich us as a society
> AS HEIRS to the social liberation struggles against all forms of domination and colonialism
> AND with a profound commitment to the present and future
> HEREBY decide to build
> A new form of public coexistence in diversity and harmony with nature, to achieve the good life, the *sumak kawsay*;
> A society that respects, in all its dimensions, the dignity of individuals and community groups

This remarkable opening recognizes difference as the basis for cooperation, rather than insisting on sameness. By using the male and female forms of "we" (still not a common practice in Spanish), the document begins with an unsettling gesture, since standard Spanish recognizes the male form (*nosotros*) to include both men and women when referring to a mixed group. By using this marked form, the writers are not only explicitly including women but also challenging the often subconscious ways in which language structures inequalities and erasures. The second line recognizes the country's millenarian roots and its distinct peoples. The third line, by paying tribute to Pacha Mama, not only points to Andean cosmologies but also, in highlighting the importance of nature to all existence, makes them relevant to today's most pressing issues and not merely a legacy of past glories. The fourth line, by invoking God, points to Western cosmologies but also explicitly recognizes the variety of religious beliefs and practices in the country. The next line again calls to the importance of all the country's cultures and the knowledge and wisdom they bring to the whole. The final two lines place the state as the inheritor not of colonial practices but as the end result of long decolonial struggles.

Furthermore, it defines the state's purpose as bringing about "sumak kawsay," an Andean concept that means living well. Here the constitution deviates from the purpose of constructing a unitary nation built strictly on Western, liberal foundations to a state open to Andean philosophy and traditional practices of reciprocity. This openness to the simultaneous multiplicity of Ecuador's cultural inheritance recognizes that the purpose of the Ecuadorian state is to find a new way for citizens to live together, respecting each other's differences and attempting to *construct* the ideal of living well.

Of course, there is often a substantial difference between the ideals expressed in a constitution and the actual practices of political actors. There has been a deep and public dispute, for instance, between leftist president Rafael Correa and CONAIE over, among other things, control of the bilingual, intercultural education system; water distribution; and mining rights in Indigenous territory. Although the constitution clearly lays out the responsibility of the state in consulting Indigenous communities that are affected by these policies, the Correa administration has often failed to do so and has accused his critics of being childish, ethnic fundamentalists, and terrorists. For their part, CONAIE believes that the administration is motivated by short-term economic interests and has fallen into familiar patterns of neocolonial attitudes and behaviors (Confederation of Indigenous Nationalities of Ecuador 2010).

If the national-level political activity of the Indigenous organizations and the idealized goals set forth in the country's new constitution have led to mixed success in promoting a truly intercultural society, it has experienced more regional success. Since the end of the twentieth century, the northern Sierra city of Otavalo has been a national (and even international) leader in establishing intercultural governance, providing an insightful example of the hopes and challenges of implementing these ideals. As Kichwa-Otavalo organizations have grown in power and as Kichwa communities begin to successfully lay claim to political representation, what becomes obvious is that even in territories where Kichwa people are a majority, they share space and institutions with non-Kichwa peoples. In other words, despite claims of national organizations that Indigenous peoples should be autonomous in their own territories, the reality is that to govern effectively, newly empowered Kichwa politicians *need* to work with white-mestizo organizations as well.

The historic domination of Indigenous communities by white and white-mestizo elites can be read in the patterns of urban settlement. Cities were traditionally the seats of power and the almost exclusive domains of the country's white and white-mestizo elites and small middle classes. Indigenous communities occupied the countryside and hinterlands, and although Indigenous individuals ventured into the cities for work, commerce, or bureaucratic obligations, they generally did not live there. This pattern was clearly in force in Otavalo until the end of the twentieth century, helping to police the boundaries of cultural differences, despite official ideologies exhorting mestizaje and a universal, mestizo nationality. Beginning in the 1940s, Otavalo's Kichwa population created and prospered from national and then global artisan trade networks. Today, Kichwa-Otavalo merchants can be found around the world and in constant communication with their locally based producers. They operate several import/export companies and seek to continually upgrade their styles, production techniques, and distribution networks (Kyle 2000; Maldonado 2004; Meisch 2002). Successful merchants not only reinvested the capital gains that accompanied this growth but also financed "retaking" the city by buying urban property and businesses. By the end of the twentieth century, Kichwa residents accounted for around 60 percent of the city's total population of fifty-two thousand and constituted an important political and economic force, which translated into the electoral victory of Mario Conejo as mayor on the Pachakutik slate in 2000.

Conejo, who is a sociologist by training, describes himself as an "urban Indian" and sees his role as mayor to govern on behalf of not just the Kichwa organizations that helped him win election but also the entire multicultural population of his city (Kowii 2006). This stance has led to criticism from some Kichwa organizations and activists, as they believe that his policies on economic development and urban renewal benefit Otavalo's urban residents more than the mainly rural communities that surround the municipality. After winning reelection in 2004, Conejo broke with Pachakutik, citing ideological disagreements with the national party, which he believed was in many ways fighting battles that it had already won. In 2009, he again won reelection—this time in an alliance with President Correa's Alianza PAIS party, which put him clearly at odds with CONAIE and many national Indigenous leaders (Lalander 2010). He acknowledges that many of his opponents "don't consider me Indigenous anymore. They say I am an 'Indian-Mestizo'" (interview by the author, Otavalo, March 1, 2007) because of his marriage to a white-mestiza woman and his ability to network among white-mestizo organizations. These tensions, however, in many ways highlight the intercultural, rather than the strictly Kichwa, agenda of politicians like Conejo. They point to the contentious processes involved in defining and forging intercultural policies, suggesting that rather than a singular Indigenous agenda, interculturality is the result of constant negotiations over meaning and relationships among and between groups (Stolle-McAllister 2013).

In Otavalo, the municipal government has actively promoted Kichwa and other ethnic communities' identities through festivals, education, and consultation processes, while simultaneously focusing on how to best advance the standard of living and life possibilities for all of its citizens. One of Conejo's major initiatives has been making the municipal Office of Citizen Participation and Intercultural Dialogue the means through which development and infrastructure needs are raised and addressed. While consulting communities and neighborhoods about infrastructure initiatives and paying attention to local decision-making processes, Conejo has also consistently employed professional technical advisors to ensure the effectiveness of mid- and long-term planning and follow-through. A second important initiative has been the municipal school, which operates outside of the national school system and has a specific focus on teaching students the importance of intercultural living by employing teachers from various ethnic backgrounds, teaching Kichwa as part of the regular curriculum, and instructing students about their human rights. Finally, the municipal government continues to be a sponsor and promoter of such important events as Inti Raymi (the Festival of the Sun) and Pawkar Raymi (the Festival of Spring) as means through which different communities can deepen and share their beliefs and their cultural histories. These and similar initiatives give voice to the multivocal dialogue within Kichwa communities and between them and non-Kichwa entities as well.

Kichwa community members in Otavalo, therefore, simultaneously promote local identities and cultural practices while seeking greater integration into global economic and cultural processes. This represents an intercultural project because the Otavalos do not accept loss of their cultural distinctiveness as the price for participation; rather, they seek to capitalize on that difference as their means of interacting with other communities. As Otavalo merchants establish networks and communities in cities around the world, they certainly adopt some of the practices and beliefs that they encounter abroad, but they bring them back home and make them uniquely theirs. Hip-hop and reggaeton in Kichwa, changing dress and hairstyles, and multilingual, cosmopolitan individuals represent cultural hybridization, but these individuals continue to consider themselves to be Kichwa and to be active participants in an ever-evolving and dynamic cultural process. Part of their intercultural experience is being able to negotiate different cultural groups, being open to constructing (and changing) their own cultural processes, and not feeling like they have to give up being different from those other cultural groups. In the case of Otavalo, because of their economic success, they are better able to engage those dialogues from a position of relative equality.

Conclusion

Mestizaje is undoubtedly an important cultural concept in Latin America and has been used as a liberating discourse for many marginalized groups as a means through which they lay claims to inclusion. However, mestizaje in the hands of elites has had the opposite effect by becoming a totalizing discourse that flattens the actual cultural diversity of the population by imposing a new homogenous national identity. This new homogeneity explicitly excludes ethnic minorities who have constructed and maintained identities distinct from the "mixed" nation. Although contact between different cultural groups inevitably ends up in transformed meanings, all too often the more powerful groups, as demonstrated by elites' use of mestizaje, dominate those transformed meanings.

Ultimately, part of the problem is that Latin American societies have not abandoned legacies of colonialism and its demarcation and stratification of people based on race and ethnicity. Although independence formally ended colonial rule, the underlying racist assumptions remained, and elites in the nation-states sought to articulate a sense of national identity based on a supposed universal melding of Indigenous and European culture, resulting in the disappearance of both and the creation of a new race, or new cultural formation. Of course, Indigenous and Afro-descendent communities did not really disappear, and their erasure from national public life was yet another form of colonial violence against them. Resistance has existed from the time of the Spanish Conquest, and in more recent years, activists and scholars from these ethnically marginalized communities have embarked on a project aimed at decolonization and a redefinition of their relationships to national society. This new definition requires that they not only eliminate the internalized ideas and practices handed down through centuries of racism and colonization but also engage a multiplicity of cultural groups in a new intercultural project.

Ecuador has been the epicenter of the region's Indigenous movements through the latter decades of the twentieth century. Although the movement has had mixed political success at the national level, it has successfully inserted some of its most fundamental demands for recognition and intercultural inclusion into the 2008 constitution. While the country takes time to put those ideals into practice and different political factions maneuver for position, in the northern Sierra, communities like Otavalo offer vivid examples of what intercultural policies and practices look like. The municipality of Otavalo includes a multicultural population, and Kichwa leaders who have assumed local office have continuously sought to negotiate with, borrow, and adapt from the plurality of their community as they attempt to advance sustainable and equitable development strategies. Inclusive development that is respectful of cultural differences and seeks to actively use those differences for everyone's well-being is a fitting goal for decolonizing an intercultural society.

REFERENCES

Albó, Javier. 2008. *Movimientos y poder indígena en Bolivia, Ecuador y Perú*. La Paz: CIPCA.

Alonso, Ana María. 2004. "Conforming Disconformity: 'Mestizaje,' Hybridity, and the Aesthetics of Mexican Nationalism." *Cultural Anthropology* 19(4): 459–90.

Alves dos Santos, Ivair Augusto. 2006. *O movimento negro e o estado (1983– 1987): O caso do Conselho de Participação e Desenvolvimento da Comunidade Negra no Governo de São Paulo*. São Paulo: Imprensa Oficial.

Anderson, Benedict. 1993. *Comunidades imaginadas*. Mexico City: Fondo de Cultura Económica.

Anzaldúa, Gloria. 1987. *Borderlands, La Frontera: The New Mestiza*. San Francisco: Aunt Lute Books.

Araya, Alejandra. 1999. *Ociosos, vagabundos y malentretenidos en Chile colonial*. Santiago: DIBAM.

Argentina. Instituto Nacional de Estadística y Censos (INDEC). 2001. *Encuesta complementaria de pueblos indígenas (ECPI) 2004–2005: Complementaria del censo nacional de población, hogares y viviendas 2001*. Buenos Aires: Instituto Nacional de Estadística y Censos. Accessed September 5, 2010. http://www.indec.mecon.gov.ar/webcenso/ECPI/index_ecpi.asp.

———. Ministerio del Interior. 1966–1968. *Censo indígena nacional* (CIN). Buenos Aires: Ministerio del Interior, República Argentina.

Arguedas, José María. 1971. *El zorro de arriba y el zorro de abajo*. Buenos Aires: Losada.

Arnold, Matthew. 1869. *Culture and Anarchy: An Essay in Political and Social Criticism*. Reprint, Cambridge: Cambridge University Press, 2011.

Arosemena, Alexander. 2004. "El proyecto agroforestal Ngäbe: Un vistazo al territorio." *La Prensa* (Panama), March 27. Accessed June 12, 2009. http://mensual.prensa.com/mensual/contenido/2004/03/27/hoy/portada/1594589.html.

Assies, Willem. 2005. "'Two Steps Forward, One Step Back': Indigenous Peoples and Autonomies in Latin America." In *Autonomy, Self-Governance and Conflict Resolution: Innovative Approaches to Institutional Design in Divided*

Societies, edited by Marc Weller and Stefan Wolff, 180–212. New York: Routledge.

Barsky, Osvaldo. 1988. *La reforma agraria ecuatoriana*. Quito: Corporación Editora Nacional.

Bebbington, Anthony, and Thomas Carroll. 2000. "Induced Social Capital and Federations of the Rural Poor." Social Capital Initiative Working Paper, no. 19. Washington, DC: World Bank.

Becker, Marc. 2008. *Indians and Leftists in the Making of Ecuador's Modern Indigenous Movements*. Durham, NC: Duke University Press.

———. 2011. *¡Pachakutik! Indigenous Movements and Electoral Politics in Ecuador*. Updated ed. Boulder, CO: Rowman & Littlefield.

Benavides, O. Hugo. 2004. *Making Ecuadorian Histories: Four Centuries of Defining Power*. Austin: University of Texas Press.

Bengoa, José. 2000. *La emergencia indígena en América Latina*. Mexico City: Fondo de Cultura Económica.

Bento, Maria Aparecida Silva. 2005. "Branquitude e poder—A questão das cotas para negros." In *Ações afirmativas e combate ao racismo nas Américas*, edited by Ana Flávia Magalhães Pinto, Maria Lúcia de Santana Braga, and Sales Augusto dos Santos, 165–77. Brasília: Ministério da Educação, Secretaria de Educação Continuada, Alfabetização e Diversidade.

Berlin, Isaiah. 1963. *Karl Marx: His Life and Environment*. New York: Oxford University Press.

Bernard, Carmen. 2001. "Mestizos, mulatos y ladinos en Hispanoamérica: Un enfoque antropológico de un proceso histórico." In *Motivos de la antropología americanista: Indagaciones en la diferencia*, edited by Miguel León Portilla, 105–33. Mexico City: Fondo de Cultura Económica.

Bernardino, Joaze. 2004. "Levando a raça a sério: Ação afirmativa e correto reconhecimento." In *Levando a raça a sério. Ação afirmativa e universidade*, edited by Joaze Bernardino and Daniela Galdino, 15–38. Rio de Janeiro: DP&A.

Berthrong, Donald. 1963. *The Southern Cheyenne*. Norman: University of Oklahoma Press.

Bhagwati, Jagdish. 2004. *In Defense of Globalization*. New York: Oxford University Press.

Bierschenk, Thomas, Jean-Pierre Chauveau, and Jean-Pierre Olivier de Sardan. 2000. *Courtiers en développement. Les villages Africains en quête de projets*. Paris: APAD and Karthala.

Blankstein, Charles S., and Clarence Zuvekas Jr. 1973. "Agrarian Reform in Ecuador: An Evaluation of Past Efforts and the Development of a New Approach." *Development and Cultural Change* 22(1): 73–94.

Bonilla-Silva, Eduardo. 2006. *Racism Without Racists: Color-Blind Racism and the Persistence of Racial Inequality in the United States*. New York: Rowman & Littlefield.

Borchart de Moreno, Christiana. 1981. "El período colonial." In *Pichincha: Monografía histórica de la región nuclear Ecuatoriano*, edited by Segundo Moreno Yánez, 193–274. Quito: Consejo Provincial de Pichincha.

Borja, Karina. 2009. "El baile del Yumbo, un símbolo de resistencia: Análisis del paisaje de San Isidro del Inca." Paper presented at the Fifty-Third International Congress of Americanists, Mexico City, July 19–24.

Bort, John R. 1976. "Guaymí Innovators: A Case Study of Entrepreneurs in a Small Scale Society." PhD diss., Department of Anthropology, University of Oregon.

Bourdieu, Pierre, and Jean-Claude Passeron. 1977. *Reproduction in Education, Society and Culture*. Translated by Richard Nice. London: Sage Publications.

Bourgois, Philippe. 1988. "Conjugated Oppression: Class and Ethnicity Among Guaymí Banana Workers." *American Ethnologist* 15(2): 328–48.

Brandão, André Augusto. 2007. *Cotas raciais no Brasil: A primeira avaliação*. Rio de Janeiro: DP&A Editora.

Brazil. Ministério da Educação. 2004. *Diretrizes curriculares nacionais para a educação das relações étnico-raciais e para o ensino de história e cultura afro-brasileira e africana*. Brasília: Ministério da Educação/SECAD.

———. 2008. *Contribuições para implementação da Lei 10.639/2003*. Brasília: Ministério da Educação/UNESCO.

Bretón, Víctor. 2001. *Cooperación al desarrollo y demandas étnicas en los Andes Ecuatorianos. Ensayos sobre indigenismo, desarrollo rural y neoindigenismo*. Quito: FLACSO.

Briones, Claudia. 2002a. "Mestizaje y blanqueamiento como coordenadas de aboriginalidad y nación en Argentina." *Runa* 23:61–88.

———. 2002b. "'We Are Neither an Ethnic Group nor a Minority, but a Pueblo-Nación Originario': The Cultural Politics of Organizations with Mapuche Philosophy and Leadership." In *Contemporary Perspectives on the Native Peoples of Pampa, Patagonia, and Tierra del Fuego: Living on the Edge*, edited by Claudia Briones and José Luis Lanata, 101–20. Westport, CT: Bergin and Garvey.

———. 2004. "Construcciones de aboriginalidad en Argentina." *Bulletin de la Société Suisse des Américanistes* 68:73–90.

———. 2005. "Formaciones de alteridad: Contextos globales, procesos nacionales y provinciales." In *Cartografías argentinas: Políticas indígenas y formaciones provinciales de alteridad*, edited by Claudia Briones, 11–43. Buenos Aires: Antropofagia.

Briones, Claudia, and Raúl Díaz. 1997. "La nacionalización/provincialización del 'desierto': Procesos de fijación de fronteras y de constitución de otros internos en el Neuquén." Paper presented at the V Congreso de Antropología Social, La Plata, Argentina, July–August. Accessed September 3, 2010. http://www.naya.org.ar.

Bruce, Jorge. 2007. *Nos habíamos choleado tanto: Psicoanálisis y racismo*. Lima: Universidad de San Martín de Porres.

Brumann, Christoph. 1998. "The Anthropological Study of Globalization: Towards an Agenda for the Second Phase." *Anthropos* 93:495–506.

Bryer, Philip. 1997. "Globalization: Advocates, Opponents and Rebels." Unpublished exit paper. Eugene: International Studies Program, University of Oregon.

Brysk, Alison. 2000. *From Tribal Village to Global Village: Indian Rights and International Relations in Latin America*. Stanford: Stanford University Press.

Carpio Muñoz, Juan Guillermo. 1996. "La identidad cultural y el nuevo mestizaje." In *Imagen y leyenda de Arequipa: Antologia 1540–1990*, edited by Edgardo Rivera Martínez, 677–79. Lima: Fundacion M. J. Bustamante de la Fuente.

Carrasco, Hernán. 1993. "Democratización de los poderes locales y levantamiento indígena." In *Sismo étnico en el Ecuador. Varias perspectivas*, edited by José Almeida Vinueza, 29–69. Quito: CEDIME; Abya-Yala.

Carroll, Thomas F. 2002. *Construyendo capacidades colectivas: Fortalecimiento organizativo de las federaciones indígenas en la Sierra ecuatoriana*. Quito: Thomas F. Carroll.

———. 2003. "Tales of Collective Empowerment in the Andes." Paper presented at the meeting of Latin American Studies Association, Dallas, March 27–29.

Carvalho, José Jorge de. 2005. *Inclusão étnica e racial no Brasil: A questão das cotas no ensino superior*. São Paulo: Attar Editorial.

Castoriadis, Cornelius. 1975. *La institución imaginaria de la sociedad*. Buenos Aires: Tusquets Editores.

Chaves, Margarita, and Marta Zambrano. 2006. "From *Blanqueamiento* to *Reindigenización*: Paradoxes of *Mestizaje* and Multiculturalism in Contemporary Colombia." *Revista Europea de Estudios Latinoamericanos y del Caribe* 80:5–23.

Cheyenne and Arapaho Planning and Development Department. 2010. *2011–2016 Comprehensive Economic Development Strategy Five Year Plan*. Concho, OK: Cheyenne and Arapaho Planning and Development Department.

Chisaguano, Silverio. 2006. *La población indígena del Ecuador: Análisis de estadísticas socio-demográficas*. Quito: Instituto Nacional de Estadística y Censos.

Cohen, Erik. 1989. "The Commercialization of Ethnic Crafts." *Journal of Design History* 2(2–3): 161–68.

Confederation of Indigenous Nationalities of Ecuador (La Confederación de Nacionalidades Indígenas del Ecuador, CONAIE). 2010. "Constitución del Parlamento Plurinacional." Accessed July 2, 2010. http://www.conaie.org/nacionalidades-y-pueblos.

CooperAcción. 2012. "Mapa: Concesiones mineras." Accessed April 22, 2013. http://www.cooperaccion.org.pe/Concesiones-Mineras.html.

Coordinadora Nacional de Pastoral Indígena (CoNaPI), Pastoral Social-Caritas Panamá (PS-C), Acción Cultural Ngóbe (ACUN), and Fe y Alegria Panamá (FyA). 2003. *Ni Ngóbe ñünadi Kóre: El pueblo Ngóbe vivirá siempre*. Panama City: Coordinadora Nacional de Pastoral Indígena (CoNaPI), Pastoral Social-Caritas Panamá (PS-C), Acción Cultural Ngóbe (ACUN), and Fe y Alegria Panamá (FyA).

Cornejo Polar, Antonio. 1983. "La literatura peruana: Totalidad contradictoria." *Revista de Crítica Literaria Latinoamericana* 9(18): 37–50.

Cosamalón, Ana Lucía. 1993. "El lado oculto de lo cholo: Presencia de rasgos culturales y afirmación de una identidad." *Allpanchis* 25(41): 211–26.

Costa, Sérgio. 2007. "Unidos e iguais? Anti-racismo e solidaroedade no Brasil contemporâneo." *Pensamiento Iberoamericano* 2(1). Accessed July 10, 2010. http://www.pensamientoiberoamericano.org/xnumeros/1/pdf/pensamientoI beroamericano-48.pdf.

Crum, Steven James. 2006. "Almost Invisible: The Brotherhood of North American Indians (1911) and the League of North American Indians (1935)." *Wicazo Sa Review* 21(1): 43–59.

Cruz, Leonardo Borges da. 2006. "Para além do racismo." In *Ethnos Brasil: Publicação semestral do NUPE, núcleo negro da UNESP para pesquisa e extensão*, 5(5). São Paulo: Núcleo Negro da UNESP (NUPE) at São Paulo State University.

Dahl, Robert Alan. 1967. *Pluralist Democracy in the United States: Conflict and Consent*. Chicago: Rand McNally.

de la Cadena, Marisol. 1998. "Silent Racism and Intellectual Superiority in Peru." *Bulletin of Latin American Research* 17(2): 143–64.

———. 2000. *Indigenous Mestizos: The Politics of Race and Culture in Cuzco, Peru, 1919–1991*. Durham, NC: Duke University Press.

———. 2001a. "The Racial Politics of Culture and Silent Racism in Peru." Paper presented at the World Conference Against Racism, Racial Discrimination, Xenophobia and Related Intolerance, Durban, South Africa, August 31–September 7.

———. 2001b. "Reconstructing Race: Racism, Culture and *Mestizaje* in Latin America." *NACLA Report on the Americas* 34(6): 16–23.

de la Torre, Luis. 2006. "La interculturalidad desde la perspectiva del desarrollo social y cultural." *Revista Sarance, Instituto Otavaleno de Antropologia* 25:62–87.

Dean, Carolyn. 1999. *Inka Bodies and the Body of Christ: Corpus Christi in Colonial Cuzco, Peru*. Durham, NC: Duke University Press.

Delgado-P., Guillermo. 1994. "Ethnic Politics and the Popular Movement." In *Latin America Faces the Twenty-First Century: Reconstructing a Social Justice Agenda*, edited by Susanne Jonas and Ed McCaughan, 77–88. Boulder, CO: Westview Press.

Deloria, Vine, Jr. 1969. *Custer Died for Your Sins: An Indian Manifesto*. New York: Macmillan.

Delrio, Walter. 2005. *Memorias de expropiación: Sometimiento e incorporación indígena en la Patagonia (1872–1943)*. Bernal, Argentina: Editorial Universidad Nacional de Quilmes.

Delrio, Walter, Diana Lenton, Marcelo Musante, Mariano Nagy, Alexis Papazian, and Pilar Pérez. 2010. "Discussing the Indigenous Genocide in Argentina: Past, Present and Consequences of Argentinean State Policies Toward Native Peoples." *Genocide Studies and Prevention* 5(2): 138–59. Dembicz, Andrzej, ed. 2004. *Interculturalidad en América Latina en ámbitos locales y regionales*. Warsaw: CESLA.

Díaz, Ramón, et al. 2009. *Análisis de la implementación del programa JUNTOS en las regiones de Apurímac, Huancavelica y Huánuco.* Lima: CIES; CARE.

Díaz Polanco, Héctor. 1997. *Indigenous Peoples in Latin America: The Quest for Self-Determination.* Boulder, CO: Westview Press.Domeyko, Ignacio. 1978. *Mis viajes. Memorias de un exiliado.* Tomo 1. Santiago: Ediciones de la Universidad de Chile.

Dorsey, George. 1905. *The Cheyenne. II. The Sun Dance.* Chicago: Field Columbian Museum.

dos Santos Vieira, Paulo Alberto. 2012. "Cotas para negros em universidades públicas no Brasil: Significados da política contemporânea de ação afirmativa." PhD diss., Programa de Pós-Graduação em Sociologia, Universidade Federal de São Carlos.

dos Santos Vieira, Paulo Alberto, and Priscila Martins Medeiros. 2008. "Ações afirmativas nas universidades brasileiras: Os críticos limites das críticas." *Revista de Faculdade de Educaçao Multi-Temática* IV(5–6): 27–52.

Duarte, Evandro Charles Piza, Dora Lúcia de Lima Bertúlio, Paulo Vinícius Baptista da Silva, and Antônio Leandro da Silva Filho. 2008. *Cotas raciais no ensino superior: Entre o jurídico e o político.* Curitiba, Brazil: Juruá Editora.

Durand, Gilbert. 1994. *Lo imaginario.* Barcelona: Ediciones del Bronce.

Ecuador. Instituto Nacional de Estadística y Censos (INEC). 2002. *Censo del año 2001.* República del Ecuador: Instituto Nacional de Estadística y Censos.

Eguren, Fernando. 2006a. "Un modelo de modernización agraria que prolonga la pobreza." In *Pobreza y desarrollo humano en el Perú 2005–2006,* 49–55. Lima: Oxfam GB, Instituto de Estudios Peruanos (IEP), Fondo de Población de las Naciones Unidas—Perú (UNFPA-Perú).

———. 2006b. "Políticas agrarias, cambios institucionales, y nuevos actores en el agro peruano." In *Construir instituciones: Democracia, desarrollo, y desigualdad en el Perú desde 1980,* edited by John Crabtree, 117–39. Lima: PUCP; UP; IEP.

Estensoro, Juan Pablo. 2003. *Del paganismo a la santidad: La incorporación de los indios del Perú al Catolicismo 1532–1570.* Lima: PUCP-IEA.

Esteva-Fabregat, Claudio. 1995. *Mestizaje in Ibero-America.* Translated by John Wheat. Tucson: University of Arizona Press.

Falaschi, Carlos, ed. 1996. *Proyecto especial de investigación y extensión U.N.C.-A.P.D.H. "Defensa y reivindicación de tierras indígenas": Informe final, Región del Comahue, Argentina, período 01.03.94–30.04.96.* Neuquén, Argentina: Asamblea Permanente por los Derechos Humanos; Universidad Nacional del Comahue; Asamblea por los Derechos Humanos.

Falaschi, Carlos, Fernando Sánchez, and Andrea Szulc. 2005. "Políticas indigenistas en Neuquén: Pasado y presente." In *Cartografías Argentinas: Políticas indígenas y formaciones provinciales de alteridad,* edited by Claudia Briones, 179–221. Buenos Aires: Antropofagia.

Fanon, Franz. 1983. *Pele negra, máscaras brancas.* Rio de Janeiro: Fator.

Farfán, P. Marcelo. 2006. *Historias desde el aula: Educación intercultural bilingüe y etnoeducación en Ecuador.* Quito: Abya-Yala.Feres Júnior, João, and

Jonas Zoninsein. 2008. "A consolidação da ação afirmativa no ensino superior Brasileiro." In *Ação afirmativa no ensino superior Brasileiro*, edited by Jonas Zoninsein and João Feres Júnior, 9–33. Rio de Janeiro: IUPERJ; Belo Horizonte: Ed da UFMG.

Fernández, Justino. 1970. *Estética del arte méxicano*. Mexico City: UNAM.

Ferrari, Andrea. 2005. "Un movimiento indígena joven en las ciudades del sur: Los mapuches punk." *Página 12* (Buenos Aires), April 24.

Fine, Kathleen. 1991. *Cotocollao: Ideología, historia y acción en un barrio de Quito*. Quito: Ediciones Abya-Yala.

Fine-Dare, Kathleen. 2007. "Más allá del folklore: La Yumbada de Cotocollao como vitrina para los discursos de la identidad, de la intervención estatal y del poder local en los Andes urbanos ecuatorianos." In *Estudios ecuatorianos: Un aporte a la discusión*. Tomo 2, *Ponencias escojidas del III Encuentro de la Sección de Estudios Ecuatorianos LASA, Quito 2006*, edited by W. F. Waters and M. Hamerly, 55–72. Quito: FLACSO; Abya-Yala.

———. 2010. "Quito Quichua." *eHRAF World Cultures*, Yale University. Accessed January 28, 2014. http://www.yale.edu/hraf/collections.htm.

———. 2013a. "Género y fricción en las prácticas y los discursos del Yumbo de y en la Yumbada de Cotocollao." Paper presented at the Sixth LASA Ecuatorianista Conference, Universidad de Cuenca, Ecuador, June 27–29.

———. 2013b. "(Neo)Indigenismo and the Transculturative Praxis of Ethnogenesis: A Case Study from Urban Ecuador." In *Indigenous and Afro-Ecuadorians Facing the Twenty-First Century*, edited by Marc Becker, 7–33. Newcastle upon Tyne: Cambridge Scholars Publishing.

First Continental Encounter of Indigenous Peoples. 1990. *Declaration of Quito*. Quito, Ecuador: The South and Meso-American Indian Information Center (SAIIC); the Confederation of Indian Nations of Ecuador (CONAIE); the Organization of Indian Nations of Colombia (ONIC); the Awakening of Indian and Campesino People of Ecuador (ECUARUNARI); and the Confederation of Indian Nationalities of the Ecuadorian Amazon (CONFENIAE). Accessed January 28, 2014. http://www.nativeweb.org/papers/statements/quincentennial/quito.php.

Fiszbein, Ariel, Norbert Schady, et al. 2009. *Conditional Cash Transfers: Reducing Present and Future Poverty*. Washington, DC: World Bank.

Flores, Juan, and Renato Rosaldo, eds. 2007. *A Companion to Latina/o Studies*. Blackwell Companions in Cultural Studies 14. Malden, MA: Blackwell Publishing.

Flores Galindo, Alberto. 1988. "República sin ciudadanos." In *Buscando a un Inca: Identidad y utopía en los Andes*, edited by Alberto Flores Galindo, 257–86. 3rd ed. Lima: Editorial Horizonte.

Fondo Ecuatoriano Populorum Progressio (FEEP). 1987. *Programa Regional Riobamba: Apoyo al autodesarrollo campesino*. Riobamba, Ecuador: FEEP.

French, Jan Hoffman. 2009. *Legalizing Identities: Becoming Black or Indian in Brazil's Northeast*. Chapel Hill: University of North Carolina Press.

Freyre, Gilberto, Fernando Henrique Cardoso, and Edson Nery da Fonseca. 2006. *Casa-grande & senzala formação da família brasileira sob o regime da economia patriarcal*. São Paulo: Global Editora.

Friedlander, Judith. 1975. *Being Indian in Hueyapan: A Study of Forced Identity in Contemporary Mexico*. New York: St. Martin's Press.

Fry, Peter, and Yvonne Maggie. 2002. "O debate que não houve: A reserva de vagas para negros nas universidades brasileiras." *Enfoques* 1(1): 93–117. Accessed March 5, 2014. http://www.enfoques.ifcs.ufrj.br/pdfs/2002-DEZ.pdf.

Gálvez, Alyshia, ed. 2007. *Performing Religion in the Americas: Media, Politics, and Devotional Practices of the Twenty-First Century*. London: Seagull Books.

Gandhi, Ajay. 2001. "Indigenous Resistance to New Colonialism." *CSQ* 25(3): 32–35.

García, José Uriel. 1937. *El nuevo indio: Ensayos indianistas sobre la sierra surperuana*. Cuzco: H. D. Rozas Sucesores.

García Canclini, Néstor. 2003. "Noticias recientes sobre la hibridación." *Trans: Revista Transcultural de Música* 7. Accessed February 2008. http://www.sibetrans.com/trans/a209/noticias-recientes-sobre-la-hibridacion.

Gerlach, Allen. 2003. *Indians, Oil and Politics: A Recent History of Ecuador*. Wilmington, DE: Scholarly Resources, Inc.

Godoy Orellana, Milton. 2007. "¡Cuando el siglo se sacará la máscara! Fiesta, carnaval y disciplinamiento cultural en el Norte Chico. Copiapó, 1840–1900." *Revista Historia* 40:5–34.

Gomes, Joaquim Barbosa. 2003. "O debate constitucional sobre as ações afirmativas." In *Ações afirmativas: Políticas públicas contra as desigualdades raciais*, edited by Renato Emerson dos Santos and Fátima Lobato, 15–57. Rio de Janeiro: Programa Políticas da Cor na Educação Brasileira.

Gomes, Nilma Lino. 2005. "Alguns termos e conceitos presentes no debate sobre relações raciais no Brasil: Uma breve discussão." In *Educação antiracista: Caminhos abertos pela lei federal no 10.639/03*, edited by Ana Flávia Magalhães Pinto, Andréia Lisboa de Sousa, Maria Lúcia de Santana Braga, and Sales Augusto dos Santos, 39–62. Brasília: SECAD-Secretaria de Educação Continuada, Alfabetização e Diversidade.

Gomez, Boris. 2004. "Mujeres comericalizan el vestido Ngäbe." *La Prensa* (Panama), July 1. Accessed June 12, 2009. http://mensual.prensa.com/mensual/contenido/2004/07/01/hoy/nacionales/1745696.html.

Gomez, R. 1967. *The Study of Latin American Politics in University Programs in the United States*. Tucson: University of Arizona Press.

Gómez Murillo, A. R. 2007. "Pueblos originarios, comunas, migrantes y procesos de etnogénesis del Distrito Metropolitano de Quito: Nuevas representaciones sobre los indígenas urbanos de América Latina." Master's thesis, La Facultad Latinoamericana de Ciencias Sociales (FLACSO), Quito, Ecuador.

Gonzales de Olarte, Efraín. 1994. *En las fronteras del mercado: Economía política del campesinado en el Perú*. Lima: Instituto de Estudios Peruanos.

———. 2006. "Economía política de la reforma del estado en el Perú." *Economía Peruana Blog*, April 17. Accessed March 5, 2014. http://blog.pucp.edu.pe

/item/2097/economia-politica-de-la-reforma-del-estado-en-el-peru-efrain
-gonzales-de-olarte.

González Holguín, Diego. 1608. *Vocabulario de la lengua general de todo el Peru llamada lengua Quichua, o del Inca; (Quichua-Spanisch und Spanisch-Quichua)*. Ciudad de los Reyes (Lima): Francisco del Canto.

González Pérez, Miguel. 2010. "Autonomías territoriales indígenas y regímenes autonómicos (desde el estado) en América." In *La autonomía a debate: Autogobierno indígena y Estado plurinacional en América Latina*, edited by Miguel González Pérez, Araceli Burguete Cal y Mayor, and Pablo Ortiz-T., 35–63. Quito: Abya-Yala.

González Pérez, Miguel, Araceli Burguete Cal y Mayor, and Pablo Ortiz-T., eds. 2010. *La autonomía a debate: Autogobierno indígena y estado plurinacional en América Latina*. Quito: FLACSO Ecuador; GTZ; Ministerio Federal de Cooperación Económica y Desarrollo; IWGIA; CIESAS; Universidad Intercultural de Chiapas.

Gose, Peter. 2004. *Aguas mortíferas y cerros hambrientos: Ritos agrarios y formación de clases en un pueblo andino*. Quito: Abya-Yala.

Gould, Jeffrey. 1998. *To Die in This Way: Nicaraguan Indians and the Myth of Mestizaje, 1880–1965*. Durham, NC: Duke University Press.

Gould, Jeffrey, Charles R. Hale, and Carol A. Smith. 1994. "Memories of Mestizaje: Cultural Politics in Central America since 1920." Unpublished manuscript.

Greene, Shane. 2005. "Incas, Indios, and Indigenism in Peru." *NACLA Report on the Americas* 38(4): 34–39.

Grinnell, George Bird. 1955. *The Fighting Cheyennes*. Norman: University of Oklahoma Press.

———. 1962. *By Cheyenne Campfires*. New Haven: Yale University Press.

———. 1972. *The Cheyenne Indians: Their History and Ways of Life*. Lincoln: University of Nebraska Press.

Groupe de Recherches sur l'Amérique Latine Toulouse-Perpignan. 1988. *Indianidad, etnocidio, indigenismo en América Latina*. Mexico City: Instituto Indigenista Interamericano; Centre d'Etudes Mexicaines et Centroamericaines.

Grupo Allpa. 2004. *Las comunidades campesinas en el siglo XXI: Situación actual y cambios normativos*. Lima: Grupo Allpa.

Gruzinski, Serge. 1999. *La pensée métisse*. Paris: Fayard.

———. 2002. *The Mestizo Mind: The Intellectual Dynamics of Colonization and Globalization*. Translated by Deke Dusinberre. New York: Routledge.

Guerrero, Andrés. 1993. "La desintegración de la administración étnica en el Ecuador." In *Sismo étnico en el Ecuador: Varias perspectivas*, edited by Andrés Guerrero et al., 91–112. Quito: CEDIME; Abya-Yala.

———. 1997. "'Se han roto las formas ventrílocuas de representación': Conversación con Andrés Guerrero." *Íconos* 1:60–66.

———. 2000. "El proceso de identificación: Sentido común ciudadano, ventriloquía y transescritura." In *Etnicidades*, edited by Andrés Guerrero, 9–60. Quito: FLACSO.

———. 2010. *Administración de poblaciones, ventriloquía y transescritura*. Lima: Instituto de Estudios Peruanos; FLACSO Ecuador.

Guerrero Arias, Patricio. 2011. "Interculturalidad y plurinacionalidad, escenarios de lucha de sentidos: Entre la usurpación y la insurgencia simbólica." In *Interculturalidad y diversidad*, edited by A. Kowii, 73–100. Quito: Universidad Simón Bolívar, Sede Ecuador; Corporación Editora Nacional. Guimarães, Antônio Sérgio A. 2003. "Como trabalhar com 'raça' em eociologia." *Educação e Pesquisa* 29(1), 93–107.

———. 2008. *Preconceito racial: Modos, temas e tempos*. São Paulo: Cortez Editora.

Guionneau, Francoise. 1988. *Movimiento profético e innovación político entre los Ngobe (Guaymí) de Panama: 1962–1984*. Panama City: Universidad de Panamá.

Guss, David M. 2006. "The Gran Poder and the Reconquest of La Paz." *The Journal of Latin American Anthropology. Special Issue: Indigenous Peoples and New Urbanisms* 11(2): 294–328.

Haddad, Fernando, and Roberto Schwarz. 1998. *Desorganizando o consenso: Nove entrevistas com intelectuais a' esquerda*. São Paulo: Editora Fundação Perseu Abramo.

Hagedorn, Katherine J. 2001. *Divine Utterances: The Performance of Afro-Cuban Santería*. Washington, DC: Smithsonian Books.

Hale, Charles. 2004. "Rethinking Indigenous Politics in the Era of the 'Indio Permitido.'" *NACLA Report on the Americas* 38(2): 16–22.

———. 2006. *Más que un indio* = More than an Indian: Racial Ambivalence and Neoliberal Multiculturalism in Guatemala. Santa Fe, NM: School of American Research Press.

Hall, Stuart. 2000. "Conclusion: The Multicultural Question." In *Un/settled Multiculturalisms: Diasporas, Entanglements, Transruptions*, edited by B. Hesse, 209–41. London: Zed Books.

———. 2006. *Da diáspora: Identidades e mediações culturais*. Belo Horizonte: EdUFMG.

Harding, Rachel E. 2000. *A Refuge in Thunder: Candomblé and Alternative Spaces of Blackness*. Bloomington: Indiana University Press.

Heckadon, Stanley. 1982. "¿Quiénes son los indígenas?" In *El Pueblo guaymi y su futuro: Quién dijo que estamos cansados de ser indios?* edited by José Agunstín Ganuza, L. G. Anderson, Kenneth Mahler, Secundino Morales, Lemuel B. Shirley, Julio Dixon, and CEASPA (Centro de Estudios y Acción Social Panamá), 85–100. Panama City: Centro de Estudios y Acción Social.

Held, David, et al. 1999. *Global Transformations: Politics, Economics and Culture*. Stanford: Stanford University Press.

Henriques, Ricardo. 2001. *Desigualdade racial no Brasil: Evolução das condições de vida na década de 90*. Rio de Janeiro: IPEA.

Herbert, Jean-Loup. 1977. Breve historia de la integración de la Indianidad al tercer mundo. Documentos, no. 3. Mexico City: CADAL.

Herlihy, Peter. 1995. "La revolución silenciosa de Panamá: Las tierras de comarca y los derechos indígenas." *Mesoamerica* 29:77–93.

Hernández, Isabel. 2003. *Autonomía o ciudadanía incompleta: El Pueblo Mapuche en Chile y Argentina.* Santiago: Naciones Unidas–CEPAL.

Herrera, Francisco A., and Raúl González. 1964. "Informe sobre una investigación ethnográfica entre los indios Bogotá [Buglé] de Bocas del Toro." *Hombre y Cultura* 1(3): 56–81.

Hofbauer, Andréas. 2004. "Raça, cultura e identidade e o 'racismo à Brasileira.'" In *De preto a afro-descendente: Trajetos de pesquisa sobre o negro, cultura negra e relações étnico-raciais no Brasil,* edited by Congresso Brasileiro de Pesquisadores Negros, Lucia Maria de Assunção Barbosa, Petronilha Beatriz Gonçalves e Silva, and Valter Roberto Silvério, 51–68. São Carlos: EdUFSCar.

Howard-Malverde, Rosaleen. 1997. "Introduction: Between Text and Context in the Evocation of Culture." In *Creating Context in Andean Cultures,* edited by R. Howard-Malverde, 3–18. New York: Oxford University Press.

Huber, Ludwig et al. 2009. *Programa JUNTOS: Certezas y malentendidos en torno a las transferencias condicionadas; estudio de caso de seis distritos rurales del Perú.* Lima: Fondo de Población de las Naciones Unidas, Perú.

Instituto de Estudios Peruanos (IEP). 2009. "Estudio de percepción sobre cambios de comportamiento de los beneficiarios y accesibilidad al programa JUNTOS en el distrito de San Jerónimo (Andahuaylas Apurímac) [informe final]." Accessed April 22, 2012. http://www.juntos.gob.pe/images/noticias /2011/01/estudio_SanJeronim01.pdf.

Jaccoud, Lucianade Barros. 2008. "Racismo e República: O debate sobre o branqueamento e a discriminação racial no Brasil." In *As políticas públicas e a desigualdade racial no Brasil: 120 anos após a abolição,* edited by Lucianade Barros Jaccoud, Rafael Guerreiro Osorio, Sergei Suarez Dillon Soares, and Mário Lisboa Theodoro, 45–62. Brasília: IPEA.

Jackson, Peter. 1999. "Commodity Cultures: The Traffic in Things." *Transactions of the Institute of British Geographers* 24(1): 95–108.

Jordán Ramos, Osvaldo. 2010a. "'Entré durante el día y salí por la noche': Relaciones de poder, ambiente y pueblos indígenas en un Panamá globalizado." In *La autonomía a debate: Autogobierno indígena y estado plurinacional en América Latina,* edited by Miguel González Pérez, Araceli Burguete Cal y Mayor, and Pablo Ortiz-T., 509–61. Quito: Abya-Yala.

———. 2010b. Indigenous Mobilization, Institutionalization and Resistance: The Ngobe Movement for Political Autonomy in Western Panama. In "The Indian Question in Latin America: A Brief History of Latin American Thought About Indigenous Peoples," chap. 2. PhD diss., Department of Political Science, University of Florida–Gainesville.

Kapchan, Deborah A. 2007. *Traveling Spirit Masters: Moroccan Gnawa Trance and Music in the Global Marketplace.* Middletown, CT: Wesleyan University Press.

Kirshenblatt-Gimblett, Barbara. 1998. *Destination Culture: Tourism, Museums, and Heritage.* Berkeley: University of California Press.

Kowii, Ariruma. 2006. "Propuestas y retos para la construcción del estado pluricultural, multiétnico y intercultural del Ecuador." In *Desarrollo e interculturalidad, imaginario y diferencia: La nación en el mundo Andino*, edited by H. Magalhães Neto, 157–74. Rio de Janeiro: Academia de la Latinidad.

Kradolfer, Sabine. 2011. "(Self)essentialization of Cultural Differences: How Peoples and States Play Hide-and-Seek." *Anthropological Notebooks* 17(2): 37–53.

Kradolfer, Sabine, and Pedro Navarro Floria. 2006. "De la difficulté d'entendre la voix de l'autre quand elle remet en question un héros national." *Carnetsde-bord* 12("Cultes du passé"): 57–66.

Krauze, Enrique. 1997. *Mexico: Biography of Power: A History of Modern Mexico, 1810–1996*. 1st ed. New York: Harper Collins Publishers.

Kropff, Laura. 2005. "Activismo Mapuche en Argentina: Trayectoria histórica y nuevas propuestas." In *Pueblos indígenas, estado y democracia*, edited by Pedro Dávalos, 103–32. Buenos Aires: Consejo Latinoamericano de Ciencias Sociales (CLACSO).

Kyle, David. 2000. *Transnational Peasants: Migrations, Networks and Ethnicity in Andean Ecuador*. Baltimore: Johns Hopkins University Press.

Lalander, Rickard. 2010. *Retorno de los Runakuna*. Quito: Abya-Yala; Universidad Polítecnica Salesiana.

Lazzari, Alex. 2009. "El indio fantasma: ¿Reconocer qué, reconocer cómo?" Paper presented at the Eighth Reunión de Antropología del Mercosur (RAM), GT 48: Bordes de Ontología y Racionalidad: Lo Emergente y lo Extraordinario en la Cultura, la Naturaleza y la Política. Buenos Aires, Argentina, September 29–October 2.

Legoas, Jorge. 2007. "Watchdogs: Ciudadanía y discursos del desarrollo." *Tabula Rasa Revista de Humanidades* 7:17–46.

Leis, Raúl. 2003. "Panamá: Condiciones políticas para los procesos de autonomía." Unpublished manuscript. Proyecto Latautonomy.

Lentz, Carola. 2000. "La construcción de la alteridad cultural como respuesta a la discriminación étnica: Caso de estudio en la Sierra ecuatoriana." In *Etnicidades*, edited by Andrés Guerrero, 201–33. Quito: FLACSO.

León, Jorge. 1998. "Contexte social et cycle politique: Les ONG en Équateur." In *ONG et développement: Société, économie, politique*, edited by Jean Paul Deler, 659–71. Paris: Karthala.

León Guzmán, Mauricio. 2003. "Etnicidad y exclusión en Ecuador: Una mirada a partir del censo de población de 2001." *Íconos* 17:116–32.

León-Portilla, Miguel. 2003. "Iberoamérica mestiza, un proceso de resonancias universales." In exhibition catalog, *Iberoamérica mestiza: Encuentro de pueblos y culturas*. Centro Cultural de la Villa, Madrid, October to November 2003, and Castillo de Chapultepec, México, January to March 2004. Madrid: Fundación Santillana; Sociedad Estatal para la Acción Cultural Exterior.

Lima, Ari. 2001. "A legitimação do intelectual negro no meio acadêmico brasileiro: Negação de inferioridade, confronto ou assimilação intelectual." *Revista Af-*

*ro*Ásia 25/26, 281–312. Salvador, Brazil: Centro de Estudos Afro-Orientaís da Universidade Federal da Bahia.

Lipschutz, Alejandro. 1963. *El problema racial en la conquista de América*. Mexico City: Austral; Edit. Siglo XXI.

Lipset, Seymour Martin. 1996. *American Exceptionalism: A Double-Edged Sword*. New York: W. W. Norton.

Llewellyn, K., and E. A. Hoebel. 1941. *The Cheyenne Way: Conflict and Case Law in Primitive Jurisprudence*. Norman: University of Oklahoma Press.

Lloyd, Elisabeth. 1983. "Marx's General Cultural Theories." In *Marxism and Native Americans*, edited by Ward Churchill, 79–90. Boston: South End Press.

Lopes, Nei. 2004. "African Religions in Brazil, Negotiation, and Resistance: A Look from Within." *Journal of Black Studies* 34(6): 838–60.

Lovato, Roberto. 2010. "Planeta o muerte—Evo Morales and the Revolutionary Politics of Mother Earth." *New America Media*. Accessed April 21, 2011. http://newamericamedia.org/2010/04/planeta-o-muerte—evo-morales-and -the-revolutionary-politics-of-mother-earth.php.

Maldonado, Gina. 2004. *Comerciantes y viajeros: De la imagen etnoarqueológico de "lo indígena al imaginario del kichwa otavalo 'universal.'"* Quito: Abya-Yala; FLACSO, Ecuador.

Mann, Henrietta. 1997. *Cheyenne-Arapaho Education 1871–1982*. Niwot: University Press of Colorado.

Martinelli, Marianella. 1994. *La mujer Ngóbe: Camino hacia la libertad*. Proyecto Agroforestal Ngóbe, Documento Ngóbe, tomo 7. San Félix, Panama: Instituto Nacional de Recursos Naturales Renovables y Agencia Alemana de Cooperación Técnica B GTZ.

Martínez Mauri, Mònica. 2005. "¿Competencia o complementariedad? Las ONG indígenas y las organizaciones tradicionales kunas en Panamá." In *Las ONGS en la reflexión antropológica sobre el desarrollo y viceversa: Perspectivas africanas y latinoamericanas*. Actas del X Congreso de Antropología. Edited by V. Bretón Solo de Zaldívar and A. López Bargados, 149–63. Seville: Federación de Asociaciones de Antropología del Estado Español; Fundación el Monte; ASANA.

———. 2007. "De Tule Nega a Kuna Yala. Mediación, territorio y ecología en Panamá, 1903–2004." PhD diss., Universitat Autònoma de Barcelona, Barcelona, and École des Hautes Etudes en Sciences Sociales, Paris.

———. 2011. *La autonomía indígena en Panamá: La experiencia del pueblo kuna (siglos XVI–XXI)*. Quito: Ediciones Abya-Yala.

———. 2012. "The Social and Political Construction of Racial and Ethnic Categories in National Censuses of Panama, 1911–2010." In *Everlasting Countdowns: Race, Ethnicity and National Censuses in Latin American State*, edited by Sabine Kradolfer and Luis Fernando Angosto, 155–84. Cambridge: Cambridge Scholars Publishing.

Martínez Novo, Carmen. 2007. "¿Es el multiculturalismo estatal un factor de profundización de la democracia en América Latina? Una reflexión desde la etnografía sobre los casos de México y Ecuador." In *Ciudadanía y exclusión: Ecuador y España frente al espejo*, edited by Víctor Bretón, Francisco García, Antoni Jové, and María José Vilalta, 182–202. Madrid: La Catarata.

Martínez Novo, Carmen, and Carlos de la Torre. 2010. "Racial Discrimination and Citizenship in Ecuador's Educational System." *Latin American and Caribbean Ethnic Studies* 5(1): 1–26.

Marx, Karl. 1904. *A Contribution to the Critique of Political Economy*. Chicago: International Library Publishing Co.

Marzal, Manuel M. 1983. *La transformación religiosa Peruana*. Lima: Pontificia Universidad Católica del Perú.

———. 1993. *Historia de la antropología indigenista: México y Perú*. Barcelona: Anthropos Editorial del Hombre; Iztapalapa, Mexico: Universidad Autónoma Metropolitana, Unidad Iztapalapa, División de Ciencias Sociales y Humanidades.

Medeiros, Priscila Martins. 2009. "'Raça' e estado democrático: O debate sóciojuridico acerca das ações afirmativas no Brasil." Master's thesis, Programa de Pós-Graduação em Sociologia, Universidade Federal de São Carlos.

Meisch, Lynn. 2002. *Andean Entrepreneurs: Otavalo Merchants and Musicians in the Global Arena*. Joe R. and Teresa Lozano Long Series in Latin American and Latino Art and Culture. Austin: University of Texas Press.

Mendoza, Zoila S. 1999. "Genuine but Marginal: Exploring and Reworking Social Contradictions Through Ritual Dance Performance." *Journal of Latin American Anthropology* 3(2): 86–117.

Mendoza B., Abdiel, Alibeth de Gracia G., and Johann Krug. n.d. "Asociaciones indígenas productivas, estimulan el desarrollo económico local." Panama: PGTZ/Empresa Consultora Keba Ambiente y Paz. Accessed June 12, 2009. http://www.infomipyme.com/docs/gt/sidel/casos/productivas.htm. Mignolo, Walter. 2011. *The Darker Side of Western Modernity: Global Futures, Decolonial Options*. Durham, NC: Duke University Press.

Mignolo, Walter, and Arturo Escobar, eds. 2010. *Globalization and the Decolonial Option*. New York: Routledge. Mijeski, Kenneth, and Scott Beck. 2011. *Pachakutik and the Rise and Decline of the Ecuadorian Indigenous Movement*. Athens: University of Ohio Press.

Miller, Andrew. 1994. *Contemporary Cultural Theory: An Introduction*. London: UCL Press Ltd.

Miller, Marylin Grace. 2004. *Rise and Fall of the Cosmic Race: The Cult of Mestizaje in Latin America*. Austin: University of Texas Press.

Millones, Luis. 2007. *Taki Onqoy, de la enfermedad del baile a la epidemia*. Santiago: DIBAM.

Miskolci, Richard. 2005. "Do desvio às diferenças." In *Teoria e pesquisa: Revista de ciências sociais* 47. São Carlos: Departamento de Ciências Sociais (DCSo), Universidade Federal de São Carlos (UFSCar).

Monroe, Javier. 2008. *Campesinado indígena y modernidad política: Cultura, ciudadanía y discriminación en los Andes peruanos*. Lima: Coordinadora Nacional de Derechos Humanos-Perú, CLACSO.

Mooney, James, and Rodolphe Petter. 1907. *The Cheyenne Indians*. American Anthropological Association Memoirs 1, pt. 6. Lancaster, PA: The New Era Press.

Moore, John H. 1992. "The Enduring Reservations of Oklahoma." In *State and Reservation: New Perspectives on Federal Indian Policy*, edited by George Pierre Castile and Robert L. Bee, 92–109. Tucson: University of Arizona Press.

Moreno Villa, José. 1942. *La escultura colonial mexicana*. Reprint, Mexico City: Fondo de Cultura Económica, 1993.

———. 1948. *Lo Mexicano en las artes plásticas*. Reprint, Mexico City: Fondo de Cultura Económica, 2004.

Morin, Françoise, and Bernard Saladin d'Anglure. 1995. "L'ethnicité, un outil politique pour les autochtones de l'Arctique et de l'Amazonie." *Études Inuit Studies* 19(1): 37–68.

Moya, Thaís Santos. 2009. "Ação afirmativa e raça no Brasil: Uma análise de enquadramento midiático do debate político contemporâneo sobre a re-definição simbólica da nação." Master's thesis, Programa de Pós-Graduação em Sociologia, Universidade Federal de São Carlos.

Murphy, Joseph M. 1994. *Working the Spirit: Ceremonies of the African Diaspora*. Boston: Beacon Press.

Muteba Rahier, Jean. 2003. "*Mestizaje, mulataje, mestiçagem* in Latin American Ideologies of National Identities." *The Journal of Latin American Anthropology* 8(1): 40–51.

Navarro Floria, Pedro. 1999. *Historia de la Patagonia*. Buenos Aires: Ciudad Argentina.

Needler, Martin. 1963. *Latin American Politics in Perspective*. Princeton, NJ: Van Nostrand.

Ovalle, Alonso de. 1888. *Histórica relación del Reino de Chile y de las misiones y ministerios que ejercita en él la compañía de Jesús*. Santiago: Imprenta Ercilla.

Paixão, Marcelo. 2008. "A Santa Aliança: Estudo sobre o consenso crítico às políticas de promoção da eqüidade racial no Brasil." In *Ação afirmativa no ensino superior Brasileiro*, edited by Jonas Zoninsein and João Feres Júnior, 135–73. Rio de Janeiro: IUPERJ; Belo Horizonte: Ed da UFMG.

Paixão, Marcelo, and Luiz M. Carvano, eds. 2008. *Relatório anual das desigualdades raciais no Brasil; 2007–2008*. Rio de Janeiro: Editora Garimond, Ltd.

Paixão, Marcelo, Irene Rossetto, Fabiana Montovanele, and Luiz Carvano, eds. 2010. *Relatório anual das desigualdades raciais no Brasil, 2009–2010: Constituição cidadã, seguridade social e seus efeitos sobre as assimetrias de raça ou cor*. Rio de Janeiro: Garamond; Rio de Janeiro: IE/LAESER.

Pajuelo Tevez, Ramon. 2002. "El lugar de la utopia: Aportes de Anibal Quijano sobre cultura y poder." In *Estudios y otras practicas intelectuales latinoamericanas en cultura y poder*, edited by Daniel Mato, 225–34. Caracas: Consejo Latinoamericano de Ciencias Sociales (CLACSO); CEAP; FACES; Universidad Central.

Pallares, Amalia. 2002. *From Peasant Struggles to Indian Resistance: The Ecuadorian Andes in the Late Twentieth Century*. Norman: University of Oklahoma Press.

Pantin Guerra, Beatriz. 2007. *Mestizaje, transculturación, hibridación: Perspectivas de historia conceptual, análisis del discurso y metaforología para los estudios y las teorías culturales en América Latina*. Berlin: Freie Universität Berlin.

Pérez-Torres, Rafael. 2006. *Mestizaje: Critical Uses of Race in Chicano Culture*. Minneapolis: University of Minnesota Press.

Peru. Defensoría del Pueblo. 2005. *Ante todo, el diálogo: Defensoría del Pueblo y conflictos sociales y políticos*. Lima: Defensoría del Pueblo.

———. 2007. *Los conflictos socioambientales por actividades extractivas en el Perú. Abril del 2007: Informe Extraordinario*. Lima: Defensoría del Pueblo.

———. Instituto Nacional de Estadística e Informática (INEI). 2008. *Censos nacionales 2007: X de población VI de vivienda. Perfil sociodemográfico del Perú*. Lima: Instituto Nacional de Estadística e Informática.

Perz, Stephen G., Jonathan Warren, and David P. Kennedy. 2008. "Contributions of Racial-Ethnic Reclassification and Demographic Processes to Indigenous Population Resurgence." *Latin American Research Review* 43(2): 7–33.

Petras, James, and Henry Veltmeyer. 2004. World Development: Globalization or Imperialism? In *Globalization and Antiglobalization: Dynamics of Change in the New World Order*, edited by Henry Veltmeyer, 11–24. Aldershot Hants, UK; Burlington, VT: Ashgate.

Pinheiro, Luana, et al. 2008. *Retrato das desigualdades de gênero e raça*. Brasília: IPEA.

Piovesan, Flávia. 2008. "Ações afirmativas sob a perspectiva dos direitos humanos." In *Cotas raciais no ensino superior: Entre o jurídico e o político*, edited by Evandro Piza Duarte, Dora Lúcia de Lima Bertúlio, and Paulo Vinicius Baptista da Silva, 15–26. Curitiba, Brazil: Juruá.

Pliny, Ludwig von Jan, and Karl Friedrich Theodor Mayhoff. 1967. *C. Plini Secundi Naturalis historiae libri XXXVII*. Stutgardiae: Teubner.

Portocarrero, Gonzalo. 2007. *Racismo y mestizaje y otros ensayos*. Lima: Fondo Editorial del Congreso del Perú.

Powell, Peter J. 1969. *Sweet Medicine: The Continuing Role of the Sacred Arrows, the Sun Dance and the Sacred Buffalo Hat in Northern Cheyenne History*. Norman: University of Oklahoma Press.

Puente Hernández, Eduardo. 2005. *El estado y la interculturalidad en el Ecuador*. Quito: Ediciones Abya-Yala; Universidad Andina Simón Bolívar.

Quijano, Aníbal. 1980. *Dominación y cultura: Lo cholo y el conflicto cultural en el Perú*. Lima: Mosca Azul Editores.

Quiroz Paz Soldán, Eusebio. 1991. "Arequipa, pasado y presente." In *Visión histórica de Arequipa (1540–1990)*, edited by Eusebio Quiroz Paz Soldán, 340–47. Arequipa, Peru: Universidad Nacional de San Agustín UNSA.

Radovich, Juan Carlos, and Alejandro Balazote. 1992. "El pueblo Mapuche en la actualidad." In *La problemática indígena*, edited by Juan Carlos Radovich and Alejandro Balazote, 159–86. Buenos Aires: Centro Editor de América Latina.

Ramírez Gallegos, Franklin. 2009. "El movimiento indígena y la reconstrucción de la izquierda en Ecuador: El caso del Movimiento de Unidad Plurinacional Pachakutik–Nuevo País." In *Los Andes en movimiento*, edited by Pablo Ospina Peralta, Olaf Kaltmeier, and Christian Büschges, 65–94. Quito: Universidad Andina Simón Bolívar; Universidad de Bielefeld; Corporación Editora Nacional.

Ramón, Galo. 2005. Comentario sobre política e interculturalidad. In *Hacia un modelo alternativo de desarrollo histórico*, edited by R. Quintero López and E. Silva Charvet, 53–62. Quito: Ediciones La Tierra.

Ramos, Gabriela. 1992. "Políticas eclesiásticas y extirpación de la idolatría: Discursos y silencios en torno al Taqui Onkoy." *Revista Andina* 10:147–97.

Rappaport, Joanne. 2005. *Intercultural Utopias: Public Intellectuals, Cultural Experimentation, and Ethnic Pluralism in Colombia*. Durham, NC: Duke University Press.

Ray, Leslie. 2007. *Language of the Land. The Mapuche in Argentina and Chile*. Copenhagen: IWGIA.

Real Academia Española. 2001. *Diccionario de la lengua española*. Madrid: Espasa.

Rémond, René. 1969. *The Right Wing in France from 1815 to de Gaulle*. 2nd ed. Translated by James M. Laux. Philadelphia: University of Pennsylvania Press.

Republic of Panama. Dirección de Estadística y Censo Contraloría General de la República (DEC). 1981. *Informe metodológico sobre el levantamiento de los censos nacionales de 1980–82*. Panama City: Imprenta Nacional.

———. (published various years). *Censos nacionales de Panamá de 1960*. Panama City: Imprenta Nacional.

———. (published various years). *Censos nacionales de Panamá de 2010*. Panama City: Imprenta Nacional.

———. Oficina del Censo, Contraloría General de la República (OC). 1943. *Censo de población 1940, informe preliminar*. Panama City: Imprenta Nacional.

Reyes-Valerio, Constantino. 2000. *Arte indocristiano*. Mexico City: Instituto Nacional de Antropología e Historia, Col. Obra Diversa.

Ricoeur, Paul. 1991. *From Text to Action: Essays in Hermeneutics, II*. Translated by Kathleen Blarney and John B. Thompson. London: Athlone.

Roitman, Karem. 2009. *Race, Ethnicity, and Power in Ecuador: The Manipulation of Mestizaje*. Boulder, CO: First Forum Press.

Roldán Ortega, Roque. 2000. *Pueblos indígenas y leyes en Colombia: Aproximación crítica al estudio de su pasado y presente*. Santafé de Bogotá, Colombia: OIT; Tercer Mundo Editores.

Saavedra, José, ed. 2007. *Educación superior, interculturalidad y descolonización*. La Paz: Programa de Investigación Estratégica en Bolivia; Comité Ejecutivo de la Universidad Boliviana.

Sábato, Ernesto. 1973. *La cultura en la encrucijada nacional*. Buenos Aires: Editorial Suramericana.

Salinas, Maximiliano. 2001. "¡En tiempo de Chaya nadie se enoja! La fiesta popular del Carnaval en Santiago de Chile, 1880–1910." *Revista Mapocho* 50:281–325.

Salomon, Frank L. 1981. "Killing the Yumbo: A Ritual Drama of Northern Quito." In *Cultural Transformations and Ethnicity in Modern Ecuador*, edited by N. E. Whitten, 161–208. Urbana: University of Illinois Press.

Sawyer, Suzana. 2004. *Crude Chronicles: Indigenous Politics, Multinational Oil, and Neoliberalism in Ecuador*. Durham, NC: Duke University Press.

Scheckel, Susan. 1998. *The Insistence of the Indian: Race and Nationalism in Nineteenth-Century American Culture*. Princeton: Princeton University Press.

Schipani, Andres, and John Vidal. 2010. "Bolivia Climate Change Talks to Give Poor a Voice: Groups on Frontline of Global Warming Head to Alternative Summit in City of Cochabamba. *The Guardian*, April 18. Accessed March 7, 2014. http://www.guardian.co.uk/environment/2010/apr/18/bolivia-climate-change-talks-cochabasmba.

Scott, James. 1985. *Weapons of the Weak: Everyday Forms of Peasant Resistance*. New Haven: Yale University Press.

Sheriff, Robin E. 2001. *Dreaming Equality: Color, Race, and Racism in Urban Brazil*. New Brunswick: Rutgers University Press.

———. 2003. "Embracing Race: Deconstructing *mestiçagem* in Rio de Janeiro." *The Journal of Latin American Anthropology* 8(1): 86–115.

Sieiro de Noriega, Felicidad. 1980. "Los indios Guaymíes frente al problema educativo y cultural." Master's thesis [1968], Facultad de Filosofía, Letras y Educación, Universidad de Panamá.

Sierra, Justo. 1969. *The Political Evolution of the Mexican People*. Translated by Charles Ramsdell. Austin: University of Texas Press.

Silva, Nelson do Valle. 2000. "Extensão e natureza das desigualdades raciais no Brasil." In *Tirando a máscara: Ensaios sobre o racismo no Brasil*, edited by Anto^nio Sérgio A. Guimarães and Lynn Huntley, 33–51. São Paulo: Paz e Terra.

Silvério, Valter Roberto. 2005a. "Ações afirmativas e diversidade étnica e racial." In *Ações afirmativas e combate ao racismo nas Américas*, edited by Ana Flávia Magalhães Pinto, Maria Lúcia de Santana Braga, and Sales Augusto dos Santos, 141–64. Brasília: Ministério da Educação, Secretaria de Educação Continuada, Alfabetização e Diversidade.

———. 2005b. "A (re)configuração do nacional e a questão da diversidade." In *Afirmando diferenças: Montando o quebra-cabeça da diversidade na escola*, edited by Anete Abramowicz and Valter Roberto Silvério, 87–107. São Paulo: Papirus Editora.

———. 2006. "Ação afirmativa: Uma política que faz a diferença." In *O negro na universidade: O direito à inclusão*, edited by Jairo Queiroz Pacheco, Maria Nilza da Silva, and Dora Lúcia de Lima Bertúlio, 21–49. Brasília: Ministério da Cultura, Fundação Cultural Palmares.

Skar, Sarah Lund. 1994. *Lives Together—Worlds Apart: Quechua Colonization in Jungle and City*. Oslo: Scandinavian University Press; New York: Oxford University Press.

Smuts, Barbara. 1992. "Male Aggression Against Women: An Evolutionary Perspective." *Human Nature* 3(1): 1–44.

Soares, Sergei. 2008. "A trajetória da desgualdade: A evolução da renda relativa dos negros no Brasil." In *As políticas públicas e a desigualdade racial no Brasil: 120 anos após a abolição*, edited by Mário Theodoro, Luciana de Barros Jaccoud, Rafael Guerreiro Osorio, and Sergei Soares, 119–29. Brasília: Instituto de Pesquisa Económica Aplicada.

Sotero, Michelle. 2006. "A Conceptual Model of Historical Trauma: Implications for Public Health Practice and Research." *Journal of Health Disparities Research and Practice* 1(1): 93–108.

Spivak, Gayatri. 1988. "Can the Subaltern Speak?" In *Marxism and the Interpretation of Culture*, edited by Cary Nelson and Larry Grossberg, 271–313. Chicago: University of Illinois Press.

Stavenhagen, Rodolfo. 2006. *Report of the Special Rapporteur on the Situation of Human Rights and Fundamental Freedoms of Indigenous People*. Paris: UNESCO.

———. 2008. *Los pueblos indígenas y sus derechos*. Mexico City: UNESCO.

Steger, Manfred. 2003. *Globalization: A Very Short Introduction*. Oxford: Oxford University Press.

Stiglitz, Joseph. 2001. *Globalization and Its Discontents*. 1st ed. New York: W. W. Norton.

Stolle-McAllister, John. 2013. "Intercultural Processes in Kichwa Governed Municipalities in Ecuador." *Journal of Intercultural Studies* 34(1): 1–17.

Stutzman, Ronald. 1981. "*El mestizaje*: An All-Inclusive Ideology of Exclusion." In *Cultural Transformations and Ethnicity in Modern Ecuador*, edited by N. E. Whitten, 46–94. Urbana: University of Illinois Press.

Swanson, Kristen K., and Timothy J. Dallen. 2012. "Souvenirs: Icons of Meaning, Commercialization and Commoditization." *Tourism Management* 33:489–99.

Taller Cultural Kinde. 2007. "Mensajero del saber: Proyecto de educación experimental." Unpublished manuscript.

Taylor, Analisa. 2009. *Indigeneity in the Mexican Cultural Imagination: Thresholds of Belonging*. Tucson: University of Arizona Press.

Tubino, Fidel. 2002. "Interculturalizando el multiculturalismo." In *Intercultur-ael. Balance y perspectivas*, edited by Yolanda Onghena, 181–94. Barcelona: Centro de Estudios y Documentación Internacional de Barcelona.

U.S. Senate. 1867. "Chivington Massacre." In *Report of the Committees*. 39th Cong., 2d Sess. Washington, DC: General Printing Office.

Valdivia, Gustavo, and Xavier Ricard. 2009. *Tejedores de espacio en el Ande: Itinerarios agropastoriles e integración regional en el sur peruano*. Cuzco: Centro de Estudios Regionales Andinos Bartolomé de las Casas.

Van Cott, Donna Lee. 2000. *The Friendly Liquidation of the Past: The Politics of Diversity in Latin America*. Pittsburgh: University of Pittsburgh Press.

———. 2001. "Explaining Ethnic Autonomy Regimes in Latin America." *Studies in Comparative International Development* 34(4): 30–58.

———. 2005. *From Movements to Parties in Latin America: The Evolution of Ethnic Politics*. Cambridge: Cambridge University Press.

Van de Port, Mattijs. 2006. "Visualizing the Sacred: Televisual Styles and the Religious Imagination in Bahian Candomblé." *American Ethnologist* 33:444–61.

———. 2007. "Reencoding the Primitive." In *Wildness & Sensation: Anthropology of Sinister and Sensuous Realms*, edited by Rob van Ginkel and Alex Strating, 177–97. Apeldoorn/Antwerpen: HetSphinhuis.

Varela, Gladys. 1981. "El acceso de las tribus indígenas del Neuquén a la tierra pública." In *Neuqué: La occupación de la tierra pública en el departamento confluencia después de la Campaña al Desierto (1880–1930)*, 89–102. Neuquén: Universidad Nacional del Comahue.

Varela, Gladys, and Luz María Font. 1995. "Reemplazos y coincidencias en el poblamiento de Neuquén: La integración de un espacio criollo." *Revista de Historia* 5:173–83.

Varese, Stefano. 1982. "Restoring Multiplicity: Indianities and the Civilizing Project in Latin America." *Latin American Perspectives* 9(2): 29–41.

Vargas Llosa, Mario. 2007. "Prólogo." In exhibition catalog, *Revelaciones: Las artes en América Latina, 1492–1820*. Mexico City: Fondo de Cultura Económica, Antiguo Colegio de San Ildefonso; Philadelphia: Philadelphia Museum of Art; Los Angeles: Los Angeles County Museum of Art.

Vasconcelos, José. 1963. *A Mexican Ulysses, an Autobiography*. Translated by W. Rex Crawford. Bloomington: Indiana University Press.

———. 1925. *The Cosmic Race: A Bilingual Edition*. Translated by Didier T. Jaén. Baltimore: Johns Hopkins University Press, 1997.

Velázquez Chávez, Agustín. 1939. *Tres siglos de pintura colonial mexicana*. Mexico City: Editorial Polis.

Ventura, Montserrat. 1996. "La organización comunal en un grupo indígena de las tierras bajas: El caso tsáchila del occidente ecuatoriano." In *La gestión comunal de recursos: Economía y poder en las sociedades locales de España y América Latina*, edited by Marie Noëlle Chamoux and Jesús Contreras, 439–73. Barcelona: Icaria.

Viaña Uzieda, Jorge, Luis Claros, Josef Estermann, Raúl Fornet-Betancourt, Fernando Garcés, Victor Hugo Quintanilla, and Esteban Ticona. 2009. *Interculturalidad crítica y descolonización: Fundamentos para el debate*. La Paz: Instituto Internacional de Integración del Convenio Andrés Bello.

Villalba O., Marcelo. 1988. *Cotocollao: Una aldea formativa del valle de Quito*. Miscelánea Antropológica Ecuatoriana, Serie Monográfica 2. Quito: Museos del Banco Central del Ecuador.

Viveiros de Castro, Eduardo. 2006. "No Brasil, todo mundo é índio, exceto quem não é." Accessed March 2, 2014. http://pib.socioambiental.org/files/file/PIB _institucional/No_Brasil_todo_mundo_%C3%A9_%C3%ADndio.pdf.

Wade, Peter. 2003. "Repensando el mestizaje." *Revista Colombiana de Antropología* 39:273–96.

———. 2005. "Rethinking Mestizaje: Ideology and Lived Experience." *Journal of Latin American Studies* 37:239–57.

Wali, Alaka. 1995. "La política de desarrollo y las relaciones entre región y estado: El caso del Oriente de Panamá, 1972–1990." *Mesoamerica* 29:125–58.

Walker, Sheila. 1990. "Everyday and Esoteric Reality in the Afro-Brazilian Candomblé." *History of Religions* 30:103–28.

Walsh, Catherine. 2007. "Interculturalidad y colonialidad del poder: Un pensamiento y posicionamiento otro desde la diferencia." In *Educación superior, interculturalidad y descolonización*, edited by José Saavedra, 175–213. La Paz: Programa de Investigación Estratégica en Bolivia; Comité Ejecutivo de la Universidad Boliviana.

———. 2009. *Interculturalidad, estado, sociedad: Luchas (de)coloniales de nuestra época.* Quito: Universidad Simón Bolivar; Ediciones Abya-Yala.

Weismantel, Mary. 2001. *Cholas and Pishtacos: Stories of Race and Sex in the Andes.* Chicago: University of Chicago Press.

Weist, Tom. 1977. *A History of the Cheyenne People.* Bozeman: Montana Council for Indian Education.

Whitten, Norman E. 1984. "Etnocidio ecuatoriano y etnogénesis indígena: Resurgencia amazónica ante la colonización andina." In *Temas sobre la contiuidad y adaptación cultural ecuatoriana*, edited by M. Naranjo Villavicencio, J. L. Pereira and N. Whitten, 169–212. Quito: EDUC.

———. 2003. "Introduction." In *Millennial Ecuador: Critical Essays on Cultural Transformations and Social Dynamics*, edited by N. E. Whitten, 1–45. Iowa City: University of Iowa Press.

Whitten, Norman E., and Dorothea Scott Whitten. 2008. *Puyo Runa: Imagery and Power in Modern Amazonia.* Urbana: University of Illinois Press.

Whitten, Norman E., Dorothea S. Whitten, and Alfonso Chango. 2003. "Return of the Yumbo: The *Caminata* from Amazonia to Andean Quito." In *Millennial Ecuador: Critical Essays on Cultural Transformations and Social Dynamics*, edited by N. E. Whitten, 184–215. Iowa City: University of Iowa Press.

Wiarda, Howard. 2001. *The Soul of Latin America: The Cultural and Political Tradition.* New Haven: Yale University Press.

Wickstrom, Stefanie. 2003. "The Politics of Development in Indigenous Panama." *Latin American Perspectives* 30(4): 43–68.

———. 2005. "The Politics of Forbidden Liaisons: Civilization, Miscegenation, and Other Perversions." *Frontiers: A Journal of Women Studies* 26(3): 168–98.

Williams, Julie L. 2007. "Celebrando el pasado del futuro: La negociación de la identidad indígena en Lumbisí, Ecuador." In *Estudios ecuatorianos: Un aporte a la discusión.* Tomo 2, *Ponencias escojidas del III Encuentro de la Sección de*

Estudios Ecuatorianos LASA, Quito 2006, edited by W. F. Waters and M. T. Hamerly, 73–86. Quito: FLACSO; Abya-Yala.

Williams, Julie L., and Kathleen Fine-Dare. 2008. "Contrastructural Strategies of Urban Indigeneity in the Quito Basin." Paper presented at the annual meeting of the American Anthropological Association, San Francisco, California, November 19–23.

Wisdom of the Elders. 2004. "Turtle Island Storyteller Gordon Yellowman, Sr." Accessed May 24, 2013. http://www.turtleislandstorytellers.net/tis_okla homa/transcript_g_yellowman.htm.

Wolf, Eric. 1959. *Sons of the Shaking Earth*. Chicago: University of Chicago Press.

Wolf, Martin. 2004. *Why Globalization Works*. New Haven: Yale University Press.

Working Group 7. 2010. "World People's Conference on Climate Change and the Rights of Mother Earth: Working Group 7: Indigenous Peoples Statement." World People's Conference on Climate Change and the Rights of Mother Earth. Accessed February 7, 2011. http://pwccc.wordpress.com/2010 /02/07/group-7-indigenous-peoples/.

World Bank. 2013. "Peru: A Country Committed to Poverty Reduction and Shared Prosperity." Accessed June 29, 2013. http://www.worldbank.org/en/ news/feature/2013/06/27/peru-comprometido-con-reducir-pobreza.

Yashar, Deborah J. 1998. "Contesting Citizenship: Indigenous Movements and Democracy in Latin America." *World Politics* 31(1): 23–42.

———. 2005. *Contesting Citizenship in Latin America: The Rise of Indigenous Movements and the Postliberal Challenge*. Cambridge Studies in Contentious Politics. Cambridge: Cambridge University Press.

———. 2007. "Resistance and Identity Politics in an Age of Globalization." *The Annals of the American Academy of Political and Social Science* 610:160–81.

Young, Iris. 1995. "Polity and Group Difference: A Critique of the Ideal of Universal Citizenship." In *Theorizing Citizenship*, edited by R. Beiner, 175–207. Albany: SUNY Press.

Young, Philip D. 1968. "The Ngawbe: An Analysis of the Economy and Social Structure of the Western Guaymi of Panama." PhD diss., Department of Anthropology, University of Illinois at Urbana-Champaign. Ann Arbor: University Microfilms International.

———. 1971. *Ngawbe: Tradition and Change Among the Western Guaymi of Panama*. Illinois Studies in Anthropology 7. Urbana: University of Illinois Press.

———. 1976. "Guaymí Nativism: Its Rise and Demise." *Actas del XLI Congreso Internacional de Americanistas* 3:95–101.

———. 1978. "La trayectoria de una religión: El movimiento de Mama Chi entre los Guaymíes y sus consecuencias sociales." *La Antigua* 11:45–75.

———. 1995. "Buglé." In *Encyclopedia of World Cultures*, 8:31–34. Boston: G. K. Hall.

Young, Philip D., and John R. Bort. 1999. "Ngóbe Adaptive Responses to Globalization in Panama." In *Globalization and the Rural Poor in Latin America*, edited by William M. Loker, 111–36. Boulder, CO: Lynne Rienner.

Zamosc, León. 1995. *Estadística de las áreas de predominio étnico de la sierra ecuatoriana: Población rural, indicadores cantonales y organizaciones de base*. Quito: Abya-Yala.

CONTRIBUTORS

Fabrizio Arenas Barchi is a specialist in citizenship for the Ministry of Education in Peru and teaches in the Humanities Department at the Pontifical Catholic University of Peru. He has worked as a researcher and lecturer at the Center for Regional Andean Studies "Bartolomé de las Casas" in Cuzco and at the Pontifical Catholic University of Peru as a consultant for the Coordinator for Andean Science and Technology (CCTA). He received undergraduate and master's degrees from the Pontifical Catholic University of Peru.

Mariella I. Arredondo is a research associate at The Equity Project, Center for Evaluation & Education Policy, Indiana University. She received her PhD in educational policy studies, with a concentration in comparative international education, in 2013 from Indiana University, Bloomington. She holds an MA in Latin American and Caribbean Studies from Indiana University, an MA in Applied Linguistics from Ohio University, and a BA in Global and Social Studies from Antioch College.

Víctor Bretón Solo de Zaldívar is professor of social anthropology at the University of Lleida, coordinator of the Interdisciplinary Group of Studies of Development and Multiculturality (GIEDEM), and a researcher with the Latin American Faculty of Social Sciences (FLACSO), headquartered in Ecuador.

Angela Castañeda is associate professor of anthropology and Latin American and Caribbean studies at DePauw University. She holds a doctorate in cultural anthropology from Indiana University. Her research and teaching interests include identity, religion, and expressive culture among communities of the African diaspora in Latin America.

Paulo Alberto dos Santos Vieira is associate professor at the Mato Grosso State University in the Graduate Program in Education. He is currently coordinator of the Center for Research on Education, Gender, Race and Otherness, which develops work on affirmative action and race relations.

273

Kathleen S. Fine-Dare is professor of anthropology and gender/women's studies and an affiliated professor in Native American and Indigenous studies at Fort Lewis College in Durango, Colorado. She received her BA from DePauw University and her PhD from the University of Illinois, Urbana-Champaign. She was a Fulbright Lecturer at the Salesian Polytechnic University in Quito, Ecuador, in 2005. She is currently writing a book on history, performance, and indigeneity in Quito.

Sabine Kradolfer is an anthropologist and sociologist. She holds a joint doctoral degree from the Universities of Lausanne (Switzerland) and Paris III–Sorbonne Nouvelle. Currently, she is working as a senior researcher at the University of Lausanne (Switzerland). Her research interests include issues of ethnicity, Indigenous people, inequalities, public policies, gender studies, and academic careers.

Jorge Legoas P. is a postdoctoral scholar in the Department of Anthropology at McGill University in Montreal and a member of the Research Group on Political Imaginaries in Latin America (GRIPAL) and the Inter-university Center for Indigenous Studies and Research (CIÉRA). He was a Wadsworth Fellow of the Wenner-Gren Foundation for Anthropological Research (2005–2013). Prior to graduate studies, he worked for ten years in management, planning, and consulting for development agencies in the Peruvian Andes.

Mónica Martínez Mauri is a postdoctoral researcher (Juan de la Cierva Program) in the Research Group on Indigenous and Afro-American Cultures (CINAF) at the University of Barcelona. She received her PhD in social anthropology from the Autonomous University of Barcelona (UAB) and the School for Advanced Study in the Social Sciences (EHESS). Since 1999, she has conducted anthropological fieldwork on cultural mediation, anthropology of nature, Indigenous rights, and the impacts of tourism on Indigenous communities in Kuna Yala (Panama).

Iván Pizarro Díaz is an anthropologist. His research focuses on the Indigenous history of the communities of the Norte Chico area of Chile, mainly in the valleys of Copiapó, Huasco, and Elqui. He is currently completing a master's degree in ethnohistory at the University of Chile. His thesis examines conflict over water in the Huasco Valley toward the end of the nineteenth century.

John Stolle-McAllister is associate professor of Spanish and Intercultural Studies and associate dean of the College of Arts, Humanities and Social Sciences at the University of Maryland, Baltimore County, where he teaches courses on Latin American social movements, popular culture, and ethnography. His current research is on intercultural changes in Kichwa communities in and around Otavalo, Ecuador.

Sofía Irene Velarde Cruz is a researcher with the Michoacán Secretariat of Culture at its Center for Documentation and Research in the Arts. She served as the director of the Museum of Colonial Art in Morelia, Michoacán, from 2008–2012. She holds a master's degree in philosophy of culture and a bachelor's degree in history from the Michoacán University of Saint Nicolas de Hidalgo.

Jennifer Whiteman is an adjunct instructor and teaches tribal constitution and tribal economics at the Cheyenne and Arapaho Tribal College. She has worked with the Cheyenne and Arapaho Tribes' Department of Education and as an adjunct professor of tribal constitution and of tribal economics at the Cheyenne and Arapaho Tribal College. She holds an MSc in sociology from the London School of Economics and a JD from the Oklahoma City University School of Law.

Stefanie Wickstrom holds a PhD in political science from the University of Oregon and an MA in Latin American Studies from the University of Arizona. She is a senior lecturer at Central Washington University. She writes and teaches about environmental politics and development, social movements, and identity politics in Latin America, Canada, and the United States.

Rex Wirth is professor of political science at Central Washington University and has served as director of the Public Policy Program. His doctoral studies focused on politics in divided societies, with an emphasis on Belgium, where he conducted dissertation research in 1975. He received his PhD in political science from the University of Tennessee in 1977.

Philip D. Young received his PhD in anthropology at the University of Illinois, Urbana, in 1968. His dissertation was based on field research in Panama with the Ngäbe in 1964–1965. He worked with them throughout his career and retirement. During leaves of absence from the University of Oregon, he worked for an NGO (1976–1978) and a for-profit consulting firm (1981–1982 and 1989–1992). He taught at the University of Oregon from 1966 until he retired from teaching in 2002. He was an ethnographer, applied anthropologist, cultural ecologist, and specialist in Indigenous cultures of Latin America. Phil continued to conduct research and write until his death in 2013. He was interested in the adaptive responses of small-scale traditional cultures to the impact of outside social, economic, and political forces, now collectively referred to as globalization—a congeries of processes that for the native peoples of the "New World" began with the European invasion.

INDEX

"American," as identity construct in
the United States, 35, 39–40
abuse: of human rights, 4, 65; sexual,
87, 98, 119; of women, 87, 162n3,
198, 205–06, 207, 208
acculturation, 13, 36, 39–40, 145,
157, 240
affirmative action, 11, 12, 14,
92–106, 122
African diaspora, 95, 182
agrarian reform in Ecuador, 147, 151,
160, 213–14, 221–23, 225, 226
Alianza PAIS party (Ecuador), 246
Allende Gossens, Salvador, 64
Anzaldúa, Gloria, 126–27
Araucanía, 57, 62, 73n9
argentinidad, 171
Armaçao de Búzios, Brazil, 180
Ascanio Villalaz Hydroelectric Center
(Bayano River in Panama), 220
assimilation, 12, 14, 15, 36, 83, 94,
134, 137, 166, 235, 237, 243
Ateneo de la Juventud, 8, 18n9
autonomy: indigenous, 9, 12, 19n21,
173, 213–16, 224–25, 231, 236,
239, 242, 243, 245; ethnic, 213–14,
236, 239, 242
Avellaneda, Nicolás, 169
axé, 183, 188
Aymara (language), 59, 83, 86, 88,
91n7
Aymara (people), 3, 114, 165
Aztec empire, 26, 29, 31
Aztlán, 11, 29

Bachelet, Michelle, 73n17
black movement (Brazil), 14, 96, 97,
100–101, 103, 104, 105n1
blanqueamiento, 145, 240
"blood quantum," 28, 141n4
boarding schools, 136–37, 140
Bolivia, 9, 12, 19n20, 19n23, 44, 60,
79, 151, 212
Bonaparte, Napoleon, 34, 41
Buenos Aires, Argentina, 164, 170,
171, 173
Buglé people, 194, 210n3, 224, 233n6
Burke, Edmund, 37

Caesar, Julius, 27, 38
Camino de Santiago. *See* Way of Saint
James
Campaña al Desierto (Desert
Campaign; Argentina), 169–70
Candomblé, 16, 180–92
capitalism: globalization of, 71, 72,
182, 190; norms and, 131, 133,
136
capitalist development, 71, 104, 109,
131, 140, 222, 228
capitalist expansion, 110, 134,
140, 238
Carnaval, 59–61, 63, 65–66, 68,
69–70, 73n13
Carrera, Cacica Silvia, 193, 208
Carthage, 26–27
Casa Kinde, 151–53
caserios (Ngäbe), 195, 211n16
castas, 58, 59, 240

277

Catholic Church, 27–29, 33, 39, 41, 49, 61, 63, 146, 184, 225–26, 228, 231

Chaco (Argentina), 169

Charlemagne, 27, 28, 33, 34, 40

Cheyenne and Arapaho Tribes, 127–28, 130, 141n3, 141n4,

Cheyenne Dog Soldiers, 130–31, 141n5

Chicano/as, 11, 29

Chimborazo Province, Ecuador, 225

Chiriquí Province, Panama, 194–95, 197, 201, 204, 205

cholos: in Peru, 58, 78, 81–88, 89, 91n12; in Panama, 218

Chubut Province, Argentina, 173, 174, 176, 177

Citizen's Proposal Group (Grupo Propuesta Ciudadana, GPC; Peru), 114–15, 121

citizenship, 9, 89, 94, 97, 107–23 passim, 163n5, 166, 172, 213, 214, 221, 225, 232n1, 235, 245, 246

civilization (paradigm), 42, 61–62, 69, 71, 170, 172–73, 175, 238, 240, 241

class, 10, 14, 58, 63–64, 66–67, 69, 72, 73n12, 73n16, 78, 83–84, 86–89 passim, 90n4, 104, 165, 177, 214, 223, 229, 236, 237, 240, 242, 243, 245

Coclé Province, Panama, 205

Collor de Mello, Fernando, 96

Colombia, 19n20, 162n2, 215, 220, 223–24

colonialism: "internalized," 89; and interculturalidad, 238–39; "new," 3; and racism, 248

comarca system in Panama, 215

Communist Party (Ecuador), 226, 227, 231

Comunidades Campesinas (Peru), 109, 110

Concho Indian Day School (Oklahoma), 135–36

Conejo, Mario, 235, 246–47

Confederated Tribes of the Colville Reservation, 159

Confederation of Indigenous Nationalities of Ecuador (La Confederación de Nacionalidades Indígenas del Ecuador, CONAIE), 12, 146, 147–48, 214, 216–17, 219, 229, 231, 242–43, 245–46

Confederation of Peoples of Kichwa Nationality (Confederación de Pueblos de la Nacionalidad Kichwa del Ecuador, ECUARUNARI), 216, 219

Conquista del Desierto (Argentina), 170, 179n6

Consejo Asesor Indígena (Río Negro, Argentina), 177

constitutionalism, Roman, 38

constitutions, 4, 12; Argentina, 166, 168, 172, 175, 177; Brazil, 93, 97, 99; Cheyenne Arapaho Tribes, 141n4; Chile, 71; Ecuador, 232n3, 235, 244–45, 248; Panama, 218, 223, 225

Convention Concerning Indigenous and Tribal Peoples in Independent Countries, 167

cooperatives, 188, 199, 201, 203, 204

Córdoba, Spain, 28, 29, 165

corporatism, 35–41 passim

Corpus Christi observances, 59, 150

Correa, Rafael, 245, 246

Cortés, Hernán, 28–33, 39, 42

Cortés, Martín (the Mestizo), 32–33

Cosmic Race: Mission of the Ibero-American Race (La raza cósmica), The, 8, 52, 107–08, 166

Cotocollao, Quito, Ecuador, 146–47, 149–51, 156–58

Creoles, 32–33, 62, 82, 91n9, 171–72, 236

criollos. *See* Creoles

Declaration of Quito, 19n23

Declaration on the Rights of Indigenous Peoples, 4, 18n12, 167

Declarations of Barbados (1971 and 1977), 9

decolonization, 12, 86, 236, 237,
245, 248
de Gaulle, Charles, 38, 41
de las Casas, Bartolomé, 32, 33
Deloria, Vine, Jr., 18n11
development: agriculture, 3–4, 109,
110–11, 114, 152, 222, 225–26;
economic, 3–4, 11, 15, 16, 71, 100,
104, 107–23 passim, 126, 148, 151,
176, 177, 197, 199, 200–201, 203–5,
209, 212, 213, 214, 226, 228–30,
231–32, 239, 246, 248; energy, 4,
109, 110, 111, 207, 219, 220, 233n7;
international, 6, 109, 114, 221;
mining, 4, 32, 58, 71, 109, 111, 207,
219, 245; neoliberal, 228–30; water,
111, 148, 248
Development Council of Indigenous
Nations and Peoples of Ecuador
(Consejo de Desarrollo de las
Nacionalidades y Pueblos del
Ecuador, CODENPE), 147–48
Díaz, Porfirio, 30, 38, 42
dictatorship: 35; Argentina, 167, 168;
Brazil, 96, 97; Chile, 65, 71
discovery of the Americas: 26, 29–31
passim; five-hundredth anniversary
of, 168, 230
Dog Soldiers, 130–31, 141n5
domestic violence, 118, 128, 152, 198,
205–6, 207, 208
Dull Knife, 132, 134, 135
Dutch Republic, 33–34

Ecuadorian Federation of Indigenes
(FEI), 226
Ecuadorian Institute of Agrarian
Reform and Colonization (Instituto
Ecuatoriano de Reforma Agraria y
Colonización, IERAC), 222
Ecuadorian Kichwa Nation
(Nacionalidad Kichwa del
Ecuador), 147
El Cid, 28
Emberá people, 220, 224, 227, 230,
233n6
Emberá-Wounaan Comarca, 220, 224

empire, 39–42
Encilhamento crisis (Brazil), 96,
105n5
encomiendas, 33, 146
Enlightenment, 35, 36, 37, 40, 41, 172
environmental organizations,
145, 146
equality: 100, 102, 107, 121, 139;
economic, 93, 97, 247; political, 39;
racial, 92, 95, 96, 97, 98, 103–4
equal opportunity, 14, 97
Erect Horns, 127, 136, 141n9
estancias, in Argentina, 169, 170,
179n5
Esteva-Fabregat, Claudio, 7, 18n7

Federal Law 23.302 (Argentina), 168,
174, 175
Federation of Ngäbe-Buglé Artisanal
Organizations (Federación de
Organizaciones Artesanales
Ngäbe-Buglé, FORANB), 204
Fernández, Justino, 45, 48–49
Fernández de Kirchner, Cristina, 165
First Continental Encounter of
Indigenous Peoples, 19n23
France, 27, 34, 36, 38, 40
free trade, 5, 17n6
Freirina (Santa Rosa del Huasco),
Chile, 58, 65, 66
French Revolution, 34, 40–41, 221
Fujimori, Alberto, 109

García Canclini, Néstor, 52, 55n10
García Pérez, Alan, 111, 123n2
Garrido, Enrique, 217
Gaul, 27, 38–39, 40
gender, 87, 91n12, 98, 99, 152, 162n4,
195–98, 201, 203, 209
General Congress system for
indigenous communities (Panama),
224–25
German Development Agency
(Deutsche Gesellschaft für
Technische Zusammenarbeit, GTZ),
194, 204, 211n14
Glorious Revolution (England), 37

Guaraní people (in Argentina),
    164–65, 176
Guatemala, 9, 19n20, 31, 210n7,
    212
Guna Yala Comarca. *See* Kuna Yala
    Comarca
Gutíerrez, Lucio, 243

Hapsburg Empire, 33–34
hierarchy: class, 14, 79, 80, 81, 83, 84,
    88, 105n2; racial, 14, 79, 80, 83, 88,
    89, 93, 96, 98, 100, 104, 105n2,
    221, 222, 233n8, 239, 241
historical materialism, 124–26,
    135, 140
Hobbes, Thomas, 37, 38
Holy Roman Empire, 33–34, 40
Huarpe people, 165, 167, 175, 176
huasipungueros, 151, 222
huasos (guazos), 71, 72n4
Hueyapan (Mexico), 160
Humala, Ollanta, 111
human rights, 4, 16, 65, 152, 167–68,
    178, 247

identity politics, introduction to, ix, 4,
    8–12, 18n13
Iglesia de Santa María Tonantzintla, 47
ILO Convention No. 169, 4, 167,
    168, 225
imaginaries, 13, 15, 61–72 passim,
    73n8, 107–8, 146, 214, 229,
    232, 243
imperialism: 8, 13, 27, 29, 30–31,
    33–34, 35, 38, 41; and Christianity,
    13, 31, 40, 42
Inca Empire, 3, 57, 60, 85
indianidad, 10, 18n14
indianismo, 10, 226, 227
indigeneity, 10–11, 15, 18n14, 145–46,
    152, 154, 157, 158, 159, 160, 165,
    166, 167–68, 172–73, 174–75,
    177, 178
indigenismo, 9–10, 18n10
indigenous autonomy, 9, 12, 19n21,
    173, 213–16, 224–25, 231, 236,
    239, 242, 243, 245

Indigenous Peoples Working Group of
    the World People's Conference on
    Climate Change and the Rights of
    Mother Earth, 19n23
indigenous self-governance, 215
indocristiano art, 49–50
Inquisition, 29, 34, 61
interculturalidad (interculturality): 12,
    16, 19n22, 160, 161, 163n5, 234–48
    passim; and education, 14, 90,
    91n10, 148, 168, 237–38, 245, 247;
    and governance, 122, 239, 245–47,
    248; and neoliberalism, 12, 236,
    238, 243; contrasted with
    multiculturalism, 12, 236–38
Inti Raymi (Festival of the Sun), 154,
    157, 247
Islam, 27–28, 46
Italy, 34, 38, 40

Jesuits, 146, 211n12
Juárez, Benito, 42

Kichwa (language), 83, 86, 88,
    116, 148, 151–52, 156, 158–59,
    242, 247
Kichwa (people), 3, 108, 114, 158,
    229, 231, 235, 242, 245–48 passim
Kuna Congress of Madungandí, 230
Kuna General Congress, 224, 230
Kuna Madungandí Comarca, 220, 225
Kuna peoples, social movements of,
    213, 215, 220, 221, 224–25,
    226–27, 230, 231, 232n4, 233n8
Kuna Wargandí Comarca, 220,
    225, 230
Kuna Workers Union (UTRAKUNA),
    233n8
Kuna Yala Comarca, 213, 215, 220,
    224, 230
Kunas United for Napguana, 232

labor movements, 10, 147 226, 233n8
ladinos, 9, 91n8, 201n7. See also
    latinos (Panama)
Lake Texcoco (Mexico), 26, 29, 30, 31
La Malinche, 29, 32

language: 8, 10, 18n14, 38–39, 46, 52,
66, 83, 88, 91n7, 93, 114, 127–28,
130, 132, 133, 136, 145, 146, 152,
166, 173, 199, 200, 201, 203, 211n15,
218–19, 221, 235, 238, 244; and
empire, 38–39, 66, 132, 136; and
nationalism, 71, 83, 88, 93, 121,
146, 166, 221, 235. *See also specific
languages*
La Pampa Province, Argentina,
171, 173
las Casas, Bartolomé de, 32, 33
Latin (language), 38–39, 51
Latinization, 27, 36, 39
latinos (Panama), 9, 198, 202, 206,
210n7
León-Portilla, Miguel, 53
Liberal Revolution (Ecuador), 241
liberation theology, 227, 232
Locke, John, 37
López, Estanislao, 224
Lula da Silva, Luiz Inácio, 95
Lumbisí, Quito, Ecuador, 154–55

Mahuad, Jamil, 217
Mama Chi movement, 197–200,
206–08, 210n8, 210n9
Mann, Henrietta, 126, 135
Mapuche lof (Argentina), 173–74
Mapuche movement,15, 73n9, 165,
167, 176–77, 178
Mapuche people: Argentina, 15, 73n9,
164–79 passim; Chile, 62, 73n9;
Mapunkies, 175, 177; Mapurbes,
176,177
Mapudungun (language), 173
Marcapata, Peru, 116–19, 123n8
Marcha de los Pueblos Originarios
(Buenos Aires, May 2010), 164, 167
marriage, 28, 34, 51, 89, 193, 196–97,
198, 202–3, 208–9, 210n5, 246
Martinelli, Marianella, 194, 198,
203, 205
Marxist theory, 5, 15, 126, 139,
140n1, 227
mashikuna, 146
Maya, 30, 173

May Revolution (Argentina), 164
melting pot (national identity):
contrasted with "salad bowl," 11, 14;
in Argentina, 15, 165, 166, 171, 173,
178; in Chile, 58; in the United
States of America, 11, 18n17, 140.
See also salad bowl
mestizaje, biological, 7–8,
51–52, 240
Mexican Revolution, 30, 38, 42
Michoacán, Mexico, 29, 33, 46, 50
migration: labor 222, 231; rural-to-
urban, 14, 72, 78, 89–90, 110–11,
123n6, 174, 200; pre-conquest
Mexico, 29
Ministry for Social Development
(Ministerio de Desarrollo Social,
MIDES; Peru), 201, 210n11
miscegenation, 6, 11, 96, 98, 104,
167, 171
modernity, 40, 67, 146, 238, 239
modernization, 64, 110–11, 121, 122
Montezuma, 31, 33
Moors, 13, 26–29, 40, 46, 52
Morales, Evo, 212, 19n23
Moreno Villa, José, 45–47, 49
Mound Builders (Mississippi River
Valley), 30
mudéjar art, 46–47
mulatto/a: in Brazil, 101–2; in Chile,
58; in Peru, 82
multiculturalism: 9, 11, 12, 16, 90, 93,
168, 178, 215, 225, 236–38, 241;
contrasted with *interculturalidad*,
12; 236–38; neoliberal, 12,
236, 238
multinational corporations, 4, 9

nagua (Ngäbe), 205, 211n15
Nahua (people), 29–31
Nahuatl (language), 46
Naso people, 220, 225, 230, 233
National Coordinating Body of
Indigenous Peoples in Panama
(Coordinadora Nacional de Pueblos
Indígenas de Panamá,
COONAPIP), 230, 232

national identity: 14, 127; in
  Argentina, 165, 169, 171–73, 174,
  178; in Bolivia, 79; in Brazil, 93–94,
  97, 98, 100, 103–4; in Ecuador, 15,
  16, 234, 236, 139–42, 247–48; in
  France, 39; in Mexico, 13, 35, 39,
  42, 166; in Panama, 16; in Peru, 79,
  82–83, 90, 108, 172; in the United
  States of America, 11, 13, 18n16,
  26, 35, 40, 127, 140
National Program of Direct Assistance
  to the Poorest (Programa Nacional
  de Apoyo Directo a los Más Pobres,
  JUNTOS) conditional cash transfer
  program (Peru), 109, 111–13,
  123n3, 123n4
National Register of Indigenous
  Communities (Registro Nacional de
  Comunidades Indígenas, RENACI)
  (Argentina), 175
nation-state, 4, 6, 7, 9, 11, 13, 28,
  34–35, 39–40, 42, 57, 62, 69, 71,
  77, 90, 92, 93, 95, 97, 99, 102, 104,
  105, 107–8, 122, 163n5, 165, 169,
  170, 171–73, 179n4, 182–83, 184,
  190, 213, 215, 217, 234–35, 236,
  240–41, 242–45, 248
Needler, Martin C., 10, 18n15
neoliberalism, 15, 109–11, 212–13,
  228–30, 243
neoliberal multiculturalism.
  See multiculturalism
Netherlands, Northern and Spanish, 34
networking, 4, 5, 147, 163n5, 213, 214,
  225–26, 246, 247
Neuquén Province, Argentina, 165,
  173, 174, 176, 177
New Spain, 13, 31–35, 43–50, 52
Ngäbe-Buglé Comarca, 193, 194, 199,
  200, 201, 205, 207, 208, 215, 220,
  225, 230
Ngäbe people, 193–211, 220, 224,
  227, 230, 233n8
Ngäbere (language), 211n15
Ngöbe Agroforestry Project (Proyecto
  Agroforestal Ngöbe, PAN), 194,
  203–4

Nicaragua, 19n20, 215
Non-formal Programs for Early
  Childhood Education (Programa No
  Escolarizado de Educación Inicial,
  PRONOEI; Peru), 119
non-governmental organizations
  (NGOs): development, 108, 114,
  148, 203, 223, 225–26, 228, 229,
  231; indigenous, 227, 230, 232n4;
  and indigenous movements, 176,
  214, 223, 225–26, 228–29
Norte Chico, Chile, 56–59

O'Higgins, Ambrosio, 72n2
O'Higgins Riquelme, Bernardo, 72n2
Omolú, 183, 188, 189
orixá, 16, 180–92 passim, 192n2
Ossaim, 138, 185, 186
Otavalo, Ecuador, 235, 245–47, 248
Ovalle, Alfonso de, 59

Pachakuti, 3, 17n2, 60
Pachakutik movement (Ecuador),
  243, 246
Pachamama, 59, 157, 244
Pampa (Argentina), 169, 170, 171, 179n6
Panamanian Revolution, 227
Paniagua, Valentín, 109
Partido Revolucionario Institucional
  (Institutional Revolutionary Party,
  PRI), 42
Patagonia (Argentina), 73n9, 165, 166,
  169–72, 173, 175–76, 179n6
pedagogy, 151, 161, 163n5
People's Party of Panama, 227
Pichincha Province, Ecuador, 146,
  147, 154
Pinochet, Augusto, 65, 71
Plan Guaymí, 201, 203
Pliny the Elder, 51, 54n6
pluralism, 7, 13, 26, 35, 36, 39, 40, 41,
  99, 163n5, 239
polygyny, 196, 179, 198, 202, 207,
  208, 209, 210n4
Pomacocha, Andahuaylas Province,
  Peru, 113
Portugal, 34

privatization, 71, 109, 228
Program of Assistance for the
   Indigenous Peoples of Central
   America (Proyecto de Apoyo a los
   Pueblos Indígenas de América
   Central, PAPICA; Peru), 119
Pueblo Kitu Kara, 145, 147–48,
   154–55, 158
Punic Wars, 26–27
Purépecha empire, 29, 31, 50

Quechua. *See* Kichwa (language);
   Kichwa (people)
Quema de Chamiza festival, 153–54
Quetzalcoatl, 30–31, 32
Quichua. *See* Kichwa (language);
   Kichwa (people)
quilombolas, 96, 105n4
Quito, Ecuador, 15, 146–47, 148,
   162n2, 219

racial democracy (Brazil), 14, 92–93,
   95–96, 98, 99, 100, 104
racism: in Brazil 14, 92–106 passim;
   and colonialism, 248; in Ecuador,
   221, 222, 231, 239–40; impact on
   Cheyenne people, in U.S., 133; in
   Peru, 77–91 passim
Ramírez de Fuenleal, Sebastián, 33
Reconquista, 27, 28, 32, 34, 46, 51
Red de Oportunidades (Network of
   Opportunities), Panama, 201,
   210n11
republicanism, 36, 38, 40–41, 63–64,
   71, 77, 166, 178, 223
Reyes-Velario, Constantino, 49–50
rights: 12, 37, 99, 103, 116, 118, 122,
   146, 232n1; civil, 11, 93; collective,
   96, 99, 111, 152, 166, 178, 215;
   human, 4, 16, 65, 152, 167–68, 178,
   247; Indigenous, 4, 9, 16, 18n12, 146,
   151, 159, 163n5, 168, 173, 174–75,
   176, 178, 207, 215, 216, 224, 228,
   242; of Mother Earth, 19n23
Rio de Janeiro, 95, 182, 184, 185–87
Río Negro Province, Argentina, 165,
   173, 174, 176, 177

Roca, Julio Argentino, 169–70
Rodríguez Lara, General
   Guillermo, 241
Rojas, Pedro, 47–48
Roman Empire, 13, 25, 26–27, 35, 36,
   38–39, 40
Roman Republic, 38
Rosela dance, 153–54
Rousseau, Jean-Jacques, 37–38

Sábato, Ernesto, 171–72
Saint James. *See* Santiago Matamoros
   ("Moor Slayer")
Saint Sebastian, and Yubada, 150, 157
salad bowl (national identity), 11, 26.
   See also melting pot
sambos, in Chile, 58
San Blas. *See* Kuna Yala Comarca
Sand Creek Massacre, 131
San Enrique de Velasco, Quito,
   Ecuador, 151–56
San Felipe de los Alzates, Michoacán,
   Mexico, 46
San Félix, Chiriquí Province, Panama,
   204, 205, 211n12
Santa Anna, Antonio López de, 42
Santa Cruz Province, Argentina,
   173, 176
Santa Rosa del Huasco (Freirina),
   Chile, 58, 65, 66
Santa Teresa, Rio de Janeiro, Brazil, 187
Santiago, Chile, 59, 61, 73n12
Santiago de Compostela, 28
Santiago Mataíndios ("Indian
   Slayer"), 29
Santiago Matamoros ("Moor Slayer"),
   28–29, 30, 31, 32
second-tier federations
   (Organizaciones de segundo grado,
   OSGs), 216, 226, 228, 229
Second Vatican Council (1963), 225
Sierra, Justo, 30, 33
social contract theory, 37–38, 104
Socialist Party (Eduador), 242
social movements, 4; indigenous, 6,
   9–10, 12, 15, 16, 18n3, 18n11,
   18n13, 19n22, 73n9, 73n11, 123n10,

social movements (*continued*)
146, 147, 154–56, 162n2, 163n5,
164–79 passim, 165, 166, 167, 168,
212–33 passim, 234–48 passim;
transnational organizing, 4, 15–16,
147, 148, 162n2, 165, 166, 168, 176,
178, 212–13, 224, 226–28, 232,
232n4, 245; and unionism, 10, 226,
233n8. *See also* black movement
(Brazil); Chicano/as; *interculturalidad*
(interculturality); Kuna peoples;
Mama Chi movement; Mapuche
movement; Pachakutik movement
(Ecuador)
South and Meso American Indian
Rights Center, 17n1
sovereignty, 38, 40
Spain, 26–29, 33, 34, 38–39, 46
Spanish (language), 10, 18n14, 38–39,
52, 88, 91n7, 173, 199, 200, 201,
203, 218, 235, 244
state of nature, 37
State University of Rio de Janeiro
(Universidade do Estado do Rio de
Janeiro, UERJ), 95
statism, 35–38, 40–42
structural adjustment policies,
17n6, 228
subjectification, 108, 114, 121
Suh'tah, 128, 130
Supreme Federal Court (Brazil), 93,
95, 99, 104
Sweet Medicine, 127, 133–39 passim,
141n6
syncretism, religious, 53, 59, 63, 184

Tarascan (Purépecha) empire, 29,
31, 50
technology, 5, 17n5, 55, 126, 169, 209
Tenochtitlán, 29, 30, 31
Teotihuacán, 26, 30–31
Tequitqui art, 45–49
Third General Conference of the
Latin American Episcopate of
Medellín (1968), 30
Toledo, Alejandro, 109
Toltecs, 26, 30–31, 32

Torrijos, General Omar, 218, 220,
227, 232
tourism, 86, 146, 157
Toussaint, Manuel, 45
Transantiago Plan, 73n12
tribute, 46–47, 52, 58, 240–41
Tsistsistas, 128–29, 141n6
Tulenega, 224
Tule Revolution, 224

Unified Black Movement (Brazil), 97
United Fruit Company, 233n8
United Nations Children's Fund
(UNICEF), 114, 116–20
United Nations Declaration on the
Rights of Indigenous Peoples, 4,
18n12, 167
University of Brasília (Universidade de
Brasília, UnB), 97, 106n7

Valle del Tránsito, Huasco Alto, Chile,
66, 73n15
Valparaiso, Chile, 61
Vandals, 26, 27, 36
Vargas Llosa, Mario, 53
Vasconcelos Calderón, José María
Albino, 8, 52, 107–8, 166
Velázquez Chávez, Agustín, 45
Viceroyalty of Peru, 58
Virgin of Guadalupe. 32

Wallmapu, 73n9, 177, 178
Way of Saint James, 28
Wiarda, Howard, 10–11
Wichí people, 164, 165, 176
World Bank, 123n3, 148, 229, 238
World People's Conference on Climate
Change and the Rights of Mother
Earth, 19n23
Wounaan people, 220, 224, 233n6

Yashar, Deborah, 213–14, 232n1, 243
Yumba, 162n3
Yumbada dance, 148–51, 153–58
Yumbo, 162n3

Zangwill, Israel, 18n17